Evidence-Informed Assessment and Practice in Child Welfare

John S. Wodarski • Michael J. Holosko
Marvin D. Feit
Editors

Evidence-Informed Assessment and Practice in Child Welfare

Springer

Editors
John S. Wodarski
College of Social Work
The University of Tennessee
Knoxville, Tennessee
USA

Marvin D. Feit
Ethelyn R. Strong School of Social Work
Norfolk State University
Norfolk, Virginia
USA

Michael J. Holosko
School of Social Work
University of Georgia
Athens, Georgia
USA

ISBN 978-3-319-12044-7 ISBN 978-3-319-12045-4 (eBook)
DOI 10.1007/978-3-319-12045-4

Library of Congress Control Number: 2014956762

Springer Cham Heidelberg New York Dordrecht London

Printed on acid-free paper

Springer is part of Springer Science+Business Media (www.springer.com)

Preface

The focus of this book is on evidence-informed social work practice. The Institute of Medicine defines evidence-informed social work practice as the consideration of empirical research evidence, clinician expertise, and client values in addition to contextual variables used in clinical decision-making. Evidence informed practice differs from evidence-based practice in that the former centers on probability; a client(s) may be likely to respond to research evidence, but may also respond to his or her own evidence. An important issue is that previous research may not be applicable to the folks in treatment.

Thus, we were very interested in what social workers do when their knowledge of research does not appear to be very applicable to those in treatment. We have suggested and learned through this work that the evidence-informed approach is a much more appropriate approach to dealing with clients. It incorporates the existing knowledge base—which must be tested in practice to learn how good fit it is with clients and to learn from the clients themselves. In this way, a client's experience and knowledge is incorporated into one's practice, enriching the work and its applicability.

As an example, evidence-based research centered on youth and young adults who are white may not apply to a similar population who are basically from a minority. They may also differ in age, race, ethnicity, etc. Such work needs to be tested to learn what, if any, research applies, and to what degree. This is important so as to be more helpful and on target. There are many ways in which clients may not "fit" research studies, in that their applicability does not "fit" properly in practice.

Evidence-informed practice is more productive as a client does not have to fit in the context of previous research. A worker can test the evidence-based knowledge to learn what is most practical, and then proceed with assisting clients. A worker can proceed to help clients without having a large background of research. Thus, the focus of this book is to take note of how evidence-informed practice can be implemented and demonstrate how it can be effective and useful when working with all types of clients.

The chapters are written by practitioners whose central focus is on evidence-informed work. The book has three distinct sections. The first centers on the context for providing evidence-informed assessments. The second centers on actual field-tested evidence-informed assessments, and the third addresses field-tested evidence-informed interventions. Together they provide a backdrop for using research in an effective manner in social work practice.

Marvin D. Feit, Ph.D.

Contents

Contributors

Jason Bostur University of Tennessee, Knoxville, TN, USA

Aaron R. Brown The University of Tennessee, Knoxville, TN, USA

Shauna Cook Children's Mental Health Services Research Center, University of TN, Knoxville, TN, USA

Rachel Cooper University of Tennessee, Knoxville, TN, USA

Joanna Cummings The University of Tennessee, Knoxville, TN, USA

Carrie Fair The University of Tennessee, Knoxville, TN, USA

Erin Faith The University of Tennessee, Knoxville, TN, USA

Marvin D. Feit Norfolk State University, Norfolk, VA, USA

Cyomara Fisher The University of Tennessee, Knoxville, TN, USA

Jaime Frimpong University of Tennessee, Knoxville, TN, USA

Kimberly High University of Tennessee, Knoxville, TN, USA

Jennifer Holmes The University of Tennessee, Knoxville, TN, USA

Michael J. Holosko University of Georgia, Athens, GA, USA

Professor at University of Georgia, Athens, GA, USA

Sandy R. Johnson University of Georgia, Athens, GA, USA

Jessica W. Johnston The University of Tennessee, Knoxville, TN, USA

R. Manon Kraus The University of Tennessee, Knoxville, TN, USA

Andrea Loy University of Tennessee, Knoxville, TN, USA

Cindy McCleary-North The University of Tennessee, Knoxville, TN, USA

Jason Minor The University of Tennessee, Knoxville, TN, USA

Kat Murphy The University of Tennessee, Knoxville, TN, USA

Johnna Ojo The University of Tennessee, Knoxville, TN, USA

Johnna E. Ojo University of Tennessee, Knoxville, TN, USA

Ashley Peery The University of Tennessee, Knoxville, TN, USA

Mary Stangarone University of Tennessee, Knoxville, TN, USA

Renee Strong The University of Tennessee, Knoxville, TN, USA

Sarah Tillotson University of Tennessee, Knoxville, TN, USA

Shannon Waldrup The University of Tennessee, Knoxville, TN, USA

John S. Wodarski The University of Tennessee, Knoxville, TN, USA

Part I
The Context for Providing Evidence-Informed Assessments for Children and Families

Chapter 1
Educating BSW and MSW Social Workers to Practice in Child Welfare Services

Michael J. Holosko and Erin Faith

Introduction

Child welfare generally refers to a broad range of services provided by agencies charged with maintaining the safety and well-being of children according to legally mandated or socially sanctioned standards of conduct. For the purpose of this chapter, child welfare specifically denotes services provided to at-risk children and their families who have been referred to Child Protective Services (CPS) agencies because of confirmed maltreatment, neglect, or the likelihood of this occurrence.

This chapter offers a basis for deciding which professional staff positions in CPS agencies are most effectively filled by social work graduates with specific levels of education. Underlying the recommendations made herein is the conviction that masters-level graduates should have direct field experience with at-risk children and their families before performing duties in the areas of supervision, evaluation, or administration. Conversely, the authors recognize that some valued employees may leave a child welfare agency if promotional opportunities are, in effect, limited by an absence of meaningful financial support for graduate education.

As federal and state resources diminish, increasing numbers of children remain under the supervision of CPS (Geeraert et al. 2004; Fink and McCloskey 1990). The reported national incidence of documented cases of children injured because of abuse or neglect (meeting Harm Standard) increased more than 149 % between 1984 and 1993 (Sedlak and Broadhurst 1996), showing only a close-to-significant decrease in total documented cases since 1993 (Sedlak et al. 2010). During the same period, according to the data collected in the *Third National Incident Study of Child Abuse and Neglect* under the agencies of the U.S. Department of Health and Human Services, an estimated 1,553,800 children were injured because of abuse or

M. J. Holosko (✉)
University of Georgia, Athens, GA, USA
e-mail: mholosko@uga.edu

E. Faith
The University of Tennessee, Knoxville, TN, USA

J. S. Wodarski et al. (eds.), *Evidence-Informed Assessment and Practice in Child Welfare*, DOI 10.1007/978-3-319-12045-4_1

neglect in 1993, having increased from an estimated 931,000 in 1986 (Sedlak and Broadhurst 1996). An update from The Fourth National Incidence Study of Child Abuse and Neglect demonstrates the stabilization of the increase in the number of children injured due to abuse and neglect, estimating in the 2005–2006 study that as many as 1,256,600 children had been injured in this manner (Sedlak et al. 2010).

A rationale is offered for deciding how to appropriately apply the competencies of both bachelor- and masters-level social work graduates. Generalist skills taught in Bachelors in Social Work (BSW) programs prepare students for employment such as; hot-line screener, foster care case managers or case workers with low-to-moderate risk families, or in a position that would allow them to recruit, screen, and train foster and adoptive parents. Comparatively, skills taught in Masters in Social Work (MSW) programs are specialized for the proficiency of conducting initial investigations, working with high-risk families, terminating parental rights, placing children with adoptive families, or for management roles such as administrative or supervisory staff.

Child Welfare Curricula in Social Work Programs

The term *social worker* is often used generically, particularly in child welfare services. In this text, it denotes those CPS workers who have degrees from accredited schools of social work. Social work has long been associated with child welfare services (Scannapieco and Connell-Corrick 2003). BSW graduates are generally attributable to entry level child welfare positions, while MSW graduates more often hold clinical and managerial positions (Scannapieco and Connell-Corrick 2003; Council on Social Work Education (CSWE) 1982).

Findings by Baer and McLean (1994) suggest that most BSW programs include course content related to child welfare functions. However, in a follow-up survey conducted by the same authors, many of the same schools reported the inclusion of limited content specifically related to child welfare laws or intervention strategies that target families with a history of maltreatment. Most of these educational institutions reported that child welfare content was infused into introduction courses on child welfare policy or that it could be broadly derived from course work in generalist practice. Further, these schools reported that elective courses specific to the topic of child welfare had not been delivered in recent years due to budget constraints, a declining population of incoming social work majors, and a failure to attract non-majors.

Under current accreditation standards, BSW graduates must have generalist training in basic social work skills. They are informed about federal, state, and local policies regarding mandated services for children and their families. They are taught to perform basic practice skills of engagement, interviewing, assessment, and problem-oriented intervention (Zlotnik 2003).

The *CSWE Curriculum Policy Statement for Master's Degree Programs in Social Work Education* charges MSW programs to prepare "students for advanced social work practice in an area of concentration" (CSWE, Standard M5.2 1995). The MSW is differentiated from the BSW by "the depth, breadth, and specificity of knowledge and skill that students are expected to synthesize and apply in practice" (CSWE, Standard M5.2 1995). MSW programs are expected to produce "advanced practitioners who can analyze, intervene, and evaluate in ways that are highly differentiated, discriminating, and self-critical" (CSWE, Standard M5.7 1995). They must be prepared to "synthesize and apply a broad range of knowledge as well as practice with a high degree of autonomy and skill" (CSWE, Standard M5.7 1995).

Many MSW programs offer focused course content on services and practice orientations, which are directly related to assessing and intervening with maltreated families at both micro and macro levels. MSW courses expand the basic content of the foundation curriculum to advanced levels, graduating practitioners skilled in working within a vast range of target population needs, including economic, health, mental health, substance abuse, and other disenfranchising conditions. MSW candidates perform two supervised field practice placements, which allow them to have additional opportunities to integrate theory with practice.

Service Continuum in Child Welfare

Before considering differential assignments of BSW and MSW educated social workers in child welfare services, three domains of child welfare practice should be defined; direct service, program development and administration, and program evaluation.

Direct service is the spectrum of firsthand services provided by CPS workers and their immediate supervisors to children, families, and caretakers. These services may include central register screening, risk assessment, problem identification, crisis intervention, needs assessment, resource identification, case planning, linkages to other services, implementation of services, advocacy, evaluation of services on a case-by-case basis, and case closures.

Program Development and Administration includes services needed to develop and manage the overall operations of child welfare organizations. This may include staffing (allocation, recruitment, and hiring), benefits management, funding, program development and implementation, management-services matrix support, organization-to-organization contract negotiations, community liaison, leases and facilities maintenance, purchasing, accounting, payroll, and similar services needed to ensure the ongoing operation of programs.

Program evaluation includes the combination of formative program needs assessments, concurrent assessment and summative program outcome assessments for the purposes of determining what programs are needed, whether designated services are indeed occurring, and the effectiveness of those services. Competent program evaluation includes analysis of the effectiveness of both direct and indirect services.

Direct Services at Intake

Decision-making occurs throughout the duration of both mandated and voluntary services and is guided by screening and risk assessment protocols from point-of-entry into the system through discharge or termination (Cash 2001). Each of the direct service stages of CPS supervision—screening, investigation, ongoing services, and direct service supervision—demand different skills and will be addressed separately herein. The training of BSW and MSW educated social workers will be associated with the basic knowledge and skills needed to accomplish each major direct service function.

State Central Registry (SCR) Screeners

The number of cases registered with the State Central Registry (SCR) has increased steadily since 1974 in all states. For example, in New York a total of 136,917 cases involving 227,543 children were registered with the SCR in 1992 (with 105,305 cases opened for investigation) compared with 29,912 cases involving 59,636 children in 1974 (with 27,597 cases opened). This number has continued to rise; 164,831 reports of child abuse and neglect were made in 2008 in New York, climbing to 164,831 reports in 2009 (New York State 2011). In 1992, 55.9% of the reports were made by mandated reporters (social workers, physicians, and other healthcare professionals, mental health workers, law enforcement workers, school personnel, and medical examiners) and 44.1% were made by neighbors, relatives, and other nonmandated reporters (New York Child Protective Services 1993). The basic skills needed by those who screen calls made to abuse registries include risk assessment for maltreatment of referred children, ability to determine where and with whom the child resides, isolating the identity of the abuser, determining the extent of neglect, locating prior reports or cases involved, and determining the existence of imminent danger to the child and whether there are substantive reasons to doubt or question the veracity of the reporters. Because of the range of mandated reporters, screeners must be able to engage people with differential educational backgrounds, be sensitive and competent in addressing cultural and social issues, and be able to deal with reporters who may be highly emotional at the time of their reports. The skills needed include abilities to (1) engage informants, (2) interview informants in order to fully understand and record their complaints, (3) determine what collateral information is needed and available to address gaps in reported information, (4) recognize inconsistencies and obtain clarification, (5) delineate essential problems in reported families, and (6) determine whether reports meet criteria for preliminary investigation.

Educational Requirement for SCR Screeners

All of the essential skills needed by SCR screeners should be learned in the generalist training of BSW programs. It is recommended that SCR screeners have at least a BSW or equivalent degree.

Risk Assessment Investigators

Preliminary assessments are generally made by implementing predetermined, structured decision-making procedures, commonly known as risk assessment instruments/tools (Gambrill and Shlonsky 2000). These instruments have been designed and refined to guide the collection of pertinent data, thus providing greater consistency and reliability in the assessment of risk (Leschied et al. 2002). However, it would be a serious mistake to assume that a risk assessment instrument could replace critical decision-making processes. The skills needed for preliminary risk assessment should not be underestimated; the ongoing safety of children at risk may depend on the accuracy of their assessments. Those assessments occur in highly stressful circumstances, requiring sophisticated knowledge about the psychodynamics of dysfunctional families relative to their external and internal stressors (Shlonsky and Wagner 2005). Workers must be attuned to cultural nuances during the course of their investigations and respond competently to cultural influences on behaviors. They must have thorough knowledge of child development within cultural and environmental contexts—knowledge that permits them to discriminate normal from abnormal development—and abilities to assess the impact these developmental delays might have on family functioning.

Risk assessment workers must determine when cases do not meet risk or harm standards and be willing to take appropriate actions in order not to overwhelm already strained resources. On the other hand, when potential risk is substantiated or indicated, these social workers often are expected to develop priorities for immediate services and interventions based on factors presumed to correlate with an imminent danger to children. During preliminary assessment of safety, investigators categorize based on degrees and types of risk; identifying contributory family and community problems, and assessing individuals in the context of their family unit as a whole for strengths and weaknesses (Shlonsky and Wagner 2005).

Integrated knowledge of psychopathology, advanced assessment techniques, and intervention strategies are needed to work effectively with resistant families. Investigators must be able to gather and synthesize complex information from families and multiple collateral contacts. This information must be gathered quickly and reliably in order to delimit or react to imminent danger. Investigators must recognize the ways in which families minimize, distort, or misrepresent histories of violence, neglect, and substance abuse—or the denial of existing problems altogether, as a natural stress response to being investigated. These families fear the removal of their children and may coalesce in order to avoid being separated. It is not surprising that workers may encounter angry, hostile, and resistant parents/caretakers who act in defiant and sullen ways, children who are frightened by the conditions that engendered investigation and potential for out-of-home placements. Regardless of the intentions of a worker, their clients are likely to avoid any apparent complicity with a process they likely feel is an intrusion into the privacy and integrity of their family.

Investigators must weigh placement of children outside the home against the impact of separation, drawing from current research and theory to inform that process. Children experiencing unhealthy attachment relationships exhibit higher levels of anxiety, fearfulness, frustration, and delinquency (Sousa et al. 2011), while abused and neglected children experience incapacitating problems throughout childhood and into adulthood, including various psychopathologies and health concerns (Rogosch et al. 2011).

Social and community support systems must be appraised by risk assessment workers. Current research suggests that family and community supports mitigate potential recurrences of abuse (McCroskey et al. 1991; McCroskey et al. 2012). In addition, assessments of living conditions are especially important in determining the level of intervention required to mitigate the effects of neglect. One study suggested that it is best to investigate the well-being of the child and family as a whole rather than to solely investigate the reported incident specifically. This study utilized a multiple response system in which the child welfare worker would identify whether the family should be required to participate in services through CPS, services through outside providers, or not recommended to participate in any services. This method was determined to allow the child welfare worker to more efficiently identify the level of services needed and the manner in which these services should be provided or referred elsewhere (Lawrence et al. 2011).

Educational Requirements for Risk Assessment Investigators

Risk assessment investigators need the knowledge and skills found in MSW level education to adequately perform this function.

Ongoing Direct Services

Services provided by direct service workers immediately following an initial risk assessment are variable and offer multiple levels of complexity. This section is organized to distinguish direct services that are best handled by BSW educated social workers from those services which are best served by MSW educated social workers. While it is tempting to argue that all at-risk and maltreating families should receive the services of the most well-trained social workers possible, it is not feasible for most agencies to use MSW graduates exclusively. If maltreating families are evaluated along a continuum of low-to-high risk, it is suggested that families among the low risk categories can be well served with BSW staff and that those at higher risk may require the more advanced skills of MSW educated staff.

Direct Services for Low-to-Moderate Risk Families

Moderate-to-low risk families are often stabilized during the risk assessment process, during the development of a preliminary remedial case plan designed to prevent any further maltreatment. Direct service workers may need to refine and clarify contracts for services initiated at the time of risk assessments as the multiple problems facing client families resolve or escalate. During supervision, workers monitor compliance with established plans, make appropriate adjustments to those plans as circumstances change, evaluate the ongoing safety of children, arrange and obtain collateral information, negotiate linkages to community resources, and file reports with the courts (Smith and Donovan 2003; Rothman 1991). They are responsible for deciding when the presenting conditions that brought families under supervision are sufficiently reduced to allow for termination of such supervision.

Workers must have the skills required to engage families in the remedial process. The worker–client relationship is fundamental to the success of the foster care outcome. The relationship that the direct staff establishes with the foster child is the main determinant of the child's success in foster care. The relationship established between the child and the staff is often the main source of consistency throughout the duration of the foster care experience. The ability for the client to trust and rely on the staff to advocate for their rights is important (De Boer and Coady 2007; Inglehart 1992). The worker must be able to employ a complex repertoire of basic direct and indirect problem identification and resolution techniques across multiple levels and systems to provide the full spectrum of services sanctioned by CPS agencies, approved by the judicial system, and appropriate for their client families (Pecora 2000). As client families frequently exist within emotionally charged and economically compromised circumstances, workers need skills to limit crises as they occur, provide general conflict mediation and resolution, use interventions based on problem solving, and provide limited individual counseling (2000). They must be able to assess for substance abuse, medical problems, mental illness, transportation needs, employment and educational training deficits, child care, and parenting skills among other target areas. High rates of poverty among client families require that social workers be skilled at facilitating linkages to general assistance programs such as: Aid to families with dependent children (AFDC), food stamps, disability services, or emergency food and shelter programs. The need for these skills is confirmed by a recent study which found that families who received higher levels of intervention that included referrals and linkages, experienced lower rates of maltreatment recidivism than those families who did not receive these services (Lawrence et al. 2011).

Matching between caseworker and child must be made carefully; supervising staff must look at the demographics of the child and the caseworker and match them accordingly. Race, economic status, and sex should be taken into careful consideration during this process. The more similar in demographics a child is to the caseworker, the shorter the duration in the child welfare system (Ryan et al. 2006).

Many children come under CPS supervision specifically because of poverty (Connell-Corrick 2002). Although poverty may be a corollary of substance abuse problems or some other type of individual attribute, in many cases inadequate economic resources engender at-risk referrals independent of other factors. Mediation and advocacy skills are necessary to ensure that mandated or identified services are appropriate, delivered, and received—especially those intended to obviate the effects of poverty. Although living in poverty does not immediately mean that a child will suffer from maltreatment, the frequency of neglect is substantially higher in impoverished families (McGuinness and Schneider 2007). The inability to provide children with basic needs becomes an issue for CPS to address. Homelessness, substance abuse, human immunodeficiency virus status, and rates of incarceration are all significantly higher in impoverished families (2007). Restricted access to resources that are necessary for the well-being of the child can become problematic, such as restricted access to healthcare. A trained social worker must be knowledgeable about available resources within the community that could be accessed to moderate any unintentional sources of neglect (2007).

As many client families are under supervision of the court, direct service workers must be able to provide the courts with adequate evaluations of current levels of functioning and risk factors. This ensures that there is sufficient information on which to base decisions about whether to continue or terminate supervision. This requires that direct service workers provide testimony related to ongoing assessments of complex family dynamics.

Foster and Adoptive Home Recruitment

Not all children under CPS supervision can be kept in the homes of their parents or relatives, regardless of service intensity or sincerity of families' desires to provide adequate care. In some high-risk cases, it is simply not in the best interest of the child to do so. Thus, in order to meet demands for substitute care, some social workers become involved in recruiting, screening, training, and monitoring foster and adoptive parents. These workers must be able to conduct selective recruitment of families and effective screening of foster and adoptive homes. The importance of conducting thorough evaluations of substitute families (foster as well as adoptive) cannot be overstated. Children may present with severe problems, such as developmental lags, self-destructive behaviors, aggressive and destructive behaviors, medical and emotional problems, and inability to establish bonding relationships, all of which create a difficult and demanding parenting experience. Assessing the ability of foster and adoptive parents to cope with the multiple needs of these children requires skilled interviewers who can develop rapport with the entire family, evaluate the presence of subtle difficulties in family functioning, and determine if the potential behaviors, beliefs, values, or conditions are problematic or pose a threat to any children placed in the home. Some experts suggest that due to the extreme need for foster home placements, individuals with a marketing background could be beneficial to the foster care recruitment process. By using the media, recruitment would be able to reach a wider subset of the population, increasing demographic diversity of potential foster parents to allow for more suitable placements for the varying needs and characteristics of the children in need of placement (Cox et al. 2002; Rodwell and Biggerstaff 1993).

There are currently a number of training models for foster and adoptive parents (Price et al. 2008, 2009). Most foster and adoptive parent training models are prescriptive, with structured learning sequences. However, the success of these programs is, in part, dependent on sophisticated understanding of small group dynamics and psychoeducational group processes (Farmer and Pollock 2003). Like all training, the success of these training models is dependent on the skills of the trainer. The training given to potential foster parents must involve therapeutic techniques and strategies to deal with the emotional trauma the foster child has likely endured. Adequate preparation for foster parents to know what they can expect and how to navigate difficult situations is absolutely necessary; this may include the development of safety plans or the completion of goal-setting templates such as those used with children who have been physically of sexually abused (2003).

The turnover rate for foster parents is high and is strongly correlated with the preliminary training they receive (Buehler et al. 2003). To be effective, the foster care trainer must be comfortable and knowledgeable in the teaching process, and must be straightforward and honest regarding the possible scenarios that the foster parents might encounter. Failure to prepare the foster parents for potential problems will decrease their trust and confidence in the foster care program and will likely result in the foster parent feeling lost and powerless in their encounters with problematic children, leaving a high likelihood that they give up and leave the program—thus adding to the high rates of turnover. Adequate training allows the foster parents to establish trust, in addition to establishing a supportive network with the social workers and other foster parents (Buehler et al. 1997). Research has shown that even when foster parents rate themselves as confident in their ability to work with foster care agencies, they also report frustration and a lack of faith in utilizing the foster care system as a resource (Cooley and Petren 2011).

Educational Requirements for Providers of Direct Services to Low-to-Moderate Risk Families

The supervision of low-to-moderate risk families and the recruitment of substitute care families are appropriate roles for BSW educated social workers who have knowledge and skills as generalist practitioners.

Direct Services for Moderate-to-High Risk Families

Foster Care and Adoptive Services

Decisions to remove children from their families' care or to terminate parental rights are serious, with life-long implications for everyone involved: the children, their birth families, and their foster/adoptive families. These decisions are made by the courts based on expert testimonies from social workers regarding the projected benefits and liabilities of in-home versus out-of-home placements. The appropriate removal of children from the home—be it a temporary or permanent effort—requires several considerations: competent preparation and presentation of legal cases, interventions to mediate smooth transitions for children and their caretakers, and the eventual decision of whether the child may be returned to the family, or requires a permanent placement outside of the home. The effectiveness of workers to provide courts with sufficient information to make informed decisions is dependent on the workers' ability to synthesize the needs of individual children in relation to the family unit (birth as well as substitute) through completion of assessments. This erudition is based on a collection of considerations: predicted long-term adjustments of each child in an alternative setting, the pathology of children's families, individual pathologies of family members, strengths and deficits in all applicable systems, and anticipated resources available to the child in an alternative placement.

When a decision is made to remove a child from the home, preparation of both the child and the family of origin requires advance clinical skills. Addressing complex emotions associated with loss and grief, as well as recognizing and understanding the different manifestations of these emotions between children and adults are skills essential to helping a family adjust. Further, social workers must often provide counseling to grieving parties to ensure that transitions of children into alternative placements proceed without incident.

Conducting comprehensive evaluations of children for best possible placements and determining the development of supportive and remedial services needed by all parties are functions that require an advanced education. Determining the quality and efficacy of external evaluations is essential to ensure that decisions made are based on the best possible information, and that this information is relatively consistent across systems. Often, it is necessary to help facilitate the understanding of evaluation materials of the child by foster or adoptive parents and to put both their strengths and problems into perspective. This requires that direct service workers be able to read and interpret psychological and medical reports and synthesize them within the context of current behaviors displayed by a child into terms easily understood by the respective parties.

Direct service workers need to help children in understanding the reasons for their removal from the family of origin and to find acceptance in the temporary placement. Workers must understand the multitude of ways that children handle loss, stress, and trauma, so they can respond appropriately and inform the child without overwhelming them. Comprehensive knowledge of the short- and long-term emotional impacts of abuse and neglect and child egocentrism should guide the worker to help the child be able to construct a balanced understanding of their life events and thus avoid the internal foci of circumstance. Monitoring of post-placement adjustment requires an understanding of healthy coping mechanisms present at various developmental stages, potential pathological responses that may require immediate intervention, and reactions within the normal or expected range for a disruption of placement.

For children who are not candidates for foster parent adoptions, CPS workers turn to potential adoptive parents on termination of parental rights. Some agencies contract adoptive services to specialized facilities; others assume this responsibility directly. Preparation of children for foster or adoptive placements is critical, requiring an understanding of the dynamics of multiple separations, complex grieving processes in children who have been moved around and the corresponding effects of multiple moves on bonding to person and place, and the stages of post-placement adjustment (Newton et al. 2000; Rittner 1995). Further, workers must be able to differentiate those behaviors, which are likely to signal problems from those that are indicative of typical idiosyncratic adjustment. In some cases, this means also having to mediate the stress experienced by foster families due to disruption of daily functioning with the transition of a child.

Foster care placement personnel and recruiters are held accountable for any negligence or harm done to a child while in foster care. These recruiters must be thoroughly trained to identify indicative behaviors in order to prevent children in custody from enduring any unnecessary harm. A majority of the children who are placed in foster care have endured past trauma and abuse, any more incidences of trauma and abuse has the potential of escalating their emotional distress (Schroeder 2002).

Intensive Family Services

As a result of the passage of the Adoption Assistance and Child Welfare Act (PL 96–272), child welfare shifted from using foster care as the primary means of protecting children to relying more on intensified family services and family preservation programs (Pecora 2000; Fanshel 1992; Testa 1992). These programs were developed, in part, to mitigate family and environmental factors associated with continued risk of harm, while not subjecting children to the innate instability of foster care (Fanshel 1992). Although there are many variants of family preservation programs, most employ a multisystem, family-based intervention approach, utilizing intensive services over a limited period (Dawson and Berry 2002). Almost without exception, these programs concentrate on keeping children with their parents or on returning them to their parents from shelters, institutions, or foster care. More recently, relative care has been used in lieu of shelter or foster placements when available (Cuddeback 2004).

There is no question that these services are costly (Bagdasaryan 2005). Intensive family services generally target high-risk families that would otherwise have their children placed in substitute care. Research has shown that intensive in-home services can be effective in helping to prevent out of home placement. For example, one study found that only 17% of children in the research group, whose family received intensive intervention services were removed from their home after the intervention was implemented, and most of these children were placed back in their home by the end of the 12-month study (Daleiden et al. 2010). Additionally, 68% of the youth in the study were no longer in need of mental health services at the end of the 12-month study (2010). This displays the effectiveness of utilizing intensive in-home services to decrease the number of out of home placements.

Criteria for participation of intensive in-home services usually includes families with demonstrable histories of maltreatment, strong evidence of probable future maltreatment, history of serious parent–child relationship dynamics, and children with psychiatric histories (Bagdasaryan 2005). These determinations are generally made by the initial investigators and referrals are implemented within 24 h to prevent out-of-home placements. Most programs provide time-limited services based on low family-worker ratios. Efficacy relies on clearly established goals and tasks, frequent family contact, 24 h/7-day availability of workers, and services provided in-home rather than in agency offices (Barth et al. 2005). In general, these cases follow a basic service continuum: intake and referral, initial family contact, development of treatment strategies (clinical, concrete, supportive, and case management services), and evaluation of goal attainments (Bagdasaryn 2005; Barth et al. 2005).

Intensified family services require highly trained social workers knowledgeable in family dynamics, family-based interventions, crisis stabilization, advocacy, and brokering services (MacLeod and Nelson 2000). Goal-oriented case planning is considered essential to preserving families and reducing potential for out-of-home placements.

Problems in these families can be magnified when children are moved from shelters to foster care to kinship settings (Oosterman et al. 2007). Preparing parents or families for the return of their children is difficult. Children may have changed from their experiences in out-of-home placements, promoting confusion about expected behaviors and roles. Children may grieve losses of attachments to foster parents, causing anger and resentment on the part of families who failed to anticipate children's emotional connection to substitute caretakers and the resulting resentment over additional losses. Workers must help families become reacquainted and assist in anticipating behaviors that might emerge, providing guidance toward appropriate responses. Once children are returned to their parents and the family has been stabilized, their risk levels should be lower. They may be shifted to more traditional and routine case management and be reassigned to BSW educated workers as this transition takes place.

Case Closures

Decisions to end supervision are initiated by direct services workers. Case closures are usually made because families cannot be located after diligent search, cases are determined to meet the criteria for no/low risk, family strengths have increased to levels which mitigate reduced potential for continuing abuse or neglect, children are cared for by nonabusing or non-neglecting family members, children reach the age of majority, or termination of parental rights and permanent alternative placements have occurred. Decisions to close cases are usually shared by unit supervisors and must be approved by the courts.

Educational Requirements for Providers of Direct Services to Moderate-to-High Risk Families

Moderate-to-high risk families present with complex problems, which place children at risk for harm. In order to serve these families, an MSW education is indicated.

Direct Services Supervision

Supervisors play key roles at all levels of direct service delivery in CPS. They are responsible for the overall quality and effectiveness of the work done by screeners, preliminary risk assessment workers, and ongoing direct service workers. The services and roles performed by line supervisors directly related to case dispositions include providing leadership, determining distribution of work and setting of priorities, making individual case decisions, and providing ongoing consultations to social workers, courts, and administrative components of CPS.

Many line supervisors are responsible for hiring and termination of staff. They establish criteria for positions and conduct interviews. Once new staff is hired, they provide some or all of the on-the-job training, follow-up with performance evaluations and personnel actions, take corrective actions with supervisees who fail to meet established standards, and coordinate and facilitate ad hoc assignments.

The morale of staff is largely depended on line supervisors' ability to provide a supportive milieu which reduces stress, enhances loyalty, increases productivity, and maintains continuity of services (Landsman 2007). Nissly et al. (2005) note that perceived social support, especially from the direction of the supervisor–supervisee relationship tended to buffer the effects of many workplace stressors experienced by child welfare workers. Ongoing in-service training provided to child welfare practitioners has proven to increase worker retention (Turcotte et al. 2008; Curry et al. 2005). It allows the staff to learn "best practices" to use with their clients to buffer the stress experienced in the role confusion between advocating for client needs and meeting agency expectations or policies. Service training also improves worker competency and allows the child welfare practitioners to voice concerns in a group, enhancing social support (2008).

The field of Child Welfare has an extremely high rate of worker burnout (Fox et al. 2003). Factors that contribute to worker burnout include: poor supervision and initial training, long hours, daily exposure to high-stress environment, and threats from the job itself. This burnout can be neutralized with a line supervisor who has adequate training skills, worker compassion, and availability. Without these, BSW front line staff can quickly become overwhelmed, commonly leaving the job within 1 year, resulting in an extremely high turnover rate (2003). An experienced MSW supervisor is beneficial in order to retain BSW employees and provide more efficient and higher quality services (2003).

Many services provided to CPS families are contracted through outside providers, and line supervisors are responsible for evaluating the performance of contract providers. As new service needs are identified, line supervisors may become actively engaged in program development and evaluations (Perry 2006). Line supervisors, more than any individual worker or upper-level administrator, can influence which services and programs are effective, and which are deemed failures. Effective and creative supervisors are designers of new services or developers of ingenious new strategies, often to cope with diminishing resources and greater client demands.

Supervising worker performance, organizing work flow, and filing reports are only small portions of the supervisory role. They also serve as trouble shooters with difficult and resistant families (Landsman 2007). They help workers set priorities as policies and procedures change, often in apparent or direct conflict with previous mandates. Supervisors assist workers in identifying how specific problems in client families can result in poor compliance with court ordered services, and then help develop interventions which circumvent such resistance. Effective supervisors teach workers how to synthesize information about family functioning collected from observations and collateral contacts to compare reported, observed, and expected behaviors against presumed patterns and to identify actions and attitudes consistent with possible existent and impending problems. Further, supervisors can continuously communicate and reinforce the need to assess families in complex rather than formulaic ways (Gambrill and Shlonsky 2000).

Line supervisors must be able to apply theories and concepts about family systems within complex social contexts to actual practice situations. To function effectively, they should have advanced knowledge of advanced policy formulations and relevant cultural and ethnic diversity influence, as well as knowledge of factors that contribute to and sustain family violence, substance abuse, maladaptive or illegal behaviors, and noncompliance. They need to be knowledgeable about symptomology and the effects of major severe and persistent mental illnesses on family functioning and must be able to draw on advanced training in family work, group work, or couples therapy when workers are confronted with difficult cases. They should be trained to differentiate the best use of various family treatment models using empirical support for the effectiveness of those models.

A positive work environment has shown correlation with improved and positive caseworker influence on their cases. Interventions performed at an organizational level can help promote effectiveness of the direct-care staff. Such interventions can promote retention, decrease turnover, and improve organizational climate in both urban and rural child welfare settings. Such interventions should be carried out by knowledgeable staff members, such as MSW educated social worker (Glisson et al. 2006). Research has shown that there is great importance for front line staff to feel that they are supported and valued by the organization. Two main areas that have been identified as diminishing the extent to which front line staff feel that they are valued by the organization are higher caseloads and lower salaries (Strand and Dore 2009). Front line supervisors must work to ensure that the concerns of front line staff are heard and that interventions are put in place to address concerns in a timely manner.

Direct services supervisors at all levels must have advanced knowledge about crisis management, family systems, family pathology, and individual psychopathology. They must help workers use and apply that knowledge within the context of larger systems (administrative, community, external organizations, judiciary settings, etc.). They must have the skills needed to help CPS workers intervene effectively at each stage of service provision, beginning with initial calls to screeners and concluding when families are discharged.

Educational Requirement for Direct Services Supervisors

It is recommended that Direct Service Supervisors, including those supervising SCR screeners, risk assessment investigators, and direct service workers, be MSW educated.

Program Development and Administration

Middle and upper level managers in human services agencies are responsible for program planning, development, organization, and coordination of services (Austin 2002). They often contract services and terminate those contracts when services are found to be redundant, ineffective, or unsatisfactory. Responding to shrinking economic resources, many administrators actively pursue fund-raising at local and national levels. In some areas, administrators present testimony to legislators, funding sources, and various boards of directors concerning programmatic needs, which justify continued economic support. Once funds have been allocated or received, middle and upper level managers are responsible for budget allocation and fiscal accountability (2002). In addition, most managers have direct line supervisory roles that include hiring, evaluating, promoting, and terminating supervisory or staff level employees. Finally, in response to greater accountability to funding sources, middle and upper level managers and administrators are responsible for providing data about the effectiveness of their programs (Austin 2002; Posovac and Carey 1997)

Goal setting, required by federal and state mandates, continues to be a major function for program developers and requires skills in structuring achievable objectives (Austin 2002). The goals must be consistent with the available resources within agencies and in communities at large, in part to prevent unnecessary duplications (Lewis et al. 2011a).

To develop and implement programs, middle and upper level administrators must be able to calculate the minimum number of full-time-equivalent positions needed to deliver services (Austin 2002). Budgetary skills are, of course, essential. Program administrators must be able to estimate the cost of starting and sustaining programs. They determine competitive salaries, payroll and capital expenditures, direct services unit costs, space allocation, and ancillary and administrative overhead costs. Once budgetary constraints are understood, they determine which services are best contracted to private service providers and which should be self-administered from cost-benefit and resource allocation perspectives. In addition, decisions must be made with attention to local and national political agenda because of the impact that such matters can have on the delivery of services (2002).

Managers and administrators must ensure that program goals and objectives are being met. The organizational structure and tables of organization they deploy should represent lines of authority, communication links, and sequencing of instrumental steps to maintain momentum and to deliver services (Austin 2002). Further, as Miller (2011) clearly established, administrators must balance authoritarian and supportive functions. Clear roles for each position ensure sufficient flow of information to and from direct staff. Role clarity is critical to fostering high levels of responsiveness in line staff and enhances their willingness to signal emerging problems early (Lewis et al. 2011a). Miller (2011) and Lewis et al. (2011a) assert that in social service organizations, preventing staff burnout requires supportive administrators who establish clear lines of responsibility and authority without eradicating creativity, flexibility, or autonomy. They must be skilled program evaluators to determine if established objectives are being attained, if the objectives serve client needs, and if changes in program designs or implementations are indicated.

Managers determine minimum training and educational criteria for entry level employees and establish minimum standards of performance for retention and promotion. Among the most difficult personnel functions are developing and implementing performance evaluation standards and ensuring that supervisors use those measures (Austin 2002; Lewis et al. 2011b).

Educational Requirements for Program Developers and Administrators

The skills needed to successfully perform the advanced functions of program administrators are mostly likely found, at minimum, in MSW graduates. Some might argue that an MSW/Juris Doctor (JD) or MSW/Master of Business Administration (MBA) education enhances successful performance in these positions.

Program Evaluation

Program evaluation is a separate function critical to effective delivery of services in CPS (Lewis et al. 2011b; Posavac and Carey 1997). Without objective evaluations, programs tend to deliver services independent of current determinations of need or demonstrations of effectiveness. It is no longer tenable to simply declare the quality or success of services without substantive proof (1997). Funders are not willing to support programs without demonstrable evidence that services are being delivered as promised and that those services are achieving established objectives. Due to the identified need for program evaluation, the Children's Bureau of the U.S. Department of Health and Human Services administers the Child and Family Services Reviews. The purpose of these reviews is to help States improve and evaluate their service delivery by reviewing safety, permanency, and child and family well-being outcomes for the children and families receiving services (Children's Bureau n.d.). This further demonstrates the importance of evaluating programs effectively.

Program evaluators regularly conduct preservice assessments that define needed services and outcome studies that determine the effectiveness of existing services (Patti 2000). They begin with problem definitions, evaluations of the extent of the problems, determinations of the short- and long-term severity of the problems (particularly if left as it is), and the range of possible interventions identified to address the problems. Once needs have been determined, program evaluators assess if appropriate community services are already available and whether the services are likely to be used by target families (Lewis et al. 2011a). Accurate assessments of existing services and providers, as well as determinations of existing barriers to their use, prevent unnecessary duplication of services while identifying specific additional or expanded service needs (2011). Training of evaluators must be extensive and rigorous to prevent any child from slipping through the cracks of the child welfare system (Budd 2001). With child welfare horror stories on the front pages of newspapers, the attention to program evaluator's specialized skills has increased. A program evaluator must constantly be making evaluations based on a best-practice model and be willing and able to implement changes immediately and effectively as problems are identified (Hall 2008).

Program planners also depend on preservice research to determine acceptable levels of staffing, service center locations, operational hours, program options, and necessary ancillary services. Such determinations are based on cost-effectiveness analyses and resource utilization reviews of similar programs located in like communities addressing analogous problems (Lewis et al. 2011a).

Evaluators play important roles in collecting and collating data for federal and local funding reports. Analyses of pooled data sources suggest trends in reportable abuse and the effectiveness of programs in preventing child maltreatment recidivism. Programs may effectively serve populations in one part of the country but fail to have comparable success in other communities, raising legitimate concerns about the consistency of program implementation, data collection problems, or regional and cultural differences, which may influence outcomes (Lewis et al. 2011a). One example of how evaluators can impact service delivery is through the examination of the impact of various funding allocations on outcomes of the children and families within a service provision. Yampolskaya et al. (2011) found that the way in which funding is allocated and the way in which case management services are provided both significantly impact risk for re-entry into out-of-home placement. Furthermore, contracted case management services were seen as being associated with higher level of reentry into custody. Such evaluations can help child welfare providers to better decide how to effectively provide services.

Program evaluators can help set attainable and measurable goals for agencies and for specific programs within agencies. They can play a significant role in defining specific variables to measure program effectiveness and in implementing data collection protocols to ensure that data are accurately collected in a timely manner. Trained to evaluate published research, they can assist administrators and program developers in selecting service programs shown to be effective in preventing or reducing maltreatment in comparable populations to those expected to be served. They can ensure that data collection procedures are in place at program implementation, determine optimal interim evaluation points, and may be instrumental in designing data collection tools. This circumvents problems many programs confront when failure to document program successes for funders results from insufficient or nonexistent data collection procedures (Lewis et al. 2011a).

As populations shift, problems mutate over time, altering environmental influences and funding resources. Program evaluators bring expertise in understanding the demonstrable impact these changes have on families and programs. Once evaluators analyze outcome trends, they can assist agency administrators in developing strategies to adjust services or measurements, compensating for changing conditions.

Most program evaluators are used in preservice needs assessments or in post-service outcome analyses. Few are used in ongoing evaluations of quality of case dispositions. As more services are contracted to community-based providers, evaluators will more commonly study patterns of service utilization by direct services staff and evaluate consistency of agreed upon services.

Educational Requirements for Program Evaluators

The advanced training that most MSW graduates receive in research, coupled with their advanced knowledge of policy, programs, and practice, enable them to focus on providing critical information to administrators about the operation and effectiveness of agencies in providing agreed upon services (Lewis et al. 2011a; Posavac and Carey 1997).

Summary

BSW and MSW graduates have important but different roles to play in CPS, where an expansive array of responsibilities demands many skills and functional competencies to perform critical activities. In an era of shrinking resources, it is incumbent on CPS administrators to determine how they can most effectively and efficiently serve at-risk families. The cases worked on a daily basis by screeners, preliminary investigators, and direct service workers are extremely complex. Supervisors and managers must ensure that program goals and mandates are satisfied and that workers are adequately trained for the services they are expected to deliver.

Children enter CPS because there is evidence of harm or because there is adequate reason to suspect that they are at risk for harm. As child welfare programs have become progressively more subject to public scrutiny, emphasis on the understandable need to balance educational requirements against resource availability has developed. The realities of administration and decision-making in CPS strongly suggest that differential educational levels should be reflected in the hiring criteria for functionally diverse professional positions. A key concern is how quality services can best be provided to children and their families while remaining responsive to the economic problems impinging on publicly funded child welfare systems. Standards for minimal educational criteria in CPS staff positions should be clearly indicated by the inherent demands of those positions and the knowledge and skills needed to effectively execute attendant responsibilities.

Additional Resources

State Registry Screeners

New York State Office of Children and Family Services
http://www.ocfs.state.ny.us/main/youth_portal.asp

Intake, Investigation, and Assessment

Department of Health and Human Services
Child Welfare and Information Gateway
https://www.childwelfare.gov/responding/iia/
Washington State Department of Social and Health Services:
Practices and Procedures Guide
Department of Child Protective Services
http://www.dshs.wa.gov/ca/pubs/mnl_pnpg/chapter2.asp
University of California at Berkeley, School of Social Welfare
Risk and Safety Assessment in Child Welfare: Instrument Comparison
http://cssr.berkeley.edu/bassc/public/risk_summ.pdf

Intensive Family Services

Institute for Family Development
http://www.institutefamily.org/programs_IFPS.asp

Case Closures

Texas Department of Family and Protective Services
http://www.dfps.state.tx.us/handbooks/cps/files/CPS_pg_1460.asp

Department of Health and Human Services

Child Welfare and Information Gateway
Child Protective Services: A Guide for Caseworkers. 2003
https://www.childwelfare.gov/pubs/usermanuals/cps/cpsk.cfm

Supervision

Direct Service Supervision
https://www.childwelfare.gov/management/administration/

Program Evaluation

Department of Health and Human Services
Child Welfare and Information Gateway
A guide to Program Evaluation
https://www.childwelfare.gov/management/effectiveness/evaluation/index.cfm

References

Austin, D. M. (2002). *Human services management: Organizational leadership in social work practice*. New York: Columbia University Press.

Baer, B. L., & McLean, A. L. (1994). *A report: Child welfare curriculum in accredited BSW programs*. Green Bay: U.S. Children's Bureau, Administration on Children.

Bagdasaryan, S. (2005). Evaluating family preservation services: Reframing the question of effectiveness. *Children and Youth Services Review, 27*(6), 615–635.

Barth, R. P., Landsverk, J., Chamberlain, P., Reid, J. B., Rolls, J. A., Hurlburt, M. S., Farmer, E. M., James, S., McCabe, K. M., & Kohl, P. L. (2005). Parent-training programs in child welfare services: Planning for a more evidence-based approach to serving biological parents. *Research on Social Work Practice, 15*(5), 353–371.

Budd, K. S. (2001). Assessing parent competence in child protection cases: A clinical practice model. *Clinical Child and Family Psychology Review, 4*(1), 1–18.

Buehler, C., Anthony, C., Krishnakumar, A., Stone, G., Gerard, J., & Pemberton, S. (1997). Interparental conflict and youth problem behaviors: A meta-analysis. *Journal of Child and Family Studies, 6*, 233-247.

Buehler, C., Cox, M. E., & Cuddeback, G. (2003). Foster parents' perceptions of factors that promote or inhibit successful fostering. *Qualitative Social Work, 2*(1), 61–83.
Cash, S. J. (2001). Risk assessment in child welfare: The art and science. *Children and Youth Services Review, 23*(11), 811–830.
Children's Bureau. (n.d.). Child and family services review fact sheet. http://www.acf.hhs.gov/programs/cb/cwmonitoring/recruit/cfsrfactsheet.htm. Accessed 12 July 2011.
Connell, C. M., Bergeron, N., Katz, K. H., Saunders, L., & Tebes, J. K. (2007). Re-referral to child protective services: The influence of child, family, and case characteristics on risk status. *Child Abuse and Neglect, 31*(5), 573–588.
Connell-Carrick, K. (2000). A critical review of the empirical literature: Identifying correlates of child neglect. *Child & Adolescent Social Work Journal, 20*(5), 389-425.
Cooley, M. E., & Petren, R. E. (2011). Foster parent perceptions of competency: Implications for foster parent training. *Children and Youth Services Review, 33*(10), 1968–1974.
Council on Social Work Education (CSWE). (1982). Curriculum policy for the master's degree programs in social work education. *Social Work Education Reporter, 30*(3), 5–12.
Council on Social Work Education (CSWE). (1995). *Handbook of accreditation standards and procedures* (rev. ed.). Washington, DC: Council on Social Work Education (CSWE).
Cox, M. E., Buehler, C., & Orme, J. G. (2002). Recruitment and foster family service. *Journal of Sociology and Social Welfare, 29*, 151–157.
Cuddeback, G. S. (2004). Kinship family foster care: A methodological and substantive synthesis of research. *Children and Youth Services Review, 26*(7), 623–639.
Curry, D., McCarragher, T., & Dellmann-Jenkins, M. (2005). Training, transfer, and turnover: Exploring the relationship among transfer of learning factors and staff retention in child welfare. *Children and Youth Services Review, 27*(8), 931–948.
Daledien, E., Pang, D., Roberts, D., Slavin, L., & Pestle, S. (2010). Intensive home based services within a comprehensive system of care for youth. *Journal of Child and Family Studies, 19*, 318–325.
Dawson, K., & Berry, M. (2002). Engaging families in child welfare services: an evidence-based approach to best practice. *Child Welfare, 81*(2), 293.
De Boer, C., & Coady, N. (2007). Good helping relationships in child welfare: Learning from stories of success. *Child and Family Social Work, 12*(1), 32–42.
Fanshel, D. (1992). Foster care as a two-tiered system. *Children and Youth Service Review, 14*, 49–60.
Farmer, E., & Pollock, S. (2003). Managing sexually abused/abusing children in substitute care. *Child and Family Social Work, 8*(2), 101–112.
Fink, A., & McCloskey, L. (1990). Moving child abuse and neglect prevention programs forward: Improving program evaluations. *Child Abuse and Neglect, 14*, 187–206.
Fox, S. R., Miller, V. P., & Barbee, A. P. (2003). Finding and keeping child welfare workers. *Journal of Human Behavior in the Social Environment, 7*(1–2), 67–81.
Gambrill, E., & Shlonsky, A. (2000). Risk assessment in context. *Children and Youth Services Review, 22*(11), 813–837.
Geeraert, L., Van den Noortgate, W., Grietens, H., & Onghena, P. (2004). The effects of early prevention programs for families with young children at risk for physical child abuse and neglect: A meta-analysis. *Child Maltreatment, 9*(3), 277–291.
Glisson, C., Dukes, D., & Green, P. (2005). The effects of the ARC organizational intervention on caseworker turnover, climate, and culture in children welfare services. *Child Abuse and Neglect, 30*, 855–880.
Glisson, C., Dukes, D., & Green, P. (2006). The effects of the ARC organizational intervention on caseworker turnover, climate, and culture in children's service systems. *Child Abuse and Neglect, 30*(8), 855-880.
Hall, H. (2008). Evaluating the evaluators in custodial dispute placements. *Forensic psychology and neuropsychology for criminal and civil cases* (pp. 527–546).
Hall, H. (2008). Evaluating the evaluators in custodial dispute placements. *Forensic psychology and neuropsychology for criminal and civil cases* (pp. 527–546).

Hutchison, E. D. (1993). Mandatory reporting laws: Child protective case finding gone awry? *Social Work, 38*(1), 56–63.
Inglehart, A. P. (1992) Adolescents in foster care: Factors affecting the worker youth relationship. *Children and Youth Services Review, 14*(3–4), 305–322.
Landsman, M. (2007). Supporting child welfare supervisors to improve worker retention. *Child Welfare, 86*(2), 105–124.
Lawrence, C. N., Rosanbalm, K. D., & Dodge, K. A. (2011). Multiple response team: Evaluating of policy change in north Carolina's child welfare system. *Children and Youth Services Review, 33*(11), 2355–2365.
Leschied, A. W., Chiodo, D., Whitehead, P. C., Hurley, D., & Marshall, L. (2002). The empirical basis of risk assessment in child welfare: the accuracy of risk assessment and clinical judgment. *Child Welfare, 82*(5), 527–540.
Lewis, J. A., Packard, T. R., & Lewis, M. D. (2011a). Management of human service programs. CengageBrain.com.
Lewis, T. L., Kotch, J., Wiley, T. R., Litrownik, A. J., English, D. J., Thompson, R., Zolotor, A. J., Block, S. D., Dubowitz, H. (2011b). Internalizing problems: A potential pathway from childhood maltreatment to adolescent smoking. *Journal of Adolescent Health, 48*(3), 247-52.
MacLeod, J., & Nelson, G. (2000). Programs for the promotion of family wellness and the prevention of child maltreatment: A meta-analytic review. *Child Abuse and Neglect, 24*(9), 1127–1149.
McCroskey, J., Nishimoto, R., & Subramanian, K. (1991). Assessment in family support systems: Initial reliability and validity testing of the family assessment form. *Child Welfare, 70*(1), 19–33.
McCroskey, J., Pecora, P., Franke, T., Christie, C., & Lorthridge, J. (2012). Can public child welfare help to prevent child maltreatment? Promising findings from Los Angeles. *Journal of Family Strengths, 12*(1), 1–23.
McGuinness, T. M., & Schnieder, K. (2007). Poverty, child maltreatment, and foster care. *Journal of the American Psychiatric Nurses Association, 13*(5), 296–303.
Miller, K. (2011). Organizational communication: Approaches and processes. CengageBrain.com.
Newton, R. R., Litrownik, A. J., & Landsverk, J. A. (2000). Children and youth in foster care: Disentangling the relationship between problem behaviors and number of placements. *Child abuse and neglect, 24*(10), 1363–1374.
New York State. (2011). 2008 & 2009 Child Protective Services Reports. Office of Children & Family Services. http://ocfs.ny.gov/main/cps/statistics.asp.
New York Child Protective Services. (1993). State Central Register: Reporting highlights 1974-1992. Unpublished report to New York governor and legislature, 1992. Quoted data were obtained through manipulation of statistics contained in Table 9 of the report.
Nissly, J. A., Barak, M. E. M., & Levin, A. (2005). Stress, social support, and workers' intentions to leave their jobs in public child welfare. *Administration in Social Work, 29*(1), 79–100.
Oosterman, M., Schuengel, C., Wim Slot, N., Bullens, R. A., & Doreleijers, T. A. (2007). Disruptions in foster care: A review and meta-analysis. *Children and Youth Services Review, 29*(1), 53–76.
Patti, R. J. (Ed.). (2000). *The handbook of social welfare management*. London: Sage.
Pecora, P. J. (Ed.). (2000). *The child welfare challenge: Policy, practice, and research*. New Jersey: Transaction Publishers.
Perry, R. E. (2006). Education and child welfare supervisor performance: Does a social work degree matter? *Research on Social Work Practice, 16*(6), 591–604.
Posavac, E. J., & Carey, R. G. (1997). *Program evaluation: Methods and case studies*. New Jersey: Prentice-Hall.
Price, J. M., Chamberlain, P., Landsverk, J., Reid, J. B., Leve, L. D., & Laurent, H. (2008). Effects of a foster parent training intervention on placement changes of children in foster care. *Child Maltreatment, 13*(1), 64–75.
Price, J. M., Chamberlain, P., Landsverk, J., & Reid, J. (2009). KEEP foster-parent training intervention: Model description and effectiveness. *Child and Family Social Work, 14*(2), 233–242.

Rittner, B. (1995). Children on the move: Placement patterns in children's protective services. *Families in Society, 76*(8), 469–477.
Rodwell, M. K., & Biggerstaff, M. A. (1993). Strategies for recruitment and retention of foster families. *Children and Youth Services Review, 15*(5), 403–419.
Rogosch, F. A., Dackis, M. N., Cicchetti, D. (2011). Child maltreatment and allostatic load: Consequences for physical and mental health in children from low-income families. *Development and Psychopathology, 23,* 1107–1124.
Rothman, J. (1991). A model of case management: Toward empirically based practice. *Social Work, 36*(6), 520–528.
Ryan, J.P., Garnier, P., Zyphur, M., & Zhai, F. (2006). Investigating the effects of caseworker characteristics in child welfare. *Child and Youth Services Review, 28,* 993–1006.
Scannapieco, M., & Connell-Corrick, K. (2003). Do collaborations with schools of social work make a difference for the field of child welfare? Practice, retention and curriculum. *Journal of Human Behavior in the Social Environment, 7*(1–2), 35–51.
Schroeder, L. O. (2002). Negligence in placement and supervision of children in foster care: Are social workers liable? *Children and Youth Review, 8*(3), 219–226.
Sedlak, A. J., & Broadhurst, D. D. (1996). *Executive summary of the third national incidence study of child abuse and neglect*. Washington, DC: DHHS.
Sedlak, A. J., Mettenburg, J., Basena, M., Petta, I., McPherson, K., Greene, A., & Li, S. (2010). *Fourth national incidence study of child abuse and neglect (NIS-4): Report to Congress.* Washington, DC: U.S. Department of Health and Human Services. http://www.acf.hhs.gov/programs/opre/abuse_neglect/natl_incid/reports/natl_incid/natl_incid_title.html.
Shlonsky, A., & Wagner, D. (2005). The next step: Integrating actuarial risk assessment and clinical judgment into an evidence-based practice framework in CPS case management. *Children and youth services review, 27*(4), 409–427.
Smith, B. D., & Donovan, S. E. (2003). Child welfare practice in organizational and institutional context. *Social Service Review, 77*(4), 541–563.
Sousa, C., Herrenkohl, T. I., Moylan, C. A., Tajima, E. A., Klika, J. B., Herrenkohl, R. C., & Russo, M. J. (2011). Longitudinal study on the effects of child abuse and children's exposure to domestic violence, parent-child attachments, and antisocial behavior in adolescence. *Journal of interpersonal violence, 26*(1), 111–136.
Strand, V. C., & Dore, M. M. (2009). Job satisfaction in stable state child welfare workforce: Implications for staff retention. *Children and Youth Services Review, 31*(3), 391–397.
Testa, M. F. (1992). Conditions of risk for substitute care. *Children and Youth Services Review, 14,* 27–36.
Titterington, L. (1990). Foster care training: A comprehensive approach. *Child Welfare, 69*(2), 157–165.
Turcotte, D., Lamonde, G., & Beaudoin, A. (2008). Evaluation of an in-service training for child welfare practitioners. *Research on Social Work Practice, 19,* 31–41.
Yampolskaya, S., Armstrong, M. I., & King-Miller, T. (2011). Contextual and individual-level predictors of abused children's reentry into out-of-home care: A multilevel mixture survival analysis. *Child Abuse and Neglect, 35*(9), 670–679.
Zlotnik, J. L. (2003). Preparing social workers for child welfare practice: Lessons from an historical review of the literature. *Journal of Health and Social Policy, 15*(3–4), 5–21.

Chapter 2
Legal Requisites for Social Work Practice in Child Abuse and Neglect

John S. Wodarski and Jessica W. Johnston

Introduction

Since 1962, when the "battered child syndrome" first began to generate national concern over the problem of child maltreatment, immense progress has been made in efforts to protect children (Kempe et al. 2013). The prevalence and negative consequences of abuse and neglect are now recognized, and systems have been established to identify and ameliorate child maltreatment. Although intervention efforts have saved lives and benefited thousands of children, the systems that address child maltreatment are still evolving, and their limitations have been widely acknowledged (Fallon et al. 2010)

There is considerable confusion and concern among social workers regarding the workings of child protective services (CPS) and the legal systems that deal with child abuse and neglect. Social workers in agencies, schools, institutions, and private practice are expected to identify and report suspected cases of maltreatment and, increasingly, to testify in court proceedings in these cases. Certainly, those in the helping professions want to comply with reporting laws and protect endangered children, yet many are unclear as to what constitutes abuse and neglect in the eyes of CPS and the law. Others know from firsthand experience that involving CPS may result in adverse consequences for children and their families, may interfere with therapeutic relationships, and may lead to reprisals by clients or employers. To make responsible and effective decisions, social workers must understand the written and unwritten laws and procedures followed in child maltreatment cases (Broadhurst et al. 2010). However, at the same time, it must be noted that literature indicates that CPS systems are overburdened by ongoing maltreatment cases, hundreds of thousands of referrals (for which many turn out to be unsubstantiated), and a high burn out rate for staff (Goldman and Grimbeek 2011).

J. S. Wodarski (✉) · J. W. Johnston
The University of Tennessee, Knoxville, TN, USA
e-mail: jwodarsk@utk.edu

J. S. Wodarski et al. (eds.), *Evidence-Informed Assessment and Practice in Child Welfare,* DOI 10.1007/978-3-319-12045-4_2

Societal efforts to protect endangered children have resulted in increased responsibilities for social workers, who are expected to identify, report, and provide testimony in suspected cases of abuse and neglect. Their decisions in these cases may have profound consequences for children, families, and themselves (Bergman 2013). This chapter will increase social workers' knowledge of legal requisites and system realities in child protection to help them make high-quality decisions.

What is Child Abuse?

There is no universal agreement on what constitutes child abuse or neglect. The 1974 Child Abuse Prevention and Treatment Act (CAPTA) established broad parameters for defining child maltreatment, but permitted each state to develop its own definition within these parameters (Price et al. 2012). The Keeping Children and Families Safe Act of 2003 is an amendment that improved and reauthorized the CAPTA through 2008, but did not change its stance on the definition of child abuse (NASW 2011; U.S. Department of Health & Human Services 2011a). Although most state definitions are clear in cases of severe or deviant maltreatment, they are vague in defining the full continuum of maltreatment. The vagueness is not necessarily inappropriate, because cases vary widely in their particulars, and local child care standards differ as well. Hence, considerable latitude may be necessary for case-by-case discretion by CPS workers and judges. Such discretion may not always be applied evenhandedly but generally reflects community and societal views regarding the protection of children (Bergman 2013).

In 1986, more than 1½ million children were abused or neglected according to the National Center on Child Abuse and Neglect U.S. Department of Health and Human Services 2011. This represented a 66% increase since 1980. During this time, the most frequently occurring subcategories of maltreatment identified by professionals are physical neglect (9.1 per 1000 children), physical abuse (5.7), educational neglect (4.6), emotional neglect (3.5), emotional abuse (3.4), and sexual abuse (2.5). Over the last 25 years, many of these definitions have changed. There are now four categories of maltreatment, which include physical abuse, sexual abuse, neglect, and emotional abuse. More recently, additional subcategories have been defined, including abandonment, which is considered to be a specific type of neglect in which the child has been left alone for an extended period of time and the whereabouts of the parents are unknown. Another recently added subcategory of child abuse and neglect is substance abuse, which is defined as when the child is exposed to the manufacturing, distribution, or use of illegal substances (U.S. Department of Health & Human Services 2011b).

Moreover, there is now a debate being waged regarding the difference between broad and narrow definitions of child maltreatment. One side argues for a narrow definition, indicating that before any state or federal agency steps into the private lives of citizens, observable and measurable harm must have been done to a child. Those advocating for a broader view indicate the long-term effects of maltreatment in any form, recognizing that sometime this "harm" might not manifest for years (Pecora et al. 2012).

This broader view idea has roots already laid within the mandated reporting framework. One aspect that cannot be ignored is that of reasonable or just cause or reporting, the belief behind this being that it is better to report suspected cases of maltreatment that turn out to be invalid then to have a child slip through the cracks with no hope of help. However, as with other frameworks, this creates problems. There is a vagueness written into child maltreatment laws that does not extend well across different circumstances, which could correlate to certain mandated reporters being unsure of the proper steps to take (Levi and Crowell 2011).

In 2006 there were approximately 3.3 million referrals to CPS, representing 6 million children, made to CPS organizations asking for an investigation into child maltreatment (U.S. Department of Health and Human Services 2008). Of these, 61.7 % (3.6 million children) received a CPS investigation or assessment (Lee et al. 2013). Of these assessments/investigations, it was determined that 30 % found that at least one child had suffered from, or was suffering from, some type of maltreatment. Moreover, it seems that, based upon the 1986 child maltreatment figures, the number of child maltreatment cases discovered actually decreased. In 2006, the U.S. Department of Health and Human Services (2008) indicates, that 905,000 children were found to have been abused or neglected. Of these 905,000 children, it was determined that 64 % were neglected, 16 % experienced some form of physical abuse, nearly 9 % experienced sexual abuse, and about 6 % experienced emotional maltreatment (U.S. Department of Health & Human Services 2008). Another staggering figure is represented by the estimated 1530 children who died as a result of maltreatment in 2006, as reported by The National Child Abuse and Neglect Data System (NCANDS). These figures have remained rather consistent in recent years, as approximately 3.3 million referrals were also made to CPS agencies in 2010, of which 90.3 % were investigated (U.S. Department of Health and Human Services 2011c).

It is clear that some areas of discovered maltreatment have decreased since 1986, while others have actually increased. However, what is not clear are the reasons why. Have the actual number of maltreatment cases decreased/increased since 1986, or have the number of mandated reporters increased therefore causing an increase in certain cases of reporting (Lee et al. 2013)?

Given the prevalence of child maltreatment, social workers can hardly avoid discovering suspected cases. To respond effectively, they must be aware not only of the legal definitions, but also of how these definitions are interpreted and practiced. For instance, legal definitions emphasize that intervention decisions should be based on acts of the parents rather than on the degree of physical or emotional harm to the child. This preventative measure is aimed at stopping maltreatment before it results in injury or death. In practice, however, overburdened CPS systems must filter out less severe cases, and evidence of harm is the primary factor in these decisions (Alter 1985). Indeed, experts support this practice, reasoning that social workers should not intervene in borderline cases when a child is functioning adequately (Kempe et al. 2013). It follows that social workers should also consider the degree of harm to the child in deciding whether a case fits the working definition of child abuse or neglect. Of course, children who are maltreated and left within the abusive environment also suffer more than just physical or emotional damage. It can affect a child's development in relation to coping skills, social interaction skills, and attachment ability (Asawa et al. 2008).

Legal and working definitions differ regarding who may be considered victims or perpetrators under the law. The 1974 Child Abuse Prevention and Treatment Act is clear that any child under the age of 18 may be a victim, and any person who is responsible for the child's health and welfare may be a perpetrator, including parents and legal guardians, other relatives, babysitters, day care workers, teachers, youth group directors, and institutional staff. However, state and local policies have sometimes circumvented the intent of the law by declaring that certain classes of individuals (especially school personnel) be immune from child maltreatment prosecution (Davidson 1988). In some states, victims who are 17 years old are not served by CPS because the juvenile courts in these states have jurisdiction over youths only until their 17th birthday. Thus, CPS cannot petition the court for custody or court-imposed conditions in these cases.

Adolescents are generally under-served by CPS because they are less likely than younger children to show signs of serious physical damage from abuse or neglect. Adolescent victims of maltreatment (especially physical abuse) are more likely to respond with antisocial or disruptive behaviors that mask the underlying family problems. These youths are often inappropriately referred to juvenile authorities and labeled offenders, with little chance of being reclassified as abused or neglected (Phillips et al. 2010). In addition, recent research in this area suggests that both Ph.D. psychologists and Masters level social workers favored some bias toward reporting potential victims of maltreatment when the child is younger rather than older (Levi and Crowell 2011). It also appears that the child's socioeconomic status affects reporting statistics, with children from a lower socioeconomic class being reported at a higher incidence (Levi and Crowell 2011). Social workers who identify cases of adolescent maltreatment must be aware of system limitations and the need to expend extra efforts (that is, advocacy, documentation) to obtain appropriate services for these youths.

While the purpose of Child Protective Services is clear, and the role they play in working with maltreated children is vital, there are a plethora of flaws within the system. Dr. Kempe, best known for "discovering" battered child syndrome, initiated the International Society for Prevention of Child Abuse and Neglect, which has influenced public policy over the last 40 years. What eventually became of this was the CPS or DCS system that is in place across the United States. However, the child protective system that was created with the help of Dr. Kempe is now outdated and obsolete when faced with child maltreatment today (Melton 2005). Moreover, it has been suggested that some referrals to CPS could be simple calls for help from neighbors or friends of a family that is struggling economically, and are not actual calls of maltreatment—further suggesting that the CPS system is outdated and obsolete (Melton 2005).

Physical Abuse and Neglect

There is no question that acts such as physical battering, torture, or the withholding of essential nourishment by parents fit the legal and working definitions of abuse or neglect. Nonaccidental, repeated, or unexplained injuries and extreme or persistent lack of adequate food, shelter, clothing, protection, supervision, or medical and dental care are grounds for official investigation. On the other hand, although less-than-optimal parenting behaviors and living conditions are cause for legitimate concern, poor child care cannot be classified as abuse or neglect. For example, the reasonable use of corporal punishment by parents is not illegal, and many working parents cannot afford child care services. Further, millions of children are damaged by living in poverty, but they cannot all be labeled neglected and provided with services. CPS funding limitations preclude such broad interpretation of child abuse and neglect statutes. Working definitions of physical abuse and neglect require evidence of a degree of harm that exceeds community standards (Phillips et al. 2010).

Emotional Abuse and Neglect

Definitional problems are particularly troublesome when harm to the child is less tangible than physical injury. Many state laws give scant attention to emotional abuse or neglect or rely on broad designations such as "mental cruelty." Yet emotional maltreatment, which may involve distorted parental behaviors such as habitual verbal assault, rejection, tying a child to a bed, or confining a child to a closet may cause severe psychological harm to children. Symptoms can include extreme anxiety, withdrawal, depression, aggression, suicide attempts, fire setting, and other serious emotional difficulties (Walker 2010).

Emotional maltreatment cases are under-served by CPS because they are difficult to substantiate and treat. To obtain services for these children and their families, concerned social workers must supplement CPS efforts by accumulating documentation by witnesses to incidents of emotional maltreatment and evidence of harm to the child. Horwtiz and colleagues offer guidelines for collecting and presenting competent evidence (2010).

Sexual Abuse

No subcategory of maltreatment continues to generate as much consternation and controversy as sexual abuse. Legal definitions encompass a wide range of activities from rape, prostitution, and child pornography to fondling and intentional exposure. Legally, sexual abuse is defined wholly on the basis of acts of the perpetrator, not specific harm to the child; it is considered inherently harmful for children to be used for the sexual gratification of older caretakers (Stoltenborgh et al. 2011). Research on sexually abused children tends to support this view, although initial symptoms of emotional damage are generally shown to be moderate rather than severe.

On the other hand, studies of adult women who are sexually abused as children indicate that the long-term effects of such abuse are serious and may include depression, anxiety, isolation, negative self-concept, self destructive behavior, substance abuse, and sexual maladjustment (Sousa et al. 2010). Studies that could guide practice by establishing the short-term effects of various forms and intensities of sexual abuse have yet to be conducted. Most likely, childhood symptoms involve dissociative processes that are difficult to detect (Sousa et al. 2010).

The number of identified sexual abuse cases increased threefold from 1980–1986 (Walker 2010), undoubtedly caused in part by greater awareness (that is, less denial) of the problem. It is now generally acknowledged that sexual abuse may involve very young children (including infants) and male children as well as adolescent females. Professionals no longer assume that natural fathers are never involved, that parental denials are reliable, or that children's allegations are fantasies (Walker 2010). However, recognition of the problem has been so recent that many communities have not yet developed adequate response mechanisms or community-based treatment programs. As a result, sexually abused children are often exposed to additional trauma through the intervention process, which may include multiple interviews, court appearances, family breakups, foster care placements, imprisonment of the perpetrator, and loss of family income (Phillips et al. 2010). Some progress has been made in this area with the establishment and growth of the National Children's Advocacy Center (NCAC) since 1985. The NCAC works to streamline the reporting and investigation of child abuse cases in a therapeutic and child friendly environment that does not prolong the traumatic experience of repeatedly describing the abuse (NCAC 2011).

Certainly, sexual abuse must be stopped, and social workers must report known cases, but advocacy, activism, and public awareness efforts are essential if children are to be spared additional victimization. Social workers must press for the implementation of interagency protocols, modified courtroom procedures, and family treatment programs, which can reduce the negative impact of interventions on sexually abused children (Sousa et al. 2010).

Since the early 1980s, a plethora of sex offender legislation has passed on both State and Federal levels. Tennessee implemented the Containment Model to Sex Offender Treatment in the late 1980s in conjunction with a community corrections/probation program. In 1996, Tennessee also implemented the Sex Offender Registry. However, the most controversial aspect of sex offender legislation came in 2006 with the Adam Walsh Act. Title 1, the Sex Offender Registry and Notification Act (SORNA) requires all states to have a sex offender registry, and further regulates the registry requirements and defines terms, etc. (National Center for the Prosecution of Child Abuse 2007). The Adam Walsh act also requires that Tennessee have a juvenile sex offender database, and mandates that if states wish to receive federal funds, they must implement this policy. The effectiveness of a juvenile sex offender database must be left for another discussion, and its implications are far reaching.

Mandatory Reporting of Child Maltreatment

Federal statutes mandate that many professionals, including social workers, report child maltreatment. The mandate requires reporting even in relationships where confidentiality is otherwise protected. For instance, the National Association of Social Workers (NASW) Code of Ethics specifically states that an exception to client confidentiality is when a social worker has reason to believe that child abuse has occurred (NASW 1999). Although state statutes vary considerably, all specify when, how, and to whom reports should be made. Typically, mandated reporters who suspect that abuse or neglect has occurred must promptly report their suspicions, in writing, orally, or both, to designated authorities (police, CPS, juvenile services, or the local child abuse and neglect council or hot line). The reporter should provide his or her name and information on the name, age, address, and whereabouts of the child, the nature and extent of the maltreatment, and any other information that led the individual to suspect abuse or neglect. The name of the reporter is confidential and cannot be released without a court order (Phillips et al. 2010).

While mandated reporting continues to cause controversy, it is without a doubt a legal and ethical issue. The very term "mandated" indicates the level of seriousness at which professionals must consider this. Again, research suggests that only a few (if any at all) professionals actually report all suspected cases of maltreatment. Several reasons are given for this phenomenon within the literature, and they include such beliefs as not having enough evidence to make a report, the belief that CPS will not intervene as needed, cultural differences/competency, and the belief that reporting suspected maltreatment will cause further harm to a child (Levi and Crowell 2011).

All state reporting statutes guarantee immunity from civil liability to mandated reporters who act in good faith (without malice) (Sousa et al. 2010). This is true even when the report is not substantiated by CPS investigators. However, immunity applies only after a report is filed with the proper authorities. Social workers and others who conduct their own investigations before reporting are not protected from civil action. In certain maltreatment cases, especially those involving emotional maltreatment or adolescent victims, the decision to intervene may depend on supplemental documentation provided by reporters. In these cases, a report should be filed early in the documentation process, as soon as there is reasonable cause to suspect abuse or neglect (Horwtiz et al. 2010).

Most states outline criminal penalties or civil penalties for failure to report suspected abuse or neglect (Phillips et al. 2010). Even so, there is evidence that professionals report fewer than half of maltreatment cases known to them. This may reflect a general lack of familiarity with reporting responsibilities or denial of the reality of child maltreatment, but other concerns also contribute to reluctance to report, including negative perceptions about the functioning of CPS, fear that the treatment process will be disrupted, and pressure from supervisors not to report. Additionally, abuse or neglect occurring in out-of-home care often goes unreported because states are still developing adequate laws and procedures to address the problem of institutional maltreatment (Sousa et al. 2010).

Negative Perceptions of Child Protective Services

Clinical experience suggests that CPS interventions may have harmful consequences. The investigation may be traumatic for the child and family, appropriate treatment may not be provided, and removal of the child or parent from the home may increase the child's sense of victimization and produce psychological difficulties. These legitimate concerns reflect the serious underfunding of CPS agencies. For instance, research has shown that family therapists report having negative experiences with CPS that can most frequently be traced to issues of underfunding and understaffing of CPS agencies (Strozier et al. 2005).

Nevertheless, there is evidence that maltreated children are helped more than harmed by CPS involvement. Social workers must carefully assess suspected cases of maltreatment and judge whether a particular case is serious enough to warrant the interventions that may follow reporting. Behavioral indicators alone, without physical evidence or statements by the child or others, should not be considered sufficient grounds for reporting. Further, observable conditions must be linked to specific caregiver behaviors or omissions to be classed as abuse or neglect (Walker 2010).

Child Protective Services plays an invaluable role in protecting children; however, just as is the case of most agencies and professionals, mistakes are sometimes made. It is not fair to CPS to judge the entire process on a few select cases that did not end as hoped. There is a belief by some professionals that CPS is useless in terms of doing good. Those who subscribe to this ideology may further believe that one reason that maltreatment statistics rise and/or fall is due to CPS screening out certain cases. Research suggests that this is not the case, and that the statistics rise and/or fall based upon the actions of the mandated reporters and nothing else (Alvarez et al. 2010).

Reluctance to report may also reflect social workers' anxiety about the possibility of testifying in court regarding their observations. At least one commentator has suggested that the principle of immunity from liability for mandated reports should be extended to include exemption from court involvement (Levi and Crowell 2011). However, a social worker's testimony may be the key component in ensuring that a child will not continue to be abused or neglected. Thus, although the majority of cases do not require the reporter to testify in court, social workers should be prepared to testify when necessary. One publication that can help alleviate anxiety is *Child Abuse and the Law: A Legal Primer for Social Workers*, which explains courtroom procedures and offers guidelines for potential witnesses (Phillips et al. 2010).

Fear of Disruption of the Treatment Process

Social workers involved in therapeutic relationships with clients may assume that reporting will lead to termination of treatment by clients. Some research has found that as many as 27 % of clients terminate therapeutic services after mandated reporting by a therapist (Bean et al. 2011). However, studies do not support this assumption (Levi and Crowell 2011). In Watson and Levine's study, fewer than one fourth of clients terminated treatment following the filing of a report by a therapist. The authors concluded that "reporting abuse is not always detrimental to the goals of therapy and under some circumstances may even be helpful" (p. 255). At the outset of treatment, of course, practitioners should openly acknowledge limits and the promise of confidentiality. When evidence has become apparent that reportable offenses have occurred, trust may be maintained through candid discussion of the dilemma faced by the therapist, who must by law file a report despite personal reluctance to do so. The client's fear that termination while under CPS investigation will negatively affect the outcome of the case may also encourage continuation in therapy.

This issue of disruption of the treatment process or therapeutic alliance after mandated reporting has not been thoroughly explored in current research, as the most recent results come from Rokop (2003). This research examined the client's perspective of how the therapeutic relationship changes after mandated reporting. Clients who had positive experiences in therapy after mandated reporting typically reported having a strong therapeutic relationship before the report was made, and reported that the therapist was direct and apologetic about having to make the report. On the other hand, clients who had negative experiences in therapy after mandated reporting generally reported having a poor alliance with the therapist pre-report, and reported that the therapist was inexperienced, indirect about making the report, and lacked empathy (Rokop 2003). This research indicates that it is not the act of mandated reporting itself that can be harmful to the therapeutic relationship, but the manner with which the reporting is handled by the therapist. However, it is critical that this issue be revisited with more current data.

Pressure from Supervisors Not to Report

Many agencies, schools, and institutions have developed written or ad hoc procedures for the management of child abuse and neglect cases identified by staff. Often, one person or a team is designated to receive information from an employee, who is discouraged or even prohibited from reporting directly. Unfortunately, the designated staff member or team may then fail to report the employee's suspicions. In most states, the law is unclear as to who is ultimately liable for the failure to report in these cases, or what recourse an employee may have for adverse job-related action taken against him or her for direct reporting (Horwitz et al. 2010). Social workers in agencies, schools, and institutions may thus find that their ability to protect child victims is seriously compromised. When in-house channels fail, workers who report their suspicions directly to the authorities may be reprimanded or fired.

Although all states provide immunity from liability for reporting in good faith, and a few states have passed specific legislation to protect employees who report, redress often proves to be time-consuming, costly, and traumatic (Horwitz et al. 2010). Complaints must show that the adverse employment action was taken in retaliation for filing the report and was not based on other factors, such as budgetary cutbacks or a history of conflict with supervisors. One CPS director suggested that employees who are dissatisfied with their agency's response can report anonymously (although this weakens the case) or can explain the situation and request that extra precautions be taken to keep their identity confidential (although this cannot be guaranteed if the case goes to court). Legislative reforms are needed that provide full protection against retaliation to mandated reporters (Levi and Crowell 2011).

Reporting Institutional Maltreatment

There is evidence that the incidence of out-of-home maltreatment may be double the rate of familial maltreatment (Walker (2010). In 1984, the Child Abuse Prevention and Treatment Act was amended to require the reporting of suspected abuse and neglect in out-of-home settings. A growing number of states now require reports of maltreatment in foster and residential care homes and day care settings. However, already overburdened CPS systems have been slow to respond. Out-of-home cases are time consuming and require specialized skills beyond the scope of CPS personnel, who were trained to investigate and manage familial maltreatment. Media attention, political pressure, and the capacity of institutions to protect themselves often increase the difficulty of these cases. Additionally, the issue of conflict of interest arises when CPS offices must investigate sites they rely on as placement resources. For the reporter, these complexities mean that complaints are likely to be discouraged or minimized (Levi and Crowell 2011).

To address these problems, CPS offices should establish specialized units for out-of-home care investigations (Horwitz et al. 2010). In the meantime, social workers who suspect institutional abuse or neglect must be aware of the current limitations in the system. Liability for failure to report is not the primary concern in these cases; the concern is over inadequate response from CPS and job-related repercussions for reporting maltreatment occurring within one's own agency. Concerned social workers should carefully document incidents of institutional abuse or neglect, consequent harm to the child, and their own actions in the matter. Expert consultation may be necessary, particularly when agency policies are questioned, such as the improper use of physical restraints and psychotropic medications in controlling child residents. Adolescent offenders in residential placement are especially likely to suffer from overlooked or ignored abuse (Walker 2010).

Implications for Social Work

Because of the growing recognition of the extent and consequences of child maltreatment, child protective legislation has been enacted in every state. However, state laws are vague in describing a variety of reportable conditions, and the interventions provided through state programs are often seen as inadequate or harmful. As with any recently discovered phenomenon, child maltreatment practice is lagging far behind child welfare professionals' level of knowledge (Horwitz et al. 2010). According to recent literature, there appears to be a disconnect between professional levels of knowledge about what happens after a maltreatment referral is made, and those individuals making the referral do so under the assumption that certain steps will be taken. These assumed steps, however, may have little or no resemblance to what actually occurs once a referral is received (Fledderjohann and Johnson 2012). One possible way to correct these assumptions is to provide education to both mandated reporters and CPS staff regarding the expectations of both sides. Lau et al. (2009) have provided an invaluable resource for social workers with ethical or legal questions regarding the mandatory reporting of child abuse and neglect which should also be utilized in these circumstances.

On the other hand, although this chapter has focused on the limitations of CPS and legal system responses to abuse and neglect, it is important to emphasize the progress that has occurred in the past few years. Measures aimed at reducing children's trauma while increasing their protection are speedily being implemented, including the use of multidisciplinary teams and interagency protocols, feedback to reporters, videotape as an investigative tool, lay volunteers to represent children in child protective cases, expert witnesses, special hearsay exceptions for children, pretrial diversion and treatment of sex offenders, and civil lawsuits brought by children against maltreating parents (Phillips et al. 2010).

Many of these innovations (which should be universally adopted by means of policy initiatives and legislative action) were prompted by the growing public awareness of deficiencies in handling the recent flood of sexual abuse cases. Similar attention should now be focused on improving system responses to abused adolescents and to children who are maltreated in residential, foster care, and other out-of-home settings. It is important that child advocates articulate these issues for the public. Other areas of immediate concern are the lack of treatment services for maltreated children, the need for training programs to guide professionals in handling suspected cases of abuse and neglect, and the need for specific legislation in every state to protect employees from retaliation for exercising the legal obligation to report.

Social workers must be aware not only of their responsibilities as set forth by child abuse legislation, but also of current system realities that determine which cases will be served and in what manner. Their considerations affect the decision-making process—and rightly so. Informed social workers can better serve their clients, protect themselves, and foster public awareness of system shortcomings.

Additional Resources

Reporting Abuse and Neglect

Child Abuse and Neglect Reporting and Requirements
http://www.tea.state.tx.us/index4.aspx?id=25769803997
Reporting Child Abuse and Neglect
http://www.dir.ct.gov/dcf/policy/Carlne33/33-3.htm

Reporting Emotional Abuse

Recognizing, Preventing, and Reporting Child Abuse
http://www.helpguide.org/mental/child_abuse_physical_emotional_sexual_neglect.htm
Department of Health and Human Services
Child Welfare and Information Gateway
Identification of Emotional Abuse
https://www.childwelfare.gov/can/identifying/emotional_abuse.cfm

Sexual Abuse

American Humane Society
Child Sexual Abuse
http://www.americanhumane.org/children/stop-child-abuse/fact-sheets/child-sexual-abuse.html

Perceptions of Social Work

The Guardian
Social Workers Should use social media to challenge public perception
http://www.theguardian.com/social-care-network/2013/jul/23/social-workers-social-media-challenge-perception

References

Alter, C. F. (1985). Decision making factors in cases of child neglect. *Child Welfare, 64*, 99–111.

Alvarez, K. M., Donohue, B., Carpenter, A., Romero, V., Allen, D. N., & Cross, C. (2010). Development and preliminary evaluation of a training method to assist professionals in reporting suspected child maltreatment. *Child Maltreatment, 15*(3), 211–218.

Asawa, L. E., Hansen, D. J., & Flood, M. F. (2008). Early childhood intervention programs: Opportunities and challenges for preventing child maltreatment. *Education and Treatment of Children, 31*(1), 73–110.

Bean, H., Softas-Nall, L., & Mahoney, M. (2011). Reflections on mandated reporting and challenges in the therapeutic relationship: A case study with systemic implications. *The Family Journal, 19,* 286–290.

Bergman, A. B. (2013). A pediatrician's perspective on child protection. *Child Maltreatment, 1,* 63–69.

Broadhurst, K., Hall, C., Wastell, D., White, S., & Pitman, A. (2010). Risk, instrumentalism and the humane project in social work: Identifying the informal logics of risk management in children's statutory services. *Community Development Journal, 40*(4), 1046–1064.

Davidson, H. & Horowitz, R. (1988). *Children and the Law.* Washington, DC: American Bar Association.

Fallon, B., Trocme, N., Fluke, J., MacLaurin, B., Tonmyr, L., & Yuan, Y. Y. (2010). Methodological challenges in measuring child maltreatment. *Child Abuse And Neglect, 34*(1), 70–79.

Fledderjohann, J., & Johnson, D. R. (2012). What predicts the actions taken toward observed child neglect? The influence of community context and bystander characteristics. *Social Science Quarterly, 93*(4), 1030–1052.

Goldman, J. D., & Grimbeek, P. (2011). Sources of knowledge of departmental policy on child sexual abuse and mandatory reporting identified by primary school student-teachers. *Educational Review, 63*(1), 1–18.

Horwitz, S. M., Chamberlain, P., Landsverk, J., & Mullican, C. (2010). Improving the mental health in children in child welfare through the implementation of evidence-based parenting interventions. *Administration and Policy in Mental Health and Mental Health Services Research, 37*(1–2), 27–39.

Kempe, C. H., Silverman, F. N., Steele, B. F., Droegemueller, W., & Silver, H. K. (2013). The battered-child syndrome. *Child Maltreatment, 1,* 23–38.

Lau, K. J., Krase, K., & Morse, R. H. (2009). *Mandated reporting of child abuse and neglect: A practical guide for social workers*. Bronx: Fordham University Publishers.

Lee, S. J., Sobeck, J. L., Djelaj, V., & Agius, E. (2013). When practice and policy collide: Child welfare workers' perceptions of investigation processes. *Children and Youth Services Review, 35*(4), 634–641.

Levi, B. H., & Crowell, K. (2011). Child abuse experts disagree about the threshold for mandated reporting. *Clinical Pediatrics, 50*(4), 321–329.

Melton, G. B. (2005). Mandated reporting: A policy without reason. *Child Abuse and Neglect, 29,* 9–18.

National Association of Social Workers (NASW). (revised 1999)/(approved 1996). Code of ethics of the National Association of Social Workers.http://www.socialworkers.org/pubs/code/code.asp.

National Association of Social Workers. (2011). Government relations update: Keeping children and families safe act of 2003. http://www.naswdc.org. Accessed 27 Oct 2013.

National Center for Prosecution of Child Abuse. (2007). Practitioner's guide to the Adam Walsh act. http://www.ojp.usdoj.gov/smart/pdfs/practitioner_guide_awa.pdf.

National Children's Advocacy Center. (2011). History of the national children's advocacy center. http://www.nationalcac.org. Accessed 6 Jan 2013.

Pecora, P. J., Sanders, D., Wilson, D., English, D., Puckett, A., & Rudlang-Perman, K. (2012). Addressing common forms of child maltreatment: Evidence-informed interventions and gaps in current knowledge. *Child and Family Social Work, 19,* 321–332 doi:10.1111/cfs.12021.

Phillips, S. D., Dettlaff, A. J., & Baldwin, M. J. (2010). An exploratory study of the range implications of families' criminal justice system involvement in child welfare cases. *Children and Youth Services Review, 32*(4), 544–550.

Price, A., Bergin, C., Luby, C., Watson, E., Squires, J., Funk, K., Wells, K., Betts, W., & Little, C. (2012). Implementing Child Abuse Prevention and Treatment Act (CAPTA) requirements to serve substance-exposed newborns: Lessons from a collective case study of four program models. *Journal of Public Child Welfare, 6*(2), 149–171.

Rokop, J. J. (2003). The effects of CPS mandated reporting on the therapeutic relationship: The client's perspective. *Dissertation Abstracts International, 64,* 2402.

Sousa, C., Herrenkohl, T. I., Moylan, C. A., Tajima, E. A., Klika, J. B., Herrnekohl, R. C., & Russo, M. J. (2010). Longitudinal study on the effects of child abuse and children's exposure to domestic violence, parent-child attachments and antisocial behavior in adolescence. *Journal of Interpersonal Violence, 26*(1), 111–136.

Stoltenborgh, M., van Ijzendoorn, M. H., Euser, E. M., & Bakermans-Kranenburg, M. J. (2011). A global perspective on child sexual abuse: Meta-analysis of prevalence around the world. *Child Maltreatment, 16*(2), 79–101.

Strozier, M., Brown, R., Fennell, M., Hardee, J., & Vogel, R. (2005). Experiences of mandated reporting among family therapists. *Contemporary Family Therapy: An International Journal, 27*(2), 177–191.

U.S. Department of Health & Human Services. (2008a). Child abuse and neglect fatalities: Statistics and interventions. http://www.childwelfare.gov. Accessed 4 Feb 2008.

U.S. Department of Health & Human Services. (2008b). Child maltreatment 2006: Summary of key findings. http://www.childwelfare.gov. Accessed 4 Feb 2008.

U.S. Department of Health & Human Services. (2011a). Administration for children & families: Keeping Children and Families Safe Act of 2003. http://www.childwelfare.gov. Accessed 16 Sept 2013.

U.S. Department of Health & Human Services. (2011b). Administration for children & families: What Is child abuse and neglect? http://www.childwelfare.gov. Accessed 16 Sept 2013.

U.S. Department of Health & Human Services. (2011c). Child maltreatment 2010. http://www.childwelfare.gov. Accessed 16 Sept 2013.

Walker, L. E. (2010). Child physical abuse and neglect. *Handbook of Clinical Psychology Competencies, 1,* 1515–1540.

Chapter 3
Child Development

Michael J. Holosko, Sarah Tillotson and Johnna E. Ojo

Introduction

To understand social work practice from a human growth and developmental perspective, knowledge must be derived and subsequently drawn from a variety of sources. These perspectives include psychoanalytic theories and stage theories, biological facts, human behavior theories, economic reports, legal issues, and specific cultural information, as well as other sources. This makes assessment somewhat of an "art" and the more choices the social worker has available, the more opportunities there are for adequate assessment and intervention. There are many stages of development throughout our life span and this chapter will be broken down into categories of development, beginning with prenatal development.

Prenatal Development

On average, the human organism undergoes a gestation period of 38 weeks characterized by rapid fetal biological development. As the unborn child develops from embryo (fertilized egg) to fetus, it is exposed to psychological and environmental stressors which may cause detrimental outcomes later in life (Trickett and McBride-Chang 1995; Grizenko, et al. 2008; Del Cerro et al. 2010). Due to plasticity of the brain, neurodevelopment of the fetus may be affected by adverse events (Sesma and Georgieff 2003). Determinants of fetal growth and functioning include: woman's age at the time of conception, hereditary characteristics, adequate nutrition, alcohol consumption, smoking habits, and ingestion of either prescribed or illicit drugs.

M. J. Holosko (✉)
University of Georgia, Athens, GA, USA
e-mail: mholosko@uga.edu

S. Tillotson · J. E. Ojo
University of Tennessee, Knoxville, TN, USA

J. S. Wodarski et al. (eds.), *Evidence-Informed Assessment and Practice in Child Welfare,* DOI 10.1007/978-3-319-12045-4_3

Physical neglect or abuse plays a role in the development of a baby, as do other environmental factors such as access to medical care, adequate financial and emotional support, and exposure to hazardous chemicals. The blood-brain barrier protects the brain from chemicals but is not developed until months after birth so it is beneficial that women do not take medications during pregnancy or labor (Azmitia 2001).

According to the National Scientific Council, the young brain is very plastic and therefore early exposure to stress can impact brain development and physical/mental health later on. Stress experienced by the mother, especially during pregnancy, also impacts the level of stress-responsivity displayed by the offspring and even subsequent generations (Champagne and Curley 2005). In addition, prenatal stress is linked to ADHD, anxiety, and language delays (Talge et al. 2007). Stress may also lead to poor immune function (Lu and Halfon 2003). Given the impact the prenatal period has on later development, it is important to take smart approaches to pregnancy. What this means to social work is that pregnancy is a critical developmental stage that requires early intervention because the circumstances of a person's pregnancy and birth can have lasting effects on their children.

Recent research has shown that cortisol levels can impact infant cognitive development in utero (Bergman et al. 2010). Anxiety or stress experienced by the mother causes prenatal cortisol levels to rise and this then passes through the placenta barrier "to influence fetal brain development" (Bergman et al. 2010, p. 5). Animal research has supported similar conclusions (Afadlal et al. 2010). Further research is needed on this subject in order to accurately predict the extent of the impact that maternal prenatal cortisol levels have on fetal cognitive development.

It will sometimes be necessary to provide the mother with education regarding prenatal development and childbirth. In addition, interventions designed to help reduce stress can help the client and family system to deal with the changes that occur with the birth of a baby. Expectant parents may need assistance in accessing and securing the resources needed (e.g., prenatal care, good nutrition, adequate financial support, and genetic counseling). Low-income families may be particularly in need of this support in terms of information and advocacy as they may have the least access to high quality prenatal, postnatal, and other medical care. Furthermore, the stresses associated with poverty put an added burden on a pregnant woman and her family, making the prebirth environment for the baby more hazardous than desired.

When a mother is told that there is a high probability that her baby will be born disabled, she may feel extreme pressure to abort or give up the child. The role of the social worker is clear in helping the mother and family understand the pros and cons of bearing and caring for all newborns including those that suffer from disabilities. Raising a child, whether the child is disabled or not, is never an easy task, but having the proper information and supports in place can make the family experience less stressful.

In providing services to the infant, the social worker's primary intervention efforts will be directed toward the parents, thus enabling them to provide a stimulating environment for their child. This will foster the child's cognitive, physical, and social-emotional growth. The parents may need education regarding the needs of the infant and support while adjusting to the demands of parenthood. This can help reduce neglect. Children need "both stable emotional attachments with and touch from primary adult caregivers, and spontaneous interactions with peers. If these connections are lacking, brain development both of caring behavior and cognitive capacities is damaged in a lasting fashion" (Perry 2002, p. 79).

Infancy

Once out of the womb, the infant brain has all of the "hardware" but must undergo processes such as migration (getting cells to appropriate location), forming synapses (points of communication between cells) and myelination or the formation of protective tissue on nerve cell (Shonkoff and Meisels 2000). The brain structure and function is extremely plastic at this time and may be altered by our experiences during this sensitive period of infancy. Since the impact of experience during infancy can cause long-term effects, it is important to look at the steps parents can take to ensure healthy development.

Infant brains depend on experience to grow and develop, which is why providing a language-rich environment is necessary to promote healthy development. Talking, singing, and reading to infants promote stimulation, which according to Keller (2003) is a necessary aspect of adequate parenting. According to Combs-Orme et al. (2003), adequate parenting may also include sensitivity (being attuned and accurately interpreting) and responsivity (appropriately responding) toward the infant, which introduces the next step for healthy development. Understanding and responding to your baby's needs informs them that you are there for them and that their needs matter as well as increase the infant's self-confidence. Understanding and responding to your infant will help them to develop levels of faith and trust which may later result in a secure attachment (Balbernie 2002).

The environmental circumstances and individual characteristics may alter the balance between future vulnerability and resilience of the infant (Balbernie 2002). The infant learns to trust or mistrust an adult according to the care given by the caregivers, and this relationship with the parent has an effect on future attachments and relationships. Parental stress is linked to less positive attachments and parent–child interactions (Magill and Harrison 2001), which speaks to the increased risk factors of being a teenage mother or being poor. According to Halpern (1993), economic demands can affect any parent and interfere with their ability to be attentive and mentally available to their infant. If the infant is neglected, there can be an adverse affect. The earlier and more pervasive the child neglect is, the more destructive the developmental problems are for the child (Perry 2002).

Infant mental health is a relatively new service that is used to reduce social and emotional disturbances in early parenthood and infancy (Weatherston 2001). There are many diverse theories for infant mental health, but their commonality speaks to how to better an infant's socio-emotional health. Mental health home visiting services allow a clinician to enter the family's world and watch the interaction between the mother and the infant. This leads to the opportunity for early intervention, which is very important to promote any kind of change (Weatherston 2001).

Early Childhood Development (2–6 Years Old)

With every stage of development comes a set of major or critical tasks to be accomplished by the individual. These tasks include social, emotional, cognitive, and physical functions which promote adaptation and optimal development. Optimal development or mastery of such tasks has been found to result from many factors such as child characteristics, caregiver adequacy, and environmental factors (Azar and Barnes 1988). Between the ages of two and six, the child continues to enlarge his repertoire of behavior. With improved physical coordination, the child now uses locomotion as a means of exploring the environment. The child learns to master such independence producing tasks as dressing and toilet training. Language grows, as does expressive social interactions with family and friends.

Family or home environment is a major contributing factor to child developmental outcomes. The social-developmental behaviors of children are often influenced by the norms, beliefs, and values of their family (Johnson et al. 2003). More importantly, emotional and cognitive development is promoted through nurturing, responsive parenting (Culbertson, et al. 2003) whereas the absence of one or both parents is a major risk factor for developmental outcomes (Putnam 2003).

The absence of one or both parents is often unavoidable because of career aspirations or financial pressures that require both parents to work. Many parents are resorting to daycare centers to care for their young children while they are at work. There are many factors to consider when choosing a daycare, and many cultures will have differing needs based on their core values. For instance, African American and Latino cultures place a greater importance on values of collectivism and spirituality (Johnson et al. 2003) as well as heritage cultural practices (Fuller and Garcia Coll 2010), when compared to Western European cultures. These characteristics play a part in which child care setting they will choose.

Middle Childhood Development (6–12 Years Old)

Cognitive developments such as solving conservation problems, ability to place objects in serial order, and concrete operational thinking is a primary task of the children aged 6–11 years (Culbertson et al. 2003). Though cognitive development is greatly impacted by environmental factors, personality and genetics continue to play a role in individual outcomes. It is during this stage that children are first exposed to the stressors associated with the school environment. Temperament plays a large role in the coping capacities of children in dealing with this new environment.

The temperament and coping abilities of school-aged children are measured in the Carson and Bittner (2001) article. The school environment can be very stressful for children and school stressors can take many forms including: academic performance, undue pressure to achieve and be perfect, peer pressures, bullies, conflicts with teachers, etc. It was predicted that a child with a more difficult temperament would have more trouble learning in school and have a harder time making friends, which may affect their self-efficacy. External factors may play a limited role in the coping capacities of children because their temperament is so influential. With proper training and working together with parents, teachers, and child-care providers, we can look for children characterized by clusters of temperament characteristics that may predispose them toward developmental problems or delays.

It is during the early school years that child maltreatment is most likely to be detected. The child is no longer restricted to family contact or family sanctioned contacts; teachers and social workers who have been trained to recognize signs of abuse and neglect are expected, and legally mandated, to report cases of abuse. Unfortunately, as social workers, we will come in contact with children who are being abused or adults who are victims of abuse at some point in our career.

During middle childhood, children find themselves encountering two environments: home and school. The school environment presents new challenges such as academics, friends, and additional authority figures (i.e., teachers). Socialization is a key component in human development. Social status can impact the level of a child's self-esteem (Davies 2004). In addition, social status can affect children's neurological and physical state. Peer exclusion in school was found to raise levels of cortisol in the hypothalamic pituitary adrenocortical (HPA) system (Peters et al. 2011). The HPA system produces cortisol when the body identifies psychological stress. Cortisol allows the body to produce energy and aid in other responses to the potential threat. Danger is reached when the HPA system remains on high alert over long periods of time. Once high levels of cortisol are maintained over extended periods of time, the HPA system has a difficult time turning off the stress response and in fact can become frozen in a high stress response state (Shonkoff and Phillips 2000 as citied in Davies 2004). Children can become stuck in high alert mode, causing the body to experience high anxiety and stress which can have dangerous consequences such as increased heart rate and difficulty concentrating.

Adolescence (13–17 Years Old)

Adolescence is the life stage marking the transition from childhood to adulthood in our culture. Like those developmental phases that preceded it, distinct biological, psychological, and social changes occur within the individual. During adolescence, teens also experience puberty, the hormonal changes responsible for maturation of genital organs and the appearance of secondary sex characters (Ramirez 2003). Walker (2002) further explains that puberty influences cognition, mood, and behavior as a result of the hormonal changes in brain structure and function that occur.

In Cicchetti and Rogosch (2002), the developmental psychopathology of adolescence is discussed. They stated that adolescence is neither only a time of storm and stress nor just a normal time for adjustment. Adolescence is a more difficult stage of development than adulthood or childhood because the boundaries between normal and abnormal or between normative struggles and psychopathology become less clear.

Key characteristics of adolescence are "impulsivity, lack of foresight, poor decision-making, elevated emotional reactivity, and sensation-seeking behavior" (Andrews-Hanna et al. 2011). The area of the brain responsible for such actions (i.e., prefrontal cortex) as decision-making is not fully developed at the stage of adolescence. Understanding the neurodevelopmental stage of adolescence is critical when working with this population. Workers can gain understanding and empathy by realizing that adolescents have decision-making restrictions due to their current development stage.

Adolescent behavior and development are clearly influenced by the physical changes occurring in the body as well as many other factors. One factor which profoundly impacts the adolescent experience is their position on the continuum of poverty and affluence (Stanton et al. 2001). Poverty is often associated with an escalation of high-risk behaviors such as smoking, drug use, and dropping out of school. As social workers, we will inevitably work with people in poverty. Stanton et al. (2001) discuss how poverty impacts an adolescent's development. Single-parent households are more common in impoverished communities and the combination of poverty and parental discord can increase the chance that an adolescent will exhibit deviant behavior.

Emerging Adulthood (18–25 Years Old)

The developmental period characterized by a period of prolonged exploration from ages 18–25, before settling into adulthood, is known as emerging adulthood (Roisman et al. 2004). During this period, emerging adults experience several defining features that differentiate this stage from both adolescence and adulthood such as identity explorations, instability, and self-focus (Arnett 2000). During emerging adulthood autonomy (making independent choices) and self-determination (determining one's own fate) help prepare one for the decisions they will make during adulthood; however, both early attachment styles and early family life adversity will be contributing factors for adult development (Kenny and Barton 2003; Luecken and Appelhans 2006).

The transition to college can be challenging for many young adults. Studies on attachment have shown links between one's attachment type (i.e., secure or insecure) with success and a healthy transition to college. Both female and male college students "who perceived a more secure attachment to parents (higher trust and communication and less anger and alienation) perceived themselves as more competent, experienced less psychological distress, and experienced better adjustment to college" (Hiester et al. 2009). On the contrary, male and female college students who felt alienated from or angry with their parents reported adjustment difficulties. In addition, these college students also were more likely to "perceive themselves negatively" (Hiester et al. 2009). Recommendations for those working with college age students involve paying special attention to the person's current relationship with their parent/guardian as well as the changes that might be currently taking place. By exploring the student's relationship with their parent/guardian, the worker can acquire vital information to help the client make a healthy transition to college.

As in middle childhood and adolescence, social support remains a major factor in the development stage of emerging adulthood. Emerging adulthood involves transitions. Most people in this state of development experience transitions from their guardian's home to college as well as from college to career. Even as young adults transition to college the need for social support remains. In a recent qualitative study, researchers examined the experiences of emerging adults' transition from college to career. The findings indicated that current life satisfaction was related to the strength of social support (Murphy et al. 2010). Social support of family and friends was found to impact participants' transition from college to career, first job expectations and well-being (Murphy et al. 2010). A recent longitudinal study suggests that global self-esteem increases during these processes, through adolescence and then more slowly throughout the twenties (Erol and Orth 2011).

Adulthood

Adulthood is traditionally associated with independence, autonomy, and physical/emotional separation from parents but is not defined consciously and may take on various definitions (Jordan and Dunlap 2001). As the individual enters into the life stage of adulthood, different developmental tasks must be undertaken. These typically include entering the work force, completing any remaining educational objectives, choosing a life partner, and deciding whether to become a parent. This stage is not marked by a specific age but rather characterized by certain life events which differ based on one's culture. The entrance into adulthood is different today than 50+ years ago. It "has become deinstitutionalized and individualization has increased, meaning that people are required to rely on their own resources and their own sense of agency" (Arnett 2000, p. 4). Regardless of the changes in timing and meaning of adulthood that occur over time, adulthood continues to be the stage of peak physiological and physical health.

Being the stage of peak health, it is important to understand that early life events may impact later life health. Our early life environments, attachments, relationships, temperament (to name a few) are characteristics to consider for later life outcomes. Several studies have been conducted which associate the relationships between early life characteristics and later life outcomes (Kumari et al. 2013; Poon and Knight 2012). One such study looked at the relationship between having emotionally supportive parents early in life and an individual's health in adulthood

(Shaw et al. 2004). According to their results, a lack of parental support during childhood is associated with increased levels of depressive symptoms and chronic conditions in adulthood. The results of this study showed that "personal control, self-esteem, and social relationships during adulthood account for a large portion of these long-term associations" (Shaw et al. 2004, p. 4). These results speak to the importance of knowing the in depth history of our adult clients.

Additional Resources

Prenatal Development Encyclopedia of Children's Health

http://www.healthofchildren.com/P/Prenatal-Development.html

Endowment of Human Development

http://www.ehd.org/prenatal-summary.php

Infancy Child Development

http://www.cdc.gov/ncbddd/childdevelopment/positiveparenting/infants.html

Infant and Newborn Development

http://www.nlm.nih.gov/medlineplus/ency/article/002004.htm

Early Childhood Development Harvard University

Center for the Developing Child

http://developingchild.harvard.edu/resources/multimedia/interactive_features/five-numbers/

Harvard University

National Forum on Early Childhood Policy and Programs

http://developingchild.harvard.edu/activities/forum/

Middle Childhood Development Middle Childhood

http://www.cdc.gov/ncbddd/childdevelopment/positiveparenting/middle.html

Adolescence Young Teens

http://www.cdc.gov/ncbddd/childdevelopment/positiveparenting/adolescence.html

Teenagers

http://www.cdc.gov/ncbddd/childdevelopment/positiveparenting/adolescence2.html

Emerging Adulthood Young Adult Development Project

http://hrweb.mit.edu/worklife/youngadult/about.html

Adolescence: The last step before becoming an adult

http://childdevelopmentinfo.com/child-development/teens_stages/

Adulthood Four Adult Development Theories and Their Implications for Practice

http://www.ncsall.net/index.html@id=268.html

References

Afadlal, S., Polaboon, N., Surakul, P., Govitrapong, P., & Jutapakdeegul, N. (2010). Prenatal stress alters presynaptic marker proteins in the hippocampus of rat pups. *Neuroscience Letters, 470,* 24–27.

Andrews-Hanna, J. R., Mackiewicz Seghete, K. L., Claus, E. D., Burgess, G. C., Ruzic, L., & Banich, M. T. (2011). Cognitive control in adolescence: Neural underpinnings and relation to self-report behaviors. *PLoS ONE, 6*(6). doi: 10.1371/journal.pone.0021598.

Arnett, J. J. (2000). Emerging adulthood: A theory of development from the late teens through the twenties. *American Psychologist, 55*(5), 469–480.

Azar, S. T., Barnes, K. T., & Twentyman, C. T. (1988). Developmental outcomes in physically abused children: Consequences of parental abuse or the effects of a more general breakdown in caregiving behaviors? *Behavior Therapist, 11,* 27–32.

Azmitia, E. C. (2001). Impact of drugs and alcohol on the brain through the life cycle: Knowledge for social workers. *Journal of Social Work Practice in the Addictions, 1*(3), 41–52.

Balbernie, R. (2002). An infant in context: Multiple risks, and a relationship. *Infant Mental Health Journal, 23*(3), 329–341.

Bergman, K., Sarkar, P., Glover, V., & O'Connor, T. G. (2010). Maternal prenatal cortisol and infant cognitive development: Moderation by infant-mother attachment. *Biological Psychiatry, 67*(11), 1026–1032.

Carson, D. K., & Bittner, M. T. (2001). Temperament and school-aged children's coping abilities and responses to stress. *The Journal of Genetic Psychology, 155*(3), 289–302.

Champagne, F. A., & Curley, J. P. (2005). How social experiences influence the brain. *Current Opinion in Neurobiology, 15,* 704–709.

Cicchetti, D., & Rogosch, F. A. (2002). A developmental psychopathology perspective on adolescence. *Journal of Consulting and Clinical Psychology, 70,* 6–20.

Combs-Orme, T., Wilson, E., Cain, D., Page, T., & Kirby, L. (2003). Context-based parenting of infants. *Child and Adolescent Social Work Journal, 20*(6), 437–472.

Culbertson, J. L., Newman, J. E., & Willis, D. J. (2003). Childhood and adolescent psychologic development. *The Pediatric Clinics of North America, 50*(4), 741–764.

Davies, D. (2004). *Child development: A practitioner's guide*. New York: Gilford.

Del Cerro, M. C., Perez-Laso, C., Ortega, E., Martin, J. L., Gomez, F., Perez-Izquierdo, M. A., et al. (2010). Maternal care counteracts behavioral effects of prenatal environmental stress in female rats. *Behavioural Brain Research, 208,* 593–602.

Erol, R. Y., & Orth, U. (2011). Self-esteem development from age 14–30 years: A longitudinal study. *Journal of Personality and Social Psychology, 101,* 607–619.

Fuller, B., & Garcia Coll, C. (2010). Learning from Latinos: Contexts, families, and child development in motion. *Developmental Psychology, 46*(3), 559–565.

Gilgun, J. F. Human development and adversity in ecological perspective, Part 1: A conceptual framework. *Families in Society*, 395–402.

Gilgun, J. F. (1996). Human development and adversity in ecological perspective, Part 1: A conceptual framework. *Families in Society, 77*, 395-402.

Grizenko, N., Rajabieh, Y., Polotskaia, A., Ter-Stepanian, M., & Joober, R. (2008). Relation of maternal stress during pregnancy to symptom severity and response to treatment in children with ADHD. *Journal of Psychiatry and Neuroscience, 33*(1), 10–16.

Halpern, R. (1993). Poverty and infant development. In C.H. Zeanath (Ed.), *Handbook of infant mental health* (pp. 73–86). New York: Guilford.

Hiester, M., Nordstorm, A., & Swenson, L. M. (2009). Stability and change in parental attachment and adjustment outcomes during the first semester transition to college life. *Journal of College Student Development, 50*(5), 521–538. doi: 10.1353/csd.0.0089

Johnson, D. J., Jaeger, E., Randolph, S. M., Cauce, A. M., & Ward, J. (2003). Studying the effects of early child care experiences on the development of children of color in the United States: Toward a more inclusive research agenda. *Child Development, 74*(5), 1227–1244.

Jordan, B., & Dunlap, G. (2001). Construction of adulthood and disability. *Mental Retardation, 39,* 286–296.

Keller, H. (2003). Socialization for competence: Cultural models of infancy. *Human Development, 46,* 288–311.

Kenny, M. E., & Barton, C. E. (2003). Attachment theory and research: Contributions for understanding late adolescent and young adult development. In J. Demick, & C. Andreoletti (Eds.), *Handbook of adult development* (pp. 371–389). New York: Kluwer/Plenum.

Kumari, M., Head, J., Bartley, M., Stansfield, S., Kivimaki, M. (2013) Maternal separation in childhood and diurnal cortisol patterns in mid-life: Findings from the Whitehall II study. *Psychological Medicine, 43*(3), 633–643.

Lu, M. C., & Halfon, N. (2003). Racial and ethnic disparities in birth outcomes: A life-course perspective. *Maternal and Child Health Journal, 7*(1), 13–30.

Luecken, L. J., & Appelhans, B. M. (2006). Early parental loss and salivary cortisone in young adulthood: The moderating role of family development. *Development and Psychopathology, 18,* 295–308.

Magill-Evans, J., & Harrison, M. J. (2001). Parent-child interactions, parenting stress, and developmental outcomes at four years. *Childrens Health Care, 30*(2), 135–150.

Murphy, K. A., Blustein, D. L., Bohlig, A. J., & Platt, M. G. (2010). The college-to-career transition: An exploration of emerging adulthood. *Journal of Counseling & Development, 88*(2), 174–181.

National Scientific Council on the Developing Child. (2005/2014). Excessive Stress Disrupts the Architecture of the Developing Brain: Working Paper 3. Updated Edition. Retrieved from www.developingchild.harvard.edu.

Perry, B. D. (2002). Childhood experience and the expression of genetic potential: What childhood neglect tells us about nature and nurture. *Brain and Mind, 3*(1), 79–100.

Peters, E., Riksen-Walraven, J. M., Cillessen, A. H. N., & de Weerth, C. (2011). Peer rejection and HPA activity in middle childhood: Friendship makes a difference. *Child Development.* doi: 10.1111/j.1467-8624.2011.01647.x

Poon, C. Y. M., & Knight, B. G. (2012). Emotional reactivity to network stress in middle and late adulthood: The role of childhood parental emotional abuse and support. *Gerontologist, 52*(6), 782–791.

Putnam, F. W. (2003). Ten-year research update review: Child sexual abuse. *Journal of the American Academy of Child Adolescent Psychiatry, 42*(3), 269–278.

Ramirez, J. M. (2003). Hormones and aggression in childhood and adolescence. *Aggression & Violent Behavior, 8,* 621–644.

Roisman, G. I., Masten, A. S., Coatsworth, J. D., & Tellegen, A. (2004). Salient and emerging developmental tasks in the transition to adulthood. *Child Development, 75*(1), 123–133.

Sesma, H. W., & Georgieff, M. K. (2003). The effect of adverse intrauterine and newborn environments on cognitive development: The experience of premature delivery and diabetes during pregnancy. *Development and Psychopathology, 15,* 991–1015.

Shaw, B. A., Krause, N., Chatters, L. M., Connell, C. M., & Ingersoll-Dayton, B. (2004). Emotional support from parents early in life, aging and health. *Psychology and Aging, 19*(1), 4–12.

Shonkoff, J. P., & Phillips, D. A. (Eds.). (2000). *From neurons to neighborhoods: The science of early childhood development*. Washington DC: National Academy Press.
Shonkoff, J. P., Meisels, S. J. (Eds). (2000). Handbook of early childhood intervention. 2nd Edition. Cambridge, U.K.: Cambridge University Press.
Stanton, B., Cuthill, S., & Amador, C. (2001). Adolescence and poverty. *Adolescent Medicine: State-of-the-Art Reviews, 12*(3), 525–538.
Talge, N. M., Neal, C., Glover, V., & The Early Stress, Translational Research and Prevention Science Network: Fetal and Neonatal Experience on Child and Adolescent Mental Health (2007). Antenatal maternal stress and long-term effects on child neurodevelopment: How and why? *Journal of Child Psychology and Psychiatry, 48*(3/4), 245–261.
Trickett, P. K., & McBride-Chang, C. (1995) The developmental impact of different forms of child abuse and neglect. *Developmental Review, 15,* 311–337.
Walker, E. F. (2002). Adolescent neurodevelopment and psychopathology. *Current Directions in Psychological Science, 11*(1), 24–28.
Weatherston, D. (2001). Infant mental health: A review of relevant literature. *Psychoanalytic Social Work, 8*(1), 39–69.

Chapter 4
Contributing Factors to Child Sexual Abuse

John S. Wodarski and Sandy R. Johnson

Perpetrators

The overwhelming majority of child sexual abuse perpetrators are men. The perpetrators are known to the child in the majority of the cases and a majority of these are members of the child's family (Elliott and Carnes 2001; Sapp and Kappeler 1993).

According to the National Incidence Studies of Missing, Abducted, Runaway and Thrownaway Children (NISMART), a child perpetrator between ages 13 and 17 was involved in 25 % of both reported and unreported cases of child sexual abuse based on data collected in 1999. Children under 12 accounted for 4 % of perpetrators.

Certain authors describe a person who sexually abuses children as a dependent, immature, inadequate individual, with an early life history of conflict, disruption, abandonment, abuse, and exploitation (Priebe and Svedin 2008). Groth (1982) sees offenders as often coming from homes characterized by physical and sexual abuse. Davis and Archer (2010) found common themes in the MMPI profiles of child sex offenders, such as feelings of insecurity, inadequacy in interpersonal relationships, dependency, and family histories of social isolation and family discord. In describing other characteristics of child sexual abuse, data vary widely. Poor impulse control, maternal deprivation, and paternal deprivation are cited frequently by authors in their descriptions of men who commit child sexual abuse (Lalor and McElvaney 2010; Hillberg and Hamilton-Gaichritsis 2011).

Whether those who sexually abuse children are satisfying sexual needs is debated. Some research views them as "me first" individuals who satisfy many "nonsexual

J. S. Wodarski (✉)
University of Tennessee, Knoxville, TN, USA
e-mail: jwodarsk@utk.edu

S. R. Johnson
University of Georgia, Athens, GA, USA

J. S. Wodarski et al. (eds.), *Evidence-Informed Assessment and Practice in Child Welfare,* DOI 10.1007/978-3-319-12045-4_4

needs" through sexual activity with children, while others sees difficulty with this description because all sexual involvement includes expression of nonsexual needs (Spataro et al. 2004). Frude (1982) also sees the unfulfilled sexual needs of perpetrators as an important factor in sexual abuse. Kluft (2011) sees parents who were victims as children as more likely to become abusers. In summary, a typical profile of the abuser is familiarity with the child, lack of self-esteem, and poor impulse control.

Family Characteristics

Child sexual abuse victims have been found to have several commonalities, and these are viewed as possible predictors of the abuse. Believed to be relevant are family dynamics, demographic factors, and personal characteristics of the victim. The importance attributed to each varies widely according to investigators of the phenomenon.

Ethnicity and socioeconomic status have not been shown to be significant risk factors for child sexual abuse (Finkelhor et al. 2008). Instead, research has pointed toward factors such as domestic violence, parenting styles, harsh punishment practices by parents, and emotional deprivation.

Families of victims of child sexual abuse are often described as dysfunctional or pathological (Putnam 2003). Though certain common themes arise from these descriptions, the specifics often differ. Sapp and Kappeler (1993) view families exhibiting sexual abuse as analogous to "character disordered" persons. Various authors have described these families as being characterized by paternal dominance, social and sexual estrangement between the father and the mother, social isolation, assignment of adult roles to children, particularly the "mothering" role to the oldest daughter, poor communication, emotional and social stress, and poor family sexual and physical boundaries (Lalor and McElvaney 2010; Hillberg and Hamilton-Gaichritsis 2011). DiLillo et al. (2000) attribute to these families abuse of power, fear of authority, denial, lack of empathy, emotional deprivation, and magical expectations. Though many of these accounts specifically refer to familial child sexual abuse, the authors identify the following avenues through which families may contribute to the event even in extrafamilial abuse: poor supervision, poor choice of surrogate caretakers or babysitters, inappropriate sleeping arrangements, and blurred role boundaries (DiLillo et al. 2000).

A study of coastal families in Colombia showed that parental communication was associated with child sex abuse (Ramierz et al. 2011). The finding was consistent with theoretical approaches, which indicate that children with parents who listen and regularly ask questions are less likely to be victims (Zielinsky and Bradshaw 2006; Belsky and Jaffe 2006.) Parental communication may be a protective factor because it equips the child to deal with potentially threatening situations and also allows parents to be alerted to warning signs of abuse (Ramierz et al. 2011).

Victim Characteristics

Descriptions of the demographic factors and personal traits of the victim differ among studies and authors. Elliott and Carnes (2001) examined the sociodemographic backgrounds of 28 sexually abused children, and described the following victim prototype: a white female, 9 years old, from a working-class family, headed by both parents or the mother only.

Finkelhor et al. (2008) estimated a history of sexual abuse in at least 7 % of females and at least 3 % of males internationally, based on a meta-analysis. A follow-up in 2009 showed continuity over the years, especially with women (Pereda et al. 2009).

Finkelhor and others listed social variables found to be associated with increased risk of child sexual abuse: living in a family with a stepfather, having lived at certain times without the mother, a lack of closeness to the mother, the mother having never completed high school, having a sexually punitive mother, receiving no physical affection from the father, the family having an income of less than US$10,000 per year, and having few close friends (2008). Additionally, having grown up on a farm and coming from a family that is experiencing marital strife are risk factors.

In a meta-analysis of students and the community who were victims of sexual abuse as children, research found their backgrounds representative of all socioeconomic levels. None of their mothers were employed outside the home, and the majority of the families were seen as apparently intact and presenting a façade of responsibility (Pereda et al. 2009).

In a demographic study of more than 4000 families seen by the Child Sexual Abuse Treatment Program in Santa Clara County, California, Giaretto (1976) found families to be representative of a cross-section of the county the program serves. Families leaned toward the professional, semi-professional, and skilled blue-collar workers, had a median education level of 12.6 years, and 76.8 % were white, 17.5 % Mexican-American, 3 % Oriental, and 1.7 % black.

Zefran et al. (1982) studied 55 families of child victims of sexual abuse referred to the Cook County Juvenile Court's Special Services Unit and found that the average age of the children was 10, 95 % were female, 39 % were Caucasian, 51 % were black, and 10 % were classified as other. Whether these percentages were representative of the population of the area was not noted.

The age of the victim at the time of the incident is most often reported as 12 or under (Lalor and McElvaney 2010; Hillberg and Hamilton-Gaichritsis 2011). Pereda et al. (2009) found data that challenge the assertion by some authors that the victims are sexually mature and develop secondary sex characteristics early (Gentry 1978), and thus may "encourage" the adult (Gagnon 1965). Other personal characteristics of the child seen as risk factors for sexual abuse are an unusually attractive and charming personality, an unusually strong need for attention, and mimicking seductive behavior (Lalor and McElvaney 2010; Hillberg and Hamilton-Gaichritsis 2011).

Assessments of the relationship of child sexual abuse to economic factors are diverse. Results of some studies indicate that children from low-income families are at higher risk (Lalor and McElvaney 2010; Hillberg and Hamilton-Gaichritsis 2011). Others report that families of child sexual abuse victims represent all social, economic, and educational strata (Putnam 2003).

Certain researchers have found that child sexual abuse tends to occur in unbroken homes (Pereda et al. 2009). However, Elliott and Carnes found a small percentage of victims were living with both parents present, and were more likely to have a stepfather or stepmother. Research also found that living with a step or foster father was a risk factor (Bonoldi et al. in press). Peter (2009) sees a weakening of the taboo against child sexual abuse in stepfamilies because the members are not blood relatives. Peter also proposes that the loosened sexual boundaries in these families is the result of a lack of proximity to the child during the years of growth and development, and the failure to develop ties with the child during the time family relationships were being formed. Thus, in summary, the available data indicate that victims generally are between the ages of 9 and 12, live for a period of time with one parent, and come from low-income families.

Effects on Victim

The effects of child sexual abuse described in the literature are many and diverse. Most are related to females, but some seem equally applicable to males. As seen in the following presentation of sequelae, a majority of the problems relate to specific periods in the victim's life, while others are observed throughout the lifetime. Priebe and Svedin (2008) assert that certain child victims may exhibit symptoms related to the abuse while it is occurring, some at disclosure, and others may have a delayed response. If the abuse is not disclosed, the effects may continue into or arise in adulthood. Perhaps the most obvious problems described are physical consequences, such as venereal disease or bodily injury (Priebe and Svedin 2008). Psychological or emotional reactions are extensive. Victims of child sexual abuse describe feeling rejected, used, trapped, confused, humiliated, betrayed, and disgraced (Putnam 2003)

Those victimized by other children experience negative later-in-life outcomes that are similar to those victimized by adults, according to numerous studies (Cyr et al. 2002; Shaw et al. 2000; Sperry and Gilbert 2005; Lalor and McElvaney 2010; Hillberg and Hamilton-Gaichritsis 2011).

Psychological Effects

Other reported victim reactions include fear, anger, phobias and mood changes, depression, hysterical seizures (Sharpe and Faye 2006), etc. While seizures have been linked to childhood sexual abuse, researchers caution drawing definitive relationships between the variables and suggest, however, that there may be a link that is inadequately understood due to research design limitations (Sharpe and Faye 2006; Duncan 2010).

Other reactions to childhood sexual abuse include hyperactivity, nightmares, anxiety, guilt, somatic complaints, instance of irritable bowel syndrome, withdrawal and isolation, self-mutilation, and suicidal tendencies (Lalor and McElvaney 2010; Hillberg and Hamilton-Gaichritsis 2011; Putnam 2003).

Research on the late-life psychological effects on the victim of childhood sexual abuse explains that victims may experience changes in physiological reactions to stress, less effective regulation of emotions, chronic depression or dysthymia, and even less adaptive beliefs about the world, the self, and the future (Davies 2003; Friedman 2002).

Interpersonal–Social Side Effects

Victims reportedly experience role confusion, poor self-image and low self-esteem, developmental lags, and learning disabilities (Lalor and McElvaney 2010; Hillberg and Hamilton-Gaichritsis 2011). The developmental and learning deficits may be directly related to truancy and other school problems described (Garber 2011). This conglomeration of problems along with difficulty in interpersonal relationships may contribute to behaviors frequently noted as developing as victims move into adolescence and adulthood (Harvey and Taylor 2010).

Social behavioral problems include delinquency, running away, substance abuse, promiscuity and prostitution (Ray 2001). Childhood sexual abuse has also been identified as a predictor for dating violence (Ko Ling et al. 2011; Ulloa et al. 2009). Sexual dysfunction and difficulty functioning in marriage and parenting roles are commonly reported among adults who were victims of child sexual abuse. While sexual dysfunction has been linked to childhood sexual abuse, research suggests that this connection may be due to factors other than childhood sexual abuse (Spataro et al. 2004; Leonard et al. 2008). To leave the discussion of the effects of child sexual abuse at this point would ignore those who contend that it has little or no ill effects on some children, little or no lasting effects on any children, or that sex between adults and children can have a positive effect (Peter 2009; Riegel 2008). Certain authors see the human service network's responses and procedures in the intervention system as a possible source of trauma and further victimization of the child (Lalor and McElvaney 2010; Hillberg and Hamilton-Gaichritsis 2011). Others see this trauma as the major cause of problems for the victims in many cases (Ray 2001).

Individual and Family Focus

Treatment programs for child sexual abuse have increased rapidly in recent years, from 20 in the USA in 1976 to 300 listed by the National Center on Child Abuse and Neglect in 1981 (Goodyear-Brown 2011). The programs differ in regard to involvement with the court and child protective service systems, treatment focus, and treatment modalities used.

The focus of treatment for the incest offender is on family relationships and their modifications. Incestual child molesters are a special case of situational offenders. They, very seldom, prefer children as sexual partners and are least likely to recidivate. Their offense is related to family dynamics and opportunism rather than inappropriate sexual preference. The procedure of treatment is the rebuilding of the marital dyad, reestablishing the mother–daughter relationship, and reframing the cognitions and affective focus of the adult–child transactions. Following these separate actions, the family often can be successfully reconstituted.

One of the foremost programs in the country is the Child Sexual Abuse Treatment Program established in Santa Clara County, California, by Henry Giarretto (1982). This program is community based and incorporates the use of the existing agencies, including the Child Protective Services and the criminal justice system. In fact, to be admitted to the treatment process, the incident must be reported and the appropriate legal course pursued. The treatment orientation is humanistic in nature, not aiming at punishment, but treatment of all family members. The goals are focused on reuniting the family and preventing recurrence of the abuse, as well as helping the family members deal with the problems that arise. The program is made up of the professional staff from officially responsible agencies in the community, a cadre of volunteers (generally undergraduate and graduate students), and self-help groups including Parents United and Daughters and Sons United. The usual order of the various treatment modalities is: (1) individual counseling, (2) mother–daughter counseling, (3) marital counseling, (4) father–daughter counseling, (5) family counseling, and (6) group counseling. Sapp and Kappeler (1993) also adhere to a community treatment model. Their procedure is to establish an authoritative position with the family through the juvenile or criminal court. Services are coordinated through a treatment team, which holds meetings to discuss problems and progress. The model is oriented around the view of the sexually abusive family as "character disordered." Close supervision is stressed to avoid family members' manipulation of the system as well as to prevent their receiving confusing, mixed messages. This model advocates removal of the victim or perpetrator from the home when necessary.

The treatment process begins with a thorough evaluation of the family and its members. Three phrases of treatment follow. In phase I, the family is broken into small units, and treatment options include individual counseling, victim groups, couple counseling, chemical dependency treatment (if appropriate), and behavior modification for the abuser. Phase II reunites the family in therapy but often not at home. Male/female co-therapists are used in marital and family therapy. In phase II, the family is reunited at home with supervision. Therapy continues with the aim of establishing new roles and ending treatment.

Sgroi (1982) uses a family treatment approach. The stated position with reference to the legal system is that it is unlikely that family treatment can effectively occur without the provision of an authoritative incentive such as the court system. This is seen as particularly important in intrafamilial abuse.

This model stresses the importance of assessing the family's contribution to the abuse, that is, whether it is extrafamilial or intrafamilial in nature. The treatment issues, though very similar, are differentiated along the lines of these two categories as well as parent, parent figure, or nonparent figure. In this model, parental sexual abuse families are also seen as "character disordered" in their functioning.

This model agrees with the view that family therapy should be used in conjunction with a variety of treatment methods and should not begin until individual therapy has been established with family members. The various therapies include individual, dyad, group (for fathers, mothers, parents, and adolescents, to provide peer support), couples, and family. Act and play therapies are also employed.

Harvey and Taylor (2010) also used a variety of treatment modalities, with the decision as to the treatment employed being based on an analysis of several factors: the child's age, developmental level, sex, diagnosis, and family situation. Group individual psychotherapy is presented as a possibility as the sole treatment modality or in conjunction with family or group therapy. The group is seen as helpful for adolescent and preadolescent victims because it incorporates peer support. Family therapy is described as useful when the family structure is "operational," and only after individual issues have been addressed. Role clarification is recommended for the victim's substitute families (such as foster homes) or group home family networks in appropriate cases. This model views the recurring themes of damaged or inadequate sense of self, problems with heterosexual relationships, guilt, anger, and sexuality as important in treatment of the victims.

Zefran et al. (1982) describe case management and treatment of child sexual abuse in a juvenile court setting. Their position is one of close cooperation between child protection service agencies, the court system, and treatment professionals. The assumptions are that the method demonstrates to the child that he or she is believed and will be protected, and helps to gain admission of the abuse from the offender.

This model is based on treatment of sexual abusing families, with primary attention on the victims. The treatment methods used and issues addressed differ according to the three categories the situation fits: (1) family without abuser, (2) family together, and (3) victim without family.

"Family without abuser" treatment involves working with families where the abuser has left home permanently. The process begins with individual therapy for the victim and proceeds at times with later placement in group therapy. Also, casework services are offered to the nonoffending parent (normally the mother) through support groups or group therapy. Later the focus shifts to work on the mother–daughter relationship.

"Family together" treatment begins with the victim in individual therapy and continues throughout. Mother–victim sessions follow. The abuser is seen in individual therapy as well and treatment is aimed primarily at acceptance of responsibility. Court sanctions are seen as important for getting the abuser to treatment. Later, the abuser begins treatment with the child and the spouse/partner. Finally, family therapy begins with either reunification of the family as a goal, or the assumption of appropriate roles in a maintained home.

"Victim without family" treatment sees the victim as the only identified client. The focus is on helping the victim deal with the abuse as well as the reality that returning home may never occur (Goodyear-Brown 2011). Individual therapy is used, but the support of victims' groups is seen as critical.

Goodyear-Brown (2011) presents family treatment as the choice for familial sexual abuse. The sessions are led by male/female co-therapists to provide modeling of appropriate behaviors. An effort is made to provide family members with positive extrafamilial relationships in order to promote growth in the individuals and total family unit. Later the groups are divided by sex in order to develop bonds and communication between same-sex family members. Individual therapy is provided in this model as needed. The emphasis is on development of self-respect and honesty. There is also focus on decreasing shaming and increasing positive reinforcement.

Group Focus

Other authors have noted the use of groups in their treatment of child sexual abuse. A program based on the model by Giarretto (1982) employs a specific group model and is used for latency-aged victims. The group contains only females, aged 7–12, with the small number of males seen individually. The group meets in 8-week cycles once per week. In the ninth session, the members engage in some activity with parent, friends, and siblings. After a week off, the sessions resume with a majority of members participating in more than one cycle. The group is open-ended with members included throughout the cycles.

The sessions are structured around separate themes considered important to the victims. The themes are: (1) believability; (2) guilt and responsibility; (3) body integrity and protection; (4) secrecy and sharing; (5) anger; (6) powerlessness; (7) other life crises, tasks, and symptoms; and (8) court attendance. According to the author, these themes should be addressed in a way that corresponds to the developmental tasks of the particular group members. Individual crises and needs are also addressed.

Misurell et al. (2010) describe the use of group psychotherapy with adolescent females who were sexually abused. The focus is on their present functioning with peers, family, and others in light of the effects of past abuse. The group is led by male/female co-therapists. The process is verbally oriented with additional use of role-play and other exercises. The group is developed around four themes seen as important for these victims: isolation, loss, anger, and hope.

Misurell et al. (2010) also propose group therapy as the primary treatment for victims of intrafamilial sexual abuse. The group revolves around the therapeutic needs of these victims to help minimize self-destructive behavior, resolve emotional conflicts, change negative self-images, and promote normal developmental tasks of adolescents.

The common themes that are deemed critical in therapy are: (1) isolation and alienation from peers, (2) distrust of adults and authority figures, (3) guilt and shame, (4) fear of intimacy with the therapist and other adults, (5) anger turned inward (i.e., depression, suicide, and self-mutilation), (6) unmet dependency needs, (7) helpless victim mentality, (8) development of social skills, and (9) developmental tasks of adolescence.

Other Treatment Approaches

Other treatment for the perpetrators of child sexual abuse includes multistage aversion therapy, social skills training, covert sensitization and other behavior modification techniques (Foster 2013). The use of chemotherapy is also reported (Groth et al. 1982).

Numerous authors suggest the need for an overall change in society's attitude toward sex, particularly in regard to sex role behavior, before the problem can be fully addressed (Spataro et al. 2004). There is also much debate over society's punitive reaction to this phenomenon. Whether it is an appropriate, helpful response or whether it contributes to the trauma and secrecy surrounding the problem is the major concern (Garber 2011).

Conclusions and Implications

Though much has been written about child sexual abuse, it is a relatively new area of empirical study. Many questions are yet to be answered: Why do some individuals or families with particular characteristics become involved in child sexual abuse, while other similar individuals and families do not? Why do some victims exhibit no apparent symptoms, while others have multiple problems? Why do the data and opinions vary so widely on different aspects of the phenomenon?

It is hoped that further research will provide the answers. Current data are almost exclusively descriptive and observations are most often clinical. The present research is also hampered by the small, convenient samples often used. Biases also seem likely in light of the characteristics of the populations studied. Moreover, the samples, generally obtained from agency clientele, limit the generalizability of the data. Empirical data derived from evaluation studies should shed valuable light on the subject (Lalor and McElvaney 2010; Hillberg and Hamilton-Gaichritsis 2011). The limited data available suggest that behavior modification techniques based on social learning theory with victims and their families should be further explored. Research that will clarify the continuum of services is likewise essential.

Current information does, however, provide useful guidelines for practice. First, treatment programs should be clear with regard to the goals of treatment, and sound measures of effectiveness should be developed so that practitioners and clients can evaluate the various treatment modalities. In the treatment of child sexual abuse, professionals must be aware of the latest findings concerning causes and effects.

Second, broader issues pertaining to interventions in child sexual abuse (as discussed earlier) are the problems arising for the child, the family, and society from: (1) the process of disclosure; (2) physical examinations for the victim, child, or abuser; (3) removal from the home; and (4) court/child protective service investigation processes. The effects of these activities, particularly on the victim, should be closely monitored, and the therapeutic intervention carried out in the least traumatic way as possible (Foster 2013; Decker and Naugle 2009). Third, society ultimately must evaluate the contribution to the problem of child sexual abuse. The effect of sex roles in our society on child sexual abuse was addressed earlier. In addition, it would seem that the place of the child in our society is crucial. Those who are seen as subordinate objects or possessions to be controlled and manipulated for the comfort and enjoyment of the "larger" world would seem more prone to various types of victimization. The "rights of the child" in our society seem to remain an issue. Not only children and adults must be educated as to the occurrence and effects of child sexual abuse and the means of prevention, but also society must begin to see the results of the "powerful use of the powerless" mentality and move to correct it. This type of broad change seems necessary before problems such as child sexual abuse can be controlled.

Additional Resources

Perpetrators of Sexual Abuse
Juvenile Sexual Offenders
https://www.childwelfare.gov/can/perpetrators/sexual_abuse/juvenile.cfm
Female Sex Offenders
https://www.childwelfare.gov/can/perpetrators/sexual_abuse/female.cfm
Center for Sex Offender management
Characteristics of Sexual Abusers
http://www.csom.org/train/etiology/3/3_1.htm
Center for Sex Offender Management
Etiology and Explanatory Theories
http://www.csom.org/train/etiology/5/5_1.htm#heading2

Side Effects of Sexual Abuse
Rape, Abuse, & Incest National Network
Effects of Sexual Assault
https://www.rainn.org/get-information/effects-of-sexual-assault

South Eastern CASA (Centre Against Sexual Assault)
The Effects of Childhood Sexual Abuse
http://www.secasa.com.au/pages/the-effects-of-childhood-sexual-abuse/

References

Belsky, J., & Jaffe, S. (2006). The multiple determinants of parenting. In D. Cicchetti & D. Cohen (Eds.), *Risk, disorder and adaptation, developmental psychopathology*, (2nd ed., vol. 3, pp. 38–85). New York: Wiley.

Bonoldi, I., Simeone, E., Rocchetti, M., Codjoe, L., Rossi, G., Gambi, F., Balottin, U., Caverzasi, E., Politi, P., & Fusar-Poli, P. (in press) Prevalence of self-reported childhood abuse in psychosis: A meta-analysis of retrospective studies. *Psychiatry Research, 13,* S0165–1781.

Chen, L. P., Murad, M. H., Paras, M. L., Colbenson, K. M., Sattler, A. L., Goranson, E. N., Elamin, M. B., Seime, R. J., Shinozaki, G., Prokop, L. J., & Zirakzadeh, A. (2010). Sexual abuse and lifetime diagnosis of psychiatric disorders: Systematic review and meta-analysis. *Mayo Clinic Proceedings, 86*(7), 618–629.

Cyr, M., Wright, J., McDuff, P., & Perron, A. (2002). Intrafamilial sexual abuse: Brother–sister incest does not differ from father–daughter and stepfather–stepdaughter incest. *Child Abuse and Neglect, 26,* 957–973.

Davies, S. (2003). The late-life psychological effects of childhood abuse. *Current Medical Literature: Health Care of Older People, 16*(4), 83–87.

Davis, K.M., & Archer, R.P. (2010). A critical review of objective personality inventories with sex offenders. *Journal of Clinical Psychology, 66*(12), 1254–1280.

Decker, S.E., & Naugle, A.E. (2009). Immediate interventions for sexual assault: A review with recommendations and implications for practitioners. *Journal of Aggression, Maltreatment & Trauma, 18*(4), 419–441.

DiLillo, D., Tremblay, G. C., & Peterson, L. (2000). Linking childhood sexual abuse and abusive parenting: The mediating role of maternal anger. *Child Abuse & Neglect, 24*(6), 767–779.

Duncan, R. (2010). Psychogenic non-epileptic seizures: Diagnosis and initial management. *Expert Review of Neurotherapeutics, 10*(12), 1803–1809.

Elliott, A.N., & Carnes, C.N. (2001). Reactions of non-offending parents to the sexual abuse of their child: A review of the literature. *Child Maltreatment, 6*(4), 314–331.

Finkelhor, D., Hammer, H., & Sedlak, A. (2008). Sexually assaulted children: National estimates and characteristics (Publication No. NCJ 214383). *Bulletin: National Incidence Studies of Missing, Abducted, Runaway, and Thrownaway Children Series.* http://www.ojj.dp.ncjrs.gov/publications/PubResults.asp. Accessed 19 March 2012.

Foster, J. M. (2013). Child sexual abuse in the United States: Perspectives on assessment and intervention. *American Journal of Humanities and Social Sciences, 1*(3), 97–108.

Friedman, M. (2002). *Post traumatic stress disorder: The latest assessment and treatment strategies*. Kansas City: Compact Clinical.

Frude, N. (1982). The sexual nature of sexual abuse: A review of the literature. *Child Abuse and Neglect, 6*(2), 211–233.

Gagnon, J. (1965). Female child victims of sex offence. *Social Problems, 13*(2), 176–*192.*

Garber, B. D. (2011). Parental alienation and the dynamics of the enmeshed parent-child dyad: Adultification, parentification, and infantilization. *Family Court Review, 49*(2), 322–335.

Gentry, C. E. (1978). Incestuous abuse of children: The need for an objective view. *Child Welfare, 62*(6), 355–364.

Giarretto, H. (1976). The treatment of father-daughter incest: a psycho-social approa*ch. Children Toda*y 5:2–6.

Giarretto, H. (1982). *Integrated treatment of child sexual abuse: A treatment and training manual*. Palo Alto: Science and Behavior.

Goodyear-Brown, P. (2011). *Handbook of child sexual abuse identification, assessment, and treatment*. New York: Wiley.

Groth, A. N., Hobson, W. F., & Gary, L. S. (1982). The child molester: Clinical observations. *Journal of Social Work and Human Sexuality, 1,* 129–144.

Harvey, S. T., & Taylor, J. E. (2010). A meta-analysis of the effects of psychotherapy with sexually abused children and adolescents. *Clinical Psychology Review, 30*(5), 517–535.

Hillberg, T., & Hamilton-Giachritsis, C. (2011). Review of meta-analyses on the association between child sexual abuse and adult mental health difficulties: A systematic approach. *Trauma Violence Abuse, 12*(1), 38–49.

Kluft, R.P. (2011) Ramifications of incest. *Psychiatric Times, 27*(12), 1–11.

Ko Ling, C., Yan, E., Brownridge, D. A., Tiwari, A., & Fong, D. T. (2011). Childhood sexual abuse associated with dating partner violence and suicidal ideation in a representative household sample in Hong Kong. *Journal of Interpersonal Violence, 26*(9), 1763–1784.

Lalor, K., & McElvaney, R. (2010). Child sexual abuse, links to later sexual exploitation/high-risk sexual behavior, and prevention/treatment programs. *Trauma Violence Abuse, 11*(4), 159–177.

Leonard, L. M., Iverson, K. M., & Follette, V. M. (2008). Sexual functioning and sexual satisfaction among women who report a history of childhood and/or adolescent sexual abuse. *Journal of Sex & Marital Therapy, 34*(5), 375–384.

Misurell, J. R., Springer, C., & Tryon, W. W. (2010). Game-based cognitive-behavioral therapy (GB-CBT) group program for children who have experienced sexual abuse: A preliminary investigation. *Child Sexual Abuse, 20*(1), 14–36.

Newton, A. S., Zou, B., Hamm, M. P., Curran, J., Gupta, S., Dumonceaux, C., & Lewis, M. (2010). Improving child protection in the emergency department: A systematic review of professional interventions for health care providers. *Academic Emergency Medicine, 17*(2), 117–125.

Pereda, N., Guilera, G., Forns, M., & Gomez-Benito, J. (2009) The prevalence of child sexual abuse in community and student samples: A meta-analysis. *Clinical Psychology Review, 29*(4), 328–338.

Pereda, N., Guilera, G., Forns, M., & Gomez-Benito, J. (2009). The international epidemiology of child sexual abuse: A continuation of Finkelhor. *Child Abuse & Neglect, 33,* 331–342.

Peter, T. (2009) Exploring taboos: Comparing male- and female-perpetrated child sexual abuse. *Journal of Interpersonal Violence, 24*(7), 1111–1128.

Priebe, G., & Svedin, C. G. (2008). Child sexual abuse is largely hidden from the adult society: An epidemiological study of adolescents' disclosures. *Child Abuse and Neglect, 32*(12), 1095–1108.

Putnam, F. W. (2003). Ten-year research update review: Child sexual abuse. *Journal of the American Academy of Child and Adolescence Psychiatry, 42*(3), 269–278.

Ramierz, C., Pinzon-Rondon, A. M., & Botero, J.C. (2011). Contextual predictive factors of child sexual abuse: The role of parent-child interaction. *Child Abuse and Neglect,* 35, 1022–1031.

Ray, S. L. (2001). Male survivors' perspectives of incest/sexual abuse. *Perspectives in Psychiatric Care, 37*(2), 49–59.

Riegel, D. L. (2008). Boyhood sexual experiences with older males: Using the internet for behavioral research. *Archives of Sexual Behavior, 38*(5), 626–630.

Sapp, A. D., & Kappeler, S. F. (1993). A descriptive study of child molestation: Victim and offender characteristics. *Journal of Police and Criminal Psychology, 9*(1), 56–62.

Sgroi, S. M. (1982). Family treatment of child sexual abuse. *Journal of Social Work and Human Sexuality, 1,* 109–128.

Sharpe, D., & Faye, C. (2006). Non-epileptic seizures and child sexual abuse: A critical review of the literature. *Clinical Psychology Review, 26*(8), 1020–1040.

Shaw, J., Lewis, J., Loeb, A., Rosado, J., & Rodriguez, R. (2000). Child-on-child sexual abuse: Psychological perspectives. *Child Abuse and Neglect, 24*(12), 1581–1600.

Spataro, J., Burgess, P. M., Wells, D. L., & Moss, S. A. (2004) Impact of child sexual abuse on mental health: Prospective study in males and females. *The British Journal of Psychiatry, 184*(5), 416–421.

Sperry, D., & Gilbert, B. (2005). Child peer sexual abuse: Preliminary data on outcomes and disclosure experiences. *Child Abuse and Neglect, 29*, 889–904.

Ulloa, E. C., Baerresen, K., & Hokoda, A. (2009). Fear as a mediator for the relationship between child sexual abuse and victimization of relationship violence. *Journal of Aggression, Maltreatment & Trauma, 18*(8), 872–885.

Weber, E. (1977). Incest: Sexual abuse begins at home. *Ms. Magazine, 5*, 64–67.

Zefran, J., Jr., Riley, H. F., Anderson, W. O., Curtis, J. H., Jackson, M., Kelly, P. H., McGury, E. T., & Suriano, M. K. (1982). Management and treatment of child sexual abuse cases in a juvenile court setting. *Journal of Social Work and Human Sexuality, 1*, 155–170.

Zielinsky, D., & Bradshaw, C. P. (2006). Ecological influences on the sequelae of child maltreatment: A review of the literature. *Child Maltreatment, 11*(1), 49–62.

Chapter 5
The Integrated Model for Human Service Delivery in Child Welfare

Marvin D. Feit, R. Manon Kraus and Aaron R. Brown

Introduction

The present child welfare system is under attack by both conservatives and liberals alike for its fragmented system resulting in less than adequate services for the children and families it serves. Multiple weaknesses of the current social service and child welfare systems have been broadly assessed. But there has been no sustained effort to create a satisfactory system of social services to meet the needs of children and their families. There is an extraordinary convergence of increased awareness of the problem, new knowledge of what works, and new openness to change the way social services are financed, organized, and delivered. The proposed "Integrated Human Service Delivery System: Child Welfare Model" will provide an innovative approach to service delivery, which will facilitate more comprehensive and effective service delivery and better meet the needs of children and families served by our child welfare system.

The Human Service Delivery System: Child Welfare Model

The present child welfare system is under attack by both conservative and liberals alike for its fragmented system resulting in less than adequate services for the children and families it serves. Meyers (1993) reports that for at least the last 30 years; policy analysts, advocates, and service providers have complained about fragmentation in children's services as demonstrated by separate systems including child welfare, juvenile justice, public school, welfare and health systems, and other

M. D. Feit (✉)
Norfolk State University, Norfolk, VA, USA
e-mail: mdfeit@nsu.edu

R. M. Kraus · A. R. Brown
The University of Tennessee, Knoxville, TN, USA

J. S. Wodarski et al. (eds.), *Evidence-Informed Assessment and Practice in Child Welfare,* DOI 10.1007/978-3-319-12045-4_5

public and private agencies. In addition, numerous professional disciplines have been criticized for creating barriers to services, duplication of effort, incomplete service plans, service redundancies, and generally fewer and less adequate services for children. More recently, Howell et al. (2004) cites Roush (1996) in stating that youth-serving systems are too crisis-oriented, too rigid in problem classification, too inflexible, insufficiently funded, and mismanaged.

The Current State of Child Welfare

There has been no sustained effort to create a satisfactory system of social services to meet the needs of children and their families (Kamerman and Kahn 1990). In 2005, under the Child and Family Services Review, there was not a single state that met the federal requirements of providing permanency and stability for children in the child welfare system (Burskas 2008). Multiple weaknesses of the current social service and child welfare systems have been broadly assessed. Weaknesses identified by O'Looney (1994) include a fractured system that has categorical programming, duplicative social services, and uncoordinated service delivery with cross-purposes that is often confusing to families. Gambrill and Shlosky (2001) suggest that risk assessments for children and families are too narrowly focused, ignoring many potential factors. The current system also has a narrow specialization of provider skills, inflexible processes and organizational structures, a lack of client involvement or participation in service plans, lost referrals, incongruent and cumbersome paperwork, and eligibility processes, combined with a lack of prevention and early intervention services. In addition, clients often are not given individualized service plans which results in either inappropriate services being mandated or needed services not being identified and provided. This fragmented system results in many of our society's most vulnerable children in the child welfare system not receiving the protection, critical services, and interventions necessary to develop into responsible, healthy adults (Bruskas 2008). Well-coordinated services are necessary in order to effectively serve children and adolescents in the child welfare system, who are significantly more likely than those not involved in the child welfare system to have significant mental health, emotional, or behavioral problems (Hussey et al. 2012).

Proposed Changes

There is an extraordinary convergence of increased awareness of the problem, new knowledge of what works, and new openness to change the way social services are financed, organized, and delivered. During the 1990s, that openness to change resulted in the passage of the Multiethnic Placement Act of 1994 and the Interethnic Adoption Provisions of 1996 (MEPA-IEP), welfare reform, and the Adoption and Safe Families Act of 1997 (ASFA). Along with welfare reform, these changes resulted in a greater degree of flexibility, but the implementation is just now being studied and published. ASFA, in particular, was passed to expand guidelines for the removal of parental rights for biological parents, modify guidelines for the involvement of relatives, and increase opportunity and support for adoption (Hollingsworth 2000). ASFA mandated the system to do what is best for the individual child (Sempek and Woody 2010). According to Mitchell et al. (2005), ASFA has had the most effect on child welfare service delivery, but the focus of the data gathering has been on outcomes, not on the implementation of the services or the emerging service delivery models. Mitchell points out that even though welfare services develop in idiosyncratic ways due to local conditions and policies, that there may exist benefits to centralization.

In 2004, Howell et al. called for the integration of all child welfare agencies to begin with the integration of substance abuse treatment with services provided in other systems. In Illinois, one study (Ryan et al. 2006) focused on intensive case management to link children and families to substance abuse services and found that their model of service increased family reunification and more efficient use of services. However, a study conducted in 2011 states that the service delivery systems in child welfare continues to remain fragmented, particularly in small counties (Drabble 2011). Howell also notes that there is a need for an integrated response as the problems of youth often come bundled up as the result of issues that are stacked up over time. The lack of an integrated response results in children and adolescents being sent in a haphazard manner through a fragmented system. Howell goes on to suggest a system that is based on a comprehensive assessment of research-based risk and protective factors, a full assessment of the client population using research-based assessment instruments to classify and position families in a continuum of program interventions. Howell finalizes his proposal with a call for local ownership of programs and strategies with each neighborhood, city, or state to develop its own strategic plan. The integration and instrument-based assessment components are in line with the current research cited in this chapter. One criticism of the Howell proposal is that complete local ownership by the neighborhood, city, or state sounds more like the current fragmented system fraught with funding conflicts and turf battles.

Junek and Thompson (1999) proposed a self-regulating service delivery system that consists of four components. First, there would be outcome measurements that reflect the mental health status of the children in service. Second, regular feedback of these measurements would be given to governments, the public, and service delivery organizations. Third, powerful rewards and incentives would be given for the most desired outcomes to motivate provider behavior, and finally, decision making that affects all entities within the system. Junek and Thompson note that children's problems frequently cut across government departments and the actual number of children at risk far exceeds the capacity of a consumer-oriented service delivery system. One of the chief issues pointed out was the glaring lack of regular indicators of outcomes relevant to the clients. Herrenkohl and Herrenkohl (2007) suggest that the few indicators that are commonly used such as co-occurring stressors, socioeconomic status, and child maltreatment are not very predictive and are overlapping.

When the issue of lack of outcome indicators is combined with political turf battles and special interests, there is little external incentive for efficiency, coherent planning, priority setting, or action.

Integrated Human Service Delivery System: Child Welfare Model

The proposed "Integrated Human Service Delivery System: Child Welfare Model" will provide an innovative approach to service delivery which will facilitate more comprehensive and effective service delivery and better meet the needs of children and families served by our child welfare system. "The Integrated Human Service Delivery System: Child Welfare Model" is presented as service delivery through a case management modality. The model incorporates state-of-the-art rapid assessment and computer technology, utilizing appropriate interventions matched to assess identified deficits. Cahill and Feldman (1993) in their study found that technological change in a social welfare setting can improve the flow and timeliness of paperwork completion and gives both labor and management better way to do their work. In 2005, North Carolina implemented a child welfare website by using knowledge discovery and data mining (KDD) technology. KDD is an area of computer science that produces an integrated method for extracting important information from data by using the collaboration of facts and patterns from different databases. A majority of the staff believed the website provided a better understanding of their cases and they were enabled to communicate the child welfare outcomes more efficiently (Duncan et al. 2008). Coordination and follow-up is also provided in an innovative approach to child welfare reform. This approach is unique in that it combines the best of the previously discussed proposals and integrates them into one unit.

The "Integrated Human Service Delivery System" model would provide appropriate assessment, intervention, and accountability for optimal delivery of integrated services. Yessian (1995) reports the US Department of Health, Education, and Welfare definition of Service Integration as follows:

> Service integration refers primarily to ways of organizing the delivery of services to people at the local level. Service integration is not a new program to be superimposed over existing programs; rather, it is a process aimed at developing an integrated framework within which ongoing programs can be rationalized and enriched to do a better job of making services available within existing commitments and resources. Its objectives must include such things as: (a) the coordinated delivery of services for the greatest benefit to people; (b) a holistic approach to the individual and the family unit; (c) the provision of a comprehensive range of services locally; and (d) the rational location of resources at the local level to be responsive to local needs.

In the United States of America, there are many levels of government involved in service delivery. Even with the trend of devolving authority away from the federal government to the states, the delivery system is a complex bureaucracy. A self-regulating system is conceptually neutral and would allow the emphasis to be on managing the outcome and not the process (Junek and Thompson 1999). Hurlburt et al. (2007) found a strong positive relationship between interagency linkage and the effectiveness, efficiency, and continuity of services for high-risk populations, in particular. These linkages can be developed from greater communication, more awareness of interagency concerns, a more simplified referral process between agencies, and when possible co-location of providers to increase all these developmental qualities. Kolko et al. (2009) discovered that programs within the Child Welfare System, which communicated through written means, continually met the needs of their clients more effectively. Thus improving their clients mental health and were found to use more evidence-based interventions. "The Integrated Human Service Delivery System" incorporates the aspects of self-regulation that will keep this client focus through the use of continuous feedback loops from providing agencies to the case manager.

The identification of the fractured child welfare service delivery system as a problem has specific features that would be addressed in this integrated service delivery system. This would include a case and system focus on whole family units rather than individuals; co-location of services and staff joint-and-cross training of staff a tightened referral system; a reduction in barriers to information sharing; a reduction in policy and practice barriers to the delivery of flexible and preventive services; joint programming; and a system-level approach to impact evaluation (Gardner 1992). This integration would allow agencies to receive feedback from key stakeholders in the client's treatment. The implementation of the stakeholders input has been found helpful in enhancing the service delivery system (Kolko et al. 2009). In addition, it would provide intensive case management to ensure the service plan is utilized and followed accurately and hold service providers responsible for effective service delivery. This system-level approach has been explored extensively by Junek and Thompson (1999) and they state that though various components of the service delivery system have appeared in the journal literature, integration into an abstract conceptual model subject to creation and testing have not yet been documented. This proposal will expand the current knowledge base and will lead to the implementation of an integrated service delivery system.

The exchange of scarce and valuable resources and information between social service agencies is an important basis for this model. Agencies are more likely to take on the added risks and costs of coordination and collaboration if doing so secures their supply of money, services, clients, information, or other resources that are critical for meeting their service goals (Meyers 1993). In human services, less attention has been given to intraorganizational coordination than to interorganizational issues of service delivery (Neugeboren 1991). In present time of welfare reform this must change. Complex organizations often face difficulties in achieving desired levels of coordination (Hall 1991). A number of supportive conditions must be present or created with specific service delivery guidelines in place for the complex act of service coordination to succeed (Meyers 1993; Howell et al. 2004; Papin and Houck 2005; Kolko et al. 2009). These conditions include leadership among the private and public sector willing to commit to a vision and mission that supports collaboration and integration. This leadership includes a centralized approach that shares information and builds trust between providers and agencies. Murphy et al.

(2006) assert that a priority for service integration and interagency collaboration should be to standardize practice expectations and education and training standards. Other conditions are a more manageable caseload per case manager and adequate pay and incentives for the professional staff as well as service providing agencies. Burns et al. (2007) found in their study that a caseload ration of 1:20 is generally best for intensive case management scenarios. Studies show the importance of staff being adequately compensated and valued. The devalued nature of the child welfare professional leads to high turnover and inadequately trained staff, which plagues the system (Kolko et al. 2009; Shdaimah 2008). Rapid assessment, evidence-based interventions, and practices must also be combined with program evaluations. With much potential for success, the Integrated Human Service Delivery System: Child Welfare Model, when customized to local conditions, does just this. It utilizes a case management modality design and implements state-of-the-art assessment technology, appropriate interventions matched to assessed identified deficits, and coordination and follow-up in providing an innovative approach to child welfare reform.

In recent years, accountability has become a primary issue in the child welfare field. Although the profession has responded well to many client needs through the use of professionals and paraprofessionals, there continues to be a most serious allegation that intervention methods lack demonstrated effectiveness in achieving positive client change. Accurate assessment of the child client and their family, worker, and agency attributes are essential for effective practice (Wodarski 1981, 1985). Rapid assessment technology is now available to assist practitioners in assessing clients and in matching effective interventions to specific deficits. The proposed model will equip the practitioner with the fundamental tools necessary for accurate assessment, an essential element of effective intervention in social work practice (Gingerich et al. 1976). Kazdin (2005) notes that as time goes on, new outcome measures, assessments, and studies for children and youth expands exponentially. This calls for the studious work of reviewing these new assessments in order to provide clients with the most up to date and accurate assessment available. Inaccurate assessment, regardless of what powerful techniques the change agent possesses, results in ineffective or irrelevant intervention when an accurate assessment of the client's difficulties has not occurred.

The Model

"The Integrated Human Service Delivery System: Child Welfare Model" utilizes a design that suspends many of the child welfare policy and procedures as we now know them. The model provides service integration delivery through a case management modality. The Integrated Service Plan Referral Flow Chart (Appendix A) maps out the flow of information and referrals and illustrates that the quality control of the model remains with the Child Welfare/Child Protection (CPS) case manager at all times.

All children and their families, who are reported to CPS and subsequently designated a founded case, would be assigned a case manager. Due to the intensive case management of each case in this model, it would be essential for the CPS worker to have a limited number of clients on their caseload to ensure adequate time to provide necessary case coordination. Once a case has been founded, the CPS case manager would do the intake and the initial assessment, utilizing the Service Provider Measurement Package (Appendix B) to determine the child/family's strengths and deficits. This measurement package includes the Hudson MPSI and Family Risk Scale. In addition, an assessment of current services of the client/family is linked to would-be attained (Appendix B). This information would be the basis of the Integrated Individualized Service Plan (Appendix C). Development of this plan would begin with the CPS worker who would do problem identification, problem selection, and goal development with the client. Based on the identified deficits in the initial assessment, the case manager would acquire necessary releases and make referrals, on the client's behalf, to various service providers (i.e., mental health, support collection, JTPA, WIC, legal aid, etc.) for further specific assessment and intervention. The service provider would provide diagnosis definition, objective creation, and intervention delivery. They would utilize a standardized rapid assessment package to further assess (Appendix B). Based on that assessment they would provide intervention/services as indicated. In addition, they would complete and provide monthly Progress/Review Reports (Appendix D) to the caseworker as the client's progress. These reports would incorporate the intervention modality and technology utilized, along with the client's overall progress toward treatment goals. This report would allow the case manager to monitor the client's compliance and progress.

Each time a new issue was identified that required a referral, the service provider would refer the client back to their case manager who would then initiate the referral (Appendix A). This information flow would require strict adherence to ensure that service providers did not make referrals between themselves on the client's behalf as this would undermine the case manager's role and inhibit the model design.

In-Service Training and Service Agreements

In-service training would be provided by CPS for all service providers as to the overall model design and protocol. This training would include use of all communication and reporting forms which would be provided to the service providers by CPS. A standardized rapid assessment measurement package, service provider specific, would be dictated by the model design and would be mandated for use in all referrals that were initiated by the CPS case worker (Appendix B).

Service agreement contracts would be established between CPS and each service provider to ensure understanding, cooperation, coordination, and compliance with the model. Payment for services would be linked to outcomes and the service provider's strict adherence to the integrated model as specified in the service agreement contract.

Rapid Assessment

Rapid assessment techniques, as of late, have become increasingly popular with practitioners and agencies alike. This trend in the use of rapid assessment techniques has been associated with the recent request by funding agencies to have evidence that clients are reaching their stated goals and that programs are effective in treating their clients. Both practitioners and agencies have realized the contribution of rapid assessment instruments in meeting these two aims. Accurately assessing clients' needs and evaluating the effectiveness of programs for clients are two necessary objectives that face the child welfare/child protection services worker. As a result, the CPS worker desperately needs easy yet reliable assessment instruments.

Social workers have begun to identify the ability of rapid assessment instruments to collect large quantities and better quality data. Studies have consistently found that these instruments are easily administered, cost effective, and can provide reliable client data (McMahon 1984). Rapp et al. (1999) concluded that the rapid assessments used in their study elicited similar results to the more lengthy and advanced assessments for the same measures. In addition, these assessment instruments are more objective than a personal interview, in that the personal biases of the worker are reduced and the subjective nature of assessment as a whole is also decreased. Flowers et al. (1993) found that clients who were given rapid assessment instruments throughout treatment, made more improvement on their goals, terminated from treatment less often, and were in general more satisfied with treatment. These instruments have also been noted to obtain more information from clients in a shorter amount of time. Consequently, these instruments are more efficient as well as more accurate.

Social workers who work with children and multiproblem families need to assess multiple sources of data across and beyond family systems. For the prevention of children reentering the child welfare system, there is a need for assessments to accurately evaluate the family and child's risk and protective factors (Kimberlin et al. 2008). For social workers who work with abused and neglected children, the need for accurate and reliable information is even more critical because of the serious decisions that must be made (Rittner and Wodarski 1995). At the present time, many social services workers use clinical interviews, personal judgment, and assumptions to make decisions about services, treatment needs, and placement. The danger in this is clear. The proposed model "Integrated Human Service delivery System: Child Welfare Model" would reduce this subjectivity and danger by providing child protective workers with a package of easy-to-use assessment instruments. Child welfare assessment involves two primary regions: risk and child/family functioning. Both of these regions are critical in aiding decisions for CPS workers. Shlonsky and Wagner (2005) assert that actuarial risk assessment instruments have the greatest potential for reliable and accurate estimates of the recurrence of child maltreatment. Still, with good assessment, the CPS worker must decide which services would be most effective. The structured decision-making (SDM) approach may help make these decisions less subjective by integrating predictive and contextual assessment strategies into child welfare practice. By utilizing these techniques with all clients, the worker can readily assess the needs of the individual client or family in multiple problem areas. The client or family would be assessed for alcohol and drug problems, mental illness, family violence, child abuse, housing needs, nutrition, financial problems, etc. This information can then be utilized to provide the client with an individualized treatment plan, appropriate referrals, and child placement if necessary. By utilizing these valid assessment instruments, the worker can increase her/his chance of making an accurate evaluation of all the client/family's needs. No area would be left out, thus making the use of these instruments much more efficient and effective than personal judgment. With an appropriate, accurate assessment, the client and/or family can receive only the services that they need, therefore making duplication of services obsolete.

The information gathered from the rapid assessment instruments would not necessarily be used solely for the intake worker. Rather, this information (with client's consent) could be forwarded to the service agencies, where the client would be referred for treatment. This process would assist the service agencies by providing reliable information about the clients' problems prior to the first meeting; it would also reduce replicated information gathering by the service agencies. Again, efficiency would be increased.

The proposed use of rapid assessment instruments is not limited to the intake child protective worker; rather these instruments should also be utilized by practitioners at the service agencies. In this proposed system, after the practitioner obtains the initial information from the intake worker, the practitioner can utilize a different set of assessment instruments to obtain more specific information regarding the clients' problem areas. This process would allow the practitioner to gather more accurate information regarding diagnosis. In addition, the use of these instruments would provide an opportunity for the client and practitioner to develop a treatment plan. The continued use of these instruments throughout the intervention sessions will also provide the practitioner and client with information regarding how the client is improving and when the interventions can be terminated. This information will be vital for the intake worker as he/she prepares to help the client/family identify what further needs they have.

The "Integrated Human Service Delivery System: Child Welfare Model" proposes the use of rapid assessment instruments to provide intake and service agency workers with quick, accurate information on their clients. These instruments can provide quantifiable means of assessment that can significantly augment data collected through traditional procedures (Rittner and Wodarski 1995). These instruments are essential for accurate assessment and hence effective intervention. In addition, these instruments are valuable for implementing the tasks of the intake worker and practitioner; which include: treatment planning, monitoring client change, and outcomes evaluation. The use of better assessment instruments would allow the practitioner to be able to evaluate the family's readiness for reunification, therefore, shaping a more reliable predictor of the family's determination of making a lasting change and reducing the child's risk of reentering the child welfare system

(Kimberlin et al. 2008). The next section will discuss these tasks in more detail and explain how they fit into the overall integrated delivery system.

Computer Assistance

The delivery system discussed above, proposes to integrate a fragmented child welfare system, to provide clients with efficient and effective services. The use of computers can make this integration even more cost-effective and accurate. Computers could be utilized at every level of the system to improve speed as well as accuracy. At the level of intake, the social services worker can begin to generate a client/family file, which could be stored directly on the computer. Included in this file would be: rapid assessment results, treatment plans and client/family goals, referrals to service providers, client/family monitoring, and improving the overall integration of services. Toche-Manley et al. (2013) argue that computers have the ability to revolutionize the child welfare system through the use of outcomes management technology. Such programs would allow for early detection of risk factors associated with involvement in the child welfare system, but various barriers prevent this technology from current utilization. The following provides a more detailed description of how a computer system will provide further integration and efficiency.

Rapid Assessments

Rapid assessment instruments can be completed by clients directly on the computer. The computer can score these and then generate a profile that can also be stored on the computer and (with consent) forwarded to all referred service providers. This procedure has been shown in studies to be just as accurate in information obtained, but quicker and easier for the clients and workers (Hays et al. 1993; Flowers et al. 1993). For the child protective worker, the computer can help with decision-making with regard to placement. This would increase accuracy by reducing human error.

Treatment Planning, Referrals, and Progress Reports

Treatment plans that have been devised by the client/family and case manager can also be stored on the computer in the client/family file. Hard copies of this plan can be forwarded to service providers who are working with the client/family. All referrals made will be recorded in the client/family file and updated frequently. Progress/Review Reports generated by the service providers will be sent to the intake worker, who will record them into the client/family file. The computer will monitor each client/family for improvements and/or problems. The computer system can also provide precise information regarding client/family goals. For instance, the computer system could statistically report improvements on goals and when these changes occurred. This information will be important for the client as well as the worker.

Client/Family Outcomes

While the computer is monitoring client/family progress, the computer can also assist with decision-making regarding termination. Upon termination, the computer can generate an overall outcome evaluation. It could report statistically what improvements occurred in what areas. This would provide workers with more objective means to validate termination. The outcome evaluation can also identify difficulties within the system and provide an assessment of the entire delivery system. As shown in North Carolina with the use of the KDD technology in the social service documentation website, the workers were able to create charts to communicate accurately the trends of children in custody (Duncan et al. 2008). This could be used later to assist administrators with program quality improvement, personnel training, and integration. The computer could also help generate useful statistics, which could further assist with agency level changes.

Service Providers

After receiving a referral from the intake worker and an initial assessment, the practitioner will be required to obtain further, more detailed assessment information, develop a treatment plan, produce progress reports (Appendix D) to the original worker, make recommendations for further referrals, monitor client/family progress, and terminate when appropriate. These tasks, similar to those of the intake worker, can be completed with the assistance of the computer.

Schoech and Fluke (2006) propose that there is a great need to advance evidence collection and evaluation processes from the individual practitioner to the organization. They assert that a technology-based evidence-based practice (EBP) model should be employed to change EBP's focus from an individual practitioner looking for relevant research on a case-by-case basis to equipping an organization with tools that provide the needed data, assessments, and research readily available for workers.

The ultimate goal in the proposed integrated social service delivery system would be to produce a completely integrated computer system. The social service workers' computer system would be integrated with each of the service providers' computer systems, thus, making efficiency one step better. This integration would eliminate hard copy information between agencies and social services and improve confidentiality of clients and families. It would also increase time efficiency because information could be simply accessed by workers through the system. The efficient use of time increases productivity and leaves more time for the social worker to develop and expand the relationship with the client (Tredeagle and Darcy 2008).

This information sharing between agencies and social services would enhance accuracy as well as service effectiveness. Ultimately, overall program evaluation would be more easily facilitated because administrators could assess the functioning of the entire system. Weak points and system flaws could be observed and modified more quickly. The single computer system could also assist administrators in affecting new policy and procedural changes with less disruption (Cash and Berry 2003).

Conclusion

The "Integrated Human Service Delivery System: Child Welfare Model" provides an innovative approach to child welfare, which facilitates comprehensive and effective service delivery. It provides solutions to the current fragmented child welfare system through a program design that utilizes a case management modality and implements state-of-the-art rapid assessment and computer technology. This allows for appropriate interventions matched to assessed deficits and improved case coordination and follow-up which will result in better meeting the needs of children and families served by the child welfare system.

Additional Resources

Child Welfare Model

Family Assessment in Child Welfare: The Illinois DCFS Integrated Assessment Program in Policy and Practice
http://www.chapinhall.org/research/report/family-assessment-child-welfare-illinois-dcfs-integrated-assessment-program-policy-a
Florida Alcohol and Drug Abuse Association
http://www.fadaa.org/resource_center/CWI.php
Integrated Care for Children with Specific Diagnoses
http://www.hdwg.org/catalyst/pay-additional-services/integrated-care
Department of Health and Human Services
Child Welfare and Information Gateway
System Reform
https://www.childwelfare.gov/management/reform/
National Conference of State Legislatures
Child Welfare
http://www.ncsl.org/research/human-services/child-welfare.aspx

Reforming the Child Welfare System

The Future of Children

http://www.princeton.edu/futureofchildren/publications/journals/article/index.xml?journalid=40&articleid=132&sectionid=868

The Child Welfare System

https://www.firststar.org/library/child-welfare-system-overview.aspx

References

Bruskas, D. (2008). Children in foster care: A vulnerable population at risk. *Journal of Child and Adolescent Psychiatric Nursing, 21*(2), 70–77.

Burns, T., Yiend, J., Doll, H., Fahy, T., Fiander, M., & Tyrer P. (2007). Using activity data to explore the influence of case-load size on care patterns. *British Journal of Psychiatry, 190,* 217–222.

Cahill, J., & Feldman, L. H. (1993). Computers in child welfare planning for a more serviceable work environment. *Child Welfare, 72*(1), 3–12.

Cash, S., & Berry, M. (2003). Measuring service delivery in a placement prevention program: An application to an ecological model. *Administration in Social Work, 27*(3), 65–85.

Drabble, L. (2011). Advancing collaborative practice between substance abuse treatment and child welfare fields: What helps and hinders the process? *Administration in Social Work, 35*(1), 88–106.

Duncan, D. F., Kum, H., Weigensberg, E. C., Flair, K. A., & Stewart, C. J. (2008). Informing child welfare policy and practice: Using knowledge discovery and data mining technology via a dynamic web site. *Child Maltreatment, 13*(4), 383–391.

Flowers, J., Booraem, C., & Schwartz, B. (1993). Impact of computerized rapid assessment instruments on counselors and client outcome. *Computers in Human Services, 10*(2), 9–18.

Gambrill, E., & Shlosky, A. (2001). The need for comprehensive risk management systems in child welfare. *Children and Youth Services Review, 23*(1), 79–107.

Gardner, S. L. (1992). Key issues in developing school-linked, integrated services. *The Future of Children, 2,* 85–94.

Gingerich, W. J., Feldman, R. A., & Wodarski, J. S. (1976). Accuracy in assessment: Does training help? *Social Work, 21*(1), 40–48.

Hall, R. H. (1991). *Organizations: Structures, processes & outcomes*. Englewood Cliffs: Prentice-Hall, Inc.

Hays, R., Hill, L., Gillogly, J., & Lewis, M. (1993). Response times for the CAGE, Short MAST, and Jellinek Alcohol Scales. *Behavior Research Methods, Instruments & Computers, 25*(2), 204–307.

Herrenkohl, T. I., & Herrenkohl, R. C. (2007). Examining the overlap and prediction of multiple forms of child maltreatment, and socioeconomic status: A longitudinal analysis of youth outcomes. *Journal of Family Violence, 22*(7), 553–562.

Hollingsworth, L. D. (2000). Adoption policy in the United States: A word of caution. *Social Work, 45*(2), 183–186.

Howell, J. C., Kelly, M. R., Palmer, J., & Mangum, R. L. (2004). Integrating child welfare, juvenile justice, and other agencies in a continuum of services. *Child Welfare, 83*(2), 143–156.

Hurlburt, M. S., Leslie, L. K., Landsverk, J., Barth, R. P., Burns, B. J., Gibbons, R. D., Slymen, D. J., & Zhang, M. S. (2007). Contextual predictors of mental health service use among children open to child welfare. *Archives of General Psychiatry, 61*(12), 1217–1224.

Hussey, D. L., Falletta, L., & Eng, A. (2012). Risk factors for mental health diagnoses among children adopted from the public child welfare system. *Children and Youth Services Review, 34*(10), 2072–2080.

Junek, W., & Thompson, A. H. (1999). Self-regulating service delivery systems: A model for children and youth at risk. *The Journal of Behavioral Health Services & Research, 26*(1), 64–79.

Kamerman, S., & Kahn, A. (1990). Social services for children, youth and families in the United States. *Children and Youth Service Review, 12*(1), 1–79.

Kazdin, A. E. (2005). Evidenced-based assessment for children and adolescents: Issues in measurement development and clinical application. *Journal of Clinical Child and Adolescent Psychology, 34*(3), 548–558.

Kemberlin, S. E., Anthony, E. K., & Austin, M. J. (2008). Re-entering foster care: Trends, evidence, and implications. *Child and Youth Services Review, 31,* 471–481.

Kolko, D. J., Herschell, A. D., Costello, A. H., & Kolko, R. P. (2009). Child welfare recommendations to improve mental health services for children who have experienced abuse and neglect: A national perspective. *Administration and Policy in Mental Health and Mental Health Services Research, 36*(1), 50–62.

McMahon, R. (1984). Behavior checklists and rating scales. In T.H. Ollendick & M. Hersen (Eds.), *Child behavioral assessment: Principles and procedures tap* (pp. 80–105). New York: Pergamon.

Meyers, M. K. (1993). Organizational factors in the integration of services for children. *Social Service Review, 67*(4), 547–575.

Mitchell, L. B., Barth, R. P., Green, R., et al. (2005). Child welfare reform in the United States: Findings from a local agency survey. *Child Welfare, 84*(1), 5–24.

Murphy, M., Shardlow, S., Davis, C., & Race, D. (2006). Standards: A new baseline for interagency training and education to safeguard children? *Child Abuse Review, 15*(2), 138–151.

Neugeboren, B. (1991). Introduction: Coordinating human service delivery. *Administration in Social Work, 14*(4), 1–7.

O'Looney, J. (1994). Modeling collaboration and social services integration: A single state's experience with developmental and non-developmental models. *Administration in Social Work, 18*(1), 61–85.

Papin, T., & Houck T. (2005). All it takes is leadership. *Child Welfare, 84*(2), 299–310.

Rapp, L. A., Dulmus, C. N., Wodarski, J. S., & Feit, M. D. (1999). Screening of substance abuse and child protective service clients: A comparative study of rapid assessment instruments vs. the SASSI. *Journal of Addictive Diseases, 18*(2), 83–88.

Rittner, B., & Wodarski, J. (1995). Clinical assessment instruments in the treatment of child abuse and neglect. *Early Childhood Development & Care, 106,* 43–58.

Roush, D. W. (1996). A juvenile justice perspective. In C. M. Nelson, R. B. Rutherford, & B. I. Wolford (Eds.), *Comprehensive and collaborative systems that work for troubled youth: A national agenda* (pp. 29–60). Richmond: National Juvenile Detention Association.

Ryan, J. P., Marsh, J. C., Testa, M. F., & Louderman, R. (2006). Integrating substance abuse treatment and child welfare services: Findings from the Illinois alcohol and other drug abuse waiver demonstration. *Social Work Research, 30*(2), 95–107.

Sempek, A. N., & Woody, R. H. (2010). Family permanence versus the best interests of the child. *The American Journal of Family Therapy, 38*(5), 433–439.

Shdaimah, C. S. (2008). Of pots of gold and pots of glue: Society's maltreatment of America's poorest children and their families. *Journal of Progressive Human Services, 19*(2), 92–111.

Shlonsky, A., & Wagner, D. (2005). The next step: Integrating actuarial risk assessment and clinical judgment into an evidence-based practice framework in CPS case management. *Child and Youth Services Review, 27*(4), 409–427.

Shoech, D., & Fluke, J. D. (2006). A technology enhanced EBP model. *Journal of Evidenced Based Social Work, 3,* 3–4.

Toche-Manley, L. L., Dietzen, L., Nankin, J., & Beigel, A. (2013). Revolutionizing child welfare with outcomes management. *Journal of Behavioral Health Services & Research,* 40(3), 317–329.

Tregeagle, S., & Darcy, M. (2008). Child welfare and information and communication technology: Today's challenge. *British Journal of Social Work, 38,* 1481–1498.
Wodarski, J. S. (1981). *Role of research in clinical practice*. Baltimore: University Park Press.
Wodarski, J. S. (1985). An assessment model of practitioner skills: A prototype. *Arete, 10*(2), 1–14.
Yessian, M. R. (1995). Learning from experience: Integrating human services. *Public Welfare, Summer, 3,* 4–42.

Part II
Field-Tested Evidence-Informed Assessments

Chapter 6
Risk Assessment: Issues and Implementation in Child Protective Services

Michael J. Holosko and Johnna Ojo

Introduction

The primary goal of child welfare is "to protect children from harm" (Pecora et al. 2010). In order to fulfill this goal the child protective services (CPS) use assessments of risk as an essential part of service. Historically, assessment of risk and investigation are what workers use to determine the likelihood of maltreatment. Therefore, the assessment of risk is a key aspect of child protective agencies (Walk and Woolverton 1990 as cited in D'andrade et al. 2008). In this chapter, the history, goal, issues, and implementation of formal risk assessments in CPS will be discussed.

History

In the past, child protective workers have heavily relied on the case study method to assess risk or the likelihood that maltreated children were in danger of future maltreatment. This method involves the examination of "case assessments, clinical experience, professional judgment, and sometimes intuition" (Hughes and Rycusa 2006). In addition, prior maltreatment was believed to indicate an increased risk for future maltreatment. Many professionals practice the "availability of heuristic" method. This method of decision making involves professionals following "rules of thumb" to make quick judgments (Littlechild and Hawley 2009). Workers rely on their professional knowledge and experience. This approach can lead to workers making conclusions based on biases or simply insufficient data.

M. J. Holosko (✉)
Professor at University of Georgia, Athens, GA, USA
e-mail: mholosko@uga.edu

J. Ojo
The University of Tennessee, Knoxville, TN, USA

J. S. Wodarski et al. (eds.), *Evidence-Informed Assessment and Practice in Child Welfare,* DOI 10.1007/978-3-319-12045-4_6

Child maltreatment is a complicated issue and an unfortunate epidemic. Due to its severity and complex nature, there is a "consensus that practitioners should not rely solely on substantiation or prior maltreatment as the basis of subsequent case decisions" (Hughes and Rycusa 2006). The unstructured style of assessing risk promoted bias and error (Hughes and Rycusa 2006). To decrease error, biases, and promote a more accurate decision-making strategy CPS began to utilize risk assessments. Even within risk assessments there is a range "from discrete, 'point-in-time' assessments of the likelihood of future harm to case management tools that promote an overarching attention to risk…" (Hughes and Rycusa 2006). This broad range from discrete to case management risk assessments can create confusion amongst professionals. Point-in-time risk assessments focus on families in which future maltreatment is likely to occur. On the other end of the continuum, case management risk assessments attempt to collect data throughout the lifespan of a case (Hughes and Rycusa 2006). Attention is given to various areas of the family's life. The danger with a broad continuum is that some workers practice at one end and other workers at the opposite end. These grand differences can lead to extremely different decisions in cases. In an effort to minimize the confusion and provide a more reliable and accurate decision-making model, CPS began to implement formal risk assessments. Formal risk assessments include those that are tested and found to be reliable and valid.

Studies suggest the interplay between risk and protective factors as contributors to maltreatment (Pecora et al. 2010). The evidence found in research has led to the use of the ecological framework in child protective agencies. The ecological framework is a systematic approach to assessing an individual's life. Systems are examined at their level of interaction with one another. The decision-making strategy can greatly affect the provision of services in a child's life (Pecora et al. 2010). Assessment of multiple domains requires an accurate strategy. The best formal risk assessments are those that contain a list of variables from numerous domains of life. These domains typically include: "child characteristics (e.g., age, disability), caretaker characteristics (e.g., substance use, access to the child, parenting skills), maltreatment characteristics (e.g., severity), environment (e.g., social support, housing and financial stability), and level of family cooperation with CPS" (Camasso and Jagannathan 1995; Fluke et al. 2005; Hindley et al. 2006; Johnson and L'Edperance 1984; Marks and McDonald 1989; McDonald and Marks 1991 as cited in Sledjeski et al. 2008). It is important for child welfare workers to remember that rarely is neglect "an isolated experience" (Mennen et al. 2010, p. 11). Therefore, conducting assessments that utilize the ecological framework are essential for accurate risk assessments.

Goal

The primary goal of CPS is to keep "children safe from child abuse and neglect" (Pecora et al. 2010). This goal corresponds with the goal of formal risk assessments. Formal risk assessments are "instruments and structured formats…" that "… aim to improve 'unassisted' professional judgment" (Broadhurst et al. 2010). Formal risk assessments possess the ability to improve the decision-making process in CPS. It was believed that accurate and effective assessments would lead to "identification of children at high risk of future harm" (Hughes and Rycusa 2006). Ultimately a more accurate method to assessing risk such as the use of formal risk assessments could improve and promote safety of children.

Added to the primary goal of risk assessments is a list of ways in which formal risk assessments are expected to improve practice. They include:

> Improving workers' decision-making at all stages of casework; improving the quality and consistency of services to families; improving the case referral and case management process; providing a forum for case discussion and supervision; delineating child welfare practice standards; increasing agency accountability; demonstrating agency accountability to the public; reducing agency liability; improving court presentations; compensating for inexperienced staff and the effects of turnover; helping manage workloads; and providing a framework for case documentation (Hughes and Rycusa 2006).

Types of Models

Most risk assessment models have four components. These components include:

> 1) the broad categories to be assessed; 2) behavioral descriptors that define and operationalize these criteria (also known as measures); 3) procedures and calculations for determining various levels of risk; and 4) standardized forms to uniformly capture and record this information (Hughes and Rycusa 2006).

As CPS and similar agencies progress there is a move towards using and implementing risk assessments and interventions that are found to be empirically valid (Shlonsky and Wagner 2005). Currently in CPS, there are two major approaches to risk assessment: Consensus-based model and an Actuarial model (D'andrade et al. 2008). These models are used as decision-making models and risk assessments are created based upon these models.

The consensus-based model is a comprehensive approach of child maltreatment theories, professional opinions as well as professional reports of child maltreatment. The collaboration of information often leads to the creation of hybrid assessments (D'andrade et al. 2008). Information from various assessments are gathered and created into one assessment. The consensus model of risk assessments is appealing due to its adaptability. However, adaptability does not equal effectiveness. In fact the flexibility of the consensus model may decrease the effectiveness of assessments by altering the validity and reliability of the various instruments used to create one hybrid risk assessment (D'andrade et al. 2008). The reliability and validity of a risk assessment model are the factors that determine its effectiveness. Without a strong level of reliability and validity, risk assessment models provide inconsistent and ultimately inaccurate data. These faulty data could potentially lead CPS professionals to make inaccurate decisions.

Actuarial-based risk assessments use measures that have been statistically proven to "have high levels of association with recurrences of maltreatment" (Hughes and

Rycusa 2006). Assessments that follow the actuarial model possess tested levels of reliability and validity. Actuarial risk assessments often provide professionals with numerical scores or an alternate method that can be used to classify a client's likelihood of risk (i.e., risk level) (Schwalbe 2008). As a result, comparative research has shown that actuarial-based assessments are better than consensus-based assessments in accurately assessing the probability of particular outcomes (Coohey et al. 2013; Shlonsky and Wagner 2005). Instead of relying on professional judgment and intuition, knowledge of empirical literature and research is the focus (Dorsey et al. 2008). In recent years, CPS have begun implementing actuarial-based risk assessments.

Despite the high validity of actuarial-based risk assessments, there are some professionals who are against the use of these assessments because they believe it undermines the use of clinical judgment (Shlonsky and Wagner 2005). These professionals are encouraged to research the development of actuarial-based risk assessments. The items used on actuarial risk assessments are often collected from professionals in the child welfare field (Shlonsky and Wagner 2005). The items then are used in an actuarial study to test the validity and reliability before being released as a formal risk assessment. Even though clinical/professional judgment is utilized in the development of the risk assessments the question remains: do actuarial-based risk assessments provide a full range of items necessary to evaluate and predict risk? Some would argue that guarding against the intrusion of clinical judgment by using a formal risk assessment eliminates the evaluation of additional or unexpected variables.

According to Baron, models of assessment should be a combination of the actuarial model and professional judgment (Littlechild and Hawley 2009). Though formal risk assessments such as actuarial-based assessments are vital to best practice, the professional judgment of workers should not be discarded. An equal mix between formal risk assessments and professional judgment based on research and practice experience is encouraged. Many workers would find it difficult to exclude or ignore their professional experience and knowledge. Some say that it is near to impossible. If workers choose to use professional judgment and experience, they must continue to keep biases in check to ensure that fair and accurate decisions are being made.

In recent years, researchers have begun to examine the use and effectiveness of decision-making models that influence the creation of formal risk assessments. A new theory that requires addition research is based on the integration of formal risk and needs assessments. Proponents of such an integrated approach to risk assessments state that the assessments would provide professionals with a thorough understanding of the client situation. This includes classification of risk (i.e., low, medium, high risk) provided by the risk assessment portion and direction for services provided by the needs assessment portion of the assessment (Schwalbe 2008). The confusion between the concepts of "risk" and "need" often interferes with the creation of such an assessment (Schwalbe 2008). A comprehensive approach to formal risk assessments is believed to prevent "misdirected casual hypotheses" (Schwalbe 2008). In this approach, professional intuition is supported by a needs assessments and an empirically tested risk assessment.

Methodological Problems in Risk Assessments

The biggest problem/barrier with risk assessments in CPS is the fact that risk assessments rely on the social process of the interaction between CPS workers and clients (Munro 2002; Gambrill and Shlonsky 2000). Interactions between workers and clients are an unavoidable component of risk assessments. However, as mentioned previously, the social aspect of risk assessments increases the likelihood that error and biases of the worker will occur.

Most risk assessments used today are based on an ecological framework. Failure to recognize the interaction of factors in one's life can lead to a poor risk assessment. Therefore, a barrier to an accurately performed risk assessment is a workers lack of knowledge of all factors of a family's life. A family's lack of access to community support services might be a contributing factor to the perception of risk (Harlington et al. 2010). While a lack of services can negatively impact a family, this issue should not be held against the family during a risk assessment. Instead the worker should make attempts to place the family in contact with community services.

Lastly, a barrier in risk assessment is the predictor of child maltreatment (Camasso and Jagannathan 2012; Harlington et al. 2010). Despite numerous studies and years of research on the topic of predicting child maltreatment, it remains a topic that is still unclear. Researchers are continuously studying predictors of child abuse and neglect. Much knowledge has been gained throughout the years but like many fields of social science the wealth of knowledge is always evolving. Therefore, the known predictors of child maltreatment should continue to be tested and researched. New predictors or risk factors should be tested extensively before being associated to predicting the likelihood of child maltreatment.

Proper Use of Risk Assessment

The term risk assessment has often been used interchangeably in CPS. The term is used to describe ongoing casework in which a CPS worker watches for signs of maltreatment and the term is also applied to formal, standardized assessment instruments (Hughes and Rycusa 2006). Professionals in CPS frequently make the mistake of labeling every contact with a client as a formal risk assessment.

Confusion also exists between family assessments and risk assessments. There is confusion and disagreements on the difference between risk assessments and family assessments in CPS (Shlonsky and Wagner 2005). According to the National Association of Public Child Welfare Administrators, risk assessment is defined as, "undertaken to determine the likelihood of future maltreatment, particularly in the absence of intervention" family assessment is defined as:

> Undertaken to determine dynamic aspects of family functioning that resulted in the family being brought to the attention of child protective services, as well as family strengths, conditions that need to be remedied, cultural issues, and other issues that should contribute to the construction of a successful service plan (1999 as citied in Kirk 2008).

It is important to establish and maintain a distinction between family assessments and risk assessments. Though both are equally important in a case, the dangers of using the two assessments interchangeably are inconsistency and poor quality practice. As the definition suggests, family assessments should be used for case planning purposes and not for assessing the level of risk (Hughes and Rycusa 2006).

Difficult to Measure

Many informal risk assessments are difficult to measure. The ambiguous scoring and poorly defined risk classifications lead to inconsistent measuring. Even more dangerous to the effectiveness of practice, the ambiguousness allows the same behaviors or conditions to be scored at more than one risk level (Rycus and Hughes 2002; Pecora et al. 2000 as cited in Hughes and Rycusa 2006). This ultimately weakens the assessment's reliability.

Some risk assessments provide examples to aid child protective worker in identifying and classifying risk levels. However, the examples have the potential to bring confusion instead of clarity. The following example was taken from a risk assessment training manual. This particular measure describes moderate risk as "Caregiver currently exhibiting behaviors which may be a sign of deteriorating mental health, and treatment is not being sought" and high risk is described as "Caregiver's current psychological state appears to pose a high level of risk to the child; caregiver is unwilling and/or refuses to seek psychiatric treatment and/or evaluation" (Los Angeles County, Family Assessment Risk Variables, 1996, adapted from Illinois Department of Children and Family Services, 1989, Risk Assessment Training Manual, as citied in Hughes and Rycusa 2006). Both could be detrimental to a child but the difference between moderate and risk hinges on the phrase "appears to pose a high level of risk to the child." Although this may be true, the assessment is forcing the worker to make a judgment about the level of risk by choosing between two similar statements. Instead the conclusion should be derived from the risk assessment and little from the professional to prevent biases and inaccurate beliefs from intruding.

The difficulty of measuring formal risk assessments varies. The difficulty often depends on the type of risk assessment. Many risk assessments have a likert scale design. Likert scales allow the rater to score a behavior or incident on a continuum (i.e., never, rarely, sometimes, often, frequently, and always). The problem with likert scales lies with the worker. It relies on the worker to collect sufficient information to place the behavior or incident on the scale accordingly. This type of scoring works better with some risk factors than other. For example, a "minor gas leak" might be considered as a moderate risk and a "severe gas leak" as high risk (Hughes and Rycusa 2006). Whether a gas leak is minor or severe all levels should be considered high risk because gas is dangerous and can kill. This example while extreme demonstrates that the likert scale does not work for all risk factors.

Clarity in Language

The problem with informal risk assessments is the lack of clarity in classifications, language, ratings, and questions. Increasing the accuracy of formal risks assessments involves clarifying the language found in the assessments. The simple terms of risk and safety are often interpreted differently by workers in CPS (Munro 2008). According to Webster, risk is defined as the possibility of injury, damage, or harm, while safety is defined as the state of being free from hurt, injury, or harm (Risk n. d.; Safety n. d.). Based upon these definitions one might assume that there should not be any misuse of these terms. However, the terms are often used differently in CPS. For example, risk factors are often understood as factors that threaten safety and safety factors are seen as "conditions that offset or mitigate risk" (Munro 2008). On the other hand, the term safety factors is also used to discuss "conditions that increase risk rather than conditions that mitigate it… (Munro 2008). Due to this discrepancy between the terms risk and safety there first must be an understanding of the two terms in CPS. There must be an understanding that risk assessments as mentioned previously are used to assess the potential risk or likelihood of child maltreatment. Whereas, safety assessments are used to assess "severe harm in the near term" (Hughes and Rycusa 2006). Safety assessments are a form of risk assessments but emphasis is placed on present harm. The proper use of the term risk with regards to assessment will lead to improving the assessments made by CPS, therefore, the safety and well being of children.

Once the use of the word risk is agreed upon an agreement on the type of risk being assessed needs to be clarified in assessments. There are two types of risk factors: static and dynamic risk factors (Schwalbe 2008). Static risk factors are "historical in nature and as such tend to remain fixed or indicate greater risk over time" (Schwalbe 2008). However, dynamic risk factors are current and "can change with changing circumstances" (Schwalbe 2008).

In addition, the word neglect is often defined differently from worker to worker (Harlington et al. 2010). Researchers often define neglect according to the legal term (Mennen et al. 2010). The legal definition of neglect is "an omission to do or perform some work, duty or act" (Neglect n. d.). According to the Child Abuse Prevention and Treatment Act as amended by the Keeping Children and Families Safe Act of 2003, child abuse and neglect is defined as:

> At a minimum, any recent act or failure to act on the part of a parent or caretaker which results in death, serious physical or emotional harm, sexual abuse or exploitation or an act or failure to act which presents an imminent risk of serious harm (US Department of Health and Human Services 2003).

Inconsistency in the definition of neglect varies across states and professions (e.g., CPS, court system) (Children's Bureau, Office on Child Abuse and Neglect and DePanfilis 2006). For example, in California neglect is defined as "the failure of a parents or caretaker to provide for a child's needs" (Mennen et al. 2010, p. 2). The question arises, who defines a child's needs? Needs may vary from culture to culture. Workers should be aware of their personal beliefs regarding the needs of a child. Research in child development can provide beneficial information to assist CPS workers regarding the needs of children.

What may be considered neglect in one state may not be in another state. CPS workers need to assess neglect carefully using formal risk assessments. A call for consistency of the term neglect is needed for developing and interpreting risk assessments. A definition that is constant will improve current and future research in child maltreatment and risk assessments. With this lack of consistency "it is nearly impossible to compare research results" (Children's Bureau, Office of Child Abuse and Neglect and DePanfilis 2006).

Implications for Practice

Implementation of Risk Assessment in Child Welfare Practice

Generally, CPS workers have a heavy caseload and therefore the time, which they can spend with each family, is limited. The limited amount of time can impact the workers' ability to perform a thorough risk assessment. Workers may shorten the risk assessment process to fit their time frame, therefore increasing the likelihood that error and biases could intrude in the decisions made from the risk assessment (Hughes and Rycusa 2006). A call for a change in policy should be made in order to lighten the caseload of CPS workers and allow workers more time to complete thorough assessments and therefore better informed decisions. In support of lighter caseloads to allow case workers more time is the timing of the implementation of risk assessments. Often risk assessments are carried out in the initial meeting. It is suggested that risk assessments should be conducted after a few meetings after rapport has begun to be established or collateral contact have been made (Hughes and Rycusa 2006).

Research on actuarial-based risk assessments has shown results to yield strong validity and reliability. Even though numerous studies have proven actuarial risk assessments promise for making more accurate decisions, implementation in CPS is problematic (Dorsey et al. 2008). Some of the barriers to agency-wide implementation of risk assessments include:

> Excessive workloads, shifting and competing priorities, poor time management, a reactive rather than planful approach to management, too few resources, poorly designed and implemented change initiatives, an unsupportive political environment, and the general resistance to change that helps maintain the status quo in may bureaucratic organizations (Hughes and Rycusa 2006).

Lastly, opposition of implementation comes from both caseworkers and supervisors. Many CPS workers believe the use of actuarial-based risk assessments hampers practice rather than improving it. This is especially true if the workers do not see the value in using formal risk assessments or a need to improve their quality of assessments, decisions, or practice (Hughes and Rycusa 2006). Although the use of formal risk assessments in CPS is progressing, the use of "clinical prediction continues to thrive" (Gambrill and Shlonsky 2000). Human service professionals are urged to "consider" risk assessment findings or even to allow risk assessment findings to supplant their intuitive judgment about future risk" (Schwalbe 2008).

Training

Research demonstrates that even with the use of risk assessments, there are discrepancies in the decisions made by social workers (Lee et al. 2013; Morgan 2007). Proper training is another barrier to implementing risk assessments in CPS. Many workers describe their training for complex cases involving child and parents as inadequate (Darlington et al. 2005 as cited in Darlington et al. 2010). Conducting risk assessments requires a considerable amount of clinical and professional skill (Hughes and Rycusa 2006). Therefore, quality training on risk assessments is needed among workers in CPS. Education and training on the use of formal risk assessments could lead to accurate implementation of the assessment tools. Training on how to read/interpret the responses and answers on risk assessments could increase the accuracy of decisions. The ultimate goal of training in risk assessments is to create consistency and improve accuracy amongst the decisions made by CPS workers.

The beliefs and values of a worker conducting the risk assessments can greatly impact the conclusion (Hughes and Rycusa 2006). One's culture shapes the way in which they interact with and view the world. For this reason, training on acknowledging and recognizing one's belief and value system is imperative. Culture awareness training can prevent one's worldview from obscuring the understanding of the client(s) being assessed.

In addition, all those involved in understanding and implementing risk assessments should receive joint training (Darlington et al. 2010). Training for all professionals involved in risk assessments (i.e., caseworkers and supervisors) would provide better practice outcomes for clients. Training should include information on each item in the assessment, areas being measured, influence of culture, values and beliefs, time management, analyzing and scoring assessments, risk classifications, and influence of self on clients during risk assessment (Hughes and Rycusa 2006). If workers view formal risk assessments as a "bureaucratic mandate" or unnecessary they are more likely to shortcut the risk assessment process (Hughes and Rycusa 2006). This attitude towards risk assessments could harm clients by providing inaccurate information and thus inaccurate decisions are being made. Professionals should be educated on the value of formal risk assessments and their importance in quality practice.

Ethical and Legal Issues of Risk Assessments

The state is obligated to support parental rights and protect the rights of children with regards to safety (Hughes and Rycusa 2006). However, it is parents that have authority and legal rights of their children. In cases of child maltreatment, "children's rights to safety supersede parents' rights to self-determination" (Hughes and Rycusa 2006). Therefore, it is the states' responsibility to protect children from child maltreatment by caregivers. Although the state has the responsibility and obligation to intervene in the life of a child, certain factors must exist. For example, there must be serious concerns about abuse or evidence of abuse.

The ethical and legal question arises to whether CPS can intervene based upon information from risk assessments (Hughes and Rycusa 2006). The argument exists to whether CPS has the legal right to intervene in a family's life against their wishes based upon risk assessment results (i.e., a high-risk classification) (Hughes and Rycusa 2006). Currently, child protective investigations focus on substantiated child maltreatment. Some argue that investigations should move from past incidents to including more risk assessments, which are aimed to prevent future child maltreatment. Supporters of such a shift argue that substantiation is confrontational and does not focus on the families' strengths and potential growth. This then inhibits the development of a collaborative relationship between the family and CPS. CPS workers must remember that "high-risk" classification even on a highly reliable and valid assessment tool does not equal certainty. High risk simply means high probability and not certainty (Hughes and Rycusa 2006). Despite the discussion of this issue the reality remains that the classification of high risk does not assure that families will maltreat their children (Baird and Wagner 2000 as cited in Hughes and Rycusa 2006). Therefore, it appears that substantiation will continue to be a "necessary part of child protective services" (Hughes and Rycusa 2006). The need to assess both past incidents and future likelihood of maltreatment are important for protecting the child.

Perhaps the most important ethical and legal issue for professionals to remember is that all actions are subject to legal action. Therefore, it is imperative that professionals do not falsely claim that their assessments are standardized and empirically tested. In addition, even standardized formal assessments have limitations and these must be acknowledged in practice. Professionals must be aware that all assessments have potential ethical and legal liabilities and it is their responsibility to ensure that the limitations of the risk assessment are recognized (Hughes and Rycusa 2006).

Conclusions

Risk assessment tools are meant to improve practice and limit harm towards children. As discussed in this chapter, tested risk assessments provide accuracy and consistency to decisions made in CPS. In a recent study by the Department of Social

Services of Virginia, the department compared data from 30 local departments using actuarial-based risk assessments and 90 local departments that used nonactuarial-based risk assessments. The researchers also conducted interviews with 25 social workers and supervisors from the local departments. Qualitative results showed that social workers "preferred actuarial based risk assessment tools to a less structured approach to the child protective services process" (Jones and Beecroft 2008). The social workers felt that the use of actuarial base risk assessments not only provided consistency but helped justify their decisions. In addition, supervisors "liked the consistent and objective framework for making decisions about cases" (Jones and Beecroft 2008).

Almost all science-based professions use empirically sound and evidence-based assessment tools in practice. The area of social work and child welfare should be no different. Currently there are many assessment tools being utilized in child welfare that have not undergone strict research protocols. Professional fields such as education, psychology, medicine, etc. use standardized and tested assessments (Hughes and Rycusa 2006). In addition, these professions have strict guidelines for administration and scoring of the assessments. CPS "should commit to the same high standards" (Hughes and Rycusa 2006). To remedy the disparity between the profession of child welfare and other professions, the national child welfare system and social work organizations should create and establish a strict protocol for the "development, administration, evaluation, and utilization of formal risk assessment technologies" (Hughes and Rycusa 2006).

Before implementing specific risk assessments into practice, the instruments must have undergone empirical testing. It is important that the assessment tool itself has been tested but in addition the risk factors being assessed should be tested as well. Often certain risk factors are mentioned to be associated with child maltreatment (Shlonsky and Wagner 2005). However, association is not adequate for quality practice. The risk factors must be proven to predict child maltreatment or increase the likelihood of child maltreatment.

Recommendations for future research include researching caseworkers' use of empirical knowledge and literature in their practice and case decisions. The current research being conducted on decision making and use of risk assessments in CPS is limited and typically involves small sample sizes as well as low generalizability to all cultures and geographical areas (Dorsey et al. 2008). The information gained through research can be used to inform and improve risk assessments.

Perhaps, the most important recommendation for future risk assessments is that each risk assessment should include a concise and descriptive training manual. CPS should attend regular training on the proper use and implementation of particular risk assessments used in their local department of CPS. The training format should include history, importance, instructions, scoring, and interpretation of the risk assessment. In addition, training should include a time of culture awareness training and question and answer time.

Just like many professions, despite good effort, CPS may have missed the mark for the proper use and implementation of formal risk assessments. To remedy this, the child welfare profession needs to reevaluate their options of best practice as well as identify and maximize its strengths as a profession. Furthermore, they should "implement strategic measures to promote the most ethical and effective use of risk assessment to promote equitable and legitimate protective decisions"...for children and their families (Hughes and Rycusa 2006).

Finally, all involved in the risk assessment process whether from analyzing, development, research, or implementation, professionals should remember the goal of risk assessments. The purpose of risk assessments in CPS is to identify those children that are at risk for future maltreatment. To sustain the recommended changes discussed in this chapter, in real life practice, CPS workers need to be educated on the importance of risk assessments. Supervisors need to provide frontline workers with adequate support to ensure that thorough risk assessments are employed. Again, child protective professionals must remember that classifying an individual or family as high risk does not mean that future maltreatment is certain (Hughes and Rycusa 2006). Identification of high risk simply allows CPS to provide services in hopes to reduce or prevent future maltreatment from occurring.

Additional Resources

Evaluation Methodology: Child Protection
http://www.aifs.gov.au/cfca/bibliographies/evaluationchildprotect.php
Consensus Based Model
http://seedsforchange.org.uk/consensus
Hartnett's Consensus Oriented Decision making Model
http://www.mindtools.com/pages/article/codm.htm

References

Broadhurst, K., Hall, C., Wastell, D., White, S., & Pithouse, A. (2010). Risk, instrumentalism and the humane project in social work: Identifying the informal logics of risk management in children's statutory services. *British Journal of Social Work, 40*(4), 1046–1064. doi:10.1093/bjsw/bcq011.

Camasso, M. J., & Jagannathan, R. (2012). Decision making in child protective services: A risky business? *Risk Analysis, 33*(9), 1636–1649.

Children's Bureau, Office of Child Abuse and Neglect, & DePanfilis, D. (2006). Child neglect: A guide for prevention, assessment and intervention. http://www.childwelfare.gov/pubs/usermanuals/neglect/index.cfm. Accessed June 22, 2013.

Coohey, C., Johnson, K., Renner, L. M., & Easton, S. D. (2013). Actuarial risk assessment in child protective services: Construction methodology and performance criteria. *Children and Youth Services Review, 35*(1), 151–161. doi:10.1016/j.childyouth.2012.09.020.

D'andrade, A., Austin, M. J., & Benton, A. (2008). Risk and safety assessment in child welfare. *Journal of Evidence-Based Social Work, 5*(1–2), 31–56. doi:10.1300/J394v05n01_03.

Darlington, Y., Healy, K., & Feeney, J. A. (2010). Approaches to assessment and intervention across four types of child and family welfare services. *Children and Youth Services Review, 32*(3), 356–364. doi:10.1016/j.childyouth.2009.10.005.

Dorsey, S., Mustillo, S. A., Farmer, E. M. Z., & Elbogen, E. (2008). Caseworker assessments of risk for recurrent maltreatment: Association with case-specific risk factors and re-reports. *Child Abuse & Neglect, 32*, 377–391.

Gambrill, E., & Shlonsky, A. (2000). Risk assessment in context. *Children and Youth Services Review, 22*(11/12), 813–837.

Hughes, R. C., & Rycusa, J. S. (2006). Issues in risk assessment in child protective services. *Journal of Public Child Welfare, 1*(1), 85–116.

Jones, B., & Beecroft, E. (2008). *The impacts of actuarial risk assessment on child protective services in Virginia*. Office of Research: Virginia Department of Social Services.

Kirk, R. S. (2008). Development and field-testing of a family assessment scale for use in child welfare practice settings utilizing Differential Response. *Protecting Children, 23*(1–2), 71–88.

Lee, S. J., Sobeck, J. L., Djelaj, V., & Agius, E. (2013). When practice and policy collide: Child welfare workers' perceptions of investigation processes. *Children and Youth Services Review, 35*(4), 634–641. doi:http://dx.doi.org/10.1016/j.childyouth.2013.01.004.

Littlechild, B., & Hawley, C. (2009). Risk assessments for mental health users: Ethical, valid, and reliable? *Journal of Social Work, 10*(2), 211–229. doi:10.1177/1468017309342191.

Mennen, F. E., Kim, K., Sang, J., & Trickett, P. K. (2010). Child neglect: Definition and identification of youth's experiences in official reports of maltreatment. *Child Abuse & Neglect, 34*(9), 647–658. doi:10.1016/j.chiabu.2010.02.007.

Morgan, J. (2007). *"Giving up the culture of blame": Risk assessment and risk management in psychiatric practice', briefing document to Royal College of Psychiatrists*. London: Royal College of Psychiatrists.

Munro, E. (2008). Assessing risks throughout the life of a child welfare case. In D. Lindsey & A. Shlonsky (Eds.), *Child welfare research: Advances for practice & policy* (pp. ADD). New York: Oxford.

Neglect. (n. d.) *West's Encyclopedia of American Law, edition 2*. (2008). http://legal-dictionary.thefreedictionary.com/neglect. Accessed June 18, 2013.

Pecora, P. J., Whittaker, J. K., Maluccio, A. N., Barth, R. P., DePanfilis, D., & Plotnick, R. D. (2010). *The child welfare challenge: Policy, practice and research* (3rd ed.). New Brunswick: Transaction.

Risk. (n. d.). In *Merriam-Webster Dictionary online*. http://www.merriam-webster.com/dictionary/risk. Accessed June 18, 2013.

Safety. (n. d.). In *Merriam-Webster Dictionary online*. http://www.merriam-webster.com/dictionary/safety. Accessed June 18, 2013.

Schwalbe, C. S. (2008). Strengthening the integration of actuarial risk assessment judgment in an evidence based practice framework. *Children and Youth Services Review, 30*, 1458–1464. doi:10.1016/j.childyouth.2007.11.021.

Shlonsky, A., & Wagner, D. (2005). The next step: Integrating actuarial risk assessment and clinical judgment into an evidence-based practice framework in CPS case management. *Children and Youth Services Review, 27*(4), 409–427. doi:10.1016/j.childyouth.2004.11.007.

Sledjeski, E. M., Dierker, L. C., Brigham, R., & Breslin, E. (2008). The use of risk assessment to predict recurrent maltreatment: A classification and regression tree analysis (CART). *Society for Prevention Research, 9*, 28–37. doi:10.1007/s11121-007-0079-0.

US Department of Health and Human Services. (2003). *The child abuse and prevention treatment including adoption opportunities and the abandoned infants assistance act as amended by the keeping children and families safe act of 2003*. Administration for Children and Families, Administration of Children Youth and Families. Children's Bureau, Office of Child Abuse and Neglect.

Chapter 7
Assessment Methods

John S. Wodarski

Introduction

In recent years, practitioners and agencies have placed a greater emphasis on documenting the effectiveness of interventions (Serbati et al. 2013). This trend toward outcome evaluation is associated, in part, with the legitimate interest by funding sources in assessing whether the promised goals of programs are being attained. In order to demonstrate the effectiveness of services delivered to targeted populations and to augment decision-making processes, program developers and practitioners need reliable instruments to provide data along a continuum of services. As a result, more independent practitioners and agency-based social workers are using rapid assessment instruments to increase the quantity and quality of data collected during the provision of services.

In certain arenas, the use of data-collection instruments has become particularly important. For those working with children, the need to assess multiple sources of data across and beyond family systems is especially relevant because of the complex interactions between environments and children. For social workers working with abused and neglected children, the need for accurate and reliable information is even more critical because of the serious decisions that must be made.

Other than the risk assessment instruments currently in place, a few exist that employ a structured method of data collection in managed care (Broadhurst et al. 2010). In making important decisions regarding the duration and nature of interventions, referrals, and termination of services, social workers tend to rely largely on personal judgment, matrix factors, structured risk assessment tools, and accepted implicit and explicit assumptions about variables associated with the risk to clients (Wells and Correia 2010). Most often, data are collected through interviews with various persons in the social environments. There are eight different interviewing types, but the one that is used most regularly for data collection is education

J. S. Wodarski (✉)
The University of Tennessee, Knoxville, TN, USA
e-mail: jwodarsk@utk.edu

J. S. Wodarski et al. (eds.), *Evidence-Informed Assessment and Practice in Child Welfare,* DOI 10.1007/978-3-319-12045-4_7

evaluation (Fallon et al. 2010). Rarely are self-report inventories or behavioral inventories used to collect information directly from parents, children, teachers, or others with specific knowledge of the family, despite the advantages of using such scales.

Self-report inventories, in particular, offer a number of advantages to workers who are intervening with families. Since child maltreatment typically occurs in the privacy of family settings and is not directly observable, gathering sufficient and reliable data about the multiplicity of problems that might exist can be very complex and challenging (Trickett et al. 2011). Instruments can record additional data on behavior and attitudes that may enhance the direction and intensity of the interventions selected. For instance, a multilevel intervention recorded in California suggests that it is most beneficial to obtain data on several aspects of children, such as learning, behavioral influences, and social competencies (Mills et al. 2013). Further, the use of scales reduces the time required by workers to collect data at the same time as it expands the sources of information across multiple systems. The broader-base information may include teachers and other school personnel, other professionals (visiting nurses, clinicians, physicians, and so forth), as well as a wider range of individual family members who may not be present at the time of the intake interview or at subsequent assessment points.

An accurate assessment is essential for effective practice. In child welfare, where assessments must depend on direct as well as indirect evidence, data on parental attitudes toward the victim, problem behaviors within the family constellation, and possible compromising psychopathologies can be obtained through the use of standard scales. A variety of objective measures pertinent to the assessment of child abuse and neglect are now available that can be used by practitioners with minimal disruption in terms of time, energy, cost, and ease of administration. The purpose of this chapter is to review a variety of instruments that child-welfare workers, specifically, and practitioners involved in children's services, in general, can use in the assessment and treatment of child abuse and neglect.

Assessment Strategies

The assessment methods reviewed here include a variety of instrument types. Some are self-report inventories, and others are behavior-rating scales, structured interviews, or observational coding systems. Traditional questionnaires are an example of the self-report approach, while behavior-rating scales, structured interviews, and observational coding systems are completed by an informed source in reference to the behavior or characteristics of another person. Both self-report inventories and behavior-rating scales have the recognized advantage of being generally easy to administer. In addition, they can provide objective evidence of client change. They are less costly and time-consuming than structured interviews or direct observation (Swenson et al. 2010).

There are several potential disadvantages to the use of paper-and-pencil self-report measures (Cohen et al. 2012). It is important to remember that when instruments are used in child-welfare settings, the informants may recognize and give socially desirable responses rather than accurate ones. This possibility should always be considered and adjusted for through complementary sources of information or alternative methods of obtaining information (Cohen et al. 2012). An important example of complementary source of information is structured interviews consisting of standardized questions, observational methods, and behavior-rating scales. Observational coding systems entail observing and recording the frequency of occurrence of specific behaviors, such as parental praise and commands during an interaction sequence in naturalistic structured situations. This approach requires more time, training, and resources than other methods but can provide accurate identification of specific parent-child problems (Park and Ryan 2008).

Selecting and Using Assessment Instruments

Instrument-based data, in concert with interviews, are useful in shaping and clarifying areas of concern, providing direction for more probing inquiry, determining possible intervention strategies, and assessing the success of interventions selected. Choosing empirical measures for child maltreatment case planning must begin with a clear understanding of the kind and purpose of the assessment, the breadth of information needed within the scope of the assessment, and the interventions available once problems are defined and the assets of the family are identified. The selection of any instruments must include evaluation of their levels of reliability and validity and understanding of the circumstances in which those levels optimally exist. This method is in cohorts with the upcoming research design called mixed methods. It triangulates the perspectives, rather than just viewing one aspect, such as the interview. Mixed methods use both qualitative and quantitative methods to come to a more valid decision (Broadhurst et al. 2010).

A valid instrument measures what it proposes to measure and includes sufficient items to be representative of the concepts to be measured. Reliability refers to the consistency of the measure; that is, the instrument yields similar results each time it is administered. All of the instruments reviewed here are regarded as having acceptable levels of validity and reliability. However, it is important to understand that these determinations are based on group data and cannot be guaranteed in each individual circumstance of potential use. An individual's score may in fact be correct. Important decisions should never be based on the results of a single assessment tool (Stith et al. 2009). Data obtained from the measures included here should supplement, not replace, traditional sources.

A practitioner using any instrument must become thoroughly familiar with how to administer and score it for effectiveness and efficient use (Corcoran and Pillai 2009). This includes knowing for which populations the instrument can be effectively used, how it is completed, how much time is required to complete it, and what kinds of equipment are needed to complete and score it. These factors must be considered in addition to the levels of reliability and validity of the instrument as a whole, as well as the reliability and validity of possible subscales. In all cases, sources for each instrument used should be reviewed in order to ensure that the optimal conditions for applying the instrument are present. Manuals or reference literature providing information about administering, scoring, and interpreting specific instruments should be obtained and scrutinized. Self-administration and structured role-play with colleagues will help practitioners gain confidence in the use of an instrument (Mezuk et al. 2010).

Many practitioners are uncertain about how to introduce the use of assessment instruments to family members or individuals in nonthreatening ways. Clients should be given general information about the purpose of the instrument—what will be involved in completing the instrument, how the information will be used, and who will have access to the information obtained. It is recommended that the results be discussed with clients in a candid manner. Practitioners who provide feedback with sensitivity can promote positive client change.

Assessment Methods

The nonunitary nature of child abuse and neglect suggests that they require multimethod, multisource assessment and interventions. There are also no special circumstances surrounding the assessment of child maltreatment (e.g., social desirability in self-report measures and reactivity in observation), which reinforce the need to seek convergent findings across multiple sources. It is recommended that the clinician select from a variety of assessment procedures dictated by the unique features of each individual case—evidence-based practice (EBP), clinical expertise, and client values. There is a correlation among the parents that maltreat their children. Depression and biases toward children lead to a type of abuse. Therefore, two models are documented to help eliminate the behavior. First is the ecological model, which views the family as a system and identifies what subsystem is creating the issue. The next method is the social situational model, which views the larger society, as opposed to the family, as a system (Storer et al. 2012).

The primary concern in any assessment of child abuse and neglect must be the assessment of immediate risk to the child. This is particularly salient in light of the finding from a review of 89 demonstration projects that one-third or more of the participating parents maltreated their children while involved in the treatment (Mannarino et al. 2012). On occasion, the child or children must be removed prior to further assessment and treatment. Currently, several empirically derived risk assessment instruments are available (Stith et al. 2009). However, none of these have a sufficient level of predictive accuracy to allow for the sole dependence in decision-making. In addition, these models have been derived to evaluate reports to child protective services, rather than for use in a clinical setting. They may, however, provide a useful adjunct to clinical judgment.

Having addressed the initial determination of child safety, the objective of parenting assessment should be the determination of "functional parenting competencies," based on what the parent or caregiver understands, believes, knows, does, and has the capacity to do (Rivas et al. 2009). This implies that in addition to the parental assumptions about the child needs and their knowledge of parenting, the current and potential future behavior of the parent becomes central to clinical assessment. Furthermore, Belsky (1993) posits that physical abuse and neglect are determined by factors operating at multiple levels of analysis. Thus, suggesting that the developmental context, the immediate interactional context, and the broader context (community, culture, and evolution) should all be examined.

Structured Clinical Interviews

The model form of clinical assessment is the interview and to the extent that the factors raised by Lu et al. (2011) are addressed—this may be appropriate. Also, the structured clinical interviews provide the basic material needed to achieve an assessment (Feindler et al. 2003). However, as a vehicle for obtaining information in situations of family violence, the interview often suffers from respondent distortion, self-serving, social desirability bias, or poor recall (Lietz et al. 2011). In an effort to guide clinicians in the assessment of abusive families, Lietz et al. (2011) devised the child abuse and neglect interview schedule (CANES). This was originally developed to use with disabled children; however, it is also designed to assess the maltreating behaviors such as corporal punishment, physical abuse, and history of maltreatment, and is utilized with the general population.

Structured interviews may also consist of various combinations of existing instruments. In choosing an empirical measure, the clinician should have a clear understanding of the purpose of the assessment, type of intervention required, interventions available, family's strengths, cultural background, and applicability of measures with diverse populations. The chapter categorizes the measures under headings such as parental assessment, child assessment, family level measures, marital assessment, environmental level measures, and ecological measures. It also provides information on the availability of each instrument and the length of time to administer.

Computerized Assessment Methods

The advent and availability of personal computers has increased the accessibility and flexibility of collecting and analyzing client information. There are many computer programs available for clinical use; however, most do not have available psychometric information. Two measures with extensive psychometric information available are listed below. Both are available in computerized format.

One measure of general individual and family functioning is the multi-problem screening inventory (MPSI) (Pelaez and Sanchez-Cabezudo 2013). The MPSI provides clinicians with a 334-item scale measuring 27 dimensions of family and individual functioning. Subscales addressing physical abuse, nonphysical abuse, depression, self-esteem, partner problems, child problems, family problems, and numerous other issues, are contained in the instrument (Pelaez and Sanchez-Cabezudo 2013).

Additionally, a family assessment screening inventory (FASI) can assess the family situation. The inventory consists of 256 items covering the following categories: housing, physical safety, economic stress, nutrition and diet, family conflict, aggressive behavior, stress, family support, extended family, previous partners, community, employment, school, people outside family, alcohol use, drug use, domestic abuse, child abuse, extrafamilial abuse, self-destructive behavior, child care, parenting, psychological conditions, health conditions, and legal involvement.

A measure more directly focused on children is the Child Well-Being Scales (Serbati et al. 2013). This scale is a multidimensional measure of potential threats to the well-being of children. The scales include both child and family measures. They were originally designed as an outcome measure for child-welfare services, rather than for clinical assessment. However, a computerized form of the scale has been in use as a clinical decision-making tool since the early 1990s (Lyons et al. 2012).

Self-Report Methods

In cases of child abuse and neglect, there is a tendency towards social desirability in self-report measures. This reinforces the need for triangulation in assessment to ensure accuracy and veracity. The Child Abuse Potential Inventory (CAPI) is the most extensively researched instrument of its kind (Walker and Davies 2010). It has a validity index designed to detect biased or random response patterns. This 160-item inventory is intended to differentiate physically abusive parents from parents who are not physically abusive. The scale includes items related to distress, rigidity, child problems, family problems, unhappiness, loneliness, negative self-concept, and negative concept of the child. The CAPI is one of the few instruments available with published validation and cross-validation information. This measure also has cross-validated data available in Spanish translation for the abuse scale (Walker and Davies 2010).

Several other self-report measures are worthy of mention, although they are not as extensively researched as the CAPI. The Parenting Stress Index (PSI) is designed to assess the extent of parenting-related stressors (Pereira et al. 2012). Although used more as a program evaluation tool, it has been used successfully with abusive parents. The Parent Opinion Questionnaire (POQ) is an 80-item instrument that assesses the extent a parent may hold unrealistic expectations about the developmental abilities of their children (Okado and Azar 2011). Significant scoring differences have been found on this instrument with abusive and non-abusive parents. Another instrument is the Rorschach test, which is a questionnaire for children. The Rorschach test is on the rise in recent years, averaging a 6 % increase in usage (Pereira et al. 2012).

The Childhood Trauma Questionnaire (CTQ) short version is a 28-item self-report inventory, which measures the physical, emotional, and sexual abuse, and physical and emotional neglect across the life of a child (Bernstein et al. 2003). The questionnaire uses several Likert scales to enhance reliability and statistical power. It takes about 5 min to complete and can be used in normal and clinical populations (Bernstein et al. 2003).

Observation Methods

Several available observational procedures are designed to assess selected behaviors or qualities of the parent-child interaction. One example of such scales is the 100-item Home Observation Measurement of the Environment (HOME) (Rijlaarsdam et al. 2012). The HOME assesses the quality of stimulation in the child's early environment. Two versions of this instrument are available—one for children from birth to age three, and another for children ages from three to six. This scale consists of some self-report items, though the majority of the items are based on the observation of the parent and child.

This is an observational system designed specifically to evaluate parental control strategies, and was developed by Schaffer and Crooke (McLeod and Weisz 2010). Examination of the parent-child interaction system using this model yields the classic, tripartite, and antecedent child behavior-parent control-consequent child behavior model.

Some caution is merited in the use of observation methods, as they require extensive training for reliable use. In addition, many were developed for research rather than clinical purposes. Yasui and Dishion (2008) report that the coder's ethnicity and the family's ethnicity represent factors that may lead to inconsistent outcomes of observations. Even so, the observation methods often yield invaluable information on parent-child behaviors and interaction systems. Richard and Luprich (2011) noted that the reactive effects might not preclude the validity of such assessments.

In contrast, some research suggests that the demand characteristics do impact observational assessments by depressing the frequency of negative interactions (Messing et al. 2012). Clearly, there is need for caution in the interpretation of observational methods. It has been suggested that this type of observation is most reliably performed in the family, home, or a structured setting, such as a clinic, and that interactions should optimally involve the whole family and take place over multiple sessions.

Rating Scales

The Childhood Level of Living Scale (CLLS) is a 99-item behavior rating scale developed as a measure for scaling the essential elements of child-care and neglect of children under age seven (Bellamy 2008). Subscales include positive child-care, state of home repair, negligence, household maintenance, health care, encouraging competence, consistency of discipline, and coldness. This scale is particularly useful in assessing how chronic and severe care giving deficits are.

The Social Competence and Behavior Evaluation Scale (SCBE-30, short form) is an 80-item Likert rating scale which measures social competence, emotional regulation and expression, and adjustment difficulties in children from three to six years old (LaFraniere and Dumas 1996). There are three factors identified including social competence, anger-aggression, and anxiety-withdrawal. This scale was found to have a high inter-rater reliability, test-retest reliability, internal consistency, and temporal stability. It is used primarily to identify high risk children. Respondents may respond to questions with never, rarely, sometimes, often, frequently, and always (LaFraniere and Dumas 1996).

The Child Exposure to Domestic Violence Scale (CEDVS) is a 42-item scale which measures the level of abuse witnessed by a child, and is of a fourth grade reading level (Edleson et al. 2007). Responses are on a Likert three-point scale—never, sometimes, or a lot. There are three sets of questions that discuss the type of violence witnessed, if the child knew about it before coming home, and basic demographics. Face, content, and convergent validity were established with the things I have heard and seen survey (Edleson et al. 2007).

Physiological Methods

Social desirability bias is less of an issue if physiological measures of arousal are used. Physiological measures of arousal may be taken in response to audio or video material, in vivo exposure to problematic child behavior, infant crying, and so forth (Stith et al. 2009). As an adjunct to complement parent self-report, physiological measures may indicate under-reporting or under-recognition of negative responses.

Family Strengths

The family or individual need for a concentration of many assessment measures means that they are often deficit focused. This can tend to color the perspective of the clinician, as well as further stigmatizing the already demoralized parents. Therefore, it is crucial that clinicians take into account the strengths and potential resources possessed by families. These may include interpersonal skills, supportive family, friends, or neighbors, motivation, or other compensatory characteristics.

"Positive attributes provide a context for understanding the severity and implications of problematic parenting features, and they provide a basis on which future parenting competence can be built" (Storer et al. 2012). Lack of warmth and rewards can also cause severe depression or suicidal tendencies in the future.

Conceptual Framework

Research findings support an ecological approach to child maltreatment with child abuse and neglect addressed as complex problems occurring within a milieu of family dysfunction, environmental stress, and societal values relating to child-rearing (Stith et al. 2009). This recognizes the futility of efforts to identify single causes or solutions to child maltreatment (Fallon et al. 2010). The ecological perspective offers the taxonomy for assessment at various levels: individual, family, and environmental. The procedures reviewed here assess parent and child factors (individual level), family interaction and marital discord (family level), as well as stress and social support (environmental level). In addition, a number of instruments, which assess child abuse and neglect at multiple levels, are discussed under the heading of "Ecological Assessment."

Individual Level

Parent Factors

Attempts to delineate distinguishing traits of abusing and neglecting parents have resulted in markedly inconsistent findings (Tolle and O'Donohue 2012). Most data suggest that only 5 to 10% of abusers can be classified as psychotic or mentally ill (Draine 2013). While it is vital to identify the presence of severe personality disorders in clients, instruments designed for this purpose are difficult to interpret without specialized training. If mental illness is suspected, an evaluation by a mental health professional is indicated.

Numerous studies suggest an association between child maltreatment and parental depression, low self-esteem, and poor interpersonal relationships (Kim and Cicchetti 2009). Assessment of these factors, where indicated, can be useful in targeting specific problem areas, establishing a baseline, and monitoring change.

Early researchers suggested that parents who mistreat their children have unrealistic expectations for their children (Broadhurst et al. 2010). Subsequent research on this issue has generally failed to support this proposal (Stith et al. 2009). Nevertheless, an assessment of a parent's knowledge and expectations of child behavior is useful in identifying clients who could benefit from the instruction in this area.

Parental Assessment Measures

The Adult-Adolescent Parenting Inventory is a 32-item self-report questionnaire measuring parenting strengths and weaknesses in four areas: inappropriate developmental expectations, lack of empathy toward children's needs, belief in the use of corporal punishment, and reversal of parent-child roles. Adult parents, adolescent parents, or prospective parents respond to each item on a five-point scale, which ranges from "strongly agree" to "strongly disagree." (Mezuk et al. 2010).

The Beck Depression Inventory is a 21-item self-report inventory, and it is one of the most-widely used measures of depression in clinical practice. Respondents indicate the severity of their current symptoms on a scale from zero to three (Broten et al. 2011).

The National Comorbidity Survey-Revised (NCS-R) is a two part self-report and interview (Medley and Sachs-Ericsson 2009). The NCS-R diagnoses are based on the Diagnostic and Statistical Manual of Mental Disorders, 4th Edition (DSM-IV) and require information on childhood abuse, assessment of parenthood, parental abuse of children, and family psychiatric history (Medley and Sachs-Ericsson 2009). The interview takes anywhere from 90 min to 6 h to complete, based on the respondent's history. Trained interviewers are needed to facilitate the survey in order to properly interpret nonverbal body language and results (Kessler et al. 2011).

The Generalized Contentment Scale (GCS) is a 25-item self-report inventory that the clients respond to on a scale ranging from one to five. The GCS measures the degree, severity, or magnitude of nonpsychotic depression and focuses largely on affective aspects of depression (Mezuk et al. 2010).

The Implicit Parental Learning Theory Interview is a 45-item, 45 min structured interview. There are 20 items for the Implicit Parental Learning Theory Interview (IPLET's) 5–6. It is designed to inventory the techniques a parent uses to deal with developmentally appropriate behaviors of preschool children. Five separate forms are available for use with parents of children aged from one to 16.

The Index of Self-Esteem is a 25-item self-report inventory rated on a one to five continuum. It measures the degree, severity, or magnitude of a client's problems with self-esteem (Mezuk et al. 2010).

The Index of Parental Attitudes is a 25-item self-report inventory rated on a one to five continuum. It measures the extent, severity, or magnitude of parent-child relationship problems perceived and reported by the parent in reference to a child of any age (Mezuk et al. 2010).

The Index of Peer Relationships is a 25-item self-report inventory rated on a one to five continuum. It measures the degree, severity, and magnitude of a client's problems in relationships with peers. It can be used as a global measure of peer-relationship problems or the practitioner can specify the peer-reference group (i.e., work associates and friends) (Mezuk et al. 2010).

The Maternal Characteristics Scale is a 35-item observational rating scale consisting of descriptive statements with which the caseworker assesses relatedness, impulse-control, confidence, and verbal accessibility. Case workers respond to true, false, mostly true, or mostly false questions (Dubowitz et al. 2011).

The Michigan Screening Profile of Parenting is a 30-item self-report inventory measuring the attitudes regarding child rearing, parental self-awareness, and self-control. Clients respond to each item on a seven-point scale ranging from strongly agree to strongly disagree (Wekerle 2013).

Child Factors

Over the years a substantial body of research focusing on the effects of maltreatment has identified an extremely large range of behaviors and characteristics frequently observed in children who are abused and neglected. However, the inherent difficulties in studying the phenomenon compromise the ability of social workers to make definitive statements regarding the effects of maltreatment. Moreover, a significant number of maltreated children show no signs of overt problems (Miller-Perrin and Portwood 2013). Nevertheless, an assessment of specific factors that have been associated with maltreatment is an important part of systematic analysis and treatment planning. Generally, studies show maltreated children exhibit depression, low self-esteem, low frustration tolerance, withdrawal, anxiety, poor social skills, developmental deficits, and other signs of maltreatment (Hur and Testerman 2012).

Recently, researchers have looked beyond the effects of abuse and neglect to focus on the role of the child in eliciting further maltreatment, particularly physical abuse (Miller-Perrin and Portwood 2013). Studies have identified specific behavioral and temperamental characteristics of the abused children that have been shown to precipitate additional abuse including aggressiveness, irritability, hyperactivity, and negativity (Moss et al. 2011). An assessment of these characteristics can be particularly useful in targeting child behavior modifications.

Child Assessment Measures

The Adolescent Alcohol Involvement Scale is a 14-item self-report inventory categorizing adolescent alcohol use and abuse along a continuum from abstinence to misuse. This instrument demonstrated high test-retest reliability in screening adolescent populations for alcohol misuse (Lipscomb et al. 2012). This scale is available from the Department of Psychiatry and Behavioral Sciences, Northwestern University, Chicago, IL 60611.

The Childhood Experiences of Violence Questionnaire (EVQ) is an 18-item self-report scale of victimization for youth aged from 12 to 18. It takes approximately 15 min to complete. The EVQ measures victimization, sexual abuse, physical abuse, physical punishment, trauma, witnessing domestic abuse, and emotional abuse (Walsh et al. 2008). Respondents answer the items with never, rarely, sometimes, or often. This scale is based on the ecological model.

The Behavior Problem Checklist is a 55-item behavior rating scale. This scale measures the types and degree of behavior problems in children and adolescents. A parent or teacher completes the three-point scale. Four subscales identify conduct problems, personality problems, inadequacy-immaturity, and socialized delinquency (Kimonis and Frick 2011).

The Child Behavior Checklist is a 118-item behavior rating scale, and is one of the most widely used measures of children's behavior problems. There are parallel forms for parents and teachers to complete about children aged from four to 16. There is also a form for children aged from 11 to 18 to self-report on their behaviors. The respondents rate a variety of behaviors on a three-point scale. The checklist measures internalizing syndromes (i.e., depressed and immature) and externalizing syndromes (i.e., aggressive and hyperactivity) (Aarons et al. 2010).

The Child's Attitude Toward Father and Mother scales are separate 25-item self-report inventories rated on one to five continuums. They measure the extent, degree, or severity of problems a child aged 12 or older has with his or her father or mother (Mezuk et al. 2010).

The Developmental Profile II is a 186-item behavior rating scale that measures the functioning of children from birth to age nine in five areas. The five areas are physical, self-help, social, academic, and communication. The age-graded items are rated pass or fail. The instrument can be completed in 20 to 40 min by a service provider employing knowledge of the child's skills, observations, and parent interviews. This scale is available from the Psychological Development Publications, P.O. Box 3798, Aspen, CO 81611.

The Rosenberg Self-Esteem Scale is a 10-item self-report inventory that measures the self-esteem of high school students. The respondents rate each item on a four-point scale (Marsh et al. 2010).

The Self-Perception Profile for Children is a 28-item self-rating inventory assessing a child's perception of his or her cognitive, social, and physical competence. The scale is for use with children in the third through ninth grades. For each item, the child is asked to first identify which two descriptions best describe him or her, then rate whether the description is sort of true or really true (Lou et al. 2013).

The Problem-Oriented Screening Instrument for Teenagers [POSIT] is a 139-item self-report rating instrument that assesses substance abuse problems, physical health status, mental health status, family relationships, peer relationships, educational status, vocational status, social skills, leisure/recreation, and aggressive behavior/delinquency. This instrument is intended for use as a screening tool to identify problems in need of further assessment (French et al. 2013).

The Sexual Abuse Exposure Questionnaire (SAEQ) can be used to retroactively measure the extent of exposure to sexual abuse in children (Keyes et al. 2011). The SAEQ is a self-report questionnaire that consists of 10 items, each of which describes a specific sexual abuse event or experience. Clients respond to each item positively or negatively to indicate whether or not they have experienced the described event. Higher scores indicate higher exposure to childhood sexual abuse. This questionnaire has been found to have high reliability and validity (Keyes et al. 2011).

The Assessing Environments-III Inventory includes the Physical Punishment Scale (AE-III-PP), which can be used to measure childhood experiences of physical abuse and corporal punishment (Berger et al. 1988; Feindler et al. 2003). This inventory consists of 12 items, each of which describes a type of physical punishment with a wide range in severity. Clients respond to each with "true" or "false," and higher scores indicate greater exposure to physical punishment during childhood. The AE-III-PP has demonstrated high reliability and validity (Berger et al. 1988; Feindler et al. 2003).

The Posttraumatic Diagnostic Scale (PDS) can be used to assess a client's childhood history of trauma (Powers et al. 2010). This 49-item scale assesses client experience of trauma based on the DSM-IV criteria for posttraumatic stress disorder. Each item represents a trauma symptom, and clients respond to each item on a scale from 0 to 3, with higher scores representing higher frequency of trauma symptoms. Higher overall scores indicate higher likelihood of posttraumatic stress disorder (Powers et al. 2010).

The Sexual and Physical Abuse Questionnaire (SPAQ) can be used to measure the extent of experiences of sexual and physical abuse across the life span. For this reason, it can be used to measure experiences of sexual and physical abuse of clients as adults, adolescents, or children (Irish et al. 2010).

The Child Abuse and Trauma Scale (CATS) can be used to measure the extent of childhood abuse and maltreatment (Pereira et al. 2012). The CATS consists of an overall score of trauma, as well as three subscales: childhood sexual abuse, childhood neglect, and childhood punishment. There are 38 items, each of which represents a specific abusive or neglectful behavior experienced within the home. Clients are asked to indicate how often each behavior occurs on a range from 0 (never) to 4 (always). This scale has high reliability and validity (Pereira et al. 2012).

The Activities of Daily Living (ADL) checklist for neglect can be used to determine the extent to which the children are being neglected within the home (Kutlay et al. 2009). This measurement tool is completed by a professional who visits the home and observes the activities of daily living. The checklist, which includes activities such as eating, sleeping, grooming, dressing, reading, and writing, is completed based on observations within the home (Kutlay et al. 2009).

Family Level

Family Interaction

Child maltreatment is often embedded in general dysfunction. In assessing parent and child factors individually, the practitioner may overlook significant family processes. The instruments discussed in this section focus on the assessment of family structure, dynamics, and interaction patterns. Parent and child self-report inventories and behavior-rating scales can provide information on such factors as degree of attachment, perception of problems, level of conflict, and communication styles within the family (Mezuk et al. 2010).

Researchers have consistently found that abusive and neglectful families display distorted patterns of parent-child interaction marked by lower rates of interaction and an emphasis on negative aspects of the relationship (Milot et al. 2010). Several observational procedures are reviewed here which can provide specific descriptions of dysfunctional processes, such as ineffectual use of punishment. These processes can then be altered using established techniques of parent-behavior training.

Family Assessment Measures

The Conflict Tactics Scale is a 19-item self-report inventory that is widely used to assess conflict among family members. A parent or child responds on a six-point scale, from never to more than 20 times, to indicate the number of times in the past year specific techniques were used during the conflict (Swenson et al. 2010).

The dyadic parent-child interaction coding system is an observational procedure that assesses the interaction of parents and young conduct problem children. A parent and child are observed during 3–15 min segments as they interact in a clinical playroom (Stith et al. 2009).

The Family Adaptability and Cohesion Scale III is a 40-item self-report inventory that assesses family cohesion, adaptability, and communication. Adults and children aged 12 and older respond on a five-point scale to each item. The first half of the scale assesses how family members see their family (perceived), and the second half assesses how they would like it to be (ideal).

The Family Assessment Form is an observational procedure including 102 items. This instrument assesses the family's physical, social, and economic environment, psychosocial history of caregivers, personal characteristics of caregivers, child-rearing skills, caregiver to child interactions, developmental status of children, and overall psychosocial functioning of the family from an ecological perspective. Family functioning is rated on a five-point Likert scale linked to child abuse and neglect (Mezuk et al. 2010).

The Index of Family Relations is a 25-item self-report inventory rated on a one to five continuum. It measures the extent, severity, or magnitude of problems that family members have in their relationship with one another. It is considered a global measure of family problems (Mezuk et al. 2010).

The Inventory of Family Feelings is a 38-item self-report inventory assessing the overall degree of attachment between each pair of family members. Family members with at least a sixth grade education respond on a three-point scale to each item (MacKenzie et al. 2011).

The Parent Adolescent Communications Inventory is a 40-item inventory that assesses the patterns and characteristics of communication between parents and adolescents. Adolescents aged 13 years and older respond to each item using a three-point scale (Williams and Bolton 2010).

The Parent Child Behavioral Coding System is an observational procedure that assesses patterns of parent-child interaction. An observer codes parent and child behaviors in a 10-min structured exercise in a clinic and/or in a 40-min unstructured home visit (Petra and Kohl 2010). (Helping the noncompliant child: A clinician's guide to parental training, New York, Guilford Press).

The Standardized Observation System III is an observational procedure that assesses interaction between a child and other members of a family. The observer codes the interaction sequence in a 1-h unstructured home visit (Waller and Bitou 2011).

The McMaster Structured Interview of Family Functioning (CRS) focuses on whether families accomplish basic tasks of daily life in six domains: problem solving, communication, roles, affective responsiveness, affective involvement, behavior control, and overall family functioning. It uses parental self-report, clinical judgment from a 2-h interview, and observation of all members of the family. The CRS has a good inter-rater reliability (Barakat and Alderfer 2011).

Marital Discord

Not surprisingly, marital discord has been found to characterize maltreating families (Broadhurst et al. 2010). Conflict in the marital relationship often precedes abusive acts against children as stress spills over from the parental dyad into the parent-child relationships (Wekerle 2013). Children and youth reflect on what is taught in a household, and frequently coping mechanisms in children rely on substances. Several self-report instruments are reviewed here that are useful primarily in determining whether the marital relationship should be targeted for intervention and providing feedback on the effectiveness of interventions.

Marital Assessment Measures

The Dyadic Adjustment Scale is a 32-item self-report inventory that uses three different types of rating responses that measure satisfaction in an intimate relationship (Sherman and Fredman 2013).

The Couples Emotion Rating Form assesses three types of negative emotions during conflict: hard, flat, and soft (Sanford 2007). This is a self-report form where the response format is on a five-point scale of disagree strongly, disagree, agree somewhat, or agree strongly. The Couples Emotion Rating Form's main strength is that it assesses emotion to a specific interpersonal conflict (Sanford 2007).

The Index of Marital Satisfaction is a 25-item self-report inventory that uses three different types of rating responses (Riesch et al. 2010). It measures the degree, severity, or magnitude of problems one spouse or partner has in the marital relationship.

The Index of Spouse Abuse is a 30-item self-report scale rated on a one to five continuum. It measures the severity or magnitude of physical or nonphysical abuse inflicted on a woman by her spouse or partner. Clinical cutting scores are suggested for both physical and nonphysical abuse subscale scores (Riesch et al. 2010).

The Revised Conflict Tactics Scale includes the Physical Assault Scale, which can be used to measure the extent of adult exposure to physical assault by a romantic partner (Swenson et al. 2010). The scale consists of 12 items, each representing a specific physically abusive behavior. Clients respond to each item on a scale from 0 (never) to 6 (more than 20 times) based on how many times they have experienced that abusive behavior in the past year. This scale has been found to have high validity and reliability (Swenson et al. 2010).

The Marital Satisfaction Inventory is a 280-item self-report inventory that assesses individual's attitudes and beliefs regarding 11 specific areas of marital relationship adjustment. It requires approximately 30 min for individual spouses to respond true-false on each item. It also includes subscales on dissatisfaction with children and conflict over child-rearing (Reyome 2010).

Environmental Level

Stress

Increasingly, research is taking into consideration the inter-relationship among individuals, family, and situational factors in examining child maltreatment. Life stresses, such as personal crisis, divorce, the death or illness of a family member, and unemployment, tend to increase the likelihood of child abuse and neglect (Allwood and Widom 2013). While not all parents react to stress by maltreating their children, an assessment of life stresses is a useful part of an evaluation of abusive and neglectful families. High levels of stress have been found to precede maltreatment in a family, and practitioners can offer training in techniques of stress reduction to prevent further dysfunction. Being less stressed causes alpha to appear, and it can assist in making conscious choices along with proper expectations (Ben-Arieh 2010).

Stress Assessment Measures

The Family Inventory of Life Events and Changes is a 71-item self-report instrument which records normative and non-normative stressors a family unit may experience within a year (Lietz and Strength 2011). Adult family members (together or separately) respond yes or no to each item. Norms are provided for families at various stages in the family life cycle.

The PSI is a 101-item self-report inventory that assesses a mother's perception of stress associated with child and parent characteristics (Pereira et al. 2012). Additional 19 optional items assess life stress events. Mothers can complete the index in approximately 20 to 30 min.

The Social Phobia and Anxiety Inventory for Children (SPAI-C) is a 26-item self-report instrument and a daily diary which records anxiety events and feelings (Pina et al. 2013). Each item is rated on a scale. Possible answers are never, hardly ever, sometimes, most of the time, or always. The SPAI-C was measured to have high internal consistency (Pina et al. 2013).

Social Support

Social isolation of families is one of the most powerful factors distinguishing families who maltreat from those who do not (Garbarino 2013). Informal support systems appear to moderate the effects of stress on families by offering material and emotional assistance and by providing parenting role models. Formal support systems, such as groups to reduce stress can also be a significant approach to not maltreating a child. Although some programs seem to help the males more than the females, a social network consisting of a group with similar problems can be beneficial (Friend et al. 2009). As assessment of the availability and utilization of social support by maltreating families is a vital part of evaluation and treatment planning.

Social Support Measures

The Inventory of Socially Supportive Behaviors is a 40-item self-report inventory assessing the frequency with which individuals have received various forms of aid and assistance from people around them (Gottlieb and Bergen 2010). Respondents answer each item using a five-point scale ranging from not at all to every day.

The Social Support Behaviors Scale is a 45-item self-report inventory that measures five models of support: emotional, socializing, practical assistance, financial assistance, and advice/guidance (Tanigawa et al. 2011). Respondents respond on a five-point scale (from no one would do this to most family members/friends would certainly do this, to the likelihood that family/friends would help in specific ways).

Ecological Assessment

A number of instruments are designed to assess maltreating families at multiple levels (individual, family, and environment). While such instruments are particularly useful for practitioners, they should always be regarded as supplemental to the client interview and case record. In a recent study, the ecological framework was used to determine the effect of child abuse. It concludes that as a society, parents with poor skills have a tendency to raise the percentage of abuse. This in turn inhibits the child from being a productive member of society (Daniel et al. 2010).

Ecological Assessment Instruments

The Child Abuse Potential Survey is a 160-item self-report inventory, completed by the parent (Walker and Davies 2010). It is designed as a screening device to differentiate physical abusers from non-abusers. Factors measured include distress, rigidity, child with problems, problems from family and others, unhappiness, loneliness, and negative concepts of child and self. Respondents are asked to agree or disagree with each item. The inventory has a reliability level of grade three and includes a lie scale to identify individuals who tend to give socially desirable answers.

The Childhood Level of Living Scale is a 99-item behavior rating scale assessing neglect of children aged seven and under (Bellamy 2008). There are nine subscales, including general positive child care, state of repair of home, negligence, quality of household maintenance, quality of health care and grooming, encouraging competence, inconsistency of discipline and coldness, encouraging superego development, and material giving. It requires approximately 15 min for a service provider who knows the family well to answer all items either yes or no.

The Child Well-Being Scale is a 43-item behavior rating scale that is a multidimensional measure of child maltreatment situations. It is specifically designed for use as an outcome measure of child maltreatment situations. It is designed for use as an outcome measure in child protective services programs rather than for individual case outcomes (Serbati et al. 2013). Most of the scales focus on actual or potential unmet needs of children. Current testing of the subscales indicates that three factors (household adequacy [10 scales], parental disposition [14 scales], and child performance [four scales]) accounted for 43 % variance and that the Child Well-Being Scale can discriminate between neglectful and non-neglectful families (Dubowitz et al. 2011). It requires approximately 25 min for a service provider to complete the scale based on direct contact with the family, including in-home visits. Each dimension is rated on a three-point or six-point continuum of adequacy/inadequacy. This scale is available from the Publication Department, Child Welfare League of America, 440 First St NW, Suite 310, Washington, DC, 20001.

The Family Risk Scale is a 26-item behavior rating scale that is designed to identify a full range of situations predictive of near-term child placement so that the preventive services can be offered and change monitored (Serbati et al. 2013). The scale is similar in design, administration, and scoring to the Child Well-Being Scale. Dimensions are limited to the areas that are potentially malleable.

The Parenting Scale is a 30-item rating scale designed to measure dysfunctional discipline style (Morawska et al. 2011). The Parenting Scale measures three types of dysfunctional parenting styles: laxness, over-activity, and verbosity. The parenting scale score correlates with observational measures of dysfunctional discipline and child misbehavior. It has accurate reliability and internal consistency (Morawska et al. 2011). It takes only about 5 to 10 min to complete and to identify the high risk parents.

The Home Observation for Measurement of the Environment Inventory is a 100-item observation/interview procedure that assesses the quality of stimulation of a child's early environment (Rijlaarsdam et al. 2012). There are two versions for children aged from birth to 3 and from 3 to 6 years old. Approximately one-third of the items are answered through a parent interview. The remainder is based on the observation of the child and the primary caretaker in the home. It requires approximately 1 h to answer all of the questions yes or no.

The Brigid Collins Risk Screener (BCRS) is a screener for prenatal child abuse, which derives information from medical records and a brief self-report instrument (Weberling et al. 2003). The BCRS covers the following areas: environmental stressors, mother's personal history of abuse, previous child abuse, Children's Protective Services (CPS) involvement, and mother's current partner. The cumulative risk factors are considered with protective factors. Individuals are rated on a 0 (no risk) to 4 (one or more risks identified) scale (Weberling et al. 2003).

Additional Resources

Department of Health and Human Services Structured Decision Making http://www.childwelfare.gov/systemwide/assessment/approaches/decision.cfm

Assessing Promising Approaches in Child Welfare: Strategies for State Legislators http://www.ncsl.org/documents/cyf/promising_approaches_childwelfare.pdf

Department of Health and Human Services Child Neglect: A Guide for Prevention, Assessment & Intervention http://www.childwelfare.gov/pubs/usermanuals/neglect/chaptersix.cfm

Annie E Casey Foundation The Child Welfare Strategy Group http://www.aecf.org/work/child-welfare/child-welfare-strategy-group/

References

Aarons, G. A., James, S., Monn, A. R., Raghavan, R., Wells, R. S., & Leslie, L. K. (2010). Behavior problems and placement changes in a national child welfare sample: A prospective study. *Child and Adolescent Psychiatry, 49*(1), 70–80.

Allwood, M. A., & Widom, C. S. (2013). Child abuse and neglect, developmental role attainment and adult arrests. *Journal of Research in Crime and Deliquency, 50*(4), 7–24.

Barakat, L. P., & Alderfer, M. A. (2011). Introduction to special issue: Advancing the science of family assessment in pediatric psychology. *Journal of Pediatric Psychology, 36*(5), 489–493.

Bellamy, J. L. (2008). A national study of male involvement among families in contact with the child welfare system. *Child Maltreatment, 14*(3), 255–262.

Belsky, J (1993). Etiology of child maltreatment: A developmental-ecological analysis. *Psychological Bulletin, 114*(3), 413–434.

Ben-Arieh, A. (2010). From child welfare to children well-being: The child indicators perspective. *From Child Welfare to Child Well-Being Children's Well-Being: Indicators and Research, 1*, 9–22.

Berger, A. M., Knutson, J. F., Mehm, J. G., & Perkins, K. A. (1988). The self-report of punitive childhood experiences of young adults and adolescents. *Child Abuse and Neglect, 12*, 251–262.

Bernstein, D. P., Stein, J. A., Newcomb, M. D., Walker, E., Pogge, D., Ahluvalia, T., Stoke, J., Handelsman, L., Medrano, M., Desmond, D., & Zule, W. (2003). Development and validation

of a brief screening version of the childhood trauma questionnaire. *Child Abuse and Neglect, 27*(2), 169–190.
Broadhurst, K., Hall, C., Wastell, D., White, S., & Pithouse, A. (2010). Risk, instrumentalism and the Humane Project in Social Work: Identifying the *informal* logics of risk management in children's statutory services. *British Journal of Social Work, 40*(4), 1046–1064.
Broten, L. A., Naugle, A. E., Kalata, A. H., & Gaynor, S. T. (2011). Depression and a stepped care model. *Stepped Care and e-health,* 17–43.
Cohen, J. S., Edmunds, J. M., Brodman, D. M., Benjamin, C. L., & Kendall, P. C. (2012). Using self-monitoring: Implementation of collaborative empiricism in cognitive-behavioral therapy. *Cognitive and Behavioral Practice, 19,* 37–57.
Corcoran, J., & Pillai, V. (2009). A review of the research on solution-focused therapy. *British Journal of Social Work, 39*(2), 234–242.
Daniel, B., Taylor, J., & Scott, J. (2010). Recognition of neglect and early response: Overview of systematic review of the literature. *Child and Family Social Work, 15*(2), 248–257.
Draine, J. (2013). Mental health, mental illnesses, poverty, justice, and social justice. *American Journal of Psychiatric Rehabilitation, 16*(2), 87–90.
Dubowitz, H., Kim, J., Black, M. M., Weisbart, C., Semiatin, J., & Magder, L. S. (2011). Identifying children at high risk for child maltreatment report. *Child Abuse and Neglect, 35*(2), 96–104.
Edleson, J. L., Shin, N., & Armendariz, K. K. (2007). Measuring children's exposure to domestic violence: The development and testing of the child exposure to domestic violence scale (CEDV). *Children and Youth Services Review, 31*(2), 249–256.
Fallon, B., Trocme, N., Fluke, J., MacLaurin, B., Tonmyr, L., & Yuan, Y. (2010). Methodological challenges in measuring child maltreatment. *Child Abuse and Neglect, 34*(1), 70–79.
Feindler, E. L., Rathus, J. H., & Silver, L. B. (2003). *Assessment of family violence: A handbook for researchers and practitioners*. Washington, DC: American Psychological Association.
French, L. A., Kovacevic, G., & Nikolic-Novakovic, L. (2013). Assessing the aftermath of war among teens in Bosnia & Serbia: measures of substance abuse and delinquency with the POSIT (Problem-Oriented Screening Instrument for Teens). *Alcoholism Treatment Quarterly, 31*(1), 95–106.
Friend, A. C., Summers, J. A., & Turnbull, A. P. (2009). Impacts of family support in early childhood intervention research. *Education and Training in Developmental Disabilities, 44*(4), 453–470.
Garbarino, J. (2013). The emotionally battered child. *Child Maltreatment, 1,* 57–61.
Gottlieb, B. H., & Bergen, A. E. (2010). Social support concepts and measures. *Journal of Psychosomatic Research, 69*(5), 511–520.
Hur, Y., & Testerman, R. (2012). An index of child well-being at a local level in the U.S.: The case of North Carolina Counties. *Child Indicators Research, 5*(1), 29–53.
Irish, L., Kobayashi, I., & Delahanty, D. L. (2010). Long-term physical health consequences of childhood sexual abuse: A meta-analysis review. *Journal of Pediatric Psychology, 35*(5), 450–461.
Kessler, R. C., Berglund, P., Chiu, W. T., Demler, O., Heeringa, S., Jin, R., Pennell, B. E., Keyes, K. M., Eaton, N. R., & Krueger, R. F. (2011). Childhood maltreatment and the structure of common psychiatric disorders. *British Journal of Psychology*. doi:10.1192/bjp.bp.111.093062.
Keyes, K., Eaton, N. & Krueger, R. (2011). Childhood maltreatment and the structure of common psychiatric disorders. *British Journal of Psychology,* doi:I 0.1 I 92/bjp.bp. I I 1.093062.
Kim, J., & Cicchetti, D. (2009). Longitudinal pathways linking child maltreatment, emotional regulation, peer relations, and psychopathology. *Journal of Child Psychology and Psychiatry, 51*(6), 706–716.
Kimonis, E. R. & Frick, P. J. (2011). Clinical Handbook of Assessing and Treating Conduct Problems in Youth. *Etiology of oppositional defiant disorder and conduct disorder: Biological, familial and environmental factors identified in the development of disruptive behavior disorders* (pp. 49–76). New York: Springer.

Kutlay, S., Kucukdeveci, A. A., Elhan, A. A., & Tennant, A. (2009). Validation of the behavioral inattention test (BIT) in patients with acquired brain injury in Turkey. *Neuropsychological Rehabilitation: An International Journal, 19*(3), 461–475.

LaFreniere, P. J. & Dumas, J. E. (1996). Social Competence and Behavior Evaluation in Children Aged Three to Six: The Short Form (SCBE-30). *Psychological Assessment, 8*(4), 369–377.

Lietz, C. A., & Strength, M. (2011). Stories of successful reunification: A narrative study of family resilience in child welfare. *The Journal of Contemporary Social Services, 92*(2), 203–210.

Lietz, C. A., Lacasse, J. R., & Cacciatore, J. (2011). Social support in family reunification: A qualitative study. *Journal of Family Social Work, 14*(1), 3–20.

Lipscomb, S. T., Lewis, K. M., Masyn, K. E., & Meloy, M. E. (2012). Child care assistance for families involved in the child welfare system: Predicting child care subsidy use and stability. *Children and Youth Services Review, 34*(12), 2454–2463.

Lou, C., Anthony, E. K., Stone, S., Vu, C. M., & Austin, M. J. (2013). *Evidence for Child Welfare Practice*. New York: Routledge.

Lu, Y. E., Ain, E., Chamorro, C., Chang, C., Feng, J. Y., Fong, R., Garcia, B., Hawkins, R. L., & Yu, M. (2011). A new methodology for assessing Social Work Practice: The adaptation for the objective structure clinical evaluation. *Social Work Education: The International Journal, 30*(2), 170–185.

Lyons, K. H., Iokenstad, T., Pawar, M., Iuegler, N., & Hall, N. (2012). *The SAGE handbook of international social work*. London: Sage.

MacKenzie, M. J., Kotch, J. B., & Lee, L. (2011). Toward a cumulative ecological risk model for the etiology of child maltreatment. *Children and Youth Services Review, 33*(9), 1638–1647.

Mannarino, A. P., Cohen, J. A., Deblinger, E., Ruyon, M. K., & Steer, R. A. (2012). Trauma-focused cognitive-behavioral therapy for children. *Child Maltreatment, 17*(3), 231–241.

Marsh, H. W., Scalas, L. F., & Nagengast, B. (2010). Longitudinal tests of competing factor structures for the Rosenberg Self-Esteem Scale: Traits, ephemeral artifacts, and stable response styles. *Psychological Assessment, 22*(2), 366–381.

McLeod, B. D., & Weisz, J. R. (2010). The therapy process observational coding system for child psychotherapy strategies scale. *Journal of Clinical Child and Adolescent Psychology, 39*(3), 436–443.

Medley, A., & Ericsson-Sachs, N. (2009). Predictors of parental physical abuse: The contribution of internalizing and externalizing disorders and childhood experiences of abuse. *Journal of Affective Disorders, 113,* 244–254.

Messing, J. T., Flair, L. L., Cavanaugh, C. E., Kanga, M. R., & Campbell, J. C. (2012). Testing posttraumatic stress as a mediator of childhood trauma and adult intimate partner violence victimization. *Journal of Aggression, Maltreatment and Trauma, 21*(7), 792–811.

Mezuk, B., Rafferty, J. A., Kershaw, K. N., Hudson, D., Abdou, C. M., Lee, H., Eaton, W. W., & Jackson, J. S. (2010). Reconsidering the role of social disadvantage in physical and mental health: Stressful life events, health behaviors, race, and depression. *American Journal of Epidemiology, 172*(11), 1238–1249.

Miller-Perrin, C. L., & Portwood, S. G. (2013). Child and family advocacy: Bridging the gaps between research practice and policy. *Child Maltreatment Prevention* (pp. 51–71). New York: Springer.

Mills, R., Scott, J., Alati, R., O'Callaghan, M., Najman, K. M., & Strathearn, L. (2013). Child maltreatment and adolescent mental health problems in a large birth cohort. *Child Abuse and Neglect, 37*(5), 292–302.

Milot, T., St. Laurent, D., Ethier, L., & Provost, M. A. (2010). *Child Maltreatment, 15*(4), 293–304.

Morawska, A., Sanders, M., Goadby, E., Headley, C., Hodge, L., McAuliffe, C., Pope, S., & Anderson, E. (2011). Is the Triple P-Positive Parenting Program acceptable to parents from culturally diverse backgrounds? *Journal of Child and Family Studies, 20*(5), 614–622.

Moss, E., Dubois-Comtois, K., Cyr, C., Tarabulsy, G. M., St-Laurent, D., & Bernier, A. (2011). Efficacy of a home-visiting intervention aimed at improving maternal sensitivity, child attachment, and behavioral outcomes for maltreated children: A randomized control trial. *Developmental and Psychopathology, 23*(1), 195–210.

Okado, Y., & Azar, S. T. (2011). The impact of extreme emotional distance in the mother-child relationship on the offspring's future risk of maltreatment perpetration. *Journal of Family Violence, 26*(6), 439–452.
Park, J. M., & Ryan, J. P. (2008). Placement and permanency outcomes for children in out-of-home care by prior inpatient mental health treatment. *Research on Social Work Practice, 19*(1), 42–51.
Pelaez, A. L., & Sanchez-Cabezudo, S. S. (2013). Empowerment, well-being and the welfare state: Family social work in spain. *Family Well-Being Social Indicators Research Services, 49*, 277–301.
Pereira, J., Vickers, K., Atikinson, L., Gonzalez, A., Wekerele, C., & Levitan, R. (2012). Parenting stress mediates between maternal maltreatment history and maternal sensitivity in a community sample. *Child Abuse and Neglect, 36*(5), 433–437.
Petra, M., & Kohl, P. (2010). Pathways Triple P and the child welfare system: a promising fit. *Children and Youth Services Review, 32*(4), 611–618.
Pina, A. A., Little, M., Wynne, H., & Beidel, D. C. (2013). Assessing social anxiety in African American youth using the social phobia and anxiety inventory for children. *Journal of Abnormal Child Psychology, 42*(2), 311–320.
Powers, M. B., Halpern, J. M., Ferenschak, M. P., Gillihan, S. J., & Foa, E. B. (2010). A meta-analytic review of prolonged exposure for posttraumatic stress disorder. *Clinical Psychology Review, 30*(6), 635–641.
Reyome, N. D. (2010). Childhood emotional maltreatment and later intimate relationships: Themes from the empirical literature. *Journal of Aggression, Maltreatment and Trauma, 19*(2), 224–242.
Richard, D. C. S., & Iuprich, S. K. (2011). *Clinical Psychology: Assessment, treatment, and research*. Burlington: Elsevier.
Riesch, S. K., Anderson, L. S., Pridham, K. A., Lutz, K. F., & Becker, P. T. (2010). Furthering the understanding of parent-child relationships: A nursing scholarship review series. Part 5: Parent-adolescent and teen parent-child relationships. *Journal of Specialists in Pediatric Nursing, 15*(3), 182–201.
Rijlaarsdam, J., Stevens, G. W., van der Ende, J., Arends, L. R., Hofman, A., Jaddoe, V. W. V., Mackenbach, J. P., Verhulst, F. C., & Tiemeier, H. (2012). A brief observational instrument for the assessment of infant home environment: Development and psychometric testing. *International Journal of Methods in Psychiatric Research, 21*(3), 195–204.
Rivas, E. M., Handler, L., & Sims, C. R. (2009). Adult attachment measures and their potential utility in custody cases. *Journal of Child Custody, 6*(1–2), 25–37.
Sanford, K. (2007). The couple's emotion rating form: Psychometric properties and theoretical associations. *Psychological Assessment, 19*(4), 411–421.
Serbati, S., Pivetti, M., & Gioga, G. (2013). Child well-being scales (CWBS) in the assessment of families and children in home-care intervention: An empirical study. *Child and Family Social Work*. doi:10.1111/cfs.12094.
Sherman, R., & Freman, N. (2013). *Handbook of measurements for marriage and family therapy*. Philadelphia: Brunner.
Stith, S. M., Liu, T., Davies, L. C., Boykin, E. L., Alder, M. C., Harris, J. M., Som, A., McPherson, M., & Dees, J. E. (2009). Risk factors in child maltreatment: A meta-analytic review of the literature. *Aggression and Violent Behaviors, 14*(1), 13–29.
Storer, H. L., Barkan, S. E., Sherman, E. L., Haggerty, K. P., & Mattos, L. M. (2012). Promoting relationship building and connection: Adapting an evidence-based parenting program for families involved in the child welfare system. *Children and Youth Services Review, 34*(9), 1853–1861.
Swenson, C. C., Schaeffer, C. M., Henggeler, S. W., Faldowski, R., & Mayhew, A. M. (2010). Multi-systemic therapy for child abuse and neglect: A randomized effectiveness trial. *Journal of Family Psychology, 24*(4), 497–507.

Tanigawa, D., Furlong, M. J., Felix, E. D., & Sharkey, J. D. (2011). The protective role of perceived social support against the manifestation of depressive symptoms in peer victims. *Journal of School Violence, 10*(4), 393–412.
Tolle, L. W. & O'Donohue, W. T. (2012). *Improving the Quality of Child Custody Evaluations: A Systematic Model*. New York: Springer.
Trickett, P. K., Negriff, S., Ji, J., & Peckins, M. (2011). Child maltreatment and adolescent development. *Journal of Research on Adolescence, 21*(1), 3–20.
Walker, C. A., & Davies, J. (2010). A critical review of the psychometric evidence base of child abuse potential inventory. *Journal of Family Violence, 25*(2), 215–227.
Waller, T., & Bitou, A. (2011). Research with children: Three challenges for participatory research in early childhood. *European Early Childhood Education Research Journal, 19*(1), 5–20.
Walsh, C. A., MacMillan, H. L., Trocme, N., Jamieson, E., & Boyle, M. H. (2008). Measures of victimization in adolescence: Development and validation of the childhood experiences of violence questionnaire. *Child Abuse and Neglect, 32,* 1037–1057.
Walters, E. E., Zaslavsky, A., & Zheng, H. (2004). The U.S. national comorbidity survey replication (NCS-R): Design and field procedures. *International Journal of Methods in Psychiatric Research, 13*(2), 69–92.
Weberling, L. C., Forgays, D. K., Crain-Thoreson, C., & Hyman, I. (2003). Prenatal child abuse risk assessment: A preliminary study. *Child Welfare League of America, 32,* 319–334.
Wekerle, C. (2013). Resilience in the context of child maltreatment: Connections to the practice of mandatory reporting. *Child Abuse and Neglect, 37*(2–3), 93–101.
Wells, M., & Correia, M. (2010). Reentry into out-of-home care: Implications of child welfare workers' assessments of risk and safety. *Social Work Research, 36*(3), 181–195.
Williams, A., & Bolton, J. (2010). Family issues. *Handbook of Clinical Psychology Competencies, 1,* 1655–1684.
Yasui, M., & Dishion, T. J. (2008). Direct observation of family management: Validity and reliability as a function of coder ethnicity and training. *Behavior Therapy, 39,* 336–347.

Chapter 8
Substance Use and Abuse: Screening Tools and Assessment Instruments

Marvin D. Feit, Cyomara Fisher, Joanna Cummings and Ashley Peery

Introduction

The present welfare system is under attack by both conservatives and liberals alike for its promotion of dependency as demonstrated by its ineffectiveness in moving recipients from welfare to work. In light of the new welfare reforms, it is now essential that welfare workers move individuals from welfare to work in an expedient fashion. Client's alcohol and/or drug use/abuse is one barrier that may inhibit this progress for some individuals. Fortunately, assessment technologies are now accessible for welfare workers to utilize in assisting them in detecting substance use/abuse in their case loads.

In recent years, accountability has become a primary issue in the social services field. Accurate assessments of clients' strengths and difficulties are essential for effective case management, treatment, and accountability. Technology is now available to assist workers in assessing clients and in referring those clients for effective interventions. Screening instruments in particular, equip the worker with the fundamental tools necessary for an accurate assessment. Inaccurate assessment, or lack of assessment, regardless of what powerful techniques the change agent possesses, results in ineffective, irrelevant, or duplicated interventions.

Currently, many social workers utilize clinical interviews, personal judgment, and assumptions to make decisions about alcohol-related problems, treatment needs, and placement. The danger in this is clear.

The use of rapid assessment instruments would reduce this subjectivity and danger by providing the worker with an efficient and cost-effective manner to screen for alcohol use by their clients. By utilizing assessment instruments, the worker increases his/her chance of making an accurate evaluation of the client's alcohol use/

M. D. Feit (✉)
Norfolk State University, Norfolk, VA, USA
e-mail: mdfeit@nsu.edu

C. Fisher · J. Cummings · A. Peery
The University of Tennessee, Knoxville, TN, USA

J. S. Wodarski et al. (eds.), *Evidence-Informed Assessment and Practice in Child Welfare,* DOI 10.1007/978-3-319-12045-4_8

abuse. This process is more efficient and effective than personal judgment. With an appropriate, accurate assessment, the client can be referred for further substance-use assessment and if indicated, subsequently receive needed treatment, thus better preparing them for successful employment.

Social workers have begun to identify the aptitude of rapid assessment instruments to collect large quantities and better quality data. Studies have consistently found that these instruments are easily administered, cost-effective, and can provide reliable client data. In addition, rapid assessment instruments are more objective than a personal interview, in that the personal biases of the worker are reduced and the subjective mature of assessment as a whole is decreased. Rapid assessment instruments, unlike other more complex instruments, provide quick screening information that do not involve intense training or advanced diagnostic skills. In addition to serving the clinician by more accurately identifying treatment needs and goals, rapid assessment instruments benefit the client as well. Reinert and Allen (2007) describe how assessment procedures improve client motivation and goal identification, retention rates of clients in treatment programs, and the value the client holds of a formal assessment procedure. These instruments have also been noted to obtain more information from clients in a shorter period of life. Consequently, rapid assessment instruments are more efficient as well as more accurate than a subjective, personal interview (Kahler et al. 2003).

Screening and Assessment Basics

For any practitioner unfamiliar with the use of scales, questionnaires, and evaluation tools used in the study and treatment of alcohol and other drugs (AOD) problems, a general overview of the basics is very helpful. Screening is the process of identifying persons who show signs of risk factors for alcohol and substance abuse. A structured face-to-face interview between medical practitioner and client is the most common screening technique. If utilizing a paper and pencil or computer-based screening method, the social worker must consider age appropriateness, education levels, and gender, as well as the client's socioeconomic status and culture. It is important to note that screening instruments function as an indicator of substance-abuse behaviors and at-risk individuals not as a diagnosis of AOD abuse or dependence (Neal et al. 2006). Information obtained in the screening process helps to guide the practitioner's decision-making process in terms of referral for further assessment and treatment. In addition, the results of the test provide the clinician with a documented source of data useful for showing a rationale for decisions.

Two case examples demonstrate the use of both screening instruments and assessment instruments in two different intervention settings. Todd is a 22-year-old single white male, living with his family, attending college full time. He visited a social worker as part of family counseling service his family had initiated based on interpersonal stressors they were experiencing. The social worker administered the four questions comprising the CAGE (describe later). This provided the practitioner with the opportunity of offering some brief education on alcohol use and its consequences while performing a biopsychosocial assessment that included use of an alcohol screen. If needed, she could refer this 22-year-old patient for more extensive interventions as necessary.

The second case involves Tom, a 28-year-old white male, living with his family after the arrest for cocaine possession and driving while intoxicated (blood alcohol level of 0.20). He had been living independently prior to his legal problems and had been working as a successful computer salesman. His drinking history included consumption since the age of 14 and marijuana use since 15 on an intermittent basis; with rare smoking by age 20. In addition, his drinking history revealed a daily pattern by age 22 with varying quantities, ranging from 1 to 12 beers a day with evidence of tolerance. His cocaine use was intermittent until age 25 when he began daily use. This coincided with increased business success and increased money to spend. After a court hearing, Tom was mandated to attend a drinking driver educational program and a counseling program run by a social work practitioner. The social worker in charge of his group administered the Michigan alcohol screening test (MAST) that indicated a possible problem with drinking. He was then referred to an AOD treatment clinic for more extensive assessment. Subsequently, further tools, specific for poly-drug use were administered for a more comprehensive assessment and as a basis for treatment decision-making.

Once the screening procedure has signaled the need for a better understanding of AOD disorders, more comprehensive tools such as diagnostic or problem-focused interviews and multi-scale questionnaires are employed to determine "the nature and severity of drug involvement" (Perepletchikova et al. 2008). Information from the assessment allows the practitioner to individualize treatment to patient needs and preferences when a variety of treatment options are available. While traditional assessment models can help monitor patient progress toward achieving treatment goals (Freimuth 2010, p. 31), it expresses support for a "new look" addiction assessment that incorporates harm reduction and prevention while broadening "the scope of addictions to include behavioral addictions." By doing so, this "new look" assessment paradigm better addresses the total physical, psychological, and economic costs of AOD misuse and abuse.

An important aspect of the screening and assessment process is the means by which it is accomplished. A major keystone to this process is the self-report. Self-report obtains subjective information from the client in a variety of different ways: face-to-face interviews, practitioner or self-administered questionnaires, and the use of collateral reports gathered from individuals associated or related to the client. Self-report can be either face-valid, in which an association with drug or alcohol problems would be obvious to the test-taker, or indirect or subtle, in which a socially desirable response would not be readily apparent. Self-reports in addiction assessments are used to gather personal information among four broad areas. These include (a) demographic variables; (b) personality traits; (c) values, beliefs, and attitudes; and (d) quantity and frequency of use (Lance and Vandenberg 2009; Miller 2009).

Since the 1970s, a hot area of debate among addictions researchers and practitioners has been the accuracy of self-report measures. This seems to be centered on the belief that denial and minimization are characteristics of the alcohol and substance abuser that can interfere with the self-report process. Some research does support the opinion that collateral reports are more credible when the collateral (e.g., spouse, parent, friends, or adult children) has greater opportunity to witness the client's alcohol or drug use (Hersen and Turner 2003). However, it has been documented that when discrepancies do exist between the self-report and the collateral report, patients "present themselves more negatively than the collaterals" (Hersen and Turner 2003, p. 218).

More recently, an additional theme in this discussion contemplates "the more heuristically useful question of under what conditions in a clinical setting are reliable and accurate self-reports most likely to occur" (Miller 2009, p. 71). Reinert and Allen (2007) concluded that the validity and reliability of alcohol abusers' self-reports are generally accurate and can be used with confidence if the data are gathered under specific conditions. These conditions include when the patient is drug or alcohol free, the individual is assessed with structured or standardized methods, when the client is aware that the medical provider will collaborate the self-report with biomarkers or reports from spouses/significant others, and when the client has complied with other aspects of the treatment program (Miller 2009).

The value of screens and assessments can be evaluated in several ways—the most important of which are reliability and validity. Reliability measures the consistency of a tool, the degree to which a measure is free from random error. Reliability within an instrument is termed the internal consistency of the measure, while reliability over time is determined by testing and re-testing (Engell and Schutt 2010). Validity, on the other hand, refers to whether the test actually measures what it purports to measure (Abell et al. 2009).

Validity can vary greatly the use of AOD measurement tools when used with different populations. The clinician must, therefore, be aware of the type of population each tool works best with. An effort has been made to include this information under the description of each tool. In terms of reliability, Wade and Neuman (2007) indicated that a reliability or *r* score, of 0.8 or greater is a good cut-off point for evaluating the precision of a measurement tool. While they concede that others have used a cut-off of 0.7, they feel that it is useful to keep in mind the simple fact that a higher correlation or percentage of agreement is always better when evaluating measurement instruments. For the purpose of this article, only three of the tools covered reported *r* scores below eight (including the composite international diagnostic interview (CIDI), alcohol use disorders identification test (AUDIT), and CAGE questionnaires, each of which is covered in the review of tools), while all of the tools had reliability scores of greater than 0.7. Those tools and all the tools covered within this chapter meet this criterion; however, some present with greater degrees of reliability than others.

Standardizing the measurement process can insure greater precision. Examples include proper training for individuals responsible for the administration of tests, limiting the number of raters used in delivering a test, and being consistent with the use of one tool to measure the change over time. The social-work practitioner needs to be aware that reliability is both a property of the test and the person administering it. If measurements taken in clinical settings are to produce useful and meaningful information, great care needs to be taken during each step in the measurement process.

As was noted earlier, instruments can be used to screen for AOD problems or to provide more detailed assessment. For this reason, tools have been grouped according to their major function. In addition, instruments have been grouped according to the type of agent for which they are appropriate—alcohol or other drugs. Finally, instruments are presented according to the population for which they are appropriate, specifically adults, adolescents, and people with dual diagnoses.

Adult Tools: Alcohol Screens

CAGE This four-item self-report screen has the advantage of being the most brief of the major alcohol tests (Aergeerts et al. 2004). The four letters of the CAGE stands for the question in the screen as they relate to the individual's alcohol use. They are: Have you ever felt the need to Cut down on your drinking? Are you ever Annoyed by criticisms of your drinking? Have you ever felt Guilty about your drinking? Have you ever needed an Eye-opener? The CAGE has proven to be an accurate tool particularly useful in primary care settings and in general population surveys. A cutting score of two or more positive responses is considered significant for alcoholism as each of these questions represents a problem area for the abusive drinker. The CAGE, however, does not possess the ability to discriminate between heavy and nonheavy drinkers, and therefore, it should be limited to individuals identified "as alcohol users rather than screening individuals in the general population" (Sarkar et al. 2009, p. 250).

Michigan Alcohol Screening Test (MAST This screening is a 24-item, true/false alcohol-screening instruments that can be used either as a structured interview or as a self-administered questionnaire (Shields et al. 2007). The screening test examines the alcohol use within the past 12 months. Asking questions that consider workplace issues and concerns related to one's drinking and any guilt associated with the users drinking are a few questions put forth by the health care professional. (Stone and Merlo 2011). The MAST can be utilized in a variety of settings with a high sensitivity to adult alcoholics in a treatment and a modest screening sensitivity in other health care settings in the general population. Similar to the CAGE assessment tool, MAST has a "poor specificity in prenatal populations" (Mengel et al. 2006, p. 497). Additional limitations include its length and scoring time which make its use somewhat cumbersome in clinical settings (Arch 2013). Also, a focus on lifelong problems and late stage indicators of alcohol abuse limits the identification of heavy drinkers who have not experienced alcohol-related problems (McBride et al. 2004). Several variations of the MAST have been developed to adjust to clinical needs and these include the shortened SMAST (Shields et al. 2007) and the 35 questions self-administered screening test, SAAST (Vickers-Douglas et al. 2005)

MacAndrew Alcoholism Scale (MAC) This 49-item, true/false self-report instrument takes 30 min to complete and is easily hand scored (Cooper-Hakim and Viswesyaran 2002). A somewhat specialized instrument, the MAC was designed to differentiate between the alcoholic outpatients and psychiatric outpatients. A high score on the MAC is indicative of alcoholism; a low score is indicative of a psychiatric problem; and a score in the middle range indicates normal. While this may have certain clinical uses where the choice of treatment is an issue, recent trends in assessing patients for dual diagnosis problems casts some doubt on to the usefulness of the MAC scale. Therefore, the comorbidity cannot be accurately assessed. The fact that up to 50% of individuals who suffer from significant mental illness show comorbid substance-abuse problems decreases the credibility of this type of scale (Neal et al. 2006). Therefore, the MAC should only be used for treatment situations where comorbidity is not present.

Alcohol Use Disorders Identification Test (AUDIT) This 10-item questionnaire is scored for each question on a scale of one to four, with a maximum score of 40 possible (Kypri et al. 2004). Questions relate to alcohol consumption, dependence symptoms, and alcohol related health problems. Its strengths include that it was developed in a primary care health setting, which makes it useful for screening done in hospitals as part of a medical history. In this way, the test can be masked as a routine medical screen, rather than an alcohol-specific questionnaire. Also, the AUDIT is the first instrument to be developed in a cross-national setting (Reinert and Allen 2007). This means that only questions that could be translated literally into multiple languages were used, making the test particularly useful in multiethnic settings. Aside from its strengths in development, the AUDIT concentrates solely on drinking habits during the past year, which helps identify the early stages of problem drinking (Mengel et al. 2006).

Adult Tools: Alcohol Assessment

Alcohol Dependence Scale (ADS) This scale is a 25-item multiple choice questionnaire that is self-administered and takes less than 10 min to complete (Kahler et al. 2003). It is easily scored by hand and is useful in the clinical setting for assessing dependence, severity of alcoholism, withdrawal symptoms and obsessive compulsive drinking styles. The ADS is useful for developing a prognosis of alcoholism, as well as tracking the course of an alcohol problem, as it can be administered at the initial screening, at intake, and during the follow-up treatment (Murray et al. 2006).

Severity of Alcohol Dependence Questionnaire (SADQ) The SADQ is a 20-item, self-report questionnaire that is scored on a four-point scale with a maximum of 60. It is composed of five sections, four of which are components of the alcohol dependence syndrome (Heather and Dawe 2005). The areas covered include: physical symptoms of withdrawal, affective symptoms of withdrawal, alcohol craving, and withdrawal-relief drinking, typical daily consumption, the rapidity of symptom return after a period of abstinence (Echeburua et al. 2005). An identified strength of the SADQ is its usefulness with late-stage drinkers found in hospital settings. A limitation of the SADQ is that with its focus on withdrawal, it is primarily sensitive to drinkers on the severe end of the dependence syndrome continuum (Echeburua et al. 2005). However, a modified questionnaire, the short alcohol dependence data questionnaire (SADD) was developed and offers a higher sensitivity "than the SADQ over the mild to moderate alcohol dependence range" (Gleeson et al. 2009, p. 392).

Munich Alcohol Test (MALT) This 24-item true–false assessment can be used in the diagnosis and prognosis of alcoholism as well as in the measurement of the severity of alcoholism (Echeburua et al. 2005). It is easy to administer and is filled out by the client except for the seven medical history questions filled out by a medical doctor. It looks at physical health factors and components of the alcohol dependence syndrome. The MALT is primarily useful for distinguishing alcoholics from less severe problem drinkers with focus on the medical and social-behavior aspects of drinking. As with other tests which focus on the physical consequences of drinking, it has the disadvantage of only targeting the long-term drinker (Wurst et al. 2006).

Alcohol Use Inventory-Revised (AUI-R) This 228-item, forced choice, self-report questionnaire is an outcome of two previous assessment instruments including the alcohol use inventory (AUI) and the alcohol use questionnaire (AUQ) (Kahler et al. 2003). Taking 40–60 min to administer, it can be scored by non-professional staff or computer but requires clinical interpretation (Longabaugh 2002). Four areas related to drinking are examined including benefits of drinking (i.e., areas of secondary gain), styles of drinking such as compulsive drinking or binge drinking, consequences of drinking, and lastly individuals' own concerns and acknowledgement around their drinking problem (Wurst et al. 2006). The strengths of the AUI-R include its comprehensive nature that allows for evaluating and intervening with nonalcoholic problem drinkers. The content of the test also makes it useful in counseling and family-centered treatment as it includes information on marital relationship and social consequences. Obvious limitations include its inapplicability to those clinical setting in which rapid assessments are needed and time management is an issue.

Adult Tools: Drug Use Screens

Drug Abuse Screening Test (DAST) This 20-item brief, self-report questionnaire is based upon the MAST screen for alcohol use disorder. Its main area is in the measurement of the extent of problems an individual has related to drug misuse. Its main focus is on the degree of drug misuse use as it yields a total score indicating a quantitative measure of problem severity. It is less specific in measuring the type of substance-use problem a person may have. This gives it a limited potential as a clinical assessment tool; however, it may serve as a useful screening instrument in both clinical and nonclinical settings. Other limitations include a vulnerability to possible client defensiveness in employment or criminal justice settings.

Adult Tools: Drug Use Assessment

Substance Abuse Subtle Screenings Inventory (SASSI) This 88-item instrument is a comprehensive assessment tool for alcohol and other drug involvement. It takes 15 min to administer and requires a trained technician for interpretation only. It was designed to be a subtle test useful, where denial or attempts at deception are factors during assessment. Primarily, it is meant to distinguish the substance abuser from the nonabuser, however, the SASSI is composed of numerous subscales covered in the interview process. Various conclusions can be made based upon the scores in each category including, level of maladjustment, level of client defensiveness, an area that identifies the codependent relationships, and discrimination between alcohol and drug involvement. Additional subscales are covered in this somewhat complex assessment tool, the results of which are interpreted using a decision tree included in the package. Strengths of this tool include its testing on male and female control groups during validation testing and its subtle versus face-valid approach.

Addiction Severity Index (ASI) This 180-item assessment tool is a structured interview requiring approximately 45 min for administration by a trained technician (Makela 2004). The index is composed of seven areas, including, medical status, level and types of drug use, alcohol use patterns, employment status, illegal activity, social relations, and psychological functioning. This comprehensive nature of the ASI gives it the strength to measure the impact of addiction in multiple areas. For this reason it is useful in settings where a detailed clinical assessment is needed as well as settings that are engaged in outcome measurement (Makela 2004). In addition, it has been found to be of particular use with older alcoholics with cognitive impairment as well as younger patients with histories of drug use and criminal activity. A study among nine hospitals of 370 Japanese, alcoholic-males utilizing the ASI-Japanese version established the ASI-J as a useful tool for designing unique treatment practices geared to individual needs, as well as performing "as a predictive tool for relapse and compliance to treatment and was shown to be useful as a comparison tool to clarify similarities and differences between substance abuser groups" (Haraguchi et al. 2009, p. 2223). The limitations of the ASI include its lengths and need for a trained technician with substance-abuse experience to administer this highly structured interview (Longabaugh 2002).

Chemical Use, Abuse, and Dependence Scale (CUAD) This 80-item assessment tool measures problems with poly-drug use. It is administered as semi-structured interviews that can be as brief as two items, if the client denies both alcohol and drug use. It has the advantages of giving individual severity scores for each type of drug used as well as a combined chemical use severity score. It also determines if a substance use disorder is present according to Diagnostic and Statistical Manual (DSM-R) diagnostic criteria. It has the limitation of being less comprehensive than other addictions assessments, which account for multiple environmental and functioning contexts, but is critically useful where an accurate and detailed drug-use measurement is needed (Conway et al. 2010). The CUAD scale has also been useful with mentally ill patients due to its ability to help in the diagnosis of both current and lifetime alcohol and drug use and abuse (Passik et al. 2008).

The Index of Drug Involvement (IDI) and the Index of Alcohol Involvement (IAI) The IDI and IAI are rapid assessment questionnaires each containing 25 questions. These instruments have been found to have a reliability score of 0.90. They have been designed to measure the degree of magnitude of problems clients have with drug and alcohol abused. The IDI and IAI do not measure how the substance use started, but rather measures to what extent the person is using and/or abusing the substance. They do not require specialized training or certification. These tools also provide the same accuracy as the SASSI with the added benefit of speed and being user friendly (Feldstein and Miller 2006).

Summary

It is clear that a variety of tools are available for use within the addictions field.

However, they are easily incorporated into various social-work settings. These include individual and family counseling centers, and school-based, health care, and mental health settings. They provide objective measurements useful for the practitioner seeking to improve the outcome focus of their treatment interventions. By matching the appropriate tool to the individual, their needs, and agency requirements, gains for client, worker, and agency can be achieved (Gastfriend and Mee-Lee 2004). The use of these instruments can facilitate the meeting of program goals, including accountability, quality assurance, and program effectiveness. Among the differing kinds of addictions and multiple treatment options, selection for optimal treatment match can be achieved through the use of screens and assessment tools.

Additional Resources

SAMHSA-HRSA Center for Integrated Health Solutions
Screening Tools—Substance Abuse
http://www.integration.samhsa.gov/clinical-practice/substance-use
Screening, Assessment and Drug Testing Resources
http://www.drugabuse.gov/nidamed-medical-health-professionals/tool-resources-your-practice/additional-screening-resources

American Society of Addiction Medicine
Screening tools for Providers: Screening, Brief Intervention and Referral to Treatment
http://www.asam.org/for-the-public/screening-and-assessment
Do I have a drug problem?
http://www.drugscreening.org/
National Council on Alcoholism and Drug Dependence, Inc
Am I an Alcoholic?
https://ncadd.org/learn-about-alcohol/alcohol-abuse-self-test
Substance Use Screening & Assessment Instruments Database
http://lib.adai.washington.edu/instruments/

References

Abell, N., Springer, D., & Kamata, A. (2009). *Developing and validating rapid assessment instruments*, p. 10. New York: Oxford University Press.

Aergeerts, B., Buntinx, F., & Kester, A. (2004). The value of the CAGE in screening for alcohol abuse and alcohol dependence in general clinical populations: A diagnostic meta-analysis. *Journal of Clinical Epidemiology, 57*(1), 30–39.

Arch, J. J. (2013). Pregnancy-specific anxiety: Which women are highest and what are the alcohol-related risk? *Comprehensive Psychiatry, 54*(3), 217–228.

Conway, K. P., Levy, J., Vanyukov, M., Chandler, R., Rutter, J., Swan, G. E., & Neale, M. (2010). Measuring addiction propensity and severity: The need for a new instrument. *Drug and Alcohol Dependence, 111*(1), 4–12.

Cooper-Hakim, A., & Viswesvaran, C. (2002). A meta-analytic review of the MaCandrew alcoholism scale. *Educational and Psychological Measurement, 62*(5), 818–829.

Echeburua, E., de Medina, R. B., & Aizpiri, J. (2005). Alcoholism and personality disorders: An exploratory study. *Alcohol and Alcoholism, 40*(4), 323–326.

Engel, R. J., & Schutt, R. K. (2010). *Fundamentals of Social Work*, p. 71. Thousand Oaks: Sage.

Feldstein, S. W., & Miller, W. R. (2006). Does subtle screening for substance abuse work? A review of the substance abuse subtle screening inventory. *Addiction, 102*(1), 41–50.

Freimuth, M. (2010). The "new look" in addiction assessment: Implications for medical education. *Annals of Behavioral Science and medical Education, 16*(1), 30–34.

Gastfriend, D. R, & Mee-Lee, D. (2004). The ASAM patient placement criteria: Context, concepts and continuing development. *Journal of Addictive Diseases, 22*(1), 1–8.

Gleeson, D., Jones, J. S., McFarlane, E., Francis, R., Gellion, C., Bradley, M. P., & Peck, R. (2009). Severity of Alcohol Dependence in decompensated alcoholic liver disease: Comparison with heavy drinkers without liver disease and relationship to family drinking. *Alcohol and Alcoholism, 44*(4), 392–397.

Haraguchi A., Ogai Y., Senoo E., Saito S., Suzuki Y., Yoshino A., Ino A., Yanbe K., Hasegawa M., Murakami M., Murayama M., Ishikawa T., Higuchi S., Ikeda K. (2009). Verification of the addiction severity index Japanese version (ASI-J) as a treatment-customization, prediction, and comparison tool for alcohol-dependent individuals. *International Journal of Environmental Research and Public Health, 6*(8), 2205–2225.

Heather, N., & Dawe, S. (2005). Level of impaired control predicts outcome of moderation-oriented treatment for alcohol problems. *Addictions, 100*(7), 945–952.

Hersen, M., & Turner, S. M. (2003). *Diagnostic interviewing*. New York: Kluwer Academic.

Kahler, C. W., Strong, D. R., Hayaki, J., Ramsey, S. E., & Brown, R. A. (2003). An item response analysis of the alcohol dependence scale in treatment-seeking alcoholics. *Journal of Studies on Alcohol and Drugs, 64*(1), 127–136.

Kypri, K., Saunders, J. B., Williams, S. M., McGee, R. O., Langley, J. D., Cashell-Smith, M. L., & Gallagher, S. J. (2004). Web-based screening and brief intervention for hazardous drinking: A double-blind randomized controlled trial. *Addiction, 99*(11), 1410–1417.

Lance, C. E., & Vandenberg, R. J. (2009). *Statistical and methodological myths and urban legends—doctrine, verity and fable in the organizational and social sciences.* New York: Rutledge.

Longabaugh, R. (2002). Involvement of support networks in treatment. *Recent Developments in Alcoholism, 16,* 133–147.

Makela, K. (2004). Studies of the reliability and validity of the addiction severity index. *Addiction, 99*(4), 398–410.

McBride, W. J, Lovinger, D. M, Machu, T., Thielen, R. J., Rodd, Z. A., Murphy, J. M., Roache, J. D., & Johnson, B. A. (2004). Serotonin-3 receptors in the actions of alcohol, alcohol reinforcement and alcoholism. *Alcoholism: Clinical and Experimental Research, 28*(2), 257–267.

Mengel, M. B., Searight, H. R., & Cook, K. (2006). Preventing alcohol-exposed pregnancies. *Journal of the American Board of Family Medicine, 19*(5), 494–505.

Miller, P. M. (2009). *Evidence-based addiction treatment.* London: Elsevier.

Murray, T. S., Goggin, K., & Malcarne, V. L. (2006). Development and validation of the alcohol-related God locus of control scale. *Addictive Behaviors, 31*(3), 553–558.

Neal, D. J., Fromme, K., Del Boca, F. K., Parks, K. A., King, L. P., Pardi, A. M., Collins, R. L., Muraven, M., Vetter, C., & Corbin, W. R. (2006). Capturing the moment: Innovative approaches to daily alcohol assessment. *Alcoholism: Clinical and Experimental Research, 30*(2), 282–291.

Passik, S. D., Kirsh, K. L., & Casper, D. (2008). Addiction-related assessment tools and pain management: instruments for screening, treatment planning, and monitoring compliance. *Pain Medicine, 9*(2), 145–166.

Perepletchikova, F., Krystal, J. H., & Kaufman, J. (2008). Practitioner review: Adolescent alcohol use disorders: Assessment and treatment issues. *Journal of Child Psychology and Psychiatry, 49*(11), 1131–1154.

Reinert, D. F., & Allen, J. P. (2007). The alcohol use disorders identification test: An update of research findings. *Alcoholism: Clinical and Experimental Research, 31*(2), 185–199.

Sarkar, M., Burnett, M., Carriere, S., Cox, L., Dell, C. A., Gammon, H, & Wood, R. (2009). Screening and recording of alcohol use among women of child-bearing age and pregnant women. *Journal of Population Therapeutics and Clinical Pharmacology, 16*(1), 250.

Shields, A. L., Howell, R. T., Potter, J. S., & Weiss, R. D. (2007). The Michigan alcoholism screening test and its shortened form: A meta-analytic inquiry into score reliability. *Substance Use and Misuse, 42*(11), 1783–1800.

Stone, A. M., & Merlo, L. J. (2011). Attitudes of college students toward mental illness stigma and the misuse of psychiatric medications. *Journal of Clinical Psychology, 72*(2), 134–139.

Vickers-Douglas, K. S., Patten, C. A., Decker, P. A., Offord, K. P., Colligan, R. C., Islam-Zwart, K. A., Wolter, T. D., Croghan, I. T., Hall-Flavin, D., & Hurt, R. D. (2005). Revision of the self-administered alcoholism screening test: A pilot study. *Substance Use and Misuse, 40*(6), 789–812.

Wade, K., & Neuman, K. (2007). Practice-based research: Changing the professional cultural and language of social work. *Social Work in Health Care, 44*(4), 49–64.

Wurst, F. M., Alling, C., Steina, A., Pragst, F., Allen, J. P., Weinmann, W., Marmillot, P., Ghosh, P., Lakshman, R., Skipper, G. E., Neuman, T., Spies, C., Javors, M., Johnson, B. A., Ait-Daoud, N., Akhtar, F., Roache, J. D., & Litten, R. (2006). Emerging biomarkers: New directions and clinical applications. *Alcoholism: Clinical and Experimental, 29*(3), 465–473.

Part III
Field-Tested Evidence-Informed Interventions

Chapter 9
The Process of Intervention with Multiproblem Families: Theoretical and Practical Guidelines

Michael J. Holosko, Rachel Cooper, Kimberly High, Andrea Loy and Johnna Ojo

Overview

The literature review defines the characteristics of the multiproblem family. A discussion of the widespread effects of economic deprivation, lack of social networks, social skills deficits, deviance, crime, and violence in the family are reviewed. Theories and interventions currently aimed at assisting multiproblem families are evaluated and an ecological-systems approach to case management is proposed to comprehensively handle the various needs of these troubled families.

Introduction

A growing, significant number of families are chronically afflicted with environmental, social, interpersonal, and economic problems, leading to family pressure, despair, and hopelessness (Curran et al. 2010). When negativism occurs between the family members, the punitive behaviors of the parents worsen, the risk of child abuse and substance abuse increases, and psychosocial problems multiply.

Recently, the intervention and implementation of services has moved away from an individual, intrapsychic approach and has embraced a "systems" orientation (DeHoyos 1989). An ecological-systems theory approach is beginning to dominate family-centered therapy. It includes individual, marital, and parent–child relationships, family system, and community-level intervention (Olson and Gorall 2003). The ecological aspect focuses on the way humans and their environments accommodate each other (DeHoyos 1989). Combining these two theoretical approaches

M. J. Holosko (✉)
University of Georgia, Athens, GA, USA
e-mail: mholosko@uga.edu

R. Cooper · K. High · A. Loy · J. Ojo
University of Tennessee, Knoxville, TN, USA

J. S. Wodarski et al. (eds.), *Evidence-Informed Assessment and Practice in Child Welfare*, DOI 10.1007/978-3-319-12045-4_9

expands our awareness of the complexity of problem situations and provides the rationale for more comprehensive interventions. The wide range of difficulties multiproblem families exhibit increases the need for workers to broaden their understanding of a diverse set of factors and causes. It is apparent that social workers must involve themselves with intra- and extrafamilial relationships, socialization of children, housing conditions, daily practices within the home, and optimal use of community resources—all at the same time (Wood and Geismar 1989).

This chapter discusses the complexities and characteristics of multiproblem families. Current intervention and a prevention strategies utilizing ecological-systems theory are then presented, and a comprehensive case management model is proposed for the treatment of these families.

Characteristics of Multiproblem Families

"The multiproblem family has a number of problems which cut across many dimensions of family life" (Sousa et al. 2006b). These problems affect the individual, family, community, and society. According to a study by Hearn (2011), a list of the most prevalent problems include income, housing, parental help, child behavior, family relationships, education, foster care, and physical and psychological health. DePanfilis and Dubowitz (2005) reported that neglectful families are lacking materially and psychologically. Multiproblem families tend to be socially isolated, disconnected with the community, and many are in need of social training to help them locate and utilize resources and supports. Other symptoms of these families are the tendency toward chaos and disorganization (Sousa 2005).

Research suggests that these families may have intergenerational patterns of abuse, and their low income level increases overall stress. Low income and persistent discrimination have been shown to have a "weathering" effect on one's health due to high levels of stress that have a cyclical effect on families. Foster et al. (2008) demonstrate that early menarche can be associated with early childhood abuse. Additional issues that lead to "weathering" in such populations including intimate partner violence, a lower chance of graduating from high school, and early parenthood. Taylor (2008) shows how the weathering hypothesis extends all the way to later life in the extreme disparities between black and white adults in morbidity, mortality, and disability.

These factors also lead to greater negativity on the part of husbands toward their wives which, in turn, increases the punitive behavior of the fathers toward the children (Curran et al. 2010). In this intensely stressful atmosphere, abusive tendencies are easily sparked and used as a convenient outlet for frustration and aggression. Tragically, it is in this atmosphere that the children are being socialized. They learn these responses and, all too often, reproduce them as adults, continuing a vicious cycle of abuse and neglect. An experience of childhood abuse can later "constitute substantial risk to the well-being of offspring; including, but not limited to, risk for maltreatment" (Noll et al. 2009). It has been measured that 47% of parents who were abused as children, abuse their own offspring later in life, which is significantly higher than the rate of abuse occurring in families where the parents did not experience abuse (Dixon et al. 2004).

Characteristics of the Family, Caregivers, and Children

When characterizing multiproblem families, studies show that describing factors can be broken down more specifically into the families, caregivers, and children.

Moxley et al. (2012) state these families overall might be "poorly educated, come from disruptive families, depressed, socially isolated, serious psychological problems, poor impulse control, and low self-esteem. Some were also abused and neglected as children, and identify strongly with their abusive parents" (Moxley et al. 2012). Miller et al. (2007) describe how multiproblem families could lack family cohesion and adaptability. Another characteristic of some multiproblem families is the single-parent household, a make-up which Kilmer et al. (2010) demonstrate to be continually on the rise for decades.

Moxley et al. (2012) goes on to explain that parents often have negative interactions with their children due to their unrealistic expectations of them. Cunnigham and Henggler (1999) explain that these are all the characteristics that have the caregivers feeling that they are incapable of changing what is desired of them. Therefore, it is the therapist's job to instill those feelings of worthiness and empowerment. These authors have also found targeting caregiver factors that could produce a difficult intervention process. These factors are those of mistrust, hopelessness, clinical problems, and low social support. They explain that mistrust is established due to past negative experiences. Hopelessness initiates from persona, failures he/she perceives. Clinical problems have been described as "depression, schizophrenia, cocaine dependence, etc." (Hogue and Liddle 2009). Low social support is among "extended family, friends, neighbors, coworkers, and community contacts" (Hogue and Liddle 2009). Sousa (2005) states, "Caregivers do not provide the kind of tangible and, advice and guidance, or social and emotional support that parents often call on, to help with parenting." All in all, the caregivers have their own barriers when assessing the multiproblem family. Feelings of empowerment may be achieved by incorporating Friere's empowerment approach that includes: ideas of self-concept, critical analysis of the world, identifying with community members, and environmental and community change efforts (Downey et al. 2009).

Moxley et al. (2012) describe children as having higher risk for maltreatment and delay in development aspects. "They may have neurological impairment, impaired auditory comprehension and verbal ability, limited cognition, social and emotional and development … also at higher risk for psychopathology" (Moxley et al. 2012).

Holman (2010) expresses that children often have conflicts with their parents as well. Therefore, one can see that the children in multiproblem families have great developmental impacts. The US Department of Health and Human Services explains, "Child Protective Services agencies investigated 2.6 million reports of child abuse or neglect in 2002. An estimated 896,000 children were victims of abuse and neglect. Neglect and physical abuse is 60%, 10% sexual abuse, and 27% other types of maltreatment."

Another important factor related to child care is the incidence of foster care in multiproblem families. Brook and McDonald (2009) note that the majority of children in foster care are there due to some level of substance abuse problems on the parents' behalf. Dozier et al. (2008) also mention that early separation of a child increases the stress hormone, cortisol, level which effects many aspects of physical and mental health. This is an especially serious problem considering the long-term effects of their intervention study showed no significant change for these children.

Income, Unemployment, and Poverty

The multiproblem family "usually lacks financial resources to meet basic family needs and provide minimal security for family members" (Wood and Geismer 1989, p. 24). Marcus-Newhall et al. (2008) state, "Roughly one in five America children lives in a poor family, a level exceeding that of virtually every other western developed country." Response to this economic pressure is manifested in maladaptive emotional, cognitive, and behavioral responses of family members (Conger et al. 2010).

Lack of adequate income further impacts upon the functional processes of the family. "There is … a strong correlation in this country at least between social class and family malfunctioning, making there truly multiproblem family … a relatively rare phenomenon among middle class and upper-class families" (Wood and Geismar 1989, p. 23). Financial instability appears to be a basic feature of multiproblem families. "That is a reasonable assumption, because poverty brings in its wake unhappiness, frustration, a lack of skill to deal with complexities of life, and a deficiency in education" (Wood and Geismar 1989, p. 31).

Many of these multiproblem families are welfare recipients, and Levine and Zimmerman (2005) cite many reasons why monetary aid may cause difficulties. "Welfare undermines recipients' self-esteem; children growing up on welfare do not develop sufficient ambition and self confidence and are therefore unlikely to become self-supporting adults" (p. 176). In a study conducted by Rofuth and Weiss (1991), a program labeled basic employment and training (BET), reviewed the feelings associated with receiving public assistance. Eleven of the the participants correlated maintaining a job with feelings of self-worth, self-esteem, confidence, and self-assurance. Six participants expressed satisfaction with completing a job rather than receiving money from the state. It is noteworthy that these working individuals maintained an average salary of US$ 4.39/h, not much more than the welfare recipients, which indicated that working rather than having money raised their spirits. When a parent finds a job and begins to work, benefits from public assistance are revoked. This leaves families with even more difficulties and stress than they experience while on public assistance, especially where Medicaid, food stamps, and

Aid to Families with Dependent Children (AFDC) are concerned. The introduction of more frustrating problems when recipients stop receiving welfare offers insight into the widespread dependency on public assistance. If holding a job brings more problematic stress to the family, there is little motivation to move in this direction. In addition, parents that hold multiple jobs may be more stressed and have more time constraints, spending the same amount of time with kids but not being able to complete other pertinent responsibilities (Bianchi et al. 2008)

Housing and Neighborhoods

Housing and the immediate environment can have a major impact on multiproblem families. Low income can lead to poor housing conditions. Hearn (2011) implemented a program entitled lower east side family union (LESFU) in New York City where research revealed an overwhelming need for adequate housing. Poor housing and crowding may lead "to a minimum of organizations beyond that of the nuclear family, familial disorganization such as absence of childhood as distinct protected stage, early introduction to sex, lack of privacy, low self-esteem, helplessness and anomie" (Hernandez-Wolfe and McDowell 2013). Fifty-six percent of the participants in LESFU cited housing as a major reason to seek help, describing a variety of reasons why poor housing affected them as parents, and the lives of their children.

The health of these inhabitants is often at risk. Poor insulation and lead poisoning affect a great number of children. It is "estimated that 2 million children under the age of 7 reside in approximately 6 million homes with deteriorating surfaces containing lead paint" (Campbell and Osterhoudt 2000). Placing children at risk for lead poisoning increases chances for both "acute encephalopathy and chronic, persistent neuropsychological sequala, such as mental retardation, seizures, and behavioral dysfunction" (Campbell and Osterhoudt 2000).

Emotional growth also suffers. McGloin (2007) recorded the emotions of inhabitants in poor areas of Milwaukee: "Some want to leave but cannot because of residential segregation or lack of affordable housing … neighborhoods are a checkerboard for a struggling working class, even on the same block, with drug houses, gangs, and routine violence" (p. 534).

Neighborhoods are where peer groups are formed and social values learned. Simons et al. (2004) developed a model for deviant behavior. "The model indicated that participation in delinquent behavior is a function associated with deviant peers" (p. 649). They reported a significant correlation between deviant behavior and a deviant peer group. "The model posited that family factors, values, social skills, and problems as school … influence delinquency indirectly through their impact on choice of peers" (Simons et al. 2004). Delinquency is often promulgated by "widespread joblessness and lack of opportunity for upward mobility" (Brown 2004). Delinquency is also more prevalent in poverty-stricken areas, but only for those who are persistently poor and not considered impoverished for a short term (Hay et al. 2007).

Homelessness is another grave concern for multiproblem families. "Homeless families constitute approximately one-third of the homeless population … and given that estimate of the total population of homeless people range from 300,000 to 3 million, 100,000–1 million parents and children may be homeless," (Barrow and Lawinski 2009). These authors calculated the needs of homeless families in a study of 94 parents in which 77 % said they needed affordable housing. The location of housing appears to be important (64 %), transportation (57 %), social service benefits (49 %), occupation (36 %), food (45 %), child care (37 %), medical (36 %), job training (35 %), and case work and advocacy (33 %).

Anderson et al. (2006) found that 80–85 % of homeless families are headed by single mothers. Davidson et al. (2000), in a study of homeless single mothers and their families, consistently found "themes of poverty, neglect, abuse, troubled interpersonal relationships, and mental health concerns" (p. 148). This study showed that multiproblem families are at serious risk of homelessness when poverty, neglect, and abuse are in combination. This is an important correlation in considering prevention programs.

Social Skills and Social Isolation

Multiproblem families view their lives as unchangeable and predetermined. They exhibit a "resentment of authority and a sense of being blamed and victimized; a sense of aloneness and inability to trust others or form lasting attachments, an inadequate sense of rigor discipline, or perseverance; a tendency toward dependency rather than self reliance; and a declination to adhere to salaried jobs" (Hernandez-Wolfe and McDowell 2013). These dynamics cause many multiproblem families to become isolated and alienated. They possess a few positive support networks (Sousa et al. 2006) and, while in crisis, have a great need for social connection.

"The term network … conveys interdependence, flow, linkage, interactions, and meshing of structures … a system" (Rueveni 1979, p. 17). Informal networks are unstable, because the families lack skills to maintain relationships. Formal networks of these families are characterized by intervention with multiplicity of practitioners and social agencies. Personal social networks of multiproblem poor families are typically homogenous, closed, unstable, and tend to be dominated by often critical unsupportive relatives (Sousa 2005).

Members of these families' social networks often share and reinforce the poor parenting patterns. Members of the family often do not have the necessary social skills to keep relationships. The weak relationships they already have tend to break down; therefore, members within the multiproblem family tend to be alone. Multiproblem families often have "critical unsupportive relative [that] often dominate these network[s]" (Sousa 2005). Multiproblem families are in a constant crisis state, usually expressing the need for help during crisis situations. The quality and adequacy of a family's social support systems and the ability to mobilize these systems, particularly during crisis situations, affects the well-being of the family and its ability to function (Rueveni 1979). When family members experience emotional stress and their relationships reach a crisis point, support for change, particularly from productive friends is essential. Livermore and Powers (2006) argue that "young mothers were more likely to finish high school if they lived with their parents" (p. 212). In addition, the kin relationships should remain intact in case of an emergency or crisis situation.

Developmental Domain

It is reported that parents with developmentally impaired children face greater challenges in parenting. Thus, developmentally impaired children are at a greater risk of maltreatment than the children with age-appropriate development (Dubowitz et al. 2011). Developmental domain should be considered an important part of risk assessment.

Depression

Maternal Depression

Maternal depression has been linked to child maltreatment in many studies. Lahey et al. (1984) found abusive mothers to be much more depressed than the control group mothers. All but one of the eight abusive mothers scored in the abuse and physical aggression. These results introduce useful concepts with important implications that are worthy of additional research.

Maternal depression can also be broken down into behavior styles. These styles are withdrawn and intrusive. Withdrawn mothers 80% of the time are disengaged from their infants. Their behaviors include: low levels of vocalizing, touching, looking away from their infant, and exhibiting disengaged behavior. Intrusive mothers use an angry, irritated manner when handling their infants, 40% of the time. Behaviors included: rough ticking, poking, and tugging their infant. In general, the depressed mothers had a negative perception of their children, but had a positive perception of their own behaviors. When vocalizing to their children, these mothers have been noted to not have intonation, contour, or changes in facial expressions (Field et al. 2009). Such behaviors may lead to insecure attachment, which may cause lower sociability, poor peer relations, anger, and poor self-control later in life (Crowell et al. 2008). In addition to insecure attachment styles, research has shown maternal depression as a predictor of later psychological problems among children (Shaffer et al. 2008).

Although a relationship between parental depression and child abuse has been indicated in many studies, the direction of this relationship is still under question. Studies that assess parents after abuse have been reported and substantiated, but cannot determine whether the depression existed at the time the abuse occurred or if it developed as a result of being turned into the authorities. Still, some studies on depression have reported that depressed mothers often interact in a rejecting and hostile manner with their children (Colletta 1983). Depressed mothers are more likely to use physical punishment. This suggests that parental depression could lead to child abuse. Colletta (1983). found no reduction in depression reported by parents in the abusive group at follow-up, implying that depression is "chronic and deep-rooted."

Child abuse and neglect has become a major societal concern over the past 30 years. There were more than 2.6 million reports of child abuse in 1991, more than a 6% increase since 1990, and a 40% increase since 1985. Considering the 1383 documented cases of fatal child maltreatment, four children a day die as a result of child abuse (Keeping Kids Safe 1992).

The combination of the problems mentioned often leads to violence and abuse in homes. Abuse tends to be the major situation in multiproblem families that comes to the attention of social service professionals. These families commonly have a history of involvement with agencies, courts, hospitals, and child-protective services (Al et al. 2012). Dembo et al. (2007) conducted a study on the family factors associated with abuse. A cross-sectional sampling of 399 youths came from a Tampa Bay detention center revealed that 46% of the youths came from families that had problem with alcohol abuse, drug abuse, emotional or mental health problem (24%), family members arrested (70%), held in jail or detentions (64%), convicted of a crime (50%), or sent to a training school or prison (29%). From the author's analysis, significant relationships were found between physical and sexual victimization and subsequent delinquency.

Thus, it can easily be understood why being a victim of child maltreatment may lead to increased risk of becoming an abusing parent. Experts in child development have clinically depressed rank on the Beck Depression Inventory (BDI) (Lahey et al. 1984). Colletta (1983). found the parental depression significantly more evident among abusive families than among nonabusive families. In a study of abusive and nonabusive families with conduct disorder children, the abusive mothers have significantly higher scores on the BDI than did the nonabusive (Webster-Stratton 1995).

DePanfilis and Zuravin (1999) investigated the role of depression and its severity in child maltreatment in greater depth. The subjects consisted of single mothers living in Baltimore, who were recipients of Aid to Families of Dependent Children (AFDC) program. Almost half of the mothers were known for maltreating one or more of their children who were receiving child protective services (CPS). The other mothers were members of the cohort receiving AFDC, but had never been reported for physical abuse and were not receiving CPS. It was hypothesized that the severity of depression may affect the type of aggressive behavior displayed. This was based on the notion that depression usually results in fatigue, with greater depression leading to greater energy loss. Also, different types of aggressive behavior are thought to require different amounts of energy. The level of aggression was measured through the use of several indices. Respondents were then divided into either "not aggressive," "low aggressive," or "high aggressive," based on their index scores. It was found that the hypothesis was supported. Moderate depression, but not severe depression, had a significant overall effect on child abuse. Moderately depressed mothers were found to be 1.35 times more likely than nondepressed mothers to display a low level of abusive behavior and 1.57 times more likely to display a low level of abusive behavior. Moderate depression, but not severe depression, also resulted in a statistically significant overall effect on physical aggression. Moderately depressed mothers were found to be 1.41 times more likely to be frequently physically aggressive than were nondepressed mothers.

These results were attributed to the general view that severely depressed mothers suffer from more severe fatigue and energy loss, as noted. Results indicate that severely depressed mothers, who may not have the energy to inflict injury on a child, are not at increased risk of child abuse and physical aggression. However, moderately depressed mothers have more energy and are able to inflict injury. Children model the behavior as they see around time, especially if they identify with the perpetrator (Daro 1988).

D'Andrade et al. (2008) did a study on risk assessment. The risk factors derived from their sample ($N = 2209$) included environmental factors, stress on parents, employment status, and social support. Some caretaker/abuser characteristics included mental, physical, and emotional impairment, substance abuse, history of criminal behavior, and poor parenting skills. Low socioeconomic status (SES), single parenting, depression social isolation, maternal age, substance abuse, low education level, and a family history of abuse are all risk factors that may lead to child abuse and neglect.

It is sadly ironic how many of these factors parallel the difficulties facing multiproblem families. This overlap causes these families to be at a greatly increased risk for child abuse and neglect.

Economic difficulties, depression, and drug/alcohol abuse are becoming epidemic in low-income minority communities. As a result, more child abuse and neglect cases are being reported in these communities (Harris and Hackett 2008). It should be noted that minority families are not the only groups prone to violence and abuse (D'Andrade et al. 2008). No family is totally immune to the accumulation of problems that increase the risk of abuse.

Theoretical Interventions

Families facing a multiproblem crisis need intrafamilial attention as well as environmental assistance. The major theories considered most instrumental with these families are systems theory, ecological theory, multisystemic therapy, and the strengths perspective. Systems theory practitioners generally focus on patterns, rules, structure, subsystems, boundaries, detouring, and restructuring of the family (Sousa et al. 2006). Crisp et al. (2006) emphasize that the worker must attempt to gain full understanding of the complex interactions between the person and the systems that surround their lives.

Two important features of ecological theory are the understanding of families within their historical, cultural, and socioeconomic background, and the understanding of the organization of the individual, the family, and surrounding society (Fife and Whiting 2007). "The ecological approach widened the focus of social work by emphasizing interaction between humans and their environment and formalized the important notion of environmental intervention" (Williams 2012). This theory "offers a conceptual framework that shifts attention from the cause and effect relationship between paired variables … to the person/situation as an interrelated whole. The person is observed as a part if his/her total life situation; person and situation are a whole in which each part is interrelated to all other parts in a complex way through a complex process in which each element is both cause and effect" (Crisp et al. 2006).

Multisystemic therapy (MST) is often used to treat multiproblem families (Cunnigham and Henggeler 1999). MST is a family-oriented treatment that engages family members in the treatment process and looks for strength in the family.

The strengths perspective offers a more in-depth approach to helping multiproblem families identify their resources. The strengths perspective helps families by looking at their strengths, both internally and externally, and shows them how to use their own resources to solve issues (Lietz 2011).

Treatment of Depression

Depression is one of the most common mental illnesses. In any 6-month period, 9.4 million Americans suffer from it. One in four women and one in ten men develop the disorder during their lifetime. Fortunately, depression is also one of the most treatable mental illnesses; it can be effectively treated in 80–90 % of the cases (American Psychiatric Association 1989).

The exact cause of depression is unknown, and it is suspected that there is no single cure. Some believe genetic factors play a role in depression; however, psychosocial factors also contribute to the frequency and severity of depressive episodes.

Once a person is diagnosed with depression, a psychiatrist may prescribe medication; the major types being tricycles (e.g., Elavil, Trofranil, and Sinequan), serotonin reuptake blockers (Prozac), and Monoamine Oxidase (MAO) Inhibitors (Marplan, Nardil, and Parnate). All of these drugs take between 10 days and 3 weeks to have an effect, and relieve depression about 65 % of the time.

There are two problems with using drug therapy for depression. First, about a quarter of depressed people avoid or refuse drugs because of their unpleasant side effects. Second, psychiatrists often prefer to prescribe medication, which may speed up treatment and ameliorate some symptomatology, but does not resolve underlying problem. Thus, patients are at a considerable risk of relapse if they discontinue drug usage. This, in effect, leaves them where they started. With this in mind, drug therapy on its own is not panacea. It is most helpful when paired with some types of psychotherapy.

Many forms of psychotherapy are used to help people suffering from depression with the common goal to help patients gain insight into and resolve their problems.

Interpersonal psychotherapy focuses on the patient's disturbed social relationships (National Institute of Mental Health 1989). The relationship between depression and interpersonal conflicts is explored in terms of four problem areas: grief, fights, role transition, and social deficits. This approach brings relief in approximately 79% of cases (Peterson et al. 1993).

Cognitive behavioral therapy is based on "the theory that people's emotions are controlled by their views and opinions of the world" (APA 1989). The therapist helps the patient change the negative thought patterns and beliefs about failure, defeat, loss, and helplessness.

Cognitive therapy, in combination with medication, is commonly seen as the treatment of choice of depression. Cognitive therapy teaches patients to change depressogenic thoughts and assumptions, and has proven to be useful in preventing relapses and recurrence of depression (Bockting et al. 2009). Wodarski and Wodarski (1993) propose a prevention package to combat depression through a life-skills training approach. Their program utilizes cognitive self-management, communication enhancement, relaxation and assertiveness training, expression of feelings, dealing with anger and conflict, and problem solving. Family and group supports are applied to enhance learning, reinforce behavior change, and foster interpersonal relationships. It is noteworthy, because it approaches the multidimensional difficulties of depression with multiple strategies.

In general, depression can usually be treated by medication or psychotherapy, or a combination of both. The critical part is getting the patients the professional help they need. Unfortunately, many do not recognize the illness or seek help. This is especially significant with depression in men who are often misdiagnosed or not diagnosed at all (Celik et al. 2011). Men are traditionally socialized to hide their feelings, so their symptoms of depression may become externalized as anger or violence, rather than the usual internal symptoms exhibited by most depressed people, such as sadness or apathy. This also has negative implications, because men have higher rates of suicide than women. Fortunately, psychotherapy, either individual, couples, or group psychotherapy and cognitive therapy, have been shown to be successful in treating depression in men (Celik et al. 2011).

Treatment of depression would result in improved self-esteem, awareness, and coping skills which, in turn, would increase parenting ability, thus benefiting the child. Based on the research linking depression to child maltreatment, it seems likely that treating depression would lead to a decrease in child abuse.

Sex Education

Sex education is directly related to the prevention of child abuse through reducing two precipitating factors—maternal age and single parenting. About 65% of boys and 51% of girls are sexually active by the time they are 8 years old (Wodarski and Wodarski 1993). Further, approximately half of American adolescents do not use contraceptives the first time they have intercourse, which contributes to the fact that 50 % of premarital pregnancies take place within the first 6 months after sexual intercourse (Wodarski and Wodarski 1993).

Children need to receive sex education in order to be aware of the possible consequences and risks of sexual intercourse. The use of contraceptives also needs to be discussed extensively. Although many feel this should be the responsibility of the parents—parents typically are not providing this information (Wodarski and Wodarski 1993). The subsequent alternative is for schools to offer sex education.

Wodarski and Wodarski (1993) have developed a program designed for preadolescents or early adolescents. Their Comprehensive Sexual Education Program includes communication with parents and a peer group experience within the school.

Not only does sex education confront the two factors of maternal age and single parenting, it helps with other child-abuse risk factors related to teenage parenting. For example, teenage pregnancy often results in less education, dependency on public assistance, poverty, and social isolation (Wodarski and Wodarski 1993). Sex education reduces the chance of unplanned pregnancies, a phenomenon also linked to child abuse (Zuravin 1987).

Employment Preparation

Employment preparation would help prevent abuse by decreasing the impact of low SES and child maltreatment. As previously noted, lowSES has frequently been found to be related to child abuse.

According to Wodarski and Wodarski (1993), research has indicated that most people view work as the "single most defining aspect of living in American society" (p. 369). It has been found to enhance mental health. Along with the obvious financial advantage, work leads to heightened feelings of self-worth.

Some people, however, lack job skills and/or the knowledge of how to get a job. Thus, job-training programs are prerequisites and, in turn, would address child maltreatment through alleviating some of the stress of poverty and employment.

In Milwaukee, Wisconsin, an experimental program called New Hope was designed to increase parent employment and reduce poverty (Wadsworth et al. 2008). The program was successful, and a 5-year follow-up showed that these successes were maintained. The program had positive effects on children's school achievement, motivation, and social behavior, mainly for boys, across the age range 6–16 years. In addition, the program resulted in improvements in the income of the families, and in the use of organized child care and activity settings.

Substance Abuse Treatment

The treatment of a parent's substance abuse problem is essential for both the parent and the family. As noted, many studies have found that alcohol or drug abuse by parents coincides with abuse/maltreatment of their children. Young et al. (2007) note that alcohol and drug abuse are at least a partial cause in why children are placed into the foster care system in about 60% of cases and is a factor in 75% of placements outside of the home. Redmond and Spoth (2002) also show that many behaviors like substance abuse are preventable in adolescents and can either be fostered or lessened by the family unit.

Thompson et al. (2005) refer to behavioral parent training, family skills training, in-home family support, brief therapy, and family education as good measures of treating substance abuse in the family setting. They also note that the family-based strategy is statistically shown to be much more effective than simply targeting children's behavior.

In one sample of female crack smokers with children, 34.3% reported that the Bureau of Child Welfare had become involved with their children as a result of their neglect and abuse (Wallace 1991). Physical or sexual abuse of a child was found in 22.5% of families with alcohol and opiate-addicted parents (Black and Mayer 1980). A great deal of research evidence indicates that child maltreatment is a major problem among substance abusers. As a result, several programs have been developed for teaching children and adolescents about the dangers of the use of alcohol and drugs.

According to Kelley and Fals-Stewart (2002), "children of parents who abuse alcohol or other drugs are at risk for developing emotional, behavioral, and social problems" (p. 417). They found that for men, behavioral-couples therapy resulted in higher psychosocial functioning of their children, compared to those treated with individual therapy or psychoeducational attention control treatment (PACT).

As citied by Craig (1993), treatment for substance abuse usually occurs in inpatient rehabilitation settings. These programs often include educational groups, group therapy, individual counseling, attendance in alcoholics anonymous (AA), and an aftercare plan including follow-up in AA (Craig 1993).

Finkelstein (1994) considered the problems faced by women who are in need of substance-abuse treatment if they have child-rearing responsibilities. The lack of services for mothers and children, and the lack of available child care are major obstacles to treatment for these women. This issue needs to be examined and addressed in substance-abuse treatment.

Parent-Training Services

According to Daro (1988), "much of what we know with respect to the specific causes of child maltreatment suggests that direct interventions with parents, preferable as close to the birth of their first child as possible, are excellent strategies for reducing levels of physical abuse, neglect and emotional maltreatment" (p. 129). Parent-training services generally included instruction in a variety of skills, such as techniques for the reduction of stress, increasing parents' knowledge of child development, and enhancing parent–child bonding, emotional ties, and communication.

Anger-management and child-management skills are also frequently addressed in such programs. These services have been offered though home- and center-based models to produce positive gains in parenting skills (Daro 1988).

Furthermore, in a literature review of the effectiveness of family therapies, it was found that the three most effective family-intervention approaches for reducing behavioral and emotional problems in children are parent-training (primarily in a cognitive-behavioral format), family skills training, and family therapy, which may be brief, manualized, structural, functional, or behavioral-family therapy (Kumpfer and Alvardo 2003). These interventions help to alleviate some of the stresses and problems that parents may face once they have children. Israel et al. (2005) provide STAR (Stop, Think, Ask, Respond) as an example of a prevention-oriented parent education program. One important parenting aspect this program provides is how to discipline a child without corporal punishment or harsh language and communication.

Prinz et al. (2007) offer the idea of parent-training programs that include all families to better reach those that need prevention programs the most. The basic assertion is that this will destigmatize programs that target at-risk families. They stress that this population level program be evidence based.

Putting it All Together

These approaches address different aspects of the problem of child maltreatment, each with significant empirical support as an intervention. Often, however, child maltreatment occurs within a complex family system in which various factors interrelate to precipitate the abuse. Thus, several interventions may be required either separately or simultaneously. In these instances, the strengths of ecological systems theory may be utilized to formulate complex solutions to the complicated problem of child maltreatment. Since physical child abuse has no determining risk factor, it follows that interventions need to be multifaceted and comprehensive.

Prevention

Wodarski and Feit (1993) state that essential components of successful interventions include both a presentation of essential knowledge, and also a means for the development of necessary skills in the implementation of the knowledge. Two foci of primary prevention that reduce the probability of interpersonal problems include teaching individuals to both cope with and reduce stress in the actual environment (Gottsfield 1972). Secondary prevention necessitates the organization of a helping system for selected candidates within the community (Nahum-Shani et al. 2011). And finally, the goal is to maintain the individual in the community and to prevent problems from recurring.

Teaching multiproblem families how to cope with stress, gives them accurate information about situations which they commonly face (e.g., drug and sex education), organizing support systems within the community, reducing the amount of stress in their environment, and preventing problems from recurring are all important strategies.

Utilizing the strengths of ecological and systems theory, Wodarski and Wodarski (1993) have synthesized prevention curricula for an array of problems. Their prevention packages were developed over two decades of research at the John Hopkins University. They approach complex problems in a comprehensive way by combining diverse techniques.

The Life Skills Training approach is proposed as the treatment of choice. It combines the essential components of health education, skills training, application of skills, peer involvement, cognitive self-management, and relaxation training. The curricula are briefly outlined below.

Sex Education The Comprehensive Sexual Education Program is designed to provide early adolescents with basic physiological knowledge about both sexes, as well as basic values concerning sexuality. This is accomplished by means of parental communication and peer-group experience, thus increasing the likelihood that the adolescents will have an enjoyable learning experience and an opportunity to strengthen the relationship with their parents.

Substance Abuse The Comprehensive Psychoactive Substance Abuse Education Program is targeted at providing essential knowledge about psychoactive substances in three ways: education, self-management skills related to substance use, and the maintenance of knowledge and behavior.

Depression and Suicide The chronic inability to cope with changing life situation has been identified as a major factor in depression and as a predictor in suicide attempts. This issue is confronted through teaching cognitive self-management, coping skills, and relaxation techniques.

Employment Preparation Development of job and psychosocial skills necessary for success in the workplace is undertaken.

Anger and Violence Management This program stresses early identification of and intervention in antisocial behavior by teaching cognitive anger control, problem solving, peer enhancement, parenting, and communication skills.

Nutrition Education This program teaches healthy nutritional behavior and provides information about food fads and fallacies.

A family component is available for each of these programs, which enables the individual not only to learn on his/her own and in peer groups, but also to involve the family systems in the prevention effort.

The multiproblem family may need several of these curricula organized into a holistic prevention and intervention package. Cusinato and L'Abate (2007) present a similar prevention program based on family interactions. Their approach, as well, emphasizes a focus on a holistic approach that does not hone in on one particular symptom, but rather the family system as a whole.

Case Management

While treatment of the individual is necessary, a worker must look beyond the personal or intrapsychic dilemmas they confront. All the factors involved in problematic situations must be understood and managed as a whole.

Case management services are popular in practice arenas in which existing services do not adequately address the full range of client needs. Services are often fragmented, dispersed, and not easily accessible. Historically, we can look at the deinstitutionalization movement as an example of how this situation evolved. Vanderplasschen et al. (2007) explain, "Many services which were once provided in the state hospital system must now be met by a host of community providers, and the former psychiatric client may have difficulty meeting needs due to illness, skill level, and lack of knowledge or resources" (p. 198). Services have become increasingly decentralized and specialized. An agency, for instance, may offer drug rehabilitation, but not family therapy. This becomes problematic for the family with multiple difficulties, which needs access to an array of services.

Incaln and Ferran (1990) assert that for proper community development, certain support services are needed. For example, adequate housing, police protection, health and preventive services, and improvement of the educational system are some of the needed services. A large part of case management involves advocating for clients, enabling them to locate needed services, and developing new services to meet emerging needs. For instance, an important factor in abuse and neglect is parents' lack of skills in rearing a family. DePanfilis and Dubowitz (2005) have noted that neglectful parents need improvement in such parenting skills as gaining empathy toward children, learning age-appropriate expectations, use of alternative child-management techniques, and appropriateness of role expectations and enactments.

Current Intervention Programs

Some current intervention projects are outlined below.

Landau (2013) offers several family-based interventions for adult substance-abuse issues. These include AA, community reinforcement and family training, and unilateral family therapy. These interventions provide family support as well as resources for the family.

The Social Network Intervention Project (SNIP) involves identifying barriers that disabled the client. Some common barriers are poor verbal and social skills, lack of a telephone and transportation, and knowledge of child care responsibilities. By using techniques such as goal setting and case management, social workers help these clients obtain basic conveniences.

Home-builders, a crisis intervention approach, work on such concerns as parental acceptance, limiting use of physical punishment, appropriate supervision of children, the family mental health needs, conditions of the family home, and drug and alcohol abuse within the home (Forsythe 1992). Intervening in issues such as abuse is the crux of helping the multiproblem family. It is important to stress that a family problem does not refer solely to struggles within the family; rather it stems from family structure.

The Short-Term Multi-Dimensional Family Intervention (STMDFI) team "concentrates on promoting interaction through the use of group, conjoint, and individual treatment modes, as well as collaborations with community systems in the family's life space" (Ponzetti et al. 2009).

Families, a home-based model intervention, provides families with "the opportunity to model behaviors in the environment in which the behaviors must be adopted, and increase family empowerment" (Lewandowski and Pierce 2002).

Sure start is a project that aspires to prevent social segregation by targeting children between 0 and 4 years of age living in areas of social and economic deficiency (Rix and Paige-Smith 2008). This program utilizes parent-management training that teaches parents how to give comprehensible and unmistakable directions. Parents are also given training in emergent management skills so that they can learn to recognize and reinforce desired behaviors, and reduce or extinguish undesired behaviors (Rix and Paige-Smith 2008). Additionally, a solution focused brief therapy is used in conjunction with the parenting-management training. This therapeutic approach helps reduce the symptoms of maternal depression, maternal stress, and poor parental perception of the significance and severity of the emotional and behavioral problems of their children (Rix and Paige-Smith 2008).

Children in multiproblem families involved in after-school programs that combine therapy and education help children develop a healthy self-image and build positive coping skills. After-school programs should help children prepare their homework, attend other enrichment programs, build social skills, participate in therapy groups, and receive individual therapy (Itzhaky and Segal 2001).

Another school-based program, Teams Games and Tournaments (TGT), may be helpful in combating drug and alcohol abuse among adolescents and children of multiproblem families (Wodarski and Feit 2011). Incorporating TGT may help children to be more knowledgeable about responsible drinking, the effects of drug and alcohol use and abuse, and teach them appropriate responses when faced with peer pressure (Wodarski and Fiet 1995). The program also acknowledges the importance of family knowledge and involvement (Wodarski and Feit 2011).

Littell and Shlonsky (2010) maintain that it is imperative to provide "high quality intervention that teaches families new skills and how to take advantage of available public and private service assistance" (p. 44).

Social Networks

Personal social networks play a primary role in any person's life, their main purpose being to shelter individuals from stress related to the environment pressure; to ease, prevent or even collaborate in the treatment of physical disease and emotional disorders (Sousa 2005). Social networks also offer support in some life event and in social integration that encourage well-being. In this framework, personal networks of multiproblem poor families can play a significant role mainly due to the particular qualities of these types of families (Sousa 2005).

Linking the family to the community through social networks is essential to the family demonstration project (1948–1968) and is based on the principle of community organization involving all systems, such as schools, other therapists, probation department, and child protective services vital to the intervention process (Sousa et al. 2006). Without this supporting network, families may fall back into isolation. The St. Paul Project "recognized that community support was intrinsic to program success; … community organizations and direct service were key program components" (Sousa et al. 2006).

Walton et al. (2004) approaches family preservation with a multisystems approach. "This model not only recognizes that the best interests of the child cannot be determined without involving the child's family, but also points out that ignoring the constraints and interactions of other systems impinging on the child's welfare jeopardizes that the best-laid plans of interventions" (p. 243). Included in Walton et al., multisystem model are the family, the extended family, the community, and the family preservation group. Community involvement includes the neighborhood, peers, church groups, and the school system (Walton et al. 2004).

The Child at Risk Program (CAR) began in several cities that concentrate on helping youths in the areas suffering from crime and violence in families and neighborhoods. The program consists of case management, community policing, safe passages, drug-free zones, and individual and family counseling (Hebert 1993). Hebert writes, "Obviously, not all youth-even from comparable environment economic levels-are equally at risk for addiction and problems of welfare dependence, domestic violence, and criminality. However, early experimentation with alcohol and drugs, delinquency, family histories of substance abuse or criminality are indicators of higher probability of risk."

From these projects, it is clear that maintaining social networks, case management, and family counseling, has the largest positive effect on the family and is the cornerstone of treatment for multiproblem families. However, practitioners should be aware of the potential consequence of families' involvement with social agencies and how it affects their ability to build social networks (Sousa 2005). Professionals have a tendency to try to substitute parents, which is especially difficult task and often promotes a shift from interpersonal dynamics to interaction with social workers. As a result, the dilution of the family process in the social services is promoted (Sousa 2005).

Self-Esteem and Strengths

Helping families locate their strengths and build self-esteem is an important part of case management. Walton et al. (2004) "People possess unused or underused competencies and resource that can be brought forth when constraints are removed

... the individual is regarded as a system that also have unique attributes" (p. 246). The development of self-image is based on a combination of self-perception and how other views him or her. Self-esteem has a dynamic nature, thus it reflects both a variety of experiences from the past and tendencies and plans for the future (Rix and Paige-Smith 2008).

Strengths are often overlooked by case workers who have been involved with the family in the past (Sousa et al. 2006), and emphasis on weaknesses may result in a poor relationship between them. Scholsberg and Kagan (1988) recognized the difficulty that can arise if the worker concentrates only on negative family traits. If respect is lacking, family members tend to become defiant. The authors recommend that the case worker identify positive aspects of the individuals. For example, when a client has suffered a job loss, Hernandez-Wolfe and McDowell (2013) emphasize working on issues of self-esteem, anger, and depression. The worker supports potentialities for empowerment rather than simply analyzing the client's skills deficits. Workers should focus on building trust with the families and should communicate to the family that he or she would only expect family trust develop following the demonstration of "trustworthy behaviors" (Hogue and Liddle 2009).

The Family Support Center and the Self-Sufficiency Project emphasized family empowerment. Workers stressed mobilization of family strengths and active involvement with services in the community (Wilson et al. 2005). Giving the family a sense of hope for the future fosters motivation.

"Grassroots organization aims at empowering all members of the family, helping attain control of, and building responsibility for their daily lives" (Miller et al. 1990). To build self-esteem, the counselor must concentrate on the internal strengths of hope, and promoted growth within the family. Indications of positive change are recognized and progress is reinforced, which encourages continued family improvement" (Sousa et al. 2006).

Goal Setting

Concentrating on realistic and relevant goals focuses the intervention. In the ST-MDFI treatment program, "goal attainment is incorporated directly into therapeutic process as an integral part of contract building ... Goals attainment provides tangible evidence of needs and a mechanism for assessing at the end of treatment whether and to what extent goals have been accomplished" (Ponzetti et al. 2009). Goal setting provides an opportunity to establish what is important to the family. When the family defines treatment goals, it is taking responsibility for an aspect of the intervention process. "Goal setting in family social work was seen as a collaborative process of negotiations, based on mutual discussion of what was wrong, why, and what could be changed" (Wood and Geismer 1989, p. 121). The family begins to discover its own priorities.

"Goal Attainment Sealing (GAS) has been the most commonly suggested method for assessing change in relation to goals flexibility targeted to fit the unique features in each case" (Wagner et al. 2003).

Littell and Shlonsky (2010) maintain that many preventive services have complicated goals that are much too extensive for the multiproblem family. A family faced with bewildering goals will not produce an effective intervention.

Many multiproblem families are treated in an evasive and confusing way by the service-delivery system. Thus, it is especially important for these families to confer with the practitioner who will spell out in specific and unambiguous terms the goals being set, the respective responsibilities of the worker, individual family members, the family as a group, and other helpers and services, so that therapy will lead to effective case management (Wood and Geismer 1989).

Length of Intervention

In multiproblem families that parents were experiencing with high levels of stress and low levels of support, the efficacy of these interventions appear to be lower (Rix and Paige-Smith 2008). However, a major difference between multiproblem interventions is the length of treatment. Wilson et al. (2005) state that "treatment of chronic neglect should last for 12–18 months, and should not be considered short-term, intensive, crisis intervention services delivered in a family's home" (Littell and Shlonsky 2010). Klevens and Whitaker also note that the interventions aimed at effectively changing parents' attitudes and strengthening their parenting skills takes at least 6 to 12 months (Klevens and Whitaker 2007)

Wilson et al. note that the chronicity of a case determines the amount of attention given to a client. Home-builders maintain that their 16-year record of preventing placement over 90 % of the time proves the effectiveness of their short-term intervention (Littell and Shlonsky 2010).The program is based on crisis-intervention theory, which holds that families are most open to change during a period of crisis when typical coping patterns can no longer maintain family stability and independence (Lewandowski and Pierce 2002).

Ponzetti et al. (2009) examined the STMDFI model, the goals of which included short-term family intervention lasting no longer than 10 months including a 4-week hiatus, was used to prevent placement of children into foster care. This model aimed at reducing the amount of time in therapy; however, since no statistical data were available on STMDFI, an evaluation was not attainable.

Harris and Hackett (2008) argue that "chronically troubled families, families unmotivated to get help, families with addicted care givers, and homeless families are among those not amendable to brief treatment." Length of treatment is based on goals. Families in fear of having a child taken away need intensive and timely treatment. Further, workers may not be available for long-term interventions, and the cost of hiring workers for intensive home-based treatment is too high for public-welfare agencies (Fuller 2004). Thus, the severity of the current crisis, as well as the chronicity of the family problems, should guide the length and intensity of treatment.

Obstacles to Intervention

Resistance is often cited as the most difficult problem encountered by workers. Families may "view mental health professionals as intimidating parental figures who are insensitive to the families' primary needs ... They can feel victimized by interventions from family courts, educators, and social service agency staff and may resist intervention as an intrusion into the family" (Sousa et al. 2006).

Practitioners working with resistant families can become exhausted, which can lead to a dead end—the covert objective of the family. Stagnation of treatment out of fear of self-protection may actually prevent family systems from becoming accessible to change.

Many families feel strongly about maintaining loyalty. Since members fear that the family will be torn apart by judges, courts, or social service workers, practitioners must keep this in mind when starting therapy. Al et al. (2012) assert that case workers should "use the family's primary pattern of resistance to help us to utilize what we feel and what we see (the emotional and behavioral transactions in family work) as clues which can help us to engage a family" (p. 49).

In defining the multiproblem family, workers must decide who is at risk. Economic deprivation, for example, is a factor, yet not every recipient of Temporary Assistance for Needy Families (TANF) can be considered a multiproblem family in need of the same degree of intervention.

Very little data can be obtained as to the actual number of multiproblem families. National data are collected on drug abuse, poverty, and crime, but not enough is known about the prevalence, intensity, and nature of malfunctioning within the multiproblem family (Wood and Geismar 1989). Who to treat, and how much intervention is needed is a difficult decision for the social worker.

Educational training presents a problem for case workers. A dilemma occurs when social workers are placed in settings other than social-services agencies. Berger (2010) feels that the use of social workers should be expanded to health care settings. This establishes an essential link between families and social workers. These settings can be crucial for location of multiproblem or at-risk families. Rather than referral, intervention can begin promptly. The obstacles lie largely in graduate social-work curricula. Students gain little knowledge concerning health care settings and are not instructed on how to teach health care providers about social, environmental, and situational symptoms of an illness.

Problems facing the multiproblem family are often attacked individually, because little information can be found regarding the collective problem. In addition, a large number of individuals affected by one dilemma, often experience still another. As a result, social workers must intervene on many levels of the family functioning to keep the problems from becoming overwhelming. This may make family linkage to available interventions difficult, but the benefits of getting families into treatment far outweigh the costs and energy expended in doing so.

Quite a few proximal caregiver influences on the engagement process include substance abuse, mental-health problems, intellectual limitations, level of comfort with receiving services (embarrassment), extent of suffering, and poor self-sufficiency expectations (Hogue and Liddle 2009).

Practice Guidelines for Social Workers

A practice model is proposed to guide the efforts of social workers engaged in helping multiproblem families. The diverse set of factors involved demand an expanded understanding of personal, interpersonal, and social conditions by the practitioners.

"The Multisystemic therapy has a strong track record in improving family functioning and decreasing long-term rates of antisocial behavior and out-of-home placement" (Hogue and Liddle 2009). Higher rates of engagement were reached by using techniques that are essential to MST framework. This technique includes using empathy, proving credibility to the family, and using scientific mindedness (Hogue and Liddle 2009).

The Social Worker's Roles

Considering the amount of assistance the multiproblem families require, it is very important to define the roles and responsibilities within the treatment setting. A single worker can hardly be expected to handle all of the family's needs alone. Optimally, bachelors-level social workers should be responsible for providing direct services such as individuals, martial, family, and group counseling. Meanwhile, this frees masters-level workers to concentrate on case management activities that address the various services required. In many cases, disparate programs and agencies will have to be coordinated to provide effective treatment. The complex nature of the presenting problems calls for complex treatment strategies.

Assessment

A great deal of social worker's challenge lies in informing a critical and insightful assessment of the most significant factors of the family's problems. This assessment should be undertaken in conjunction with as many of the family service providers as possible. The most critical problems should be assessed.

An excellent place to begin working with multiproblem families is to create an eco-map. Zastrow (2007) defines this tool as "a drawing of the client family in its social environment … drawn jointly by the social worker and the client" (p. 216). This type of assessment focuses not solely on the problems of the family, but rather on the strengths, resources, and assets of the family unit.

Another assessment approach in line with a social-work perspective is the dynamic systems approach. This approach emphasizes the complexity, the interacting levels of organization, and self-organization of a family system (Lichtwark-Aschoff and Van Geert 2005). The dynamic systems approach highlights self-determination and the role the family itself plays in solving their problems. Carr's (2009) meta-analysis also shows that systemic interventions in a family setting are effective for many different problems that could affect a multiproblem family.

Goals Setting

Problems must be prioritized and treatment goals should be negotiated in simple, unambiguous terms. Responsibilities of the workers, the family members, and the family as a whole need to be delineated and delegated. Family and individual strengths should be addressed as much as their difficulties. The most attainable goal should be worked on first in order to foster a sense of accomplishment. The worker should avoid overwhelming the family by expecting too much too quickly. Manageable goals should be agreed upon in a trusting, supportive way. For instance, an initial contract may be negotiated for a runaway youth to return home for 1 week, if his father agrees not to drink in the house during that day. Once progress occurs, longer time periods, rational dynamics, and ultimately the alcohol problem can be addressed.

Treatment

Multiple problems need multiple solutions. Workers become case managers, brokering appropriate services and referrals. While understandably diverse, the treatment needs to remain focused and pertinent to the negotiated goals and priorities.

Specific treatment modalities are indicated for various aspects of the multiproblem family's needs. Family and marital counseling can be used in interpersonal relationship issues. Group counseling, social skills training, and linkage to community organizations are all important in improving impoverished support systems and preventing social isolation. Cognitive-behavioral therapy can be used to deal with self-esteem and depression. Relaxation techniques can be taught to ameliorate anxiety and stress. Alcohol and drug rehabilitation may be necessary in many instances, as well as parenting classes and job skills training.

Poverty and inadequate housing are more difficult problem areas. However, the social workers can act as an advocate for the family members as well as refer them to community agencies.

Information and Referral

As a case manager, social workers must be knowledgeable about the community resources. An array of referrals is often necessary to address the various needs for intervention. An intervention should include referrals to concrete services, marital counseling, and daycare (Holman 2010). On the macro level, workers may be advocating for support from a variety of sources (organizations, agencies, and legislatures) to help the client population with environmental problems such as unemployment and housing.

Conclusion

The formidable task of helping multiproblem families has long been the subject of social concerns (Holman 2010). There is no straightforward solution to the challenges they offer. Many families are afflicted with interrelated environmental, social, interpersonal, and economic problems. These multiproblem families need to be viewed in a systemic and ecological way in order to provide treatment solutions. Some effective interventions exist but, for the most part, the growing phenomenon of multiproblem families, their stress, and therapeutic needs, require further research. A comprehensive practice model based on case-management techniques is indicated in order to address the diverse areas of intervention.

Additional Resources

SAMHSA-HRSA Center for Integrated Health Solutions

Screening Tools—Substance Abuse

http://www.integration.samhsa.gov/clinical-practice/substance-use

Screening, Assessment and Drug Testing Resources

http://www.drugabuse.gov/nidamed-medical-health-professionals/tool-resources-your-practice/additional-screening-resources

American Society of Addiction Medicine

Screening tools for Providers: Screening, Brief Intervention and Referral to Treatment

http://www.asam.org/for-the-public/screening-and-assessment

Do I have a drug problem?

http://www.drugscreening.org/

National Council on Alcoholism and Drug Dependence, Inc

Am I an Alcoholic?

https://ncadd.org/learn-about-alcohol/alcohol-abuse-self-test

Substance Use Screening & Assessment Instruments Database

http://lib.adai.washington.edu/instruments/

References

Al, C. M, Stams, G. J., Bek, M. S., Damen, E. M., Asscher, J. J., & van der Lann, P. H. (2012). A meta-analysis of intensive family preservation programs: Placement prevention and improvement of family functioning. *Children and Youth Services Review, 34*(8), 1472–1479.

Anderson, L., Stuttaford, M., & Vostanis, P. (2006). A family support service for homeless children and parents: User and staff perspectives. *Child and Family Social Work, 11*(2), 119–127.

Barrow, S. M & Lawinski, T. (2009). Contexts of mother-child separations in homeless families. *Analyses of Social Issues and Public Policy, 9*(1), 157–176.

Berger, R. (2010). EBP: Practitioners in search of evidence. *Journal of Social Work, 10*(2), 175–191.

Bianchi, S., Robinson, J., & Milkie, M. (2008). Changing rythms of American family life. *Industrial and Labor Relations Review, 61*(3), 1–3.

Bockting, C. L., Spinhoven, P., Wouters, L. F., Koeter, M. W., & Schene, A. H (2009). Long-term effects of preventive cognitive therapy in recurrent depression: A 5.5 year follow-up study. *Journal of Clinical Psychiatry, 70*(12), 161–168.

Brook, J., & McDonald, T. (2009). The impact of parental substance abuse on the stability of family reunification from foster care. *Children and Youth Services Review, 31*(2), 193–198.
Brown, B. (2004). Juveniles and weapons: Recent research, conceptual considerations and programmatic interventions. *Youth Violence and Juvenile Justice, 2*(2), 161–184.
Campbell, C. & Osterhoudt, K. (2000). Prevention of childhood lead poisoning. *Pediatrics, 12*(5), 428–437.
Carr, A. (2009). The effectiveness of family therapy and systematic interventions for adult focused problems. *Journal of Family Therapy, 31*(1), 46–74.
Celik, H., Lagro-Janssen, T., Widdershoven, G., & Abma, T. A. (2011). Bringing gender sensitivity into healthcare practice: A systematic review. *Patient Education and Counseling, 84*(2), 143–149.
Colletta, N.D. (1983). A trisk for depression: A study of young mothers. Journal of Genetic Psychology, Child behaviour, Animal behaviour, and Comparative Psychology, *142,* 301–310.
Conger, R. D., Conger, K. J., & Martin, M. J. (2010). Socioeconomic status, family processes and individual development. *Journal of Marriage and Family, 72*(3), 685–704.
Crisp, B. R., Anderson, M. R., Orme, J., & Lister, P. G. (2006). What can we learn about social work assessment from the textbooks. *Journal of Social Work, 6*(3), 337–359.
Crowell, J. A., Fraley, R., Cassidy, J., & Shaver, P. R. (2008) Measurement of individual differences in adolescent and adult attachment. *Handbook of attachment: Theory, research, and clinical applications* (2nd ed.). New York: The Guilford Press.
Cunnigham, P. B., & Henggeler, S. W. (1999). Engaging multi problem families in treatment: Lessons learned throughout the development of multi systemic therapy. *Family Process, 38,* 265–286.
Curran, M., Totenhagen, C., & Serido, J. (2010). How resources (or lack thereof) influence advise seeking on psychological well-being and marital risk: Testing pathways of the lack of financial stability, support and strain. *Journal of Adult Development, 17*(1), 44–56.
Cusinato, M., & L'Abate, L. (2007). Linking theory with practice: Theory-derived interventions in prevention and family therapy. *The Family Journal, 15*(4), 318–327.
D'Andrade, A., Austin, M. J, & Benton, A. (2008). Risk and safety assessment in child welfare. *Journal of Evidence-Based Social Work, 5*(1–2), 31–56.
Daro, D. (1988). *Confronting child abuse: Research for effective program design.* New York, NY: The Free Press.
Davidson, L., Janoff-Bulman, R., & Styron, T. (2000). "Please ask me how I am": Experiences of family homelessness in the context of single mothers' lives. *Journal of Social Distress and the Homeless, 9*(2), 143–165.
DeHoyos, G. (1989). Person-in-environment: A tri-level practice model. *Social Casework, 70,* 131–138.
DePanfilis, D., and Zuravin, S. (1999). Predicting child maltreatment recurrences during treatment. *Child Abuse and Neglect, 23*(8), 729–743.
Dembo, R., Schmeidler, J., & Childs, K. (2007). Correlates of male and female juvenile offender abuse experiences. *Journal of Child Sexual Abuse, 16*(3), 75–94.
DePanfilis, D. & Dubowitz, H. (2005). Family connections: A program for preventing child neglect. *Child Maltreatment, 10*(2), 108–123.
Dixon, L., Brown, K., & Hamilton-Giachritsis, C. (2004). Risk factors of parents abused as children: A mediational analysis of the intergenerational continuity of child maltreatment. *Journal of Child Psychology, 46*(1), 47–57.
Downey, L., Anyaegbunum, C., & Scutchfield, D. (2009). Dialogue to deliberation: Expanding the education empowerment model. *American Journal of Health Behavior, 33*(1), 26–36.
Dozier, M., Laurenceau, J., Levine, S., Lewis, E., & Peloso, E. (2008). Effects of an attachment based intervention of the cortisol production of infants and toddlers in foster care. *Development and Psychopathology, 20*(3), 845–859.
Dubowitz, H., Kim, J., Black, M. M., Weisbart, C., Semiatin, J., & Magder, L. S. (2011). Identifying children at high risk for a child maltreatment report. *Child Abuse and Neglect, 35,* 96–104.
Field, T., Diego, M., & Hernandez-Reif, M. (2009). Depressed mothers' infants are less responsive to faces and voices. *Infant Behavior and Development, 32*(3), 239–244.

Fife, S. T. & Whiting, J. B. (2007). Values in family therapy practice and research: An invitation for reflection. *Contemporary Family Therapy, 29,* 71–86.
Finkelstein, N. (1994). Treatment issues for alcohol- and drug-dependent pregnant and parenting women. *Health & Social Work, 19*(1), 7–15.
Forsythe, P. (1992). Homebuilders and family preservation. *Children and Youth Services Review, 14,* 37–47.
Foster, H., Hagan, J., & Brooks-Gunn, J. (2008). Growing up fast: Stress exposure and subjective "weathering" in emerging adulthood. *Journal of Health and Social Behavior, 49*(2), 162–177.
Fuller, A. (2004). Crisis: home-based family therapy. *Australian and New Zealand Journal of Family Therapy, 25*(4), 177–182.
Gottsfield, J. (1972). *The critical issues of community mental health.* New York: Behavioral Publications.
Harris, M. S. & Hackett, W. (2008). Decision points in child welfare: an action research model to address disproportionality. *Children and Youth Services Review, 30*(2), 199–215.
Hay, C., Fortson, E. N., Hollist, D. R., Altheimer, I., & Schaible, L. M. (2007). Compounded risk: The implications for delinquency coming from a poor family that lives in a poor community. *Journal of Youth and Adolescence, 36*(5), 593–605.
Hearn, J. (2011). Unmet needs in addressing child neglect: Should we go back to the drawing board? *Children and Youth Services Review, 33*(5), 715–722.
Hebert, E. E. (1993). Doing something about children at risk. *National Institute Of Justice Journal, (227),* 4–9.
Hernandez-Wolfe, P. & McDowell, T. (2013). Social privilege and accountability: Lessons from family therapy educators. *Journal of Feminist Family Therapy, 25*(1), 1–16.
Hogue, A. & Liddle, H. A. (2009). Family-based treatment for adolescent substance abuse: Controlled trials and new horizons in services research. *Journal of Family Therapy, 31*(2), 126–154.
Holman, W. D. (2010). Talking out the rage: An ego-supportive intervention for work with potentially abusive parents. *Child and Family Social Work, 16*(2), 219–227.
Inclan, J., & Ferran, E. (1990). Poverty, politics, and family therapy: A role for systems theory. In M. P. Mirkin (Ed.), *The social and political contexts of family therapy.* Boston: Allyn & Bacon. 193–214.
Hubert, E. (1993). Doing something about children at risk. *National Institute of Justice Journal,* 227.
Israel, B. A., Parker, E. A., Rowe, Z., Salvatore, A., Minkler, M., Lopez, J., Butz, A., Mosley, A., Coates, L., Lambert, G., Potito, P. A., Brenner, B., Rivera, M., Romero, H., Thompson, B., Coronado, G., & Halstead, S. (2005). Community-based participatory research: Lessons learned from the centers of children's environmental health and disease prevention research. *Environmental Health Perspective, 113*(10), 1463–1471.
Itzhaky, H., & Segal, O. (2001). Models of after-school treatment programs as agents of empowerment. *The Journal of Family Social Work, 5*(4), 51–67.
Kelley, M., & Fals-Stweart, W. (2002). Couples-versus individual-based therapy for alcohol and drug abuse: Effects on children's psychological functioning. *Journal of Consulting and Clinical Psychology, 70*(2), 417–427.
Kilmer, R. P., Cook, J. R., & Munsell, E. P. (2010). Moving from principles to practice: recommended policy changes to promote family-centered care. *American Journal of Community Psychology, 46*(3–4), 332–341.
Klevens, J. & Whitaker, D. J. (2007) Primary prevention of child physical abuse and neglect: Gaps and promising directions. *Child Maltreatment, 12*(4), 364–377.
Kumpfer, K., & Alverado, R. (2003). Family-strengthening approaches for the prevention of youth problem behaviors. *American Psychologist, 58*(6/7), 457–465.
Lahey, B., Conger, R., Atkeson, B., & Treiber, F. (1984). Parenting behavior and emotional status of physically abusive mothers. *Journal of Consulting and Clinical Psychology, 52*(6), 1062–1071.
Landau, J. L. (2013). Family and community resilience relative to the experience of mass trauma: Connectedness to family and culture of origin as the core components of healing. *Handbook of Family Resilience*, 459–480.

Levine, P. B. & Zimmerman, D. J. (2005). Children's welfare exposure and subsequent development. *Journal of Public Economics, 89*(1), 31–56.
Lewandowski, C. A. & Pierce, L. (2002). Assessing the effect of family-centered out-of-home care on reunification outcomes. *Research on Social Work Practice, 12*(2), 205–221.
Lichtwark-Aschoff, A., & Van Geert, P. (2005). A dynamic systems approach to family assessment. *European Journal of Psychological Assessment, 21*(4), 240–248.
Lietz, C. A. (2011). Theoretical adherence to family centered practice: Are strengths-based principles illustrated in families' description of child welfare services? *Children and Youth Services Review, 33*(6), 888–893.
Littell, J. H. & Shlonsky, A. (2010). Toward evidence-informed policy and practice in child welfare. *Research on Social Work Practice, 20*(6), 723–725.
Livermore, M. M & Powers, R. S. (2006). Employment of unwed mothers: The role of government and social support. *Journal of Family and Economic Issues, 27*(3), 479–494.
Marcus-Newhall, A., Halpern, D. F, & Tan, S. (2008). *The changing realities of work and family.* London: Wiley-Blackwell.
McGloin, J. M. (2007). The continued relevance of gang membership. *Criminology and Public Policy, 6*(2), 231–240.
Miller, S., Rein, M., & Levitt, P. (1990). Community action in the United States. *Community Development Journal, 25*(4), 356–368.
Miller, R. B., Anderson, S., & Keals, D. K. (2007). Is Bowen theory valid? A review of basic research. *Journal of Marital and Family Therapy, 30*(4), 453–466.
Moxley, K. M., Squires, J., & Lindstrom, L. (2012). Early intervention and maltreated children: A current look at the child abuse prevention and treatment act and part c. *Infants and Young Children, 25*(1), 3–18.
Nahum-Shani, I., Bamberger, P. A., & Bacharach, S. B. (2011). Social support and employee well-being: The conditioning effect of perceived patterns of supportive exchange. *Journal of Health and Social Behavior, 52*(1), 123–139.
Noll, J. G., Trickett, P. K., Harris, W. W., Putnam, F. W. (2009). The cumulative burden born by offspring whose mothers were sexually abused as children. *Journal of Interpersonal Violence, 24*(3). doi:10.1177/0886260508317194.
Olson, D. H & Gorall, D. M. (2003). Circumplex model of marital and family systems. In F. Walsh (Ed.) *Normal family processes* (3rd ed., pp. 514–547). New York: Guilford
Peterson, C., Maier, S., and Seligman, M.E.P. (1993). Learned helplessness: A theory for the age of personal control. New York: Oxford.
Ponzetti, J., Charles, G. J., Marshall, S., & Hare, H. (2009). Family-centered early intervention in North America: Have home-based programmes lived up to their promise for high-risk families? *Irish Journal of Applies Social Studies, 8*(1), 12–20.
Prinz, R., Sanders, M., & Shapiro, C. (2007). Population-wide parenting intervention training: Initial feasibility. *Journal of Child and Family Studies, 17*(4), 457–466.
Redmond, C., & Spoth, R. (2002). Project family prevention trials based in community-universal partnerships: Toward scaled up preventive interventions. *Prevention Science, 3*(3), 203–221.
Rix, J., & Paige-Smith, A. (2008). A different head? Parental agency and early intervention. *Disability and Society, 23*(5), 211–221.
Rofuth, W., & Weiss, H. (1991). Extending health care to AFDC recipients who obtain jobs: Results of a demonstration. *Health and Social Work, 16*(3), 162–169.
Rueveni, U. (1979). *Networking families in crisis.* New York: Human Sciences Press.
Schlosberg, S. B., & Kagan, R. M. (1988). Practice strategies for engaging chronic multiproblem families. *Social Casework, 69,* 3–9.
Shaffer, A., Huston, L., & Egeland, B. (2008). Identification of child maltreatment using prospective and self-report methodologies: A comparison of maltreatment incidence and relation to later psychopathology. *Child Abuse and Neglect, 32*(7), 682–692. doi:10.1016/j.chiabu.2007.09.010
Simons, R. L., Chao, W., Conger, R. D., & Elder, G. H. (2004). Quality of parenting as mediator of the effect of childhood defiance on adolescent friendship choices and delinquency: A growth curve analysis. *Journal of Marriage and Family, 63*(1), 63–79.

Sousa, L. (2005). Building on personal networks when intervening with multi-problem poor families. *Journal of Social Work Practice, 19*(2), 163–179.
Sousa, L., Riberio, C., & Rodrigues, S. (2006a). Are practitioners incorporating a strengths-focused approach when working with multi-problem poor families? *Journal of Community and Applied Social Psychology, 17*(1), 53–66.
Sousa, L., Ribeiro, C., & Rodrigues, S. (2006b). Intervention with multi-problem poor clients: Towards a strength-focused perspective. *Journal of Social Work Practice, 20*(2), 189–204.
Taylor, M. G. (2008). Timing, accumulation, and the black/white disability gap in later life: A test of weathering. *Research on Aging, 30*(2), 226–250.
Thompson, S. J., Pomeroy, E. C, & Gober, K. (2005). Family-based treatment models targeting substance use and high-risk behaviors among adolescents. *Journal of Evidence-Based Social Work, 1*(1–2), 207–223.
Vanderplasschen, W., Rapp, R. C., Wolf, J. R., & Broekaert, E. (2007). The development and implementation of case management for substance use disorders in North America and Europe. *Psychiatry Services, 55*(8), 913–922.
Wadsworth, M. E., Raviv, T., Reinhard, C., Wolff, B., Santiago, C. D, & Einhorn, L. (2008). An indirect effects model of the association between poverty and child functioning: The role of children's poverty-related stress. *Journal of Loss and Trauma: International Perspectives on Stress and Coping, 13*(2–3), 156–185.
Wagner, B. M., Silverman, M. A., & Martin, C. E. (2003) Family factors in youth suicidal behaviors. *American Behavioral Scientist, 46*(9), 1171–1191.
Walton, E., Roby, J., Frandsen, A., & Davidson, R. (2004). Strengthening at-risk families by involving the extended family. *Journal of Family Social Work, 7*(4) 1–21.
Webster-Stratton, C. (1995). Preventing conduct problems in Head Start children: Short-term results of intervention. Paper presented at the Society for Research and Child Development.
Williams, C. C (2012). The epistemology of cultural competence. *Families in Society: The Journal of Contemporary Social Services, 87*(2), 209–220.
Wilson, S. L., Kuebli, J. E., & Hughes, M. H. (2005). Patterns of maternal behavior among neglectful families: Implications of research and intervention. *Child Abuse and Neglect, 29*(9), 985–1001.
Wodarski, J. S., & Feit, M. D. (2011). Adolescent preventive health and Team-Games-Tournaments: Five decades of evidence for an empirically based paradigm. *Journal of Social Work in Public Health, 26*(5), 482–512.
Wodarski, J., & Wodarski, L. (1993). *Curriculums and practical aspects of implementation: Preventive health services for adolescents*. Lanham, MD: University Press of America.
Wood, K. & Geismer, L. (1989). *Family at risk: Treating the multiproblem family*. New Jersey: Human Sciences Press.
Young, N. K., Boles, S. M., & Otero, C. (2007) Parental substance use disorders and child maltreatment: Overlaps, gaps and opportunities. *Child Maltreatment, 12*(2), 137–149.
Zastrow, C. (2007). *The practice of social work: A comprehensive worktext* (8th ed.). Pacific Grove: Thomson Brooks/Cole.
Zuravin, SJ. (1987). Unplanned Pregnancies, Family Planning Problems, and Child Maltreatment. *Family Relations 36*(2), 135–139.

Chapter 10
Comprehensive Treatment Model for Child Maltreatment

Marvin D. Feit

Introduction

Currently various approaches such as psychopathological, sociological, social–situational, family systems, and social learning are used in the treatment of parents who abuse their children.

The *psychopathological model* of child abuse emphasizes direct services (Kim and Cicchetti 2010). The services provided may consist of individual, group and lay treatment, volunteer companions, and self-help groups. These services focus on the psychopathology of the parent and provide him/her with the necessary supports for maintaining the family intact. Treatment goals include helping the parent establish trusting, gratifying relationships with the therapist and with other adults, improving the parent's chronically low self-esteem, enabling the parent to derive pleasure from the child and from his or her own accomplishments, and helping the parent to understand the relationship between his or her own painful childhood and current actions and attitudes toward the child (Swenson et al. 2010).

The *sociological model's* approach to intervention in child abuse emphasizes the need for wide-ranging changes in social values and structures. Klein (2005) states that the prevention of child abuse, according to this model, would require reconceptualization of childhood, of children's rights and of child-rearing. Major sources of stress and frustration, which are felt to trigger child abuse episodes, would need to be eliminated (Kim and Cicchetti 2010). Some of the general suggestions offered by proponents of this model include:

- Providing adequate income through employment and/or guaranteed income maintenance
- Comprehensive health care and social services
- Decent and adequate housing

M. D. Feit (✉)
Norfolk State University, Norfolk, VA, USA
e-mail: mdfeit@nsu.edu

J. S. Wodarski et al. (eds.), *Evidence-Informed Assessment and Practice in Child Welfare*, DOI 10.1007/978-3-319-12045-4_10

- Comprehensive educational opportunities geared toward the realization of each person's potential
- Cultural and recreational facilities

Other proposals that are more specific to child abuse, involve comprehensive family planning programs, family-life education programs, and support services such as day-care and homemaker services.

In the *social–situational model* the approach to treatment is based upon the assumption that the cause of child abuse lies not in the individual, but in the social situation, which may, in turn, by maintaining abusive patterns of behavior (Turner et al. 2010). This model focuses upon the negative attributes of a family's circumstances and the associated risks for the development of child maltreatment. Additionally, this model also works on the development of family and strength and resiliency to mitigate the risk of maltreatment in a community and environmental context (Coles 2008). It emphasizes that there is a high degree of interdependence between the abusive parent and the child and, therefore, both must be involved in treatment. This model advocates the use of techniques to modify the child's behavior such as reinforcement, time out, and verbal reasoning. Programs for parent education and retraining are suggested as a means of modifying the parent's disciplinary methods (Dufour et al. 2011).

The *family system model's* approach to treatment resembles that of the social–situational model in that, it too emphasizes that the underlying structure and organization of the family must change to prevent the recurrence of the same destructive patterns (Swenson et al. 2010). The therapist must work with the family to find new, more attractive roles for all members of the family. The role of the therapist is collaborative, and the parents are respected as the source of the control in the family.

Finally, the *social learning* approach to treatment involves the identification of behavioral goals, specific techniques for achieving these goals, and the use of social reinforcers to facilitate this process. This approach recommends the use of treatment personnel who are of similar socioeconomic and racial background as the abusive parents as it is felt that the parents are more likely to respond positively to these workers.

These approaches are characterized by their focus on only certain elements contributing to child abuse. This singular focus limits the effectiveness of various treatment regimens. This chapter provides the empirical rationale based on behavioral science literature for comprehensive treatment program consisting of child management, marital enrichment, vocational skills enrichment, and interpersonal enrichment components. The chapter concludes with a discussion of the implications of employing such an approach.

Effective Social Work Interventions

Unlike neglect, which is often a readily observable condition, child abuse is most often a private phenomenon. This makes it almost impossible to observe, at least until after the event. Consequently, most child abuse treatment programs are aimed at the amelioration of the correlates of maltreatment, such as parent–child conflict, anger, vulnerability to stress, and social isolation, rather than maltreatment per se. Reflecting the multicausal nature of child abuse and neglect, including substance abuse, mental illness, domestic violence, and child conduct problems, many of the empirically validated interventions that follow consist of multiple components offered simultaneously, to parents, children, and families, in both group and non-group settings (Barth 2009). Additionally, many of the studies contrast two types of interventions (cognitive behavior therapy, CBT, and multisystemic therapy; casework and play therapy; parent training; family therapy, etc.). According to Johnson (2004), an effective means to preventive would begin with educating all children throughout their childhood and continue it through high school about child abuse, but once again, a parental aspect is included throughout this process thus not making it solely child-focused intervention. Furthermore, there are multiple settings and modalities in which these prevention programs can be delivered, such as in hospitals and community health clinics, school-based programs, and parent training (MacMillan et al. 2009). Therefore, the following sections are divided between child-focused interventions. However, overlap and duplication of one or other components has led to some arbitrary allocation based on the predominant component.

Child-Focused Interventions

Concern and some consternation have been expressed at the lack of systemic research on children who have suffered child abuse and neglect (Bjornstad et al. 2010). Kort-Bulter et al. (2011) have argued cogently that there is a large body of literature on the treatment of the general population of those with childhood psychological complaints, which may be very similar to the complaints of those who have been maltreated, and that this expertise should be brought to bear on the needs of the maltreated child. The focus in child abuse treatment has generally been on the parents, with very little research directed toward the development of treatment interventions for children (Fantuzzo et al. 2011). McIntrye and Widom (2010) signify this need through a literature review they did on the effectiveness of certain treatments on identified targets—they reviewed 30 studies and only 17 of the studies were based on child-focused interventions.

Although it is appropriate that parents should be held accountable for child abuse and neglect, and that a significant proportion of societal efforts should be targeted at helping them alter their behavior, there seems to be an unreasonable and unacceptable paucity of research into the treatment needs of their children (Humphreys and Absler 2011).

Even so, there are now a handful of studies, primarily therapeutic day treatment and peer-mediated social skills that provide some preliminary guidance in interventive choice to redress the deficits sustained through maltreatment. In the first of many studies, Miller-Perrin and Portwood (2013) compared 35 maltreated children under age 6 with a matched control group. The treatment group has been in a cognitive development-based, therapeutic day-treatment program for an average of 7.6 months. Posttreatment scores were compared across the groups with significant developmental differences in favor of the treatment. The posttest-only comparison is a relatively weak design to draw firm conclusions about the impact of the program; however, in the second analysis, pre- and post- scores for the treatment group were used and indicated significant gains.

In another study, the perceived competence and social acceptance of a group of 17 maltreated children in day treatment were compared with those of a matched comparison group of 17 other children (Miller-Perrin and Portwood 2013). The study reported significant improvement in perceived competence and social acceptance for the treatment group, as compared to their own pretreatment scores and the scores of the no-treatment group.

According to the McIntyre and Widom study (2010), in the 17 studies that were child-focused interventions, 7 of these evaluated the effectiveness of a single training program offered under standard conditions and 2 studies evaluated the effects of a program with children in different age groups. The studies included boys and girls—12 years old and younger. Training of the children occurred in group and behavioral settings where 25 distinct training conditions were presented. The studies that exclusively targeted children showed significant gains in 20 of these 25 treatment conditions; however, the programs that were considered the most effective were multisystemic and targeted not only children, but also parents and teachers. They concluded that child abuse prevention programs can lead to substantial gains in a child's safety knowledge and skills.

In a study by Mannarino et al. (2012), they evaluated the impact of child and family characteristics in regards to treatment outcomes of sexually abused children. Their study consisted on 49 recently sexually abused children in the age range of 7–14 years that were randomly assigned to either abuse-focused CBT or nondirective supportive therapy. They concluded that therapeutic attention to children's sexual abuse-related ascription and enhancing parental support could be important factors in maximizing treatment outcomes in the noted sample.

Another child-focused intervention examines the role of the occupational therapist in dealing with abused or neglected children with developmental delays (Anderson 2005). Anderson's findings emphasized the specific need to tailor developmental interventions based on the child's emotional and psychological needs. Anderson notes that some occupational therapists might have to sacrifice some performance elements in order to pay special attention to helping children heighten their coping resources.

Barlow and Stewart-Brown (2005) suggest that there is some evidence that shows the potential effectiveness of the prevention of child abuse; however, there is less known about what is effective, once abuse has already occurred. The effectiveness of home visits as it pertains to eliminating abuse in the home seems to be a controversial topic, as some studies find that it prevents the reoccurrence of physical abuse, while other studies indicate that home visits exacerbate physical abuse occurring in the home (Donelan-McCall 2009). According to one study, the effectiveness of home visits by nurses in deterring abuse in the home suggests that home visits did not lessen the frequency of abuse, but actually increased the frequency of abuse; data from hospital records indicated that the children had more abuse-related injuries (Barlow and Stewart-Brown 2005). While this research suggests that home visits are not effective means of preventing further abuse, a study by Hahn et al. (2005) suggests otherwise. In their research, they believe that home visits as a means of intervention is effective, but needs further improvement regarding the effectiveness of home visitor and supervisor training, and implementation. Despite the fact that this intervention is not solely focused on the child because it involves the parents and outside community, it is a rather new research which lends itself to further investigation as a means of reducing the frequency of maltreatment once maltreatment has already been established in the home (Olds 2013).

As is common with many studies of child abuse and neglect, other services were also provided to the parents of these children. While this is socially desirable, it makes for some difficulty in identifying the precise contribution made by individual components of the intervention.

In another series of child-focused studies, Fantuzzo et al. (2011) compared peer and adult social initiation procedures designed to increase positive social behavior in a sample of maltreated children. The sample consisted of 36 preschool children (28 boys and 11 girls) who either had experienced maltreatment (physical abuse or neglect) or were thought to be at high risk of maltreatment. The treatment conditions consisted of peer-initiated social interaction, adult-initiated social interaction, and a control group. Each condition consisted of eight sessions over an approximate 3–4-week period. The peer conditions were significantly more effective in improving positive social behaviors. One other finding from this study is worthy of note. The adult treatment condition was not superior to the control condition; in fact, the oral and motor responses in this condition were lower after the treatment. This suggests that the positive initiation of the adults may have suppressed that of the participants in this condition.

Four withdrawn preschoolers who have been victims of neglect were treated in a study by Fantuzzo et al. (2011). Using a combined reversal and multiple-baseline design, the authors assessed an intervention in which two maltreated children with high levels of prosocial behavior were trained to initiate positive interaction with the withdrawn children. The results indicate an improvement in prosocial behavior in both treatment and generalization settings.

In a study established to replicate these findings, MacMillan et al. (2009) used an alternating treatment design with two withdrawn, nonmaltreated participants, two withdrawn, neglected participants, and three, aggressive, abused participants. Using alternating play sessions with a peer and an adult, during the treatment phase, the peer and adults made programmed social initiations to the child. During the baseline and follow-up phases, no positive initiations were made, but confederates responded strongly to child-initiated play interactions. The neglected children made improvements in the level of their interactions. The aggressive children, however, ultimately showed improved interactions with adults, but showed an increase in noncooperative and hostile behavior with peers.

This latter finding highlights with some specificity the need for prescriptive treatments based on the client's characteristics. These programs also demonstrate some preliminary success in meeting child victim needs in relation to the prosocial behavior, self-concept, and cognitive development. Services to children may also make some contribution to breaking the intergenerational transmission of abuse (Berlin et al. 2011)

Parent-Focused Interventions

Parent Training

The form of interventions for parents appearing most frequently in the empirical literature is parent training. This has been presented in videotaped demonstrations, discussion, modeling, and role playing, and is allied with contingency contracts. Sessions often include information on human development, child management, and problem solving, as well as instruction, modeling and rehearsal, and self-control strategies (relaxation training and use of self-statements). The training is based on a social learning model targeted at problems in child management and child development, and in the literature has often been accompanied by home visits in order to facilitate generalization (Alvarex et al. 2010).

The Centers for Disease Control and Prevention recognizes child maltreatment as a serious public health problem with extensive short- and long-term health effects. In their research brief, prevention activities are examined and Behavioral Parent Training (BPT) and Positive Parenting Program (Triple P) are presented as models that can be used effectively to prevent child maltreatment. Both BPT and Triple P were found to be successful programs that parents can participate in and make a difference in the lives of their children (Sanders and Pidgeon 2011).

An example of a parent training program to prevent child maltreatment can be found in SafeCare, an evidence-based program for at-risk and maltreating parents established in Atlanta, GA. The program addresses the social and family ecology where child maltreatment occurs. Trained service workers are located in participants' homes and communities that focus on skills development in parenting areas such as child health care, safety, hygiene, and psychological risk (Edwards and Lutzker 2008).

Another parent training program, referred to as the Nurturing Parenting Program, was involved in a research study examining the relationship between program dosage and subsequent child maltreatment. The study found that participants who received program dosage more frequently were less likely to have a repeated incidence of child maltreatment. Thus, addressing various contributing aspects to child maltreatment should be coupled with adequate program dosage (Maher et al. 2011).

In a 2010 study, O'Reilly et al. studied 89 federally funded demonstration programs for child abuse and neglect treatment. Although 3253 families were studied, the treatment efforts were not very successful, and up to half of the families may still be at risk for child maltreatment when services ended.

Research by MacMillan et al. (2009) outlined specific areas that offer help to various segments of the society providing parent training. Modern parent training programs are identified, research on effective and humane parenting is presented, and information on what parent training can achieve is also acknowledged. Using tables to illustrate parent training programs and their effectiveness, the authors argue that parental training is socially necessary.

According to Cavaleri et al. (2011), training parents in child management skills is a widely explored application due to the practical application of learning principles. Thus, as the years of research continued, new approaches have developed. These researchers reviewed 11 studies, and reported that the evidence favoring successful intervention to meet the needs of caregivers is abundant for the cognitive behavioral approaches (Cavaleri et al. 2011).

In an early study, O'Reilly et al. (2010) used a combination of parent training and self-control training for two minority families, in both of which the mothers had been charged with child abuse. They were able to demonstrate a reduction in aversive behavior and a corollary increase in prosocial behaviors evident at the 3-month follow-up.

This was further developed by Wolfe and McIssac (2011) who utilized a parent training intervention. One study used parent training and contingency contracting with abusive mothers that showed a reduction in high risk interactions with stability at 3-, 8-, and 12-month follow-ups. In another study, families identified as high risk for abuse, following investigation or suspicion of abuse by a child-welfare agency, received parent training. This was a controlled study in which the first group of families received the treatment and subsequent families were allocated to a waiting list control group. Parent training was provided in 2-h sessions on a weekly basis for 8 weeks. The control group received the standard packages of services normally provided by the child welfare agency. Direct observation of the treatment group indicated improved child management skills. However, measures of child behavior and worker ratings did not indicate any differences, although none of the treated families had been reported or suspected of abuse at the 1-year follow-up.

Some of the outstanding issues in this research—nonrandom assignment, pretest differences, small sample size, and no follow-up comparison group—were addressed in an expanded version of this program (Wolfe and McIssac 2011). Thirty mother–child dyads, who were subject to supervision by a child protection agency, were randomly assigned to one of two conditions: the control group received information from the child protection agency; the treatment group received the same information and behavioral parent training.

Posttreatment, 3-month and 1-year follow-up data were obtained. Results indicated that parent training was associated with reduction in child behavior problems as reported by the mother. Caseworker evaluations at a 1-year follow-up also favored the treatment group. Interestingly, home observations of target behaviors did not confirm the gains reported by mothers or caseworkers. The authors point out that structured observation may provide more relevant and efficient information than unstructured observations of parent–child interactions.

One of the issues of concern in the treatment of child abuse and neglect is the impact of the legal system on therapeutic accessibility. Tanaka et al. (2010) examined the effects of voluntary versus court-mandated participation in a child abuse and neglect treatment program. The treatment for parents consisted of a weekly parent training group and, for the children, a therapeutic day-care program. Based on pre- and post- improvements for each group, scored on an observational checklist, the authors concluded that both groups of parents increased the level of praise directed at the children, reduced their levels of criticism, but continued to attend to their children's annoying behavior. In other words, the court-ordered nature of some of the parents' involvement did not adversely impact their participation.

Swenson et al. (2010) made a comparison of group-based parent training with multisystemic therapy. Multisystemic therapy is based upon the belief that the behavior problems are both multiply determined and multidimensional. As a result, the intervention in the study varied based upon individual family needs and strengths. Family therapy techniques, such as reframing, joining, and tasks aimed at family restructuring, were included in all cases. Many of the families also received parent education, information about appropriate expectations, marital therapy, advocacy services, coaching, and emotional support. This component was delivered in the family home. Forty-three families, from each of which at least one parent had been investigated for abuse or neglect, were randomly assigned to one of the treatment conditions.

Families in both conditions revealed reduced stress, reduced severity of problems, and fewer psychiatric symptoms. Multisystemtic therapy was associated with more effective restructuring of parent–child relations. Parent training was more effective at reducing the number of identified social problems. It is interesting that the setting in which each of these components was delivered appears to have provided some secondary gain. For example, the group treatment condition appears to have been associated with improved social relations, and multisystemic therapy, delivered in the client's home, with greater generalization.

Carr (2009), "presents evidence from meta-analyses, systematic literature reviews and controlled trials for the effectiveness of systemic interventions for families of children and adolescents with various difficulties. In this context, systemic interventions include both family therapy and other family-based approaches such as parent training. The evidence supports the effectiveness of systemic interventions either alone or as part of multimodel programmes for sleep, feeding and attachment problems in infancy; child abuse and neglect; conduct problems (including anxiety, depression, grief, bipolar disorder and suicidality); eating disorders (including anorexia, bulimia and obesity); and somatic problems (including enuresis, encopresis, recurrent abdominal pain, and poorly controlled asthma and diabetes)."

These interventions have demonstrated some efficacy in the remediation of high-risk and aversive behavior, child behavior problems, and criticism, as well as improving child management skills, increasing praise, and increasing prosocial behavior. What is more, many of the changes persisted through the follow-up, and none of the studies reported further incidents of abuse in this period. Training parents in the application of the learning theory-based child management skills is the most widely reported empirical intervention. Building on this, other behavioral and cognitive–behavioral approaches have been applied (Patterson and Chamberlain 2006).

Behavioral and Cognitive–Behavioral Interventions

Tanaka et al. (2010) reported a study with 14 people from a public agency who had "some credible evidence" of physical abuse and 40 people from a private agency who were thought to be at risk of abuse. Subjects were divided into four different treatment conditions and a control group. The control group continued to receive a service from the agencies, but did not receive the treatment interventions, which were cognitive restructuring, relaxation procedures, problem solving, and a composite package consisting of all three interventions. Treatment took place in the client's own home and was provided by doctoral students, all of whom had graduate degrees in social work.

Results indicated that the composite treatment was the most effective in alleviating anger. However, the authors suggest that the relaxation technique might be omitted from the composite package, as individually it was the least effective. This treatment package is very encouraging, because the gains were made in only six sessions.

Another study that tested the efficacy of time-limited, cognitive–behavioral, group-based treatment has been reported (Ingram et al. 2013). Parents who had been referred by the state child protection agency met for eight bi-weekly group sessions led by graduate social work students. A nonequivalent comparison group was recruited from a well-baby clinic; however, this group had some significant pretest differences. The comparison group did not receive the self-control training.

The parents were taught self-control training, consisting of early recognition of cues to provocative situations, identifying the signs of anxiety or anger, abusing and taking deep breaths, employing alternative thoughts and actions, and rewarding their own self-coping behavior. This material was presented in a group format, with the self-control training consisting of several components aimed at increasing the number of calming self-statements. Another component was aimed at identifying and practicing actions that are not compatible with anger, and at relaxation training. One further component consisted of communication training.

Results indicated that social interaction was increased, although this is likely to have been an intended but secondary gain of the group format. Parents' evaluation of their own irritability, nervousness, and calm, as measured by a paper-and-pencil test, showed that the treatment group anger levels declined more than those of the control group, although this is possibly explained by pretreatment differences. Similar differences were noted as measured by performance on role plays of parent–child interactions, with treatment parents demonstrating their ability to remain calm under provocation. However, as Wolfe and McIssac (2011) noted, there is no substitute for in-home, real-life observations.

Kolko et al. (2010) combined monitoring of high-risk behaviors during the course of treatment with a comparison of child and parent CBT and family therapy.

Participants were randomly assigned to one of the two treatment conditions. CBT was provided for both children and parents by separate therapists using similar treatment protocols. Treatment for the children treatment covered stressors and violence, coping and self-control, and interpersonal skills. The parent treatment included stress and the use of physical punishment, attributions, self-control techniques, and behavioral principles. The family therapy conditions emphasized family functioning and relationships, the enhancement of cooperation, motivation, and an understanding of coercive behavior.

In addition to 12-one-hour-per-week clinic sessions, each condition involved home sessions, following one or two clinic sessions. These home sessions provided the opportunity for review and application of the skills and knowledge developed in the clinic sessions.

Participants in this study consisted of 38 physically abused children from age 6 to age 13 and their caregivers. Twenty-nine of the families were referred by child protective services (CPS). Results indicated that the CBT parents and children reported less use of physical discipline during treatment and greater reduction in family problems. In addition, the average length of time until the first use of force of physical discipline was nearly twice as long for the CBT condition.

A study was designed to test the impact of a program to help abused children modify aggressive and increase cooperative behavior (Storer et al. 2012). Measures were taken after each session of a 15-week program. Treatment consisted of both cognitive and behavioral components designed to address self-awareness, empathy, behavior management, and developmental awareness. Weekly group meetings, lasting 2.5 h, in which the parent and child groups met simultaneously, followed by a structured program of activities. Parental activities included learning to praise themselves and their children, learning "time out" as an alternative to physical discipline, stress reduction, and interpersonal skills. Activities for the children varied by age but included art activities, discussion of their fears of being abused, guidelines on how to keep safe, and suggestions for how to ask for help. Points were awarded based an initial increase in aggressive behavior followed by a significant increase in cooperative behaviors.

A study by Hodges et al. (2013) combined treatment for parents with the treatment for children that made a comparison between a focused casework approach and structured play therapy. The theory-driven study used a randomized designed with 38 families in which physical abuse had taken place. Through attrition, this was reduced to only 21 families by completion. Families were randomly assigned to each condition; treatment lasted 6–8 weeks, with three sessions per week for the focused casework group and two sessions per week lasting 2–3 months for the play therapy group. Focused casework was essentially behaviorally oriented, task-centered casework utilizing instruction, reinforcement by the therapist, modeling, confrontation, and problem analysis. The findings showed support for the use of the focused casework approach, which appeared to lessen coercive behaviors and improve positive behaviors.

A study of trauma focused cognitive behavior therapy (TF-CBT) with 82 sexually abused children and their primary caretakers found that those participants receiving TF-CBT showed improvements in anxiety, depression, sexual problems, and dissociation when compared to a group receiving nondirective support (Hodges et al. 2013). The study involved 12 sessions with both primary caretakers and children aged 8–15. Participants were found to show improvement in both 6- and 12-month follow-up.

A 10-year review of empirical research on child sexual abuse by Putnam (2003) found cognitive behavioral therapy to be the most effective with the child and non-offending parent both involved. The study named the parent dysfunctional as a risk factor to child sexual abuse. The review also suggested that prevention programs involving home visitation to assess safety and decrease risk factors are helpful.

A metaanalysis testing the effectiveness of interventions for child maltreatment by Skowron and Reinemann found that the treatment effects were strongest when they were associated with studies focusing on both the attitudes and behaviors of parents. The metaanalysis looked at 21 studies, most of which were multicomponent modalities. The study indicates the need for assessing families and children for multiple forms of victimization, as abuse comorbidity is frequent.

As is common with many studies of child abuse and neglect, these studies suffered from having dissimilar comparison groups and high rates of attrition. However, they offer some promising directions for treatment, being associated with reduction in anger, greater self-control, reduced irritability, reduced coercion, and increased cooperative behaviors. In addition, there was some secondary gain in reduced social isolation, arising from the group format used in certain interventions.

Parent Education

A study by O'Reilly et al. (2010) used a video-based group format to provide parent education. The video tape, *Hugs and Kids: Parenting your Preschooler*, consists of 13 episodes showing common parent-child interaction problems and several options for how to deal with them. Of the alternative endings, one is clearly inappropriate and likely to lead to violence.

Participants in the weekly program were largely clients who had been referred by the court because of abusive, neglectful, or high-risk behavior, or because the child had been removed from the home for some other reason. Results of client response to a videotaped vignette indicated that, compared to a pretest, participants suggested fewer coercive strategies, more positive power responses, and a general reduction in proposed physical punishment. Although the results showed that the parents learned something from the program, this did not measure whether the parents' actual behavior changed.

A study by Chaffin et al. (2011) found that parent education via direct coaching is an effective means of helping abusive parents learn appropriate parenting skills. The study involved 110 abusive parents and utilized parent–child interaction therapy. The program consisted of multiple parent training components including direct coaching of desired behaviors. A decrease in negative parent–child interactions were observed in the groups receiving parent–child interaction therapy over a group assigned to a standard community group.

Ecobehavioral Intervention (Project 12 Ways)

In the treatment of child neglect, several studies from Project 12 Ways, a multifaceted, in-home assessment and treatment services, are worthy of note (Webster-Stratton and Reid 2010). Many of the interventions described to ameliorate neglect are, of necessity, very practical in nature; however, this should in no way detract their contribution to improved well-being for the children involved. For example, in an effort to improve the personal hygiene and cleanliness for two children aged 5 and 9, the authors report the use of a multifaceted intervention (Webster-Stratton 2014). Several treatment phases involving different combinations of treatment (counselor, visits, contingent allowance, laundry assistance) were compared to the normal routine in a single-system design. The phases combined all three strategies produced the highest cleanliness score, assessed by the teacher ratings.

Two studies that improved the home safety and cleanliness of client families utilized a treatment and education program also from Project 12 Ways (Damasek et al. 2011). The study targeted the reduction of hazards, such as poisons, fire electricity, suffocation, and firearms. The program was generally successful in the reduction of serious hazards in the homes of six families. The treatment component in this study consisted of information about hazards and making them inaccessible to children, as well as feedback regarding the number and type of hazards present in the home. An elaboration of this program used iPhones for home safety sessions, rather than the personalized educational component (Jabaley et al. 2011). Using multiple-baseline design across the homes and unannounced follow-up visits, the researchers were able to report zero hazards in each home.

A common feature of child neglect is the inability or unwillingness of parents to provide a clean enough home environment (Kim and Cicchetti 2010). Three families presenting with the problem were assessed using a specifically designed measure, the Checklist for Living Environments to Assess Neglect (CLEAN). In a successful effort to improve the personal hygiene and cleanliness of families who had been adjudicated for child neglect, the authors established multiple baselines using various behavioral techniques, feedback positive reinforcement, and shaping. Following several months of active intervention, the families' home conditions improved.

Application of a multifaceted, ecobehavioral approach to the prevention of child physical abuse has also been reported (Edwards and Lutzker 2008). In-home treatment, consisting of stress reduction, parent training, and behavioral marital counseling, was assessed in a single subject design and determined to be effective in reduction of the mother's migraine headaches and the development of a less coercive environment.

An overall examination of the ecobehavioral services provided by Project 12 Ways looked at the reincidence and recidivism data from a random sample of former clients, compared with a sample of non-project clients (Kim and Cicchetti 2010). Both groups were involved with CPS and had at least one previous incident of child abuse or neglect, or were considered at high risk for such behavior. Results of this study indicated that families who have received services from the project were less likely to be reported for repeat incidents in the 1-year follow-up period. Services offered by the project during this period included parent–child training, stress reduction, self-control, social support, assertiveness training, and other basic skills like health maintenance, home safety, job placement, and marital counseling (Edwards and Lutzker 2008).

A manual for prevention of child maltreatment by Carr (2009) looks at years of research involving over 1500 families at risk for child abuse or neglect. The ecobehavioral model is used with Project 12 Ways as a means for creating safer homes and responding appropriately to child care needs. The manual emphasizes the multifaceted problems of abusive families and the need of interventions addressing a family's social ecology.

Social Network Interventions

In a study by Tanaka et al. (2010), the effectiveness of social network interventions were assessed and found to reduce neglect, increase size and supportiveness of social networks, and improve parenting knowledge and skills. A culturally diverse sample of families from existing CPS case loads, in which neglect had been verified, were randomly assigned to one of two conditions. The control group (36 families) received traditional agency services. The treatment group (52 families) received a multicomponent intervention consisting of: (a) direct network, (b) mutual aid groups, (c) volunteers, (d) the development of relationships with functionally adequate neighbors, and (e) social skills training. The median intervention period was 10 weeks and the range was 2–23 months.

Results indicated that the combination of the social network intervention program and intensive casework, advocacy, and case management was successful at 6- and 12-month follow-up in strengthening informal networks and in improving parenting adequate of low socioeconomic status (SES), neglectful families in both urban and rural settings. The authors stress that although the research had initially posited the use of the program as an alternative to conventional casework, their experience with this program suggested that it would be more appropriately utilized as an adjunct to traditional services.

Summary

The empirical literature on the treatment of physical abuse and neglect consists of several broad types: child-focused interventions aimed at social and cognitive development; parent-focused interventions, primarily behavioral and cognitive–behavioral; social network interventions; a multiservice of multicomponent treatments. However, the current empirical evidence is still preliminary. These studies contained numerous methodological weaknesses, often arising from the sensitivity and difficulty of research in this area. There were considerable variance in terms of characteristics of clients, referral sources, and severity and duration of maltreatment. A major problem with several of the studies was the lack of follow-up to determine the maintenance of any changes made in the treatment phase. The small sample sizes and absence of appropriate controls all contributed to a degree of healthy caution in selecting interventions. Differential dropout rates were also a major problem, as group difference may have been due to differences in the remaining participants rather than in the treatment itself. Unfortunately, but predictably, the existing research seems to indicate that those likely to remain in treatment are the most motivated and the least chronic child abusers (Tanaka et al. 2010).

There are also significant gaps in our knowledge. For example, most of the studies involving parents were aimed at mothers, even though fathers and others are associated with significant numbers of abusive incidents (Chaffin et al. 2011). There were no empirical interventions dealing with macro level or socioeconomic variables, although the multiservice and social network interventions may have something to offer in this regard in the future. Substance abuse and culturally diverse treatments are also noticeably absent. Even the intervention with the most empirical support (parent training) necessitates being able to specify the cause of maltreatment; also, the intervention recipient must be capable of learning the appropriate skills. As an illustration, none of these interventions is clinically tested with the seriously psychiatrically disturbed client. In fact, this was an exclusion criterion in many of the studies.

With the possible exception of parent training, the current state of the empirical literature makes it virtually impossible to determine the precise impact of individual treatment components. In addition, treatment success has been defined differently, often measured by the learning of a particular behavior, skills, or knowledge, rather than its utilization in a real-world setting, or by the assessment of future abuse. In essence, most of these studies identified abuse as the dependent variable, there are no substantial conclusions to be drawn about which treatment eliminated abuse. Progress had undoubtedly been made with behavioral and cognitive-behavioral interventions clearly emerging as the treatment of choice for many child-, parent-, and family-level problems associated with child abuse and neglect.

Rationale for Comprehensive Treatment Program

The long-term effects of abuse may be determined by the general conditions under which the child abuse is raised. Abused children raised outside of their own homes had fewer long-term deficits than those within their homes, and children raised in homes characterized as stable suffered fewer long-term effects than did those raised in less stable homes. The influence of the overall living condition is greater than the influence of the actual abuse itself.

It appears that the behavioral and psychological effects of abuse may be reversible, but unless the environment is improved, either through an effective treatment program or removal of the child to a new home, the abused child will likely develop severe mental and physical health problems (MacMillan et al. 2009). Thus, the effects of child abuse are not only immediately evident, but unfortunately the consequence endured.

Data indicate that parents who abuse their children face multiple social and psychological difficulties. The clearest empirical finding with regard to child abuse seems to be the lack of consistency by the parent or parents in the handling of their children and the consequent lack of effectiveness in managing the child's behavior. It has also been pointed out that another common feature of relationships between abusive parents and their children is unrealistic expectations by the parents about what constitutes an appropriate behavior at each developmental stage, such as when the child can respond to reasonable requests, length of attention-span ability to entertain themselves, and so forth. These data provide support for the position that abusive parents would stand to benefit from specific training in what to expect from their children, in procedures for teaching social skills and tasks to their children, and the appropriate application of child management procedures.

Another empirical finding of substance has been the high degree of marital strain evidence in abusive families (and the interpersonal strain between unmarried adult parents) (Pitman and Buckley 2006). In view of this finding, a comprehensive treatment approach should include appropriate interventions that teach communication skills, problem solving, conflict resolution, and so forth, to marital or unwed partners.

Recent evidence suggests that many parents who abuse their children are dissatisfied with their vocational occupations and their interpersonal relationships with others, i.e., have poor self-concepts, feelings of worthlessness, and so forth (Storer et al. 2012). Additionally, in a metaanalytic study examining the risk factors associated with child maltreatment, it was discovered that there were large effect sizes for parent anger/hyperreactivity, family conflict and family cohesion. Large effect sizes were also found between child neglects parent–child relationship, parent perceives child as a problem, parent's level of stress, parent anger/hyperreactivity, and parent self-esteem (Stith et al. 2009).

It has been suggested that the reason why treatment programs have not produced significant results in treating parents who abuse their children is that they focus on only one of the factors that operate to produce child abuse, i.e., lack of child management skills, marital dissatisfaction, or vocational or interpersonal skills dissatisfaction. It is logical that a treatment approach to abuse must view the problem as multidetermined and services should be structured in such a manner. Previous research conducted by the principal investigator and a number of others suggest that treatment programs that focus on a variety of difficulties would be beneficial in reducing the abuse. Thus, the comprehensive treatment program should consist of the following:

1. Child management program
2. Marital enrichment program
3. Vocational skills enrichment program
4. Interpersonal skills enrichment program

Programs to accomplish the acquisition of requisite skills in each area are chosen from the technology of applied behavioral analysis. Recent reviews of parent-training programs and interpersonal skills training based on behavioral technologies have shown that their effectiveness is substantial as compared to other programs from the behavioral perspective are accumulating.

Behavioral Group Work Approach

Even though recent years have witnessed a growing emphasis on group treatment, relatively a few clients who abuse their children are treated in this manner as compared to those treated individually. The provision of services in group offers the following positive aspects. The group interactional situation more frequently typifies many kinds of daily interactions. Services that facilitate the development of behaviors which enable people to interact in groups are likely to better prepare them for participation in large society; that is, it will help them learn social skills necessary for secure reinforcement (Ingram et al. 2013). From a social learning theory perspective, it is posited that if a behavior is learned in a group context, it is likely to come under the control of a greater number of discriminative stimuli; therefore, greater generalization of the behavior can occur for a broader variety of interactional contexts. There are additional substantial rationales for working with individuals in groups. Groups provide a context, where new behaviors can be tested in a realistic atmosphere. Clients can get immediate peer feedback and support regarding their problem-solving behaviors. They are provided with role models to facilitate the acquisition of requisite social behavior. Groups provide a more valid locus of accurate diagnosis and a more potent means for changing client behavior (Ingram et al. 2013). Additionally, many parents who abuse their children feel guilt, emptiness, social isolation, and a sense of failure, and could benefit from the support derived from the group (Wolfe and McIssac 2011). Finally, the provision of services through groups greatly increases the number of clients who can be served by an effective treatment program.

Treatment Packages

Child Management Program

The child management program is based on Patterson and Chamberlain (2006). The general components that are emphasized include:

1. General introduction to the behaviors that are appropriate for children at different developmental stages. For example, initial language skills, ability to identify objects, ability to carry out requests and so forth.
2. General introduction to how the provisions of certain consequences in term of rewards and punishments can control behavior. For example, verbal praise, eye contact, or verbal reprimands.
3. How to isolate and define a behavior to be changed, such as throwing of objects, increased sibling interaction, and increased verbalization.
4. The use of appropriate consequences to either increase or decrease a behavior such as rewards, punishment, time out, and extinction.
5. Use of stimulus control techniques to influence rates of behaviors, e.g., restructuring physical aspects of the home, or helping parents to see how certain behaviors, such as raising their voices, losing eye contact, praise, facial expressions, and so forth control behavior.
6. Use of simple graphs and tables to chart behavioral change and to show parents the effectiveness of the intervention.

Martial Enrichment Program

The marital enrichment program is based on Wodarski's and Bagarozzi's work on behavioral treatment of marital discord. The general components emphasized include the following:

Problem Identification, Assessment, and Determination of Treatment Procedures In the initial sessions, it is essential for therapists to determine whether the couple's presenting problems are those, which he/she has the expertise to treat. For example, alcoholism, drug abuse, and a variety of sexual dysfunctions in either or both spouses may require referral to agencies which specialize in the treatment of such problem behaviors.

Formalizing the Treatment Process Once it has been determined that behavioral intervention is the appropriate course of action, the therapist outlines the entire treatment process for the couples, so that both spouses will know precisely what will be required by each of them (e.g., keeping charts, graphs, and records, practicing newly acquired behaviors in a variety of settings to facilitate transfer, and completing homework assignments) as well as what role the therapist will play in the treatment process (e.g., teacher, model, and consultant).

Preliminary Training in Communication Training in basic communication skills is often necessary before behavioral contracting can be undertaken successfully. The ability to listen actively and nonjudgmentally, and to make open, direct, and nondefensive statements to one's mate which is not hostile personal attacks, and provides the foundation for the problem-solving process of contingency contracting. Since marital contracting is seen as a structured learning experience that follows a definite sequence, the establishment of a functional communication system is essential if more complex problem solving behaviors are to be mastered.

Locating Relationship Reward Inequities Once open communication has been established, spouses are trained to locate specific areas of their relationship where conflicts have developed over exchange inequities. Spouses are taught to identify how each contributed to maintaining a particular conflict or set or problem behaviors through the use of reciprocally reinforcing coercive interpersonal strategies. Once this is done, treatment goals for each spouse can be formulated in terms of specific observable behaviors, which are to increase, decrease, or acquire in order to reduce exchange inequities and to secure desired behavioral changes in the spouse.

Formulation of Exchange Contracts At this juncture the couple is helped to formulate and implement a contingency contract, which both members consider fair, equitable, and rewarding. In order to facilitate the couple's learning of the contractual process a variety of techniques may be utilized, such as assigned readings, observation of live and filmed models, coaching, shaping through successive approximation, supervised practice using feedback, homework exercises to increase the possibility to transfer, and generalization of newly acquired skills to a variety of environmental setting.

Phasing Out and Building The final phase of the treatment process if concerned with helping each spouse becomes less dependent upon concrete tangible reinforcements and to accept social reinforcements in their place. For example, a spouse who is contingently rewarded for time spent with his or her partner in after-dinner conversation by a specially prepared meal with continue to spend time with the partner in exchange for praise and appreciation. This can be accomplished by pairing social reinforcement for the performance of desired behavioral responses with tangible reinforcements and withdrawing gradually the concrete reinforcers, and increasing the ratios for which a spouse is contingently rewarded with tangible objects.

Follow-Up Evaluation Follow-up evaluations can be undertaken periodically be clinicians in order to determine whether the equitable balance is being maintained and whether the behaviors that both spouses had learned to perform during the course of treatment are skills that are being utilized. This follow-up may take the form of mailed self-report questionnaires, telephone contacts, or home and office visits where the behavioral skills learned by the spouses can be observed and evaluated according to objective criteria.

Vocational Enrichment Program

The vocational program is based on the work of Barlow et al. (2012). The general components emphasized are:

1. Group discussions involving strong motivation for vocational enrichment. These discussions involve mutual assistance among job seekers, development of a supportive buddy system, family support, sharing of job leads, and widening the variety of positions considered.

2. Employment securing aids such as searching wanted ads, role playing interview situation, instruction in telephoning for appointments, procedures for motivating the job seeker, developing appropriate conversational competencies, ability to emphasize strong personal attributes in terms of dress and grooming, and securing transportation for job interviews.

The Social Enrichment Program

This program is based on work of Storer et al. (2011) involving interpersonal skills training and development of assertive behavior for appropriate situations. Specific elements that are emphasized include:

1. Skills on how to introduce oneself in terms of appropriate verbal and nonverbal behaviors.
2. Skills in how to initiate conversations and continue them, i.e., the ability to employ open-ended statements.
3. Skills in giving and receiving compliments, that is developing appropriate verbal and nonverbal competencies.
4. Enhancing appearance in terms of dress, posture, and other relevant behaviors.
5. Skills in asking and refusing reasonable requests.
6. Spontaneous expression of feelings that are appropriate to the contexts.
7. Appropriate use of nonverbal behavior such as posture, gestures, eye contact, touching, interpersonal distance, body language, face, hands, and foot movement, and smiling.

Program Implementation and Evaluation: Selection Criteria

Parents are referred by a network of agencies including the department of human resources, family services, and community mental health centers.

Parents are administered a battery of self-inventories assessing the following:

1. Parental attitudes toward child
2. Martial satisfaction
3. Vocational satisfaction
4. Social satisfaction
5. Family satisfaction

Previous research by Stith et al. (2009) indicates that a score of 30 or above on the Parental Attitude Toward Child Scale, Martial Satisfaction Scale, Social Satisfaction Scale, and Index of Family Relations, provides a criteria for selecting those who should benefit from the service program. A similar criterion is being established for vocational satisfaction. Parents who score above the necessary criteria on three of these measures are asked to participate in the program. If the requirement were imposed that parents had to score above the necessary criterion on all five measures; the procedural difficulties involved in securing the participants for the program might be too costly. However, the data are secured on all five measures to assess whether such stringent criteria can be imposed and how they are related to treatment outcome.

Behavioral observation scales are administered to assess the following parental behaviors directed toward their children: directions and commands, physical contact, praise, positive attention, holding, criticisms, threats, negative attention, and so forth; and to determine the incidence of prosocial, nonsocial, and antisocial behavior exhibited by the children.

Discussion

Despite the recent attention the problem of child abuse has received, there is a lack of well-developed and evaluated treatment programs that can offer concrete assistance to mental health and protective service workers.

To reduce or prevent child abuse, it will be necessary to offer new way of developing behaviors that will bring parents reinforcement. The proposed program combines several means of effectively changing behavior for parents who abuse their children. Each aspect is chosen for the strong empirical base upon which it rests.

This chapter elucidates the relationship between conceptual knowledge, research, evaluation, and possible subsequent alteration of services provided. It has been illustrated how conceptual knowledge can be used in the foundation of a treatment program. Currently, we are implementing a program based on this model. Our data will enable the determination of what aspects of the program are relevant and essential to the capability of the comprehensive program in reducing child abuse.

Additional Resources

Emerging practices in the Prevention of Child Abuse and Neglect
https://www.childwelfare.gov/preventing/programs/whatworks/report/emerginga.cfm

Emerging practices in the Prevention of Child Abuse and Neglect
https://www.childwelfare.gov/preventing/programs/whatworks/report/

Risk and protective factors for Child Abuse and Neglect
http://www.aifs.gov.au/cfca/pubs/factsheets/a143921/

Behavioral Parent Training and Child Maltreatment

The California Evidence Based Clearinghouse for Child Welfare
http://www.cebc4cw.org/topic/parent-training/
Parent Education Programs
https://www.childwelfare.gov/preventing/programs/types/parented.cfm
Positive Parenting Program
http://www.triplep.net/glo-en/home/
Cognitive Behavioral Therapy and Parenting
http://www.nrepp.samhsa.gov/ViewIntervention.aspx?id=213
Child Maltreatment: Prevention Strategies
http://www.cdc.gov/violenceprevention/childmaltreatment/prevention.html
Child Maltreatment is a Public Health Issue
http://vetoviolence.cdc.gov/childmaltreatment/phl/index.html#.VAtNE4BdVIU

References

Alvarez, K. M., Donohue, B., Carpenter, A., Romero, V., Allen, D. N., & Cross, C. (2010). Development and preliminary evaluation of a training method to assist professionals in reporting suspected child maltreatment. *Child Maltreatment, 15*(3), 211–218.

Anderson, T. (2005). Occupational therapy in treating children with development delays who have been abused or neglected: A case study. *Australian Occupational Therapy Journal, 52*(1), 75–77.

Barlow, J., & Stewart-Brown, S. (2005). Child abuse and neglect. *Lancet, 365*(9473), 1750–1752.

Barlow, J., Smailagic, N., Huband, N., Roloff, V., & Bennett, C. (2012). Group-based parent training programmes for improving parental psychosocial health. *The Cochrane Library*. doi: 10.1002/14651858.CD002020.pub3.

Barth, R. P. (2009). Preventing child abuse and neglect with parent training: Evidence and opportunities. *The Future of Children, 19*(2), 95–118.

Berlin, L. J., Appleyard, K., & Dodge, K. A. (2011). Intergenerational continuity in child maltreatment: Mediating mechanisms and implications for prevention. *Child Development, 82*(1), 162–176.

Bjornstad, G. J., Ramchandani, P., Montgomery, P., & Gardner, F. (2010). Child-focused cognitive behavioral therapy for children who have been physically abused. *Cochrane Database of Systematic Reviews, 2,* 1–11.

Carr, A. (2009). The effectiveness of family therapy and systemic interventions for child-focused problems. *Journal of Family Therapy, 31*(1), 3–45.

Cavaleri, M. A., Olin, S. S., Kim, A., Hoagwood, K. E., & Burns, B. J. (2011). Family support in prevention programs for children at risk for emotional/behavioral problems. *Clinical Child and Family Psychology Review, 14*(4), 399–412.

Chaffin, M., Funderburk, B., Bard, D., Valle, L.A., & Gurwitch, R. (2011). A combined motivation and parent-child interaction therapy package reduces child welfare recidivism in a randomized dismantling field trial. *Journal of Consulting and Clinical Psychology, 79*(1), 84–95.

Coles, L. (2008). Prevention of physical child abuse: concept, evidence, and practice. *Community Practice, 81*(6), 18–22.

Damashek, A., Doughty, D., Ware, L., & Silovsky, J. (2011). Predictors of client engagement and attrition in home-based child maltreatment prevention services. *Child Maltreatment, 16*(1), 9–20.

Donelan-McCall, N., Eckenrode, J., & Olds, D. L. (2009). Home visiting for the prevention of child maltreatment: Lessons learned in the past 20 years. *Pediatric Clinics of North American, 56*(2), 389–403.
Dufour, S., Clement, M., Chamberland, C., & Dubeau, D. (2011). Child abuse in a disciplinary context: A typology of violent family environments. *Journal of Family Violence, 26*(8), 595–606.
Edwards, A., & Lutzker, J. R. (2008). Iterations of the SafeCare model: An evidence-based child maltreatment prevention program. *Behavior Modification, 32*(5), 736–756.
Fantuzzo, J. W., Perlman, S. M., & Dobbins, E. K. (2011). Types and timing of child maltreatment and early school success: A population-based investigation. *Children and Youth Services Review, 33*(8), 1404–1411.
Hahn, R., Mery, J., Bilukha, O., & Briss, P. (2005). Assessing home visiting programs to prevent child abuse: Taking silver and bronze along with gold. *Child Abuse and Neglect, 29*(3), 215–218.
Hodges, M., Godbout, N., Breire, J., Lanktree, C., Gilbert, A., Kletzka, N. T. (2013). Cumulative trauma and symptom complexity in children: A path analysis. *Child Abuse and Neglect, 37*(11), 891–898.
Humphreys, C., & Absler, D. (2011). History repeating: Child protection responses to domestic violence. *Child and Family Social Work, 16*(4), 464–473.
Ingram, S. D., Cash, S. J., Oats, R. G., Simpson, A., & Thompson, R. W. (2013) Development of an evidence-informed in-home family services for families and children at risk of abuse and neglect. *Child and Family Social Work.* doi:10.1111/cfs.12061.
Jabaley, J. J., Lutzker, J. R., Whitaker, D. J., Self-Brown, S. (2011). Using iPhones to enhance and reduce face-to-face home safety sessions within SafeCare: An evidence-based child maltreatment prevention program. *Journal of Family Violence, 26*(5), 377–385.
Johnson, C. (2004). Child sexual abuse. *Lancet, 364*(9432), 462–470.
Kim, J. & Cicchetti, D. (2010). Longitudinal pathways linking child maltreatment, emotion regulation, peer relations, and psychopathology. *Journal of Child Psychology and Psychiatry, 51*(6), 706–716.
Klein, R. C. A. (2005). *Multidisciplinary perspectives of family violence*. New York: Routledge.
Kolko, D. J., Hurlburt, M. S., Zhang, J., Barth, R. P., Leslie, L. K., & Burns, B. J. (2010). Posttraumatic stress symptoms in children and adolescents referred for child welfare investigation: A national sample of in-home and out-of-home care. *Child Maltreatment, 15*(1), 48–63.
Kort-Bulter, L. A., Tyler, K. A., & Melander, L. A. (2011). Childhood maltreatment, parental monitoring, and self-control among homeless young adults: Consequences for negative social outcomes. *Criminal Justice and Behavior, 38*(12), 1244–1264.
MacMillan, H. L., Wathen, C. N., Barlow, J., Fergusson, D. M., Leventhal, J. M., & Taussig, H. N. (2009). Interventions to treat child maltreatment and associated impairments. *The Lancet, 373*(959), 250–266.
Maher, E. J., Marcynszyn, L. A., Corwin, T. W., & Hodnett, R. (2011). Dosage matters: The relationship between participation in the nurturing parenting program for infants, toddlers, and preschoolers and subsequent child maltreatment. *Children and Youth Services Review, 33*(8), 1426–1434.
Mannarino, A. P., Cohen, J. A., Deblinger, E., Runyon, M. K., & Steer, R. A. (2012). Trauma-focused cognitive behavioral therapy for children: Sustained impact of treatment 6 and 12 months later. *Child Maltreatment, 17*(3), 231–241.
McIntyre, J. K., & Widom, C. S. (2010). Childhood victimization and crime victimization. *Journal of Interpersonal Violence, 26*(4), 640–663.
Miller-Perrin, C. L., & Portwood, S. G. (2013). Child maltreatment prevention. In A. McDonald Culp (Ed.), *Child and Family Advocacy* (pp. 51–71) (Issues in Clinical Child Psychology).
Olds, D. L. (2013). Moving toward evidence-based preventive interventions for children and families. *Child Maltreatment, 1,* 165–173.
O'Reilly, R., Wilkes, L., Luck, L., & Jackson, D. (2010). The efficacy of family support and family preservation services on reducing child abuse and neglect: What the literature reveals. *Journal of Child Health Care, 14*(1), 82–94.

Patterson, G. R., & Chamberlain, P. (2006). A functional analysis of resistance during parent training therapy. *Clinical Psychology: Science and Practice, 1*(1), 53–70.

Pittman, J. J., & Buckley, R. R. (2006). Comparing maltreating mothers and fathers in terms of personal distress, interpersonal functioning, and family climate. *Child Abuse and Neglect, 30*(5), 481–496.

Putnam, F. W. (2003). Ten year research update review: Child sexual abuse. *Journal of the American Academy of Child and Adolescent Psychiatry, 42*(3), 269–278.

Sanders, M., & Pidgeon, A. (2011). The role of parenting programmes in the prevention of child maltreatment. *Australian Psychologist, 46*(4), 199–209.

Stith, S. M., Liu, T., Davies, L. C., Boykin, E. L., Alder, M. C., Harris, J. M., Som, A., McPherson, M., & Dees, J. E. (2009). Risk factors in child maltreatment: A meta-analytic review of the literature. *Aggression and Violent Behavior, 14*(1), 13–29.

Storer, H. L., Barkan, S. E., Sherman, E. L., Haggerty, K. P., & Mattos, L. M. (2012). Promoting relationship building and connection: Adapting an evidence-based parenting program for families involved in the child welfare system *Children and Youth Services Review, 34*(9), 1853–1861.

Swenson, C. C., Schaeffer, C. M., Henggeler, S. W., Faldowski, R., & Mayhew, A. M. (2010). Multi-systemic therapy for child abuse and neglect: A randomized effectiveness trial. *Journal of Family Psychology, 24*(4), 497–507.

Tanaka, M., Jamieson, E., Wathen, N., & MacMilan, H. L. (2009). Methodological standards for randomized controlled trials of interventions for preventing recurrence of child physical abuse and neglect. *Child Abuse Review, 19*(1), 21–38.

Turner, H. A., Finkelhor, D., & Ormrod, R. (2010). Child mental health problems as risk factors for victimization. *Child Maltreatment, 15*(2), 132–143.

Webster-Stratton, C. L. (2014). Incredible years parent and child programs for maltreating families. In S. Timmer & A. Urquiza (Eds.), *Child maltreatment: Vol. 3. Evidence-based approaches for the treatment of maltreated children child maltreatment* (pp. 81–104). New York: Springer.

Webster-Stratton, C., & Reid, M. (2010). Adapting the incredible years, an evidence-based parenting programme, for families involved in the child welfare system. *Journal of Children's Services, 5*(1), 25–42.

Wolfe, D. A. & McIssac, C. (2011). Distinguishing between poor/dysfunctional parenting and child emotional maltreatment. *Child Abuse and Neglect, 35*(10), 802–813.

Chapter 11
Child Maltreatment

Michael J. Holosko and Jason Bostur

Introduction

Our understanding of child maltreatment has increased markedly since the radiologist Caffey first noticed a correlation between multiple long bone fractures and subdural hematoma in infants (Bross and Mathews 2013). This was followed by Kempe's contribution, which focused attention on the battered child syndrome in the 1960s (Kempe et al. 2013). Currently, the literature recognizes four major types of maltreatment: physical abuse, physical neglect, emotional maltreatment, and sexual abuse (Tickett et al. 2011).

Child physical abuse and neglect, the twin foci of this chapter are often co-terminal but independent entities with separate, though similar, etiologies and trajectories (Pecora et al. 2012). In reviewing the empirical literature on the treatment of physical abuse and neglect, one should make frequent distinctions between the two, (e.g., physical abuse as event, neglect as condition; physical abuse as commission, neglect as omission). However, the two are dealt with simultaneously here, as many studies have combined both types of maltreatment because of unclear definitions. In addition, physical abuse and neglect are often comorbid manifestations (Stith et al. 2009).

Child maltreatment is a significant problem in the USA. Its significance derives from its prevalence and the serious consequences of maltreatment for individuals, families, neighborhoods, and for societies as a whole. It has been suggested that child abuse is a fundamental sensitive marker of the strength of the social fabric; it denies the worth of children (Pasztor and Thomlison 2011). It is clear that for individuals there are very profound negative sequelae. These include psychologi-

M. J. Holosko (✉)
University of Georgia, Athens, GA, USA
e-mail: mholosko@uga.edu

J. Bostur
University of Tennessee, Knoxville, TN, USA

J. S. Wodarski et al. (eds.), *Evidence-Informed Assessment and Practice in Child Welfare,* DOI 10.1007/978-3-319-12045-4_11

cal, social, academic, and emotional problems and deficits, juvenile and/or criminal behaviors (Ausbrooks et al. 2011; Loftholm et al. 2013; Henggeler 2011)

Taylor et al. (2008) attempted to identify child abuse and neglect in the UK. They found correlations with various types of harm, with low birth weight, continuing health problems, poor school achievement, delinquency, mental health problems, and teenage pregnancy. These problems tend to cluster in socially disadvantaged communities.

In addition to the potent negative impact on the welfare of specific individuals and families, society bears enormous financial costs associated with child abuse and neglect in the USA. The total annual cost of child abuse and neglect in the USA was estimated to be in excess of $ 24 billion in 2001 (Prevent Child Abuse America). The costs include hospitalization, chronic health problems, mental health care, child welfare system, law enforcement, and the judicial system (Fromm 2001). An estimation of financial spending on the child welfare system alone in 1999 was $ 14.4 billion (Lee and Barth 2011). Individuals may face enduring economic consequences into adulthood (Currie and Widom 2010). Childhood abuse victims have lower levels of education, earnings, employment, and fewer assets compared to adults who were not maltreated as children.

Incidence

When the battered child syndrome was first promulgated, it was estimated to be affecting about 300 hospitalized children (Kempe et al. 2013). This proved to be a gross underestimation to the true extent of the problem. Since the 1960s the number of reported victims of all types of maltreatment has steadily increased. By 1984, 1.7 million children were reported as victims, 2.4 million were reported in 1989, and 2.9 million reported in 1993 (Bross and Mathews 2013). Allowing for duplicated counts, an estimated 2.3 million individual children were subjects of report in 1993. Of these, just over 1000 were fatalities related to child maltreatment (Bross and Mathews 2013). Miller-Perrin and Portwood states that 160,000 children suffer severe or life-threatening injuries and between 1000 and 2000 children die as a result of abuse (Miller-Perrin and Portwood 2013). Of these children, 80 % involve children younger than 5 years old. Homicide is the third leading cause of death in children from 5 to 14 years of age and neonatacide (infant murder during the first 24 h of life) accounts for 45 % of child death during the 1st year of life (Miller-Perrin and Portwood 2013). According to the Department of Health and Human Services 3 million referrals concerning the welfare of 5 million children were reported to child protection agencies in 2001. Physical abuse (18.6 %) and neglect (59.2 %) were the most common types of substantiated cases of child maltreatment in 2002 (Brookes and Thornburg 2003).

Based on several national reports approximately 18,000 serious disabilities and 141,000 serious injuries arise annually from maltreatment (Rymph 2012). In 1993, about 24 % of victims suffered from physical abuse and about 48 % from neglect.

The most recent national statistics show that over 900,000 children in 2001 were victims of abuse and neglect; 1300 children died of abuse or neglect (Rymph 2012; Fantuzzo et al. 2007). In relation to age groups of those reported as maltreated, the youngest group, aged birth to 3 years, are more likely than any other age group to be subjected to a recurrence of maltreatment (Fantuzzo et al. 2007).

According to Fantuzzo et al., children from families with the lowest income levels (below $ 15,000) were 22 times more likely to be abused or neglected than children from families with higher incomes (2007); children in a single parent home have over 70 % chance of being victimized than children with both parents in the home (Fantuzzo et al. 2007). Other risk factors have been identified as well.

In the end of September 2006, more than 500,000 children nationwide were considered to be in out-of-home care (Rymph 2012). African American children are more likely than white or Hispanic children to be placed in out-of-home care and "... at each decision point in the child welfare process the disproportionality of African American children grows" (Rymph 2012).

American children have lower rates of adoption than other children—of the 130,000 children free and awaiting adoption, more than one-third are African American (Rymph 2012). For more than 70 years, Congress and more presidents have proposed changes in the child welfare system aimed at improving goals or safety, permanency, and well-being for all children in out-of-home care.

As a case in point, on October 7, 2008, President George W. Bush signed into law H.R. 6893, the Fostering Connections to Success and Increasing Adoptions Act of 2008. Prior to PL 110–351, and dating as far back as the 1935 enactment of the Social Security Act of 1935 (which limited funds for child welfare services under Title V, there have been approximately 20 major federal child welfare policy enactments (Rymph 2012).

While child welfare advocates would endorse federal provisions that address the common good, there is little disagreement that the single group most detrimentally affected by the child welfare system is African American children (Rymph 2012). The plight of these children has not been effectively addressed through consideration of federal law or other regulatory reform (Rymph 2012). Despite the disproportionate rates of entry into the foster care system, slow departure rates, and other well-documented adverse conditions of care, there are no specials provisions for African American children experiencing the child welfare system (Rymph 2012).

Definition of Child Abuse and Neglect

This proliferation of reports is also a function of the malleable definition of the phenomenon. The Child Abuse Prevention and Treatment Act (CAPTA) of 1974, while establishing broad parameters for defining child abuse and neglect, gave autonomy to individual states to articulate their own definitions. Consequently, there is some agreement in extreme cases about what is and what is not child maltreatment. This precision fades, however, with the complexity of cases, in which decisions are not often between optimal parenting and abuse, but between shades of behavior (Lee and Barth 2011).

Abuse has been defined as the degree to which parents may use an inappropriate or aversive strategy to control their child or children; neglect has been defined as the degree to which parents provide little stimulation or structure or fail to provide minimal standards of nurturing and care giving in the crucial area of education, nutrition, supervision, health care, emotional availability, and general safety (Lee and Barth 2011). This definition encapsulates the twin concepts of commission (abuse) and omission (neglect) that often characterize these two phenomena.

Rymph (2012) has suggested that definitions of maltreatment have been developed to meet four interrelated purposes: social policy and planning, legal regulations, research, and case management. Confusion surrounding the definition of maltreatment is in part a function of the variety of competing explanations for its causes. It is generally recognized that maltreatment is multicausal and multiply determined, although there is no such agreement about the relative weight or combination of these multiple contributors (Stith et al. 2009). A recent review identified 46 causal models for child maltreatment (Baumann et al. 2011). The definitional consequences of these competing ontologies for the treatment of physical abuse and neglect are manifold. Selection of treatment is often determined by theoretical subscription or orientation, thus setting the parameters for intervention. In order to minimize these impediments, Gladstone and colleagues have suggested that a prerequisite for the future child protection research agenda is the development of "commonly accepted, sufficiently specific definitions of maltreatment and injury that can be used uniformly in the field" (Gladstone et al.2012).

Research can positively change the child welfare system by "extending and broadening the knowledge of the etiology, effects, and prevention of child maltreatment" (Berrick et al. 2011). Further, it can deepen our understanding of the differential effectiveness of various intervention technologies to maximize the appropriateness and utility of our intervention efforts. Unfortunately, child welfare is often presented in a narrow, piecemeal manner that limits its applicability. Practitioners believe that if groups/agencies work together, multiple systems that are involved with the same family can minimize duplication of efforts, effectively identify and provide appropriate services, minimize blaming of the non-offending parent, hold batterers accountable, and advocate on behalf of all family members (Banks et al. 2008; Curtis and Derby 2011). Moreover, Leichtman (2008) believes that residential treatment services require that a community of "treaters" comprised chiefly of childcare workers assume a combination of parental and therapeutic roles. Cunningham et al. (2009) believe that residential treatment facilities organize into three interrelated domains: client attitudes, client-provider affective relationship, and client behavioral contributions toward treatment objectives. They believe that future research needs to be done to improve the understanding of the dynamics of these relationships.

This chapter attempts to formulate a comprehensive assessment of the effectiveness of child welfare services. First, factors that would put a family at risk of child welfare service intervention are examined. Then various levels of service intervention, including family preservation, foster care, group care, and residential treatment, are analyzed. Because they are arguably the fastest growing population with the greatest needs, neglected and abused children whose family backgrounds involve multiple problem situations are focused on as the yardstick for judging program effectiveness. Finally, conclusions are drawn and research and practice recommendations are given.

Putting Children at Risk

Numerous variables have been considered in child abuse and neglect research in an attempt to determine risk factors for child maltreatment. Child maltreatment is now widely accepted as multiply determined (Stith et al. 2009). Dodge (2005) reports that risk factors for child abuse accumulate and paths to child abuse are divergent. "One abusive parent may follow a path from childhood victimization to current marital violence to the abuse of child, whereas another parent may begin the course by being a single, teenage, socially isolated parent." Dodge (2005) further states, "… evidence has shown that the more risk factors a family has, the greater the likelihood of committing or experiencing child abuse."

Ouyang et al. (2008) found that there was a high correlation between ADHD and other inattentive symptoms with child abuse. This factor has to be taken into consideration when creating an intervention plan for children of abuse. Holt et al. (2008) discuss that children living with domestic violence are at increased risk of experiencing emotional, physical, and sexual abuse, and developing emotional and behavioral problems and that the impact of the event can affect them even after measures have been taken to help the child.

A meta-analytic review of the literature suggests risk factors for physical abuse and risk factors for neglect may be very different (Stith et al. 2009). There are five risk factors for physical abuse, which have been commonly identified in the research literature. The five to be considered based on significant research are history of abuse, depression, socioeconomic status (SES), social isolation, and substance abuse. Below, each of these risk factors will be highlighted to examine how they may contribute to the need for child welfare service interventions.

History of Childhood Abuse

Bugental et al. (2010) stated, "Of all the casual factors of maltreatment identified in the literature, the childhood abuse of the parent is perhaps the factor most consistently cited." Stith et al. (2009) found that significantly more abusive families reported that they had been abused as children (46 %) than did non-abusive families (6 %). Lindo et al. (2012) indicated similar significant results in a later study. An overall comparison between a group of abusing families receiving services and a control group of non-abusing families indicated that a significantly greater percentage of the abusing families had a genealogical history of abuse than did the controls (Mullins et al. 2012).

A study that compared pregnant low-income women with a history of childhood abuse to those with no history of abuse found that women who had reported being abused as children has more tendency toward aggressive behavior than those who had not reported childhood abuse (Rafferty and Griffin 2010).

Robboy and Anderson (2011) conducted a study of the intergenerational transmission of harsh parenting by grandparents and both self- and adolescent-report measures of mothers' harsh parenting.

Rodriguez and Tucker (2011) identified variables that distinguish mothers who were abused as children, but did not abuse their own children, from those who were abused as children and did abuse their own children. They found significantly more mothers had broken the cycle by not abusing their own children and reported having a supportive relationship with some adult during their childhood and having gone to therapy (Pecora et al. 2012).

In an important review and critique of intergenerational transmission of abuse, Robboy and Anderson (2011) estimated the rate of intergenerational transmission to be approximately 30 % (give or take 5 %), far lower than other estimates in the scholarly literature or the popular press. In acknowledging yet de-emphasizing the intergenerational link, they concluded, "Undoubtedly, a history of abuse is a considerable risk factor associated with the etiology of child maltreatment, but the pathway to abusive parenting is far from inevitable or direct."

Carter (2005) reports that child abuse and domestic violence often occur in the same families and are highly associated with similar risk factors. Additional literature exists on the association of child abuse and domestic violence, particularly citing the combined effects of child abuse and exposure to domestic violence on children (Dong 2004; Herrenkohl et al. 2008; Sousa et al. 2011). Children's dual exposure to child abuse and domestic violence increases their risk for internalizing and externalizing outcomes in adolescence, such as anxiety, depression, aggressive and delinquent behaviors (Moylan et al. 2010; Sternberg et al. 2006). Chang et al. (2008) found that children were more likely at risk for abuse when there was fighting and abuse between parents. Aside from the increased likelihood of child abuse occurring by the parent who perpetrates domestic violence, children in homes where violence between parents is witnessed by the children are at increased risk to become perpetrators of abuse as adults (Carter 2005). This data further indicates that not only are parents who were abused as children twice as likely to abuse their children, but mothers currently being abused by a spouse are twice as likely to abuse their children than mothers whose husbands do not assault them (Carter 2005).

It seems likely then that being abused as a child or witnessing abuse as a child may put one at greater risk for later being a perpetrator of abuse, but many factors must also be considered.

According to Vig and Kaminer (2002), causes of child maltreatment are complex and stressors of various kinds of interact with family, parent, and child characteristics to increase risk of maltreatment for children with or without disabilities.

Parental substance abuse is a major contributing factor to increasing child welfare caseloads (Freisthler et al. 2006). For almost half of the 8.3 million children living with a substance-abusing parent, alcohol was the substance being abused; an additional 28 % lived with a parent who abused a combination of both alcohol and illicit drugs (Freisthler et al. 2006). Eisengart et al. (2008) found that older youths, girls, and adolescents with substance abuse issues had the highest probability to run away from residential treatment facilities.

Depression

Maternal depression has been linked to child maltreatment in many studies (Windham et al. 2004; Whitson et al. 2011). Research found parental depression significantly more evident among abusive families than among non-abusive families (Loftholm et al. 2013; Henggeler 2011). In a study of abusive and non-abusive families with conduct-disordered children, the abusive mothers had significantly higher scores on the Beck Depression Inventory than the non-abusive mothers (Stith et al. 2009).

Kohl et al. (2011) found moderate depression, but not severe depression, had a significant overall effect on child abuse. Moderately depressed mothers were found to be 1.35 times more likely than non-depressed mothers to display a low level of abusive behavior and 1.57 times more likely to display a high level of abusive behavior.

Household Composition

Family structure, including single parent and large family size, are commonly found to be a significant demographic characteristic of abusive families (Mersky et al. 2009; Sidebotham and Heron 2006). Statistics on child abuse and neglect indicated that 40 % of the cases occurred in single, female-headed families. However, only 19 % of the total number of families in the USA with children under the age of 18 were headed by single females (Rafferty and Griffin 2010; Whitson et al. 2011).

Mustaine et al. (in press) found abuse rates to be higher in counties with large proportions of unmarried mothers. This did not necessarily mean that these women were the perpetrators of the abuse, but could signify the considerable demands on the mothers in these counties and the extent to which these women are available to help others (Wilson et al. 2010). These results were consistent with those of previous studies, which have found a large proportion of single mothers among perpetrators of maltreatment.

Mersky et al. (2009) attempted to determine predictors of abuse by interviewing women registered at a prenatal clinic. When their infants were born, they were followed for reports of abuse for 21–48 months. The predictor "never married" was significantly correlated with abuse. However, the reasons for increased maltreatment in single parent homes were not conclusive.

Stiffman et al. (2002) utilized a case control study including data from the MO Child Fatality Review Panel System to determine if child maltreatment death was related to household composition. Their findings indicated that children living in households with one or more unrelated adult males were eight times more likely to die of maltreatment than children in households with two biological parents. Risk of maltreatment death was also elevated for children residing with step, foster, or adoptive parents and in households with other adult relatives present (Wilson et al. 2010). In addition, risk of maltreatment death was not increased for children living with only one biological parent. Although assumptions regarding increased maternal stress resulting in abuse have historically been made, perhaps single mother households increase risk to children due to the risk factor, "unrelated adult male residing in the home" (Dubowitz et al. 2011). In addition, correlations between single mothers and child maltreatment may be significantly correlated for physical abuse and physical neglect, but this correlation does not appear to exist at the level of maltreatment death (Stith et al. 2009).

Although there has historically been significant data regarding single parent households, specifically mothers, there is insufficient conclusive data regarding single father households as a risk factor for child maltreatment. The literature does not encompass the single father household as a significant population and frequently does not distinguish between mother only households, father only households or single parents who are involved in cohabitating relationships (Dubowitz et al. 2011). Due to the current trend in an aging population, divorce, and remarriage, it would be beneficial to consider the number of additional adults and children residing in the household for whom the parent is also a caregiver. A high correlation between child maltreatment and parental stress related to being a caregiver for both parents and children or an adult household member dependent on others for care may precipitate additional intervention strategies for specific household compositions (Stith et al. 2009; Whitson et al. 2011).

Understanding the risks or benefits of different household compositions and correlations with physical abuse and neglect is essential for effective interventions to occur. Family composition may include one or more grandparents residing in the home in addition to a primary caregiver or as head of household, one or two foster parents, one or two adoptive parents, older sibling or other relative as primary caregiver, or one or both biological parents. In addition, households including one adult as head of household may include a significant other who may be of the same or different gender (Dubowitz et al. 2011). Another household composition factor to be considered is the presence of siblings or unrelated children as potential protectors from harm by perpetrators.

Due to recent research, an increase in household diversity and exclusions imposed on discussion and education by terminology, it would be more accurate to discuss risk factors related to "household composition" rather than "single parenting."

Maternal Age

The literature frequently indicates that abusive mothers are significantly younger than non-abusive mothers (Mersky et al. 2009; Stith et al. 2009). Kohl et al. (2011) found that abusive mothers have their first child at a significantly younger age.

A study investigating the effects of maternal age on the parenting role found that increased maternal age was significantly related to "greater satisfaction with parenting, to greater time commitment to that role, and to more optimal observed behavior" (Platt 2012).

Mersky et al. (2009) found that teenage mothers are at least slightly overrepresented among maltreating mothers as compared with the national population. However, it was also noted that mothers in the early 1920s and 1930s were overrepresented among maltreating mothers, and mothers 45 years of age or older were underrepresented. Maltreatment was found to be more serious (including life threatening or fatal) when inflicted on children whose mothers were teenagers or were 55 years and older (Mersky et al. 2009). However, one must take into account that children 2 years of age and younger predominated among teenage mothers, and children 15–17 years of age predominated among the oldest mothers. These were the age groups to most often suffer serious injuries, impairments or fatalities.

Even though Dubowitz et al. (2011) found teenage mothers to be slightly overrepresented among maltreating mothers, the inclusion of the mother's age as a screening factor for the identification of families at high risk for child maltreatment was not recommended. Rafferty and Griffin (2010) suggests that the overreporting of teenage mothers for maltreatment may lead child-rearing behavior of young mothers to be more closely scrutinized than that of older mothers.

Stith et al.'s (2009) meta-analysis showed parental age had a small relationship to both physical abuse and child neglect. One can see the lack of consensus over the impact of maternal age as a risk factor for abuse. Still, according to past research, it does appear to be a major factor.

Socioeconomic Status

According to Rymph (2012), children from families with income less than $ 15,000 were 3.5 times more likely to experience physical abuse in 1986 than children from families with higher incomes. Many studies have identified income as a significant factor in physical child abuse (Wilson et al. 2010).

Recent research in the Netherlands indicates that there is a correlation between socioeconomic risks, associated with low levels of education, and child maltreatment (Euser et al. 2011).

Bugental et al. (2010) found that of the families whose primary type of maltreatment was physical abuse, 77.4 % experienced financial difficulties. They reported, "The vast majority of fatalities from maltreatment occur among the very poor."

Because the association between SES and maltreatment is so strong, most studies use various methods to control its effects (Sternburg et al. 2006). This is done to separate the unique effects of maltreatment from the effects of low SES. Even with SES controlled in a substantial number of studies, however, low-income groups consistently exhibit more abuse.

Social Isolation

Social isolation is considered one of the problems associated with, and related to, all types of child maltreatment (Dubowitz and Bennett 2007). Research indicates that rates of child abuse are associated with lower levels of community integration, participation in social activities and use of formal or informal community organizations (Gracia and Musitu 2003). Research also found the existence of social isolation as the primary problem in 68.5 % of families with physical abuse (Bugental et al. 2010).

Dubowitz et al. (2011) investigated the characteristics of a neighborhood at low risk of child maltreatment and a neighborhood at high risk of child maltreatment. The two neighborhoods were matched for socioeconomic levels. The high-risk neighborhood was found to have a general pattern of "social impoverishment" in comparison with the low-risk neighborhood.

Several studies have examined the effects of social support on the mother-child relationship. A significant relationship between the social support and security of the infant-mother attachment has been found, particularly where irritable babies were concerned (Costa and Figueiredo 2012). O'Reilly et al. (2010) found an inverse relationship between maternal social support and mother–child stress. They also found social support to be correlated with the amount of stimulation provided in the children's homes. Lack of social support appears to increase the risk of maltreatment, but its exact impact is unclear. It seems likely that the role of social support is related to the amount of stress existing in the family. The risk of maltreatment generally increases when the number and severity of stressors outweigh the amount of support (Sternburg et al. 2006).

Substance Abuse

Recent studies indicate a very strong association between substance abuse and child maltreatment (Costello et al. 2006). According to Freisthler et al. (2006), abusive mothers were more likely to report both an alcohol and a drug abuse history. Mersky et al. (2009) found that abusive families had experienced a significant number of stressful events particularly related to the use of alcohol or drugs within the family.

In 1991, a ten-state survey of public child welfare agencies found that 36.8 % of 305,716 children served were from families in which a member abused alcohol or drugs. Of the 111,927 child welfare cases, 57.4 % involved alcohol or drug use and approximately 32 % of substantial child abuse cases involved alcohol or drug abuse (Stith et al. 2009).

The profound effects of substance abuse on the child welfare system have also been well documented. Personnel shortages, limited availability of foster homes, unwieldy case loads, and lack of efficient and appropriate services are all challenges the overwhelming glut of substance abuse cases have brought to the system (Sternburg et al. 2006). Problems related to substance abuse both lengthen and complicate the investigative process for child protective services agencies. Younger children who are at increased risk for severe or fatal maltreatment often become the focus of child protective services (Ausbrooks et al. 2011). Because of this, older children and adolescents often fail to receive services. This contributed to the massive problems with runaway, homeless youth.

In interviewing 31,000 youths served in youth crisis centers, it is found that 40 % of their cases were caused by their parent's alcohol or substance abuse (Flemons et al. 2010). Parental substance use continues to be a serious issue in the child welfare system. Maltreated children of parents with substance use disorders often have poorer outcomes and stay in the child welfare system longer (U.S. Department of Health and Human Services 2009; Flemons et al. 2010).

Multiproblem Families

Very little data can be obtained about the actual number of multiproblem families. National data is collected on drug abuse, poverty, and crime. Information, however, is not directly calculated totaling the number of serious problems in any given home. Not enough information is known about prevalence and even less information is presented regarding the intensity and nature of malfunctioning within the multiproblem family (Loftholm et al. 2013).

What is known, however, is that combinations of the stressors mentioned above (e.g., social isolation, depression, history of abuse) and others (e.g., unemployment, poor housing, single parenting, mental illness) often lead to violence and abuse in the home. Unfavorable income levels, for instance, increase economic pressure and therefore overall success. These events may lead to greater frustration and negativity for parents, which increases punitive behavior toward children (Dutton 2012). A variety of undesirable family situations evolve within this atmosphere of intense stress. Abusive tendencies, substance abuse, and depression may easily be used as convenient outlets to relieve stress; however, these behaviors tend to further exacerbate the already complex, systemic problems. In 2001, a joint research study matched birth records including a prenatal risk assessment for 839 residents against a database of child abuse and neglect 2 years later. Although this study concluded that risk factors for abuse differed from neglect, mothers of abused or neglected infants combined reported double the number of risk factors than did mothers with no reports of abuse or neglect (Epstein 2001).

Robboy and Anderson (2011) in analyzing transmission of abuse, emphasized interrelating risk factors and compensatory factors. Variables such as high IQ, having a supportive spouse, having physically healthy children, having good social supports and good interpersonal skills, and being financially stable, help to break any possible transmission and to prevent the development of an abusive atmosphere. Meanwhile, at risk factors such as low self-esteem, marital discard, poverty, and isolation bring further stress and possibility for abusive situations to occur.

In various proportions and combinations, environmental, interpersonal, and psychosocial stressors often lead families into crises that precipitate intervention by child welfare agencies. The risk factors delineated above also have an intense impact on the children who are the unfortunate victims of physical, psychological, and emotional abuse and neglect.

The research on the effects of abuse and neglect shows that abused/neglected children exhibit low self-esteem, depression, withdrawal, anxiety, poor social skills, and developmental deficits (Stith et al. 2009). These effects further possible risk factors for intergenerational transmission of abuse (Robboy and Anderson 2011).

These abused and neglected children and their multiproblem families are the consumers that child welfare services are attempting to serve. With this background in mind, we move our discussion into exploring the effectiveness of child welfare program strategies that seek to help.

Effective Social Work Interventions

Unlike neglect, which is often a readily observable condition, child abuse is most often a private phenomenon. This makes it almost impossible to observe, at least until after the event. Consequently, most child abuse treatment programs are aimed at amelioration of the correlates of maltreatment, such as parent–child conflict, anger, vulnerability to stress, and social isolation, rather than maltreatment per se.

Reflecting the multicausal nature of child abuse and neglect, many of the empirically validated interventions that follow consist of multiple components offered simultaneously to parents, children, and families, in both group and non-group settings. Additionally, many of the studies contrast two types of interventions (cognitive behavioral therapy (CBT) and multisystemic therapy, casework and play therapy, parent training and family therapy, etc.). Therefore, the following sections are divided between child-focused interventions, parent-focused interventions, and multiple-component interventions. However, overlap and duplication of one or other components has led to arbitrary allocation based on the predominant component (Reynolds et al. 2009).

CPS Interventions with Modern Views

According to Saint-Jacques et al., the modern view of child protection services implies that to help young people, simply intervening on their behalf is not sufficient. It suggests that involving parents in the assistance process is essential in order to ensure that they are most likely to play their role as parents to their children in the fullest possible way (2006). The social service philosophy in child protection services has changed in recent years—the idea of taking over from parents who are "incapable of taking care of their children" is now considered passé (Saint Jacques et al. 2006). There have been several empirical studies which have demonstrated that the presence and active involvement of parents is essential and that, in most situations, the child's original family remains the environment most conducive to his or her development; any interruption in that relationship having a negative effect on the child (Saint-Jacques et al. 2006; Gladstone et al. 2012).

The idea of parent involvement can be found in different social work perspectives, including ecological, family preservation, network intervention, strengths perspective or empowerment. By focusing on parents' skills and strengths, rather than on their shortcomings, parent involvement is the springboard for a process of empowerment (Saint-Jacques et al. 2006; Huebner et al. 2012).

Practices whose goals are to involve parents within an empowerment perspective must be based on values, knowledge, skills, attitudes, and behavior that are not only adopted by practitioners, but conveyed by the establishment in which they work (Saint-Jacques et al. 2006).

Research has shown that both parents and the child reap benefits from parent involvement. One example can be seen in the case of foster care. Parent involvement decreases the length of time the child is placed and facilitates the child's reintegration into the family unit (Saint-Jacques et al. 2006; Cross et al. 2013). Research asserts that parent involvement is an essential condition for improving parenting skills (Saint-Jacques et al. 2006). Since each family is different, caseworkers may need many different strategies for involving parents (Gladstone et al. 2012).

In relation to CPS involvement, Saint-Jacques et al. state that the main strategies of successful intervention include: initiate contact, introduce oneself, clarify one's role and social service philosophy, and inform parents of the program, inform parents of their rights and responsibilities; encourage parents to visit the residential treatment center and to take the child home for visits during the placement period; let parents know how their child is doing during the placement period; draw up a case plan in collaboration with the parents and encourage them to actively participate in applying it; give parents homework in order to encourage them to take responsibility for the changes that need to be made; telephone regularly to check how they are doing; praise parents for the strategies they use that prove effective; help parents to interpret their situation in a more positive light; share one's personal experiences, emotions or difficulties; take time; offer to arrange transportation for parents if needed; check whether parents are satisfied with the services (Saint-Jacques et al. 2006)

Child-Focused Interventions

Concern and some consternation have been expressed at the lack of research on children who have suffered child abuse and neglect (Pecora et al. 2012). Some research has argued cogently that there is a large body of literature on the treatment of the general population of those with childhood psychological complaints, which may be very similar to the complaints of those who have been maltreated, and that this expertise should be brought to bear on the needs of the maltreated child (Fallon et al. 2010). The focus in child abuse treatment has generally been on the parents, with very little research directed toward the development of treatment interventions for children (Reynolds et al. 2009).

Although it is appropriate that parents should be held accountable for child abuse and neglect and that a significant proportion of societal efforts should be targeted at helping them alter their behavior, there seems to be an unreasonable and unacceptable paucity of research into the treatment needs of their children.

Even so, there are now a handful of studies, primarily therapeutic day treatment and peer-mediated social skills that provide some preliminary guidance in interventive choices to redress the deficits sustained through maltreatment. In one study that compared 35 maltreated children under age 6 with a matched control group, the treatment group had been in a cognitive developmental-based, therapeutic day treatment program for an average of 7.6 months (Mendelsohn et al. 2011). Post-treatment scores were compared across the groups with significant developmental differences in favor of the treatment. The posttest-only comparison is a relatively weak design to draw firm conclusions about the impact of the program; however, in the second analysis, pre- and postscores for the treatment group were used and indicated significant gains.

In another study, the perceived competence and social acceptance of a group of 17 maltreated children in day treatment were compared with those of a matched comparison group of 17 other children (Mendelsohn et al. 2011). The study reported significant improvement in perceived competence and social acceptance for the treatment group, as compared to their own pretreatment scores and the scores of the no-treatment group.

As is common with many studies of child abuse and neglect, other services were also provided to the parents of these children. While this study is socially desirable, it makes for some difficulty in identifying the precise contribution made by individual components of the intervention.

In another series of child-focused studies, Fantuzzo et al. (2007) compared peer and adult social initiation procedures designed to increase positive social behavior in a sample of maltreated children. The sample consisted of 39 preschool children (28 boys and 11 girls) who either had experienced maltreatment (physical abuse or neglect) or were thought to be at high risk of maltreatment. The treatment conditions consisted of a peer-initiated social interaction, adult-initiated social interaction, and a control group. Each condition consisted of eight sessions over an approximate 3–4-week period. The peer condition was significantly more effective in improving positive social behaviors. One other finding of this study is worthy to note. The adult treatment condition was not superior to the control condition; in fact, the oral and motor responses in this condition were lower after treatment. This suggests that the positive initiation of the adults may have suppressed that of the participants in this condition.

Four withdrawn preschoolers who had been victims of neglect were treated in a related study (Fantuzzo et al. 2007). Using a combined reversal and multiple-baseline design, the authors assessed an intervention in which two maltreated children with high levels of prosocial behavior were trained to initiate positive interaction with the withdrawn children. The results indicated an improvement in prosocial behavior in both treatment and generalization settings.

In a study established to replicate these findings, Fantuzzo et al. (2003) used an alternating treatment design with two withdrawn, non-maltreated participants, two withdrawn, neglected participants, and three, aggressive, abused participants. Using alternative play sessions with a peer and an adult, during the treatment phase, the peer and adults made programmed social initiations to the child. During the baseline and follow-up phases, no positive initiations were made, but confederates responded strongly to child-initiated play interactions. The neglected children made improvements in the level of their interactions. The aggressive children, however, ultimately showed improved interactions with adults, but showed an increase in non-cooperative and hostile behavior with peers.

This latter finding highlights with some specificity the need for prescriptive treatments based on client characteristics. These programs also demonstrate some preliminary success in meeting child victim needs in relation to prosocial behavior, self-concept, and cognitive development. Services to children may also make some contribution to breaking the intergenerational transmission of abuse.

Renner and Slack conducted a study to assess the extent to which intimate partner violence and different forms of child maltreatment occur within and across childhood and adulthood for a high-risk group of women (2006). Low-income adult women were interviewed (with the benefit of hindsight) on their experiences with intimate partner violence and child maltreatment in childhood and adulthood. Both intra- and intergenerational relationships between multiple forms of family violence were identified. The outcome of this study favored assessments of those children identified for one form of victimization to determine if other forms of victimization were present; also, interventions should address learned behaviors or beliefs associated with continued or future victimization.

Parent-Focused Interventions

Parent Training

The form of intervention for parents appearing most frequently in the empirical literature is parent training. This has been presented in videotaped demonstrations, discussion, modeling, and role playing and is allied with contingency contracts. Sessions often include information on human development, child management, and self-control strategies (relaxation training and use of self-statements). The training is based on a social learning model targeted at problems in child management and child development, and in the literature has often been accompanied by home visits in order to facilitate generalization.

In an early study, O'Reilly et al. (2009) used a combination of parent training and self-control training with two minority families, in both which the mothers had been charged with child abuse. They were able to demonstrate a reduction in aversive behavior and a corollary increase in prosocial behaviors evident at 3-month follow-up.

This was further developed in three studies by Miller-Perrin and Portwood (2013) which also utilized parent training. The first study used parent training and contingency contracting with three abusive mothers. Using a two-variable withdrawal design, the authors were able to demonstrate a reduction in high-risk interactions, stable at 3-, 8-, and 12-month follow-up. In the second study families who had been identified as at risk for abusive situations, following investigation or suspicion of abuse by a child welfare agency, received parent training. This was a controlled study in which the first group of families received the treatment and subsequent families were allocated to a waiting-list control group. Parent training was provided in 2-h sessions on a weekly basis for 8 weeks. The control group received the standard package of services normally provided by the child welfare agency. Direct observation of the treatment group indicated improved child management skills. However, measures of child behavior and worker ratings did not indicate any differences, although none of the treated families had been reported or suspected of abuse at 1-year follow-up.

Some of the outstanding issues in this research—nonrandom assignment, pretest differences, small sample size, no follow-up comparison group—were addressed in an expanded version of the program (Miller-Perrin and Portwood 2013). Thirty mother-child dyads, who were subject to supervision by a child protection agency, were randomly assigned to one of two conditions: The control group received information from the child protection agency; the treatment group received the same information and behavioral parent training.

Posttreatment, 3-month, and 1-year follow-up data were obtained. Results indicated that parent training was associated with reductions in child behavior problems as reported by the mother. Caseworker evaluations at 1-year follow-up also favored the treatment group. Interestingly, home observations of target behaviors did not confirm the gains reported by mothers or caseworkers. The authors point out that structured observation may provide more relevant and efficient information than unstructured observations of parent–child interactions (Scarborough et al. 2013).

One of the issues of concern in the treatment of child abuse and neglect is the impact of the legal system on therapeutic accessibility. Synder and Anderson (2009) examined the effects of voluntary versus court-mandated participation in a child abuse and neglect treatment program. The treatment for parents consisted of weekly parent training group and, for the children, a therapeutic day care program. Based on pre and post improvements for each group, scored by an observational checklist, the authors concluded that both groups of parents increased the level of praise directed at the children, reduced their level of criticism, but continued to attend to their children's annoying behavior. In other words the court-ordered nature of some of the parents' involvement did not adversely impact their participation.

Mendelsohn et al. (2011) made a comparison of group-based parent training with multisystemic therapy. Multisystemic therapy is based upon the belief that behavior problems are both multiply determined and dimensional (Henggeler 2011). As a result, the intervention in this study varied based upon individual family needs and strengths. Family therapy techniques, such as reframing, joining, and tasks aimed at family restructuring, were included in all cases. Many of the families also received parent education, information about appropriate expectations, marital therapy, advocacy services, coaching, and emotional support (Horwitz et al. 2010).

This component was delivered in the family home. Forty-three families, from each of which at least one parent had been investigated for abuse of neglect, were randomly assigned to one of the treatment conditions.

Families in both conditions revealed reduced stress, reduced severity of problems, and fewer psychiatric symptoms. Multisystemic therapy was associated with more effective restructuring of parent–child relations. (Barth 2009). Parent training was more effective at reducing the number of identified social problems. It is interesting that the setting in which each of these components was delivered appears to have provided some secondary gain. For example, the group treatment condition appears to have been associated with improved social relations, and multisystemic therapy, delivered in the client's home, with greater generalization.

These interventions have demonstrated some efficacy in the remediation of high-risk and aversive behavior, child behavior problems, and criticism, as well as improving child management skills, increasing praise, and increasing prosocial behavior. What is more, many of the changes maintained through to follow-up, and none of the studies reported further incidents of abuse in this period. Training parents in the application of learning theory-based child management skills is the most widely reported empirical intervention (Loftholm et al. 2013). Building on this, other behavioral and cognitive-behavioral approaches have been applied.

In response to risk factors associated with child maltreatment, much of the intervention literature has focused on child behavior management with the central focus on parent training programs include increasing child compliance with parental requests and reducing child behavior problems (Fantuzzo et al. 2007). Recently, developers of these programs have focused on other aspects of parental well-being, including improving parental social skills, expanding social networks and resources for maltreating offenders, and teaching coping skills to reduce the negative impact of daily stressors (Fantuzzo et al. 2007; Barth 2009).

Evaluation of Parenting Interventions

In the evaluation of parenting interventions, there is definitional variation in terms such as "parenting training" or "parenting program," which have been used to describe the wide range or program intensities from brief didactic teaching to long-term comprehensive multifaceted interventions into diverse aspects of a family's life (Russell et al. 2008; Horwitz et al. 2010). It has been found that parents are experiencing a range of other problems such as family disorganization and distrust of child protection services, as well as poverty, physical and/or mental health problems, and/or addictions when child maltreatment is the identified as the primary issue (Russell et al. 2008; Gladstone et al. 2012). Interventions frequently include a range of other services, sometimes referred to as family preservation services or intensive family preservation services (Al et al. 2012; O'Reilly et al. 2010; Reynolds et al. 2009).

According to Russell et al., when families are exposed to different intensities of multiple interventions, evaluation of such service requires a more individualized approach that seeks to understand the components of interventions that parents find beneficial or detrimental (2008).

Behavioral and Cognitive-Behavioral Interventions

Sanders et al. (2004) reported a study with 14 people from a public agency who had "some credible evidence" of physical abuse and 40 people from a private agency who were thought to be at risk of abuse. Clients were divided into four different treatment conditions and a control group. The control group continued to receive service from the agencies, but did not receive the treatment interventions, which were cognitive restructuring, relaxation procedures, problem solving, and a composite package consisting of all three interventions. Treatment took place in the client's own home and was provided by doctoral students, all of whom had graduate degrees in social work.

Results indicated that the composite treatment was the most effective in alleviating anger. However, the authors suggest the relaxation technique might be omitted from the composite package, as individually it was the least effective. This treatment package is very encouraging, because the gains were made in only six sessions.

Another study that tested the efficacy of time-limited, cognitive-behavioral, group-based treatment is reported by Al et al. (2012). Parents who had been referred by the state child protection agency met for eight twice-weekly group sessions led by graduate social work students. A nonequivalent comparison group was recruited from a well-baby clinic; however, this group had some significant pretest difference. The comparison group did not receive the self-control training.

The parents were taught self-control training, consisting of early recognizing of cues to provocative situations, identifying the signs of anxiety and anger, pausing and taking deep breaths, employing alternative thoughts and actions, and rewarding their own self-coping behavior. This material was presented in a group format, with the self-control training consisting of several components aimed at increasing the number of calming self-statements. Another component was aimed at identifying and practicing actions that are not compatible with anger, and at relaxation training. One further component consisted of communication training.

Results indicated that social interaction was increased, although this is likely to have been intended but secondary gain of the group format. Parents' evaluation of their own irritability, nervousness, and calm, as measured by a paper-and-pencil test, showed that the treatment-group anger levels declined more than those of the control group, although this is possibly explained by pretreatment differences. Similar differences were noted as measured by performance on role plays of parent–child interactions, with treatment parents demonstrating their ability to remain calm under provocation. However there is no substitution for in-home, real-life observations (Horwitz et al. 2010).

A recent study combined the monitoring of high-risk behaviors during the course of treatment with a comparison of child and parent CBT and family therapy (Burns et al. 2004). Participants were randomly assigned to one of the two treatment conditions. CBT was provided for both children and parents by separate therapists using similar treatment protocols. Treatment for the children covered stressors and violence coping and self-control, and interpersonal skills. The parent treatment included stress and the use of physical punishment, attributions, self-control techniques, and behavioral principles. The family therapy conditions emphasized family functioning and relationships, the enhancement of cooperation, motivation, and an understanding of coercive behavior.

In addition to 12 one-h-per-week clinic sessions, each condition involved home sessions following every one or two clinic sessions. These home sessions provided the opportunity for review and application of the skills and knowledge developed in the clinic sessions.

Participants in this study consisted of 38 physically abused children from age 6 to 13 and their caregivers. Twenty-nine of the families were referred by CPS. Results indicated that CBT parents and children reported less use of physical discipline during treatment and greater reduction in family problems. In addition, the average length of time until the first use of force or physical discipline was nearly twice as long for the CBT condition (Scarborough et al. 2013).

In a study designed to test the impact of a program to help abused children modify aggressive and increase cooperative behavior reported on a sample of 16 physically abused children between ages 3 and 13 and their parents (Runyon et al. 2004). Measures were taken after each session of the 15-week program. Treatment consisted of both cognitive and behavioral components designed to address self-awareness, empathy, behavior management, and developmental awareness. Weekly group meetings, lasting 2½ h, in which the parent and child groups met simultaneously, followed a structured program of activities. Parental activities included learning to praise themselves and their children, learning time out as an alternative to physical discipline, stress reduction, and interpersonal skills. Activities for the children varied by age but included art activities, discussion of their fears of being abused, guidelines on how to keep safe, and suggestions for how to ask for help. Points were awarded based on the child's level of cooperation and ability to abide by simple group rules. The author reported an initial increase in aggressive behavior followed by a significant increase in cooperative behaviors.

A British study combining treatment for parents with treatment for children made a comparison between a focused casework approach and structured play therapy (Phillips 2010). This theory-driven study used a randomized design with 38 families in which physical abuse had taken place. Through attrition, this was reduced to only 21 families by completion. Families were randomly assigned to each condition; treatment lasted 6–8 weeks, with three sessions per week for the focused casework group and two sessions per week lasting 2–3 months for the play therapy group. Focused casework was essentially behaviorally oriented, task-centered casework utilizing instruction, reinforcement by the therapist, modeling, confrontation, and problem analysis. These findings showed support for the use of the focused casework approach, which appeared to lessen coercive behaviors and improve positive behaviors.

As in common with many studies of child abuse and neglect, these studies suffered from having dissimilar comparison groups and high rates of attrition. However, they offer some promising directions for treatment, being associated with reduction in anger, greater self-control, reduced irritability, reduced coercion, and increased cooperative behaviors. In addition, there was some secondary gain in reduced social isolation, arising from the group format used in certain of the interventions.

Parent Education

A study by Barlow et al. (2012) used a video-based group format to provide parent education. The videotape, Hugs and Kids: Parenting Your Pre-Schooler, consists of 13 episodes showing common parent–child interaction problems and several options for how to deal with them. Of the alternative endings, one is clearly inappropriate and likely to lead to violence.

Participants in this weekly program were largely clients who had been referred by the court because of abusive, neglectful, or high-risk behavior or because the child had been removed from the home for some other reason. Results of client response to a videotaped vignette indicated that, compared to a pretest, participants suggested fewer coercive strategies, more positive power responses, and a general reduction in proposed physical punishment. Although the results show that the parents learned something from the program, this does not measure whether the parents' actual behavior changed.

Ecological, Family-Centered Perspective

The need to provide effective social services for children and their families at high risk for substance abuse problems has been a growing concern at the federal, state, and local community levels according to Ruffolo et al. (2003). New models of human service delivery have surfaced that: (1) Encourage the provision of services that deal holistically with the multiple needs of children and families; (2) Bring multiple agencies together to provide coordinated services; and (3) Develop partnerships between vulnerable families and service providers. The delivery of services to children and families in the social services system has increasingly focused attention on addressing individual (both biological and psychological), family, neighborhood, and broader contextual conditions that produce childhood problems (Ruffolo et al. 2003; Dubowitz et al. 2011).

Ecobehavioral Interventions (Project 12 Ways)

In the treatment of child neglect, several studies from Project 12 Ways, a multifaceted, in-home assessment and treatment service, are worthy of note. Many of the interventions described to ameliorate neglect are, of necessity, very practical in nature; however, this should in no way detract from their contribution to improved well-being for the children involved. For example, in an effort to improve personal hygiene and cleanliness of two children aged 5 and 9, the authors report the use of multifaceted intervention (Henggeler 2011). Several treatment phases involving different combinations of treatment (counselor visits, contingent allowance, laundry assistance) were compared with the normal routine in a single-system design. The phases that combined all three strategies produced the highest cleanliness score, assessed by teacher ratings.

Two studies that improved the home safety and cleanliness of client families utilized a treatment and education program also from Project 12 Ways. The first of these targeted the reduction of hazards, such as poisons, fire, electricity, suffocation, and firearms (Silovsky et al. 2011). The program was generally successful in the reduction of serious hazards in the homes of six families. The treatment component in this study consisted of information about hazards and making them inaccessible to children, as well as feedback regarding the number of type of hazards present in the home. An elaboration of this program used a 35 mm slide presentation, rather than the personalized educational component, as well as stickers, a home safety review manual, safety plates, and electrical tape (Jabaley et al. 2011). Using a multiple-baseline design across the homes and unannounced follow-up visits, the researchers were able to report zero hazards in each home.

A common feature of child neglect is the inability or unwillingness of parents to provide a clean enough home environment. Three families presenting with this problem were assessed using a specifically designed measure, the Checklist for Environments to Assess Neglect (Chaffin et al. 2012). In a successful effort to improve the personal hygiene and cleanliness of the families who had been adjudicated for child neglect, the authors established multiple baselines using various behavioral techniques, feedback positive reinforcement, and shaping. Following "several months of active intervention with each family" (p. 77) conditions in the three homes improved.

Application of a multifaceted, ecobehavioral approach to the prevention of child physical abuse has also been reported (Horwitz et al. 2010). In-home treatment, consisting of stress reduction, parent training, and behavioral marital counseling, was assessed in a single-subject design and determined to be effective in reduction of the mother's migraine headaches and the development of a less coercive environment (Scarborough et al. 2013).

An overall examination of the ecobehavioral services provided by the Project 12 Ways looked at the reincidence and recidivism data from a sample of former clients, compared with a sample of non-Project clients (Mullins et al. 2012). Both groups were involved with CPS and had at least one previous incident of child abuse or neglect, or were considered at high risk for such behavior. Results of this study indicated that families who had received service from the Project were less likely to be reported for repeat incidents in the 1-year follow-up period. Services offered by the Project during this period included "parent–child training, stress reduction, self-control, social support, assertiveness training, basic skills"…"leisure time, health maintenance and nutrition"…"home safety"…"job placement," marital counseling, and alcohol referral (p. 520).

Social Network Interventions

A framework for understanding child maltreatment in terms of complex and interacting factors from the individual to the societal level can aid in conceptualizing and implementing prevention efforts (Loftholm et al. 2013). In order to succeed in preventative measures, it will be necessary to also increase the level of investment placed in both one's family and in one's community (Henggeler 2011). At the level of the individual, the family, the community, the environment, the culture, and the society, are risk factors as well as protective factors which have unlimited possibilities of cross-interaction leading to child maltreatment (Henggeler 2011). Henggeler also states that child maltreatment is an extreme on a continuum, a severe manifestation of dysfunction in the interplay between a child's development and the conditions and relationships that affect development … which … make it difficult to promote social change, and challenge our efforts to devise, conduct, and disseminate research on societal interventions and initiatives.

One study assessed the effectiveness of social network interventions to reduce neglect, to increase the size and supportiveness of informal support networks, and to improve parenting knowledge and skills (Fallon et al. 2010). A culturally diverse sample of families from existing CPS caseloads in which neglect had been verified, were randomly assigned to one of two conditions. The control group (36 families) received traditional agency services. The treatment group (52 families) received a multicomponent intervention consisting of: (a) direct interventions in the family members' existing relationships to improve the family support network, (b) mutual aid groups, (c) volunteers, (d) the development of relationships with "functionally adequate" (p. 105) neighbors, and (e) social skills training. The median intervention period was 10 weeks and the range was 2–23 months.

Results indicated that the combination of the Social Network Intervention Program and intensive casework, advocacy, and case management was successful at 6- and 12-month follow-up in strengthening informal networks and in improving the parenting adequacy of low SES, neglectful families in both urban and rural settings. The authors stress that, although the research had initially posited the use of the program as an alternative to conventional casework, their experience with this program suggested that it would be more appropriately utilized as an adjunct to traditional services.

Children who are physically maltreated are at risk of a range of adverse outcomes in both childhood and adulthood (Jaffee et al. 2007). However, some children who are maltreated manage to function well despite their history of adversity. Jaffee et al. also found that for children who are residing in multiproblem families, personal resources may not be sufficient to promote their adaptive functioning (2007).

Summary

The empirical literature on the treatment of physical abuse and neglect consists of several broad types: child-focused interventions aimed at social and cognitive development; parent-focused interventions; and multiservice or multicomponent treatments. However, the current empirical evidence is still preliminary. These studies contained numerous methodological weaknesses, often arising from the sensitivity and difficulty of research in this area. There was considerable variance in terms of how physical abuse and neglect were reported. This was also true for demographic characteristics of clients, referral sources, and severity and duration of maltreatment. A major problem with several studies was the lack of follow-up to determine the maintenance of any change made in the treatment phase. The small sample size and absence of appropriate controls all contribute to a degree of healthy caution in selecting interventions. Differential dropout rates were also a major problem, as group differences may have been due to differences in the remaining participants rather than in the treatment itself. Unfortunately, but predictably, the extant research seems to indicate that those likely to remain in treatment are the most motivated and the least chronic child abusers (Wilson et al. 2010).

There are also significant gaps in our knowledge. For example, most of the studies involving parents were aimed at mothers, even though fathers and others are associated with significant numbers of abusive incidents (Rypme 2012). Nor were there any empirical interventions dealing with macrolevel or socioeconomic variables, although the multiservice and social network interventions may have something to offer in this regard in the future. Substance abuse and culturally diverse treatments are also noticeably absent. Even the intervention with the most empirical support (parent training) necessitates being able to specify the cause of maltreatment; also, the intervention recipient must be capable of learning the appropriate skills. As an illustration, none of these interventions is clinically tested with seriously psychiatrically disturbed clients. In fact, this was an exclusion criterion in many of the studies.

With the possible exception of parent training, the current state of the empirical literature makes it virtually impossible to determine the precise impact of individual treatment components. In addition, treatment success has been defined differently, often measured by the learning of a particular behavior, skill, or knowledge, rather than its utilization in a real-world setting, or by the assessment of future abuse. In essence, most of these studies focused on corollary outcomes and because none of these studies identified abuse as the dependent variable, there are no substantial conclusions to be drawn about which treatment eliminated abuse. Progress has undoubtedly been made, however, with behavioral and cognitive-behavioral interventions clearly emerging as the treatment of choice for many child, parent, and family-level problems associated with child abuse and neglect.

A closing note: The CPS and other social service agencies are typically not in a position to help or provide sufficient support to preserve the family units. They have been transformed to investigative agencies that respond mostly to cases of imminent danger.

Additional Resources

Guidelines for working traumatized children
http://teacher.scholastic.com/professional/bruceperry/working_children.htm
Social work and Child abuse and Neglect
http://www.socialworkers.org/advocacy/briefing/ChildAbuseBriefingPaper.pdf
Early intervention options for Maltreated Children
http://aspe.hhs.gov/hsp/07/children-cps/litrev/part2.htm
The National Child Traumatic Stress Network
http://www.nctsn.org/trauma-types/physical-abuse
Safety of Subsequent Children
http://www.familiescommission.org.nz/web/safety-subsequent-children/part-four_family-focused-interventions.html
Primary Care interventions to Prevent Child Maltreatment
http://www.uspreventiveservicestaskforce.org/uspstf13/childabuse/childmaltreatfinalrs.htm

References

Al, C. M. W., Stams, G. J., Bek, M. S., Damen, E. M., Asscher, J. J., & van der Laan, P. H. (2012). A meta-analysis of intensive family preservation programs: Placement prevention and improvement of family functioning. *Children and Youth Services Review, 34*(8) 1472–1479.

Ausbrooks, A., Gwin, D., & Brown, J. (2011). Legislative advocacy for and by youth transitioning from foster care: A practice/education collaboration. *Journal of Public Child Welfare, 5*(2–3), 234–250.

Banks, D., Dutch, N., & Wang, K. (2008). Collaborative efforts to improve system response to families who are experiencing child maltreatment and domestic violence. *Journal of Interpersonal Violence, 23*(7), 876–902.

Barlow, J., Smailagic, N., Ferriter, M., Bennett, C., & Jones, H. (2010). Group-based parent-training programmes for improving emotional and behavioral adjustment in children from birth to three years old. *Cochrane Database of Systematic Reviews, 17*(3). CD003680. doi:10.1002/14651858.CD003680.pub2.

Barlow, J., Smailagic, N., Huban, N., Roloff, V., Bennett, C. (2012 Jun 13). Group-based parent training programmes for improving parental psychosocial health. *Cochrane Database Systematic Review.* doi:10.1002/14651858.CD002020.pub3.

Barth, R. P. (2009). Preventing child abuse and neglect with parent training: Evidence and opportunities. *The Future of Children, 19*(2) 95–118.

Baumann, D. J., Grigsby, C., Sheets, J., Reid, G., Graham, J. C., Robinson, D., Holoubek, J., Farris, J., Jeffries, V., & Wang, E. (2011). Concept guided risk assessment: Promoting prediction and understanding. *Children and Youth Services Review, 33*(9), 1648–1657.

Berrick, J., Shauffer, C., & Rodriguez, J. (2011). Recruiting for excellence in foster care: Marrying child welfare research with brand marketing strategies. *Journal of Public Child Welfare, 5*(2–3), 271–281.

Brookes, S. J., & Thornburg, K. R. (2003). The state of child welfare in America: 2003–2004. *Center for Family Policy and Research.*

Bross, D. C., & Mathews, B. (2013). The battered-child syndrome: Changes in the law and child advocacy. *Child Maltreatment, 1,* 39–50.

Bugental, D. B., Ellerson, P. C., Lin, E. K., Rainey, B., Kokotovic, A., & O'Hara, N. (2010). A cognitive approach to child abuse prevention. *Psychology of Violence, 1*(S), 84–106.

Burns, B. J., Phillips, S. D., Wagner, H. R., Barth, R. P., Kolko, D. J., Campbell, Y., & Landsverk, J. (2004). Mental health needs and access to mental health services by youths involve with child welfare: A national survey. *Child and Adolescent Psychiatry, 43*(8), 960–970.

Carter, J. (2005). *Domestic violence, child abuse, and youth violence: Strategies for prevention and early intervention.* San Francisco: Family Violence Prevention Fund.

Chaffin, M., Hecht, D., Bard, D., Silovsky, J. F., & Beasley, W. H. (2012). A statewide trial of the SafeCare home-based services model with parents in child protective services. *Pediatrics, 129*(3), 509–515.

Chang J. J., Theodore A. D., Martin S. L., & Runyan D. K. (2008). Psychological abuse between parents: Associations with child maltreatment from a population-based sample. *Child Abuse and Neglect, 32,* 819–829.

Costa, R., & Figueiredo, B. (2012). Infants' behavioral and physiological profile and mother-infant interaction. *International Journal of Behavioral Development, 36*(3), 205–214.

Costello, E. J., Foley, D. L., & Angold, A. (2006). 10-year research update review: The epidemiology of child and adolescent psychiatric disorders: II developmental epidemiology. *Journal of the American Academy of Child & Adolescent Psychiatry, 45*(1), 8-25.

Cross, T. P., Koh, E., Rolock, N., & Eblen-Manning, J. (2013). Why do children experience multiple placement changes in foster care? Content analysis on reasons for instability. *Journal of Public Child Welfare, 7*(1), 39–58.

Cunningham, W. S., Duffee, D. E., Huany, Y., Steinke, C. M., & Naccarato, T. (2009). On the meaning and measurement of engagement in youth residential treatment centers. *Research on Social Work Practice, 19*(1), 63–76.

Currie, J., & Widom, C. S. (2010). Long-term consequences of child abuse and neglect on adult economic well-being. *Child Maltreatment, 15*(2), 111–120.

Curtis, C., & Denby, R. (2011). African American children in the child welfare system: Requiem or reform. *Journal of Public Child Welfare, 5*(1), 111–137.

Dodge, K. A. (2005). Risk and protection in the perpetration of child abuse. *North Carolina Medical Journal, 66,* 364–366.

Dong, M., Anda, R. F., Felitti, V. J., Dube, S. R., Williamson, D. F., Thompson, T. J., et al. (2004). The interrelatedness of multiple forms of childhood abuse, neglect, and household dysfunction. *Child Abuse and Neglect, 28,* 771–784.

Dubowitz, H., & Bennett, S. (2007). Physical abuse and neglect of children. *Lancet, 369,* 1891–1899.

Dubowitz, H., Kim, J., Black, M. M., Weisbart, C., Semiatin, J., & Magder, L. S. (2011). Identifying children at high risk for a child maltreatment report. *Child Abuse and Neglect, 35*(2), 96–104.

Dutton, Y. E. C. (2012). Butting in vs. being a friend: Cultural differences and similarities in the evaluation of imposed social support. *The Journal of Social Psychology, 152*(4), 493–509.

Eisengart, J., Martinovich, Z., & Lyons, J. (2008). Discharge due to running away from residential treatment: Youth and setting effects. *Residential Treatment for Children and Youth, 24*(4), 327–343.

Epstein, M. (2001). *Perinatal predictors of early child abuse and neglect. Maternal Child & Adolescent Health*. Department of Health and Child Welfare Services. Department of Employment and Social Services. Executive summary: County of Yolo, 4–8.

Euser, E. M., van IJzendoorn, M. H., Prinzie, P., & Bakermans-Kranenburg, M. J. (2011). Elevated child maltreatment rates in immigrant families and the role of socioeconomic differences. *Child Maltreatment, 16*(1), 63–73.

Fallon, B., Trocme, N., Fluke, J., MacLaurin, B., Tonmyr, L., & Yuan, Y. (2010). Methological challenges in measuring child maltreatment. *Child Abuse and Neglect, 34*(1), 70–79.

Fantuzzo, J., Tighe, E., McWayne, C., & Childs, S. (2003). Peer-reviewed papers: Parent involvement in early childhood education and children's peer-play competencies: An examination of multivariate relationships. *NHS Dialog: A Research-to-Practice Journal for the Early Childhood Field, 6*(1), 3–21.

Fantuzzo, J. W., & Fusco, R. A. (2007). Children's direct exposure to types of domestic violence crime: A population-based investigation. *Jounral of Family Violence 22*(7), 543-552.

Flemons, D., Liscio, M., Gordon, A. B., Hibel, J., Gutierrez-Hersh, A., & Rebholz, C. L. (2010). Fostering solutions: Bringing brief-therapy principles and practices to the child welfare system. *Journal of Martial and Family Therapy, 36*(1), 80–95.

Freisthler, B., Merritt, D. H., & LaScala, E. A. (2006). Understanding the ecology of child maltreatment: A review of the literature and directions for future research. *Child Maltreatment, 11*(3), 263–280.

Fromm, S. (2001). *Total estimated cost of child abuse and neglect in the United States*. Chicago: Prevent Child Abuse America

Gladstone, J., Dumbrill, G., Leslie, B., Koster, A., Young, M., & Ismaila, A. (2012). Looking at engagement and outcome from the perspectives of child protection workers and parents. *Children and Youth Services Review, 34*(1), 112–118.

Gracia, E., & Musitu, G. (2003). Social isolation from communities and child maltreatment: A cross-cultural comparison. *Child Abuse and Neglect, 27*(2), 153–168.

Henggeler, S. W. (2011). Efficacy studies to large-scale transport: The development and validation of multisystemic therapy programs. *Annual Review of Clinical Psychology, 7,* 351–381.

Herrenkohl, T. I., Sousa, C., Tajima, E. A., Herrenkohl, R. C., & Moylan, C. A. (2008). Intersection of child abuse and children's exposure to domestic violence. *Trauma, Violence, and Abuse, 9,* 84–89.

Holt, S., Buckley, H., & Whelan S. (2008). The impact of exposure to domestic violence on children and young people: A review of the literature. *Child Abuse and Neglect, 32,* 797–810.

Horwitz, S. M., Chamberlain, P., Landsverk, J., & Mullican, C. (2010). Improving the mental health of children in child welfare through the implementation of evidence-based parenting interventions. *Administration and Policy in Mental Health and Mental Health Services Research, 37*(1–2), 27–39.

Huebner, R. A., Robertson, L., Roberts, C., Brock, A., & Geremia, V. (2012). Family preservation: Cost avoidance and child and family service review outcomes. *Journal of Public Child Welfare, 6*(2), 206–224.

Jabaley, J. J., Lutzker, J. R., Whitaker, D. J., & Self-Brown, S. (2011). Using iphones to enhance and reduce face-to-face home safety sessions within SafeCare: An evidence-based child maltreatment prevention program. *Journal of Family Violence, 26*(5), 377–385.

Jaffee, S. R., Caspi, A., Moffitt, T. E., Polo-Tomas, M., & Taylor, A. (2007). Individual, family, and neighborhood factors distinguish resilient from non-resilient maltreated children: A cumulative stressors model. *Child Abuse and Neglect, 31*(3), 231–253.
Kempe, C. H., Silverman, F. N., Steele, B. F., Droegemueller, W., & Silver, H. K. (2013). The battered-child syndrome. *Child Maltreatment, 1,* 23–38.
Kohl, P. L., Jonson-Reid, M., & Drake, B. (2011). Maternal mental illness and the safety and stability of maltreated children. *Child Abuse and Neglect, 35*(5), 309–318.
Lee, B. R, & Barth, R. P. (2011). Defining group care programs: An index of reporting standards. *Child and Youth Care Forum, 40*(4), 253–266.
Leichtman, M. (2008). The essence of residential treatment: II. Implications for the ideology and structure of treatment teams. *Residential Treatment for Children and Youth, 24*(4), 283–298.
Lindo, N. A., Akay, S., Sullivan, J. M., & Meany-Walen, K. (2012). Child-parent relationship therapy: Exploring parents' perceptions of intervention, process and effectiveness. *International Journal of Humanities and Social Sciences, 2*(1), 51–61.
Loftholm, C. A, Brannstrom, L., Olsson, M., & Hansson, K. (2013). Treatment-as-usual in effectiveness studies: What is it and does it matter? *International Journal of Social Welfare, 22*(1), 25–34.
Mendelsohn, M., Ierman, J. L., Schatzow, E., Kallivayalil, D., Levitan, J., & Coco, M. (2011). *The trauma recovery group: A guide for practitioners.* New York: Guilford Press.
Merksy, J. P., Berger, L. M., Reynolds, A. J., & Gromoske, A. N. (2009). Risk factors for child and adolescent maltreatment: A longitudinal investigation of a cohort of inner-city youth. *Child Maltreatment, 14*(1), 73–88.
Miller-Perrin, C. L., & Portwood, S. G. (2013). Child maltreatment prevention. *Issues in Clinical Child Psychology, 2,* 51–71.
Moylan, C. A., Herrenkohl, T. I., Sousa, C., Tajima, E. A., Herrenkohl, R. C., & Russo, M. J. (2010). The effects of child abuse and exposure to domestic violence on adolescent internalizing and externalizing behavior problems. *Journal of Family Violence, 25,* 53–63.
Mullins, J. L., Cheung, J. R., & Lietz, C. A. (2012). Family preservation services: Incorporating the voice of families into service implementation. *Child and Family Social Work, 17*(3), 256–274.
Mustaine, E. E., Tewksbury, R., Huff-Corzine, L., Corzine, J., & Marshall, H. (in press). Community characteristics and child sexual assault: Social disorganization and age. *Journal of Criminal Justice, 41,* 173–183.
O'Reilly, R., Wilkes, L., Luck, L., & Jackson, D. (2010). The efficacy of family support and family preservation services on reducing child abuse and neglect: What the literature reveals. *Journal of Child Health Care, 14*(1), 82–94.
Ouyang, L., Fang, X., Mercy, J., Perou, R., & Grosse, S. (2008). Attention-deficit/hyperactivity disorder symptoms and child maltreatment: A population-based study. *The Journal of Pediatrics, 153*(6), 851–856.
Pasztor, E., & Thomlison, B. (2011). Challenging messages about advocacy and public relations. *Journal of Public Child Welfare, 5*(2–3), 139–144.
Pecora, P. J., Sanders, D., Wilson, D., English, D., Puckett, A., & Rudlang-Perman, K. (2012). Addressing the common forms of child maltreatment: Evidence-informed interventions and gaps in current knowledge. *Child and Family Social Work, 19*(3), 321–332. doi:10.1111/cfs.12021.
Phillips, R. D. (2010). How firm is our foundation? Current play therapy research. *International Journal of Play Therapy, 19*(1), 13–25.
Platt, D. (2012). Understanding parental engagement with child welfare services: An integrated model. *Child and Family Social Work, 17*(2), 138–148.
Rafferty, Y., & Griffin, K. W. (2010). Parenting behaviours among low-income mothers of preschool age children in the USA: Implications for parenting programmes. *International Journal of Early Years Education, 18*(2), 143–157.
Renner, L. M., & Slack, K. S. (2006). Intimate partner violence and child maltreatment: Understanding intra- and intergenerational connections. *Child Abuse and Neglect, 30*(6), 599–617.
Reynolds, A. J., Mathieson, L. C., & Topitzes, J. W. (2009). Do early childhood interventions prevent child maltreatment? A review research. *Child Maltreatment, 14*(2), 182–206.

Robboy, J., & Anderson, K. G. (2011). Intergenerational child abuse and coping. *Journal of Interpersonal Violence, 26*(17), 3526–3541.
Rodriguez, C. M, & Tucker, M. C. (2011). Behind the cycle of violence, beyond abuse history: A brief report on the association of parental attachment to physical child abuse potential. *Violence and Victims, 26*(2), 246–256.
Ruffolo, M. C., Evans, M. E., & Lukens, E. P. (2003). Primary prevention program for children in the social service system. *Journal of Primary Prevention, 23*(4), 425–450.
Runyon, M. K., Deblinger, E., Ryan, E. E., & Thakkar-Kolar, R. (2004). An overview of child physical abuse: Developing an integrated parent-child cognitive-behavioral treatment approach. *Trauma Violence Abuse, 5*(1), 65–85.
Russell, M., Harris, B., & Gockel, A. (2008). Parenting in poverty: Perspectives of high-risk parents. *Journal of Children and Poverty, 14*(1), 83–98.
Rymph, C. E. (2012). From "Economic Want" to "Family Pathology": Foster family care, the new deal, and the emergence of a public child welfare system. *Journal of Policy History, 24*(1), 7–25.
Saint-Jacques, M. C., Drapeau, S., Lessard, G., & Beaudoin, A. (2006). Parent involvement practices in child protection: A matter of know-how and attitude. *Child and Adolescent Social Work Journal, 23*(2), 196–215.
Sanders, M. R., Pidgeon, A. M., Gravestock, F., Connors, M. D., Brown, S., & Young, R. W. (2004). Des parental attributional retraining and anger management enhance the effects of the triple P-positive parenting program with parents at risk of child maltreatment. *Behavioral Therapy, 35*(3), 513–535.
Scarborough, N., Taylor, B., & Tuttle, A. (2013). Collaborative home-based therapy (CHBT): A culturally responsive model for treating children and adolescents involved in child protective services systems. *Contemporary Family Therapy, 35*(3), 465–477.
Sidebotham, P., & Heron, J. (2006). Child maltreatment in the "children of the nineties": A cohort study of risk factors. *Child Abuse and Neglect, 30,* 497–522.
Silovsky, J. F., Bard, D., Chaffin, M., Hecht, D., Burris, L., Owora, A., Beasley, L., Doughty, D., & Lutzker, J. (2011). Prevention of child maltreatment in high-risk rural families: A randomized clinical trial with child welfare outcomes. *Child and Youth Services Review, 33*(8), 1435–1444.
Snyder, C. M., & Anderson, S. A. (2009). An examination of mandated versus voluntary referral as a determinant of clinical outcome. *Journal of Marital and Family Therapy, 35*(3), 278–292.
Sousa, C., Herrenkohl, T. I., Moylan, C. A., Tajima, E. A., Klika, J. B., Herrenkohl, R. C., & Russon, M. J. (2011). Longitudinal study on the effects of child abuse and children's exposure to domestic violence, parent–child attachment, and anti-social behavior in adolescence. *Journal of Interpersonal Violence, 26*(1), 111–136.
Sternberg, K. J., Baradaran, L. P., Abbot, C. B., Lamb, M. E., & Guterman, E. (2006). Type of violence, age, and gender differences in the effects of family violence on children's behavior problems: A mega-analysis. *Developmental Review, 26,* 89–112.
Stiffman, M. N., Schitzer, P. G., Adam, P., Kruse, R. L., & Ewigman, B. G. (2002). Household composition and risk of fatal child maltreatment. *Pediatrics, 109,* 1–14.
Stith, S. M., Liu, T., Davies, C., Boykin, E. L., Alder, M. C., Harris, J. M., Som, A., McPherson, M., & Dees, J. E. M. (2009). Risk factors in child maltreatment: A meta-analytic review of the literature. *Aggression and Violent Behavior, 14*(1), 13–29.
Taylor, J., Baldwin, N., & Spencer, N. (2008). Predicting child abuse and neglect: Ethical, theoretical and methodological challenges. *Journal of Clinical Nursing, 17,* 1193–1200.
Tickett, P. K., Negriff, S., Ji, J., & Peckins, M. (2011). Child maltreatment and adolescent development. *Journal of Research on Adolescence, 21*(1), 3–20.
U.S. Department of Health and Human Services. (2009). Parental substance abuse and the child welfare system. http://www.childwelfare.gov/pubs/factsheets/parentalsubabuse.cfm. Accessed 21 Dec 2011.
Vig, S., & Kaminer, R. (2002). Maltreatment and developmental disabilities in children. *Journal of Developmental and Physical Disabilities, 14*(4), 371–386.

Whitson, M. A., Martinez, A., Ayala, C., & Kaufman, J. S. (2011). Predictors of parenting and infant outcomes for impoverished adolescent parents. *Journal of Family Social Work, 14,* 284–297.

Wilson, S. R., Norris, A. M., Shi, X., & Rack, J. J. (2010). Comparing physical abused, neglected and non-maltreated children during interactions with their parents: A meta-analysis of observational studies. *Communication Monographs, 77*(4), 540–575.

Windham, A. M., Rosenberg, L., Fuddy, L., McFarlane, E., Sia, C., & Duggan, A. K. (2004). Risk of mother-reported child abuse in the first 3 years of life. *Child Abuse and Neglect, 28*(6), 645–667.

Chapter 12
Parent Training

John S. Wodarski, Mary Stangarone and Jaime Frimpong

Referrals

The social worker must be aware of the indicators of maltreatment and must continually monitor such indicators. There are numerous indicators to look for; child characteristics such as race or children with disabilities, family characteristics including being a single parent or the presence of a nonbiological caregiver, and extrafamilial factors including unemployment or low levels of social support (Mersky et al. 2009). A researcher, Barth, narrowed down the characteristics to four common co-occurring issues; parental substance abuse, parental mental illness, domestic violence, and child conduct problems (2009). Competency in detecting child maltreatment can be tested using a checklist of indicators and practical applications of those indicators. In other words, does the trainer know what to look for, what to overlook, or what to report regarding child maltreatment? Adequate knowledge of these indicators on a written quiz may be one test of competency, but the test must go further than simply measuring the worker's knowledge. The trainer will not ensure an effective program if he or she does not pursue the principles in practice settings. Competency, especially in this area, is hard to judge. A decrease in the number of recurring child maltreatment cases and of recurring maltreatment reports in the community can be used to measure the success or failure of the trainer's ability to detect child maltreatment.

The successful prevention of child maltreatment relies on community referrals. Competency in establishing adequate referral systems can be judged by the following:

Does the trainer have community contacts....

Within the court system?
Within the educational system?
With the Public Health Department?

J. S. Wodarski (✉) · M. Stangarone · J. Frimpong
University of Tennessee, Knoxville, TN, USA
e-mail: jwodarsk@utk.edu

J. S. Wodarski et al. (eds.), *Evidence-Informed Assessment and Practice in Child Welfare*, DOI 10.1007/978-3-319-12045-4_12

With the Department of Family and Children Services?
With other local mental health centers?
With hospitals in the area?
With family planning clinics?
With local drug and alcohol programs?
With day care centers in the area?

If the answer to any of these questions is no, then the trainer must establish such contacts. It becomes evident then that a considerable amount of groundwork must be done before the implementation of any training.

Content Knowledge

Subsequent instructions apply directly to services or training rendered by the community mental health social worker. These instructions are similar to those outlined by Gordon in his book, *Parent Effectiveness Training* (Gordon 2008). Certain steps have been simplified and broken down to increase understanding on the part of the clientele. In addition, a great deal of information has been gathered from the theories of the Triple-P Positive Parenting Approach (Sanders 2008).

In addition to these works, there are other intervention methods that have been repeatedly referenced in literature, including: *Multisystemic Therapy* (Henggeler et al. 2003), *The Incredible Years* (Webster-Stratton and Reid 2010), *Parent-Child Interaction Training* (Eyberg et al. 2001; Eyberg and Robinson 1982), *Parent Management Training* (Mabe et al. 2001), *Behavioral Parent Training* (Pfiffner and Kaiser 2010; Serketich and Dumas 1996), and *Parent Effectiveness Training* (Lemmens 2011; Pinsker and Geoffroy 1981). These are the leading evidence-based training programs for parents (Barth et al. 2005).

The techniques in which a participant may possess competency include the following: reinforcement, punishment, time-out, stimulus control techniques, listening skills, and the application of all of these. First, parents must understand the meaning of reinforcement; what constitutes positive reinforcement, how to use it, when to use it, and how to get results (Cohen 2010). The importance of consistency must be stressed in reference to reinforcement. Methods to test for competency in these areas include written or verbal quizzes, class exercises, class examples, role model examples, and the use of videotapes (Cohen 2010; Webster-Stratton 1994). The ability of the individual to understand and apply these principles in the classroom will be judged by the instructor. Emphasis should be placed on the mastery of skills, instead of passing or failing. To be judged as competent, the participant must (1) make 70 % or above on all of the quizzes; (2) demonstrate mastery of the positive reinforcement techniques in four or more class exercises; (3) attend class regularly; and (4) make a videotape with the child and the trainer-observer in the room, using behavior modification techniques. Four to six sessions should be spent concentrating on reinforcement techniques, because they are critical to an intervention program. In the seventh session, the concept of shaping should be introduced, explained, and demonstrated to the class. Testing for competency with regard to shaping can be accomplished through role-plays with other class members, role-plays with children, written/verbal quizzes, and/or class exercises. Competency can be judged in a manner similar to that explained above. It is important for parents to complete a training program for true success to be established (Sandler et al. 2011).

The technique of punishment is likewise very important to behavior modification. After all have mastered the concept of reinforcement, punishment techniques should be introduced. Parents must be able to sense when and when not to use punishment. The administration of punishment such as timeout should take place in a positive loving environment to be effective. The parents need to stay calm and in control of their emotions while providing their child with reinforcements (Morawska and Sanders 2011). They should understand the dynamics of punishment, as well as be able to differentiate various kinds of punishment for different situations (Shaffer et al. 2013)

Competency can be judged through written/verbal quizzes, group exercises, lists of behaviors that call for the use of punishment, and use of charts to determine how often punishment is used at home (see Tables 12.1 and 12.2). Again, competency will be judged by the trainer according to these criteria: attendance at sessions, 70% or better quiz scores, lists of behaviors turned into the counselor, participation in group discussion and exercises.

Time-out procedures constitute an important aspect of successful behavior modification. Time-out is an effective evidence based practice, with researchers and

Table 12.1 Identify the reinforcer and the behavior that should increase.

Johnny goes to bed on time and he gets a nickel
Susie does all of her homework and she gets to go shopping with mom
For every time that John comes home sober, his wife will have sex with him
Each day that Mary keeps the dishes washed, her husband marks it on the calendar. When she has five marks on the calendar, she gets to go to dinner
Each morning that Billy gets up with dry pants and dry sheets, he gets pancakes for breakfast

Table 12.2 Day(s) of the week when behavior was exhibited

	Times exhibited SMTWThFS	Times exhibited SMTWThFS
Behavior		
Picked up clothes		
Spitting		
Cursing		
Kiss at the door		
Spending time with the children		
Appropriate compliments for tasks accomplished		

parents supporting its success when properly administrated (Morawska and Sanders 2011). Parents must understand the concept of time-out and when to apply it. Competency can be judged through: (1) scores of 70 % or higher; (2) group discussions in which each group member presents a problem for which time out would be the appropriate intervention; 3) making a list of acceptable instances to use time-out; and (4) making a complete list of resources that the parents can use for time out activity. Stimulus control techniques for altering behavior can be reviewed in Chap 4 of text entitled *Behavioral Social Work*. Time out is defined as time away from rewarding incentives, including attention from parents, due to some form of misbehaving (Morawska and Sanders 2011). Time out needs to be consistent and is most effective when it is only used in brief segments where the child is isolated from normal activities (2011).

The last step in instruction and clinical application centers on listening skills. A key element to a successful program is teaching parents to listen to their children. They need to know how to reflect what their child says and identify with the emotions of their children. This will reduce the amount of negative communication within the family (Kaminski et al. 2008). The majority of clients need to learn to listen to their children. They must practice listening to each other before they can listen to their children. The parents participate in group presentations about listening and engaging in two-person exercises. Competency in the area can be judged by: (1) attendance at meetings; (2) successful two-person exercises; (3) participation in at least two group listening exercises; and (4) through an interview with the trainer.

Clients must master these techniques before attempting to change their children's behaviors. In addition, clients may know the principles like the back of their hands, but they will not be able to use them if they are not practiced at home. Practice is vital to the success of the program, and it must be tested and thoroughly monitored.

Cultural Challenges and Difficult Settings

In a 2002 article published in *Journal of Child and Family Studies*, Forehand and Kotchick speak to the different challenges that impede the effectiveness of parent training programs. The authors suggest that many of the parenting interventions include techniques that may not apply to families of diverse ethnic backgrounds. In 2008, researchers found that the ethnicity and social economic status of the trainer were significant predictors of the different aspects of engagement. They suggested addressing these barriers in the first class to allow the participants time to come to terms with the differences, thus leading the parents to be more likely to continue the classes (Dumas et al. 2008). In order to ensure the effectiveness of the program, a thorough assessment of the family must include questions about the parents' existing attitudes and cultural beliefs about parenting. Once sufficient information regarding the family's cultural orientation has been gathered, the practitioner can alter language, reinforcements, and other aspects of the program as necessary to achieve the best results.

When dealing with cultural challenges to effective parent training, it is important to have an understanding of how culture influences parenting practices (Coard et al. 2004). There needs to be a disentanglement of ethnicity, culture and contextual processes of parenting to increase the trainer's understanding of the unique challenges the different aspects bring (Le et al. 2008). Sorkhabi (2005) suggests that parents socialize their children to be competent in their particular cultural group. Thus, the context in which parenting practices occur must be assessed and understood. In addition, parents will instinctively seek to protect their children from the dominant culture's discriminatory views, employing what is known as "racial socialization" strategies to help their children navigate their environment (Ward 2000). These practices must be taken into account when seeking to implement a successful parent-training program.

In addition to these challenges, the practitioner is likely to encounter a possible myriad of other difficulties when seeking to train parents. Researchers have found that only 30–80 % of parents most at risk for child maltreatment actually complete a parenting program (Calam et al. 2008). In a child welfare setting, the main reasons that parent training fails in some populations is due to poor incentives to attend and inadequate program implementation (Aarons et al. 2011; Webster-Stratton 1998). There is an increased need for monitoring and accountability for the private agencies providing parents with training (Barth 2009). Smagner and Sullivan (2005) offer some helpful suggestions for dealing with difficult settings. First, make sure to gain supervisor support and approval. Second, make sure that both the parents and the caseworker are active participants in the program. Third, make sure there are incentives for attending the program. Fourth, make sure that your staff is stable and that safety precautions have been taken into consideration. Finally, make sure to be adaptable to realistic time constraints and other demands.

Implementing the Program

The first step is to be able to correctly define a problem. The client must be able to recognize a problem, and then break it down into observable, measureable behaviors. The problems to be worked on must be real to each family and each family's needs. Competency for defining problems is measured by: (1) input in group discussions about problem behaviors; (2) oral presentation and analysis of a problem; (3) compiled lists of age-specific problems that are common to one or more families and (4) oral or written quizzes. The client must describe at least one problem to the trainer, pass the quizzes (70 % or better), participate in group discussions of problem behaviors, and present one problem behavior to the group. Competency will be judged by the trainer and in group situations by the group members.

The next step is taking ownership of the problem. Parents must be able to recognize and separate their problems from their children's. Competency in this area will be judged on the basis of group participation, role plays, and a quiz (written or oral) and will be determined by the trainer or, when appropriate, by the group.

The final and most important step is the implementation of principles in the home. All of what the parents have learned must be implemented and practiced at home for any success to occur. Competency will be judged by several methods. Each client must describe a real problem behavior at home, define it, own up to it, break it down, decide what to do about it, and then follow through with implementation of the solution. Problems will be presented to the group and the trainer for feedback. Behavioral contracts will be drawn up. Charts on children's behaviors will be maintained. Where possible, videotapes of parents interacting with their children should be made. Children will come to class at designated meetings so parents can practice programs within sight of the group and the trainer. Finally, the trainer will make home visits to each of the houses to observe parents in action and to provide feedback necessary to correctly implement the techniques.

Competency in the most vital areas will be judged by the instructor and the group and will include the following: (1) The client must describe at least one problem to the class, define it and present a treatment plan. (2) Behavior contracts will be written and signed by parent and child (if the child is over 7); progress or changes will be brought up before the group and the trainer. (3) Behavior charts marking increases or decreases in behaviors and the type of intervention must be presented and approved by the group and the trainer. (4) One videotape (to be reviewed by the trainer) of a successful intervention between the parent and child will be presented to the trainer. (5) Children must attend three classes; parents will be observed by the trainer while interacting with the children. (6) There must be at least three successful home visits. Success is defined as observing at least one appropriate interaction and implementation of one or more behavior modification techniques. Also, target behaviors are altered as a result of the intervention.

Outline of Each Program Session

Presession I

The success of the program is often judged through home visits. One visit should take place before the training begins, if possible, to provide baseline data. The trainer then has an idea of the baseline activity of the trainee, as well as the existing parental structure and discipline procedures. These visits are strongly urged but not totally necessary.

Session I

The first session must be an informal, information sharing, trust-building session. Many of the clients may have been forced, or strongly encouraged to participate in the group. In any event, almost everyone will be feeling anxious, perhaps threatened, reluctant, and/or angry that they have to be there. The trainer must not rush the training. There must be genuine effort and participation from the parents for this program to work. Therefore, it is extremely necessary for the trainees to feel at ease and accepted. The trainer should spend some time at the beginning of the session just chatting with the group, perhaps providing coffee and/or iced tea and baked goods to stimulate interaction. The following should be included in the first session:

1. Praise or thanks for coming to the meeting.
2. Introduction of the trainer in a personal, straightforward manner.
3. Introduction of parents and encouragement of interaction between them in loosely structured, nonthreatening ways.
4. A successful or positive experience for each couple during the first night is very important-whether the parents are voluntary or involuntary clients.
5. Discussion of children with regard to problems, appropriate behaviors at developmental stages, past histories and so on.
6. Late in the meetings- a basic outline of the course, with reference to the clients as student or trainees.
7. Talk about any transportation problems, the need for any changes in time or dates of meetings, problems with childcare during meetings (the worker can facilitate a joint sitter for the families or a child care service).
8. Discussion of fees, with an explanation of the sliding fee scale, including its purpose as well as problems associated with it.
9. A phone number for emergencies with encouragement to use it.
10. If rewards are to be given to parents, the reward system can be determined by finding out what will be appreciated or appropriate for each client (examples are course credit, money, prizes at the end, or a certificate).

Most important, the trainer must become established as a friend to participants to facilitate open lines of communication. Make sure they leave feeling good about themselves, the trainer, and the program.

A test to judge competency in this area would be to include a checklist to determine if the trainer followed all of these suggestions. The trainer may be rated by an observer to determine competency, or rated by the group. Roll taken the second session could indicate how successful the instructor was during the first meeting.

Session II

In the second session the trainer needs to begin introducing basic behavior modification principles. The key word here is simplicity. The principles must be broken down into very small, simplistic terms. The steps should be broken into easily attainable goals and presented in plain, simple language.

The first principle to be introduced is reinforcement. This is a vital part of the behavior modification system, and it must be understood thoroughly for any success to be realized in the training. The trainees must understand what reinforcement is, how it works, and when and how to use it. The trainer should gather clients around a table and talk facing all of them in a casual manner. The trainees should be able to face each other and feel comfortable talking to each other. The trainees should be provided with paper and pencils, and a blackboard may be helpful as well. The instructor should explain reinforcement verbally to the group, using the blackboard for diagrams and examples.

The following is an example of a lesson plan for use by the trainer. First, ask the trainees what they think reinforcement is. Get everyone to answer or provide input to the discussion. Then elucidate: reinforcement increases behavior. It makes behavior happen more often. The technical definition states that reinforcement is an event that happens just after a behavior occurs that increases the chances of that behavior happening again. Stress that the key point is reinforcement, which makes behavior more likely to happen. If the reinforcement does not increase the behavior, then you are not really reinforcing anything. Now stress that reinforcement can be many things. It can be candy, food, attention, money, a kind word, praise, and so on. Ask the group for examples of what would be reinforcing to them. What would make them exhibit a behavior more often? Write the examples on the board and talk about them. Talk about the behaviors that will increase as a result of such reinforcement. Then give these examples, or some similar to these.

1. If Betty gets a piece of candy for completing her homework after supper, she is being reinforced for doing her homework. The candy is the reinforcement. The behavior being increased is completing the homework.
2. If Bobby makes his bed each morning, he gets to play softball with has father from 5 to 6 each evening. The reinforcement is playing ball with his dad. The behavior that is increasing is the bed making.
3. If mom gives Billy a big hug and kiss each day that he comes home from school clean, Billy is being reinforced for coming home clean. The hug and kiss is the reinforcement. The behavior being increased is coming home clean.

Draw the diagrams and discuss. Then have each person identify one behavior to be changed and reinforcement to be used to change it. Go around the room and get individuals to describe the situation they would like to change, and how. You draw the diagrams, or let them draw one for their situation. Discuss each example in terms of the behavior diagram and the reinforcement.

Close the session with a review of the meaning of reinforcement. Set the meeting time for the next session. Get feedback from the group on how they felt about this session. Were you too fast? Too slow? Make it personal.

Session III

Assemble the group around a table with pencils and paper. Spend adequate time talking about the major problems or upsets that have occurred in the past week. Then review the last session (*What is reinforcement?*). Ask for answers from the group. Retrace briefly what happened from the last session. Then draw this diagram on the board:

Suzy completes one household chore (dishes)........................30 min of TV time

Ask what Suzy is being reinforced for doing. Make sure that if a participant does not understand, you go over the example, pointing out both behavior and the reinforcement. Then ask for a problem behavior from the group and diagram it. Ask for examples of reinforcement and when to give the reinforcement. Discuss this. Break into teams of two people. Give each team a problem behavior to be worked out in written or in oral form. Reconvene the group and ask each team to discuss their problem behavior, and reinforcement.

There are a few important points to be made here by the instructor. For reinforcement to be effective, it must be positive. The child or parent must view the reinforcement as something good, an item to work towards. For example: giving Johnny spinach as reinforcement for doing his homework when he does not like it is not likely to increase his homework behavior. Also, different behaviors may require different sizes or values for reinforcement. For example, one cannot offer a piece of candy as a reward for good grades for an entire semester. Moreover, the reinforcement must be consistent. The parents must reinforce the desired behavior each time that it occurs, and as soon as possible. It is hard to reinforce a child for taking out the trash when you just wrecked the car, the baby's diaper is wet, or you feel nauseous-but TRY! Try very hard, especially at first, to be quick and consistent with rewards. The child must be able to count on immediate reinforcement for the child to want to exhibit certain behaviors. If you simply cannot reinforce immediately, explain why and be sure that you follow through with a reward later.

The following is a good exercise for a group of parents. Send one of the participants out of the room. The rest of the group will decide on one behavior they want the absent person to do, then ask the person to return to the room. Explain that you will clap when the person exhibits the behavior that the group has decided they want the participant to do. Alternatively, if the behavior is complex, tell the person that the group will clap when he or she exhibits a behavior that is close to what they want. When the exact behavior occurs, get the group to stand up and clap. The clapping is a positive reinforcement. Be sure to explain that. This exercise encourages parent participation and unites them as a group. Try it two or three times.

Another exercise for teams is conducted as follows. Divide the participants into pairs. Have one of the partners decide on a behavior that he or she wants the other partner to increase. In other words, one person gives the other an M&M or verbal praise whenever the correct behavior is emitted. Give the individual the reward quickly and consistently after the behavior. Then, let the participant guess the behavior that you are trying to increase.

After you try these exercises, again reiterate how important consistency and immediacy of reinforcement can be to success. Spend a few minutes just talking with the group before you let them go. Ask about any problems or needed changes.

Session IV

Open the session as usual, talking about any substantial problems that have come up in the past week. Now is a good time to evaluate the learning that is taking place. Do this by asking the parents if they have noticed any changes that have happened at home. Next, review reinforcement. Ask for a definition and an example from the group. Check this definition and example with the rest of the group, getting as much input as you can. Then, ask for examples of reinforcement that could be used on these behaviors:

1. Good grades in school
2. Making beds
3. Quiet time after supper
4. Saying please and thank you
5. Reduced aggressive behavior

Remind the group that the reinforcement should increase these behaviors. One of the many ways to use positive reinforcement is through a token economy (Doughty and Shields 2009).

Next, the concept of shaping is introduced. For most behaviors, one cannot expect perfection at first. Just as one cannot expect a child to tie his or her shoes perfectly the first time, one must learn to shape the behavior that one wants. If one expects perfection for the first time, it serves to set oneself up for failure and frustration. If, for example, you want to teach a child to make the bed each morning, you may need to reinforce him or her for straightening the sheet first. Then, you may have to reinforce the child for folding the bedspread, and so on until the terminal goal is achieved. Explain all of this to the group. Ask for examples of behaviors that may need to be shaped. Discuss these behaviors. Then, ask the group to participate in this exercise: Start by picking one behavior. Give everyone a pencil and paper to write the behavior down in stepwise fashion. Write the behavior in as small, simple steps as possible, then talk about the steps. Ask everyone to pick a separate behavior and do the same with it. Discuss the behaviors.

Now, quiz the group. Ask them to fill out the quiz in Table 12.1. If the clients cannot read, read the test to them aloud. Have them check the answers or tell you, the trainer, the answers. Discuss the quiz with the group by comparing answers. Accent positive points, right answers, and so forth. Correct wrong answers on the spot.

What are two very important words to remember when you are reinforcing your child?

____and____________________

____

What does reinforcement actually do?

Draw a diagram for this problem: John and his little sister, May, fight all the time. Their mother has about had it with them. Every time they spend one hour together without fighting, she gives them a cookie.

What are certain things that would be reinforcing to you?

1.
2.
3.
4.
5.

What are items that would be reinforcing to your child?

Session V

In this session the concept of negative reinforcement is introduced. Reinforcement does not always have to be positive or desirable. Although positive reinforcement is much preferred over negative reinforcement because it works faster and creates fewer harsh feelings, negative reinforcement can be used to change behaviors. Negative reinforcement is more confusing, and may create hostile feelings and mistrust. The first thing to remember is that negative reinforcement increases behavior. It is still reinforcement. The difference is that negative reinforcement increases a behavior when it is taken away. In other words, the behavior increases when the reinforcement is taken away or stopped. The child behaves to avoid negative reinforcement. Explain this to your group and then present these exercises.

> Little Johnny has a cat. He frequently forgets to change the kitty's litter box. So, the parents put the litter box in Johnny's room. If he doesn't change it, it smells. The smell is a negative reinforcement. The behavior that increases is changing the litter box. The boy behaves to avoid the bad smell.

Another example of negative reinforcement is an alarm clock. When the alarm clock goes off in the morning, you push the button to stop it (to avoid the negative reinforcement). The alarm sound serves as a negative reinforcement. The behavior that increases is the turning off of the alarm. Diagram that situation on the board.

Give the class some examples of negative reinforcement and ask for the behaviors that could increase as a result of them.

Examples include:

1. Getting wet on rainy mornings (increased behavior is wearing a raincoat).
2. Burned finger on an iron (moving hand away from the iron).
3. Whining child (parent giving cookie to stop whining child especially in supermarkets).
4. Weight gain (dieting).

At this point, begin scheduling home visits with the group members.

Session VI

Review positive and negative reinforcement. Contrast and compare them verbally. What things are alike about the two procedures? What things are different? Ask for group input. This session is designed specifically for reviewing all of the principles presented thus far. It is up to the trainer to informally judge how well the trainees know these concepts. After talking about the differences and similarities of this type of reinforcement, list these examples on the board that everyone can see. Positive reinforcements include: candy, privileges, and money. Then write these examples of negative reinforcers: alarm clock ring, telephone ring, and car horn. Ask for other examples relevant to home interactional situations.

Then, divide the larger group into three or four smaller groups with at least three to a group. Give each group a piece of paper with a situation on it. Instruct them to decide on a positive or negative reinforcer that can be used to change the behavior. Have them describe how to do it, and role-play the situation in front of the group.

Next, call out the situations below. Ask the group to write a positive or negative reinforcement used on a piece of paper. Discuss their responses. For each of the situations, talk about how one might shape the behaviors.

Indicate to the participants that a quiz is coming up. Plan an extra session or two here if the group needs to review concepts.

1. You want to increase the time your son spends on homework.
2. You want to increase the pleasant things that your daughter says.
3. You want to get your son up in the morning with little or no hassle.

Call out situations

1. You give your son a dime for every time he takes out the trash.
2. You agree to spend 30 min playing ball after he has done his chores.
3. You take the phone off the hook to keep it from ringing.
4. Each time your spouse comes home sober you fix him or her a favorite meal.
5. Your son takes too long in the shower, so you turn off the hot water after 4 minutes.
6. You brush your teeth to get the onion taste out of your mouth.
7. You buy yourself a new dress after you lose 5 pounds.
8. You keep forgetting to take your umbrella to work and you get all wet.
9. Your hair gets itchy and greasy when it is dirty so you wash it every night.
10. You give your daughter a piece of gum every time she feeds the dog.
11. Your child yells and you give him or her what he or she wants.

Session VII

Written and/or oral quizzes. Discuss answers after the quiz.

Quiz

1. Reinforcement of any kind has what effect on behavior?
2. Explain the difference between positive and negative reinforcement.
3. Johnny is having problems taking out the trash, his nightly or bi-weekly duty. How would you tackle that problem?
4. Your husband comes home at 11:30 p.m. three or four nights a week smashed on alcohol. How would you handle that?
5. You want to change one of your child's behaviors. You want little Johnny to stop being such a smart alec. First, narrow the problems to a manageable set of behaviors to work on. List them. Then state your strategy.
6. You are visiting a friend's house. Your child wants a piece of candy. Upon being refused, he or she throws him or herself on the floor and begins to cry, scream, kick, etc. What do you do?
7. Your daughter is playing with older children that you do not approve of. What method of reinforcement could you use to change that?
8. Get with a partner and act out a situation calling for positive reinforcement, and then negative reinforcement.
9. Name three behaviors that your child does now that could be reduced by ignoring them. Name three that you think are pleasant and that you want to increase. State how you might go about shaping these behaviors.
10. What is shaping?

Session VIII

This session focuses on punishment. Sometimes punishment must be used, but it should be limited to certain circumstances and to specific types of punishment. Punishment is a negative reaction to a behavior. It can be a frown, a loss of privileges, and so forth. Punishment reduces the chances that the behavior will occur again (Gershoff 2002). For example, if you stay out late and you are grounded for it, the frequency of your being late usually decreases. The difficulty is that most people over-use punishment and under-use positive reinforcement. There are times when punishment is appropriate, for example, for intolerable or dangerous behaviors. For instance, when a little tot reaches for a hot stove, he or she must be stopped quickly and forcefully. A smack on the hand is acceptable, along with an explanation. Tell the child why he or she is being punished. Punishment, as well as reinforcement, must be consistent. Emphasize this point. It should also be as immediate as possible to be effective with small children. One of the mistakes that parents consistently make in discipline is the "wait till daddy gets home" approach. When daddy gets home, he is faced with disciplining a child for a behavior that happened a long time ago and did not involve dad himself. The key to successful parenting is to punish quickly, sparingly, adequately and consistently (Morawska and Sanders 2011).

There are many behaviors that can be dealt with by ignoring them (called extinction). By using the positive reinforcement method for prosocial behavior, the probability of nonsocial and/or antisocial behavior occurring is substantially reduced. Many children whine and cry in public places for treats or attention. For example, Joey may whine for a candy bar in the grocery store. Ignore him. He may cry, he may even cause a scene-but ignore him. It may be embarrassing for you, but bear with it; it will pay off in the end. Do not give in. When you give in and buy the candy, toy, or whatever, you are teaching your child that his crying will eventually get him what he wants. When he exhibits appropriate behavior in the store, use positive reinforcement extensively.

Conduct this exercise:

Circle the behaviors that must be treated through punishment and cross out behaviors that can/should be ignored. List the appropriate behavior that positive reinforcement increases. Then discuss the participants' answers.

Running in the street	Playing with matches
Whining	Refusing to eat
Crying (not due to physical pain)	Snapping fingers at you
Hitting a smaller brother	Smart aleck remarks
Stomping foot	Telling tall tales
Tantrums	Touching a hot iron

Try this exercise with partners. Give one partner a list of six to seven behaviors to do at once. The list can include behaviors such as tapping fingers, licking lips, messing with hair, swinging a crossed leg, and coughing. Have one partner exhibit all of the behaviors, one right after the other or intermingled. Have the other partner ignore the behaviors. Pick one particularly annoying behavior to punish. Decide on a punishment; a tasteful verbal remark, an ugly face, a pinch on the arm, and so forth. Engage in this interaction for 5 min. One person should be engaging in behaviors, one should be ignoring and/or punishing behaviors. After 5 min, discuss the exercise. Talk about how the person exhibiting the behaviors felt when the punisher was ignoring/punishing the behaviors. Did he or she feel like continuing the behavior? Was the punishment strong enough? Did it make any difference in the number of times the person engaged in the behavior?

Try role-plays with the group in which participants ignore unattractive behaviors. The idea here is that many people behave the way they do to get attention. Any attention, even gasping or staring at a person, may reinforce the behavior and increases the likelihood that it will happen again. Be careful not to reinforce what you do not want to continue. Be strong and use consistent positive reinforcement for appropriate behavior.

Session IX

Review the concept of punishment. Ask for examples of behaviors in which punishment is appropriate. Get class input on how and why punishment is used.

One procedure that should be utilized is time-out. Time-out is exactly what it sounds like, time-out from the situation. If nothing else works, remove either the child or yourself from the situation. Taking a child home when he or she is misbehaving in a grocery store is a good example of time-out. Sit the child in a quiet, separate place, until he or she calms down or stops the misbehavior. Do not send a child to his or her room if there are toys, puzzles, or TV to entertain. Time out should be age appropriate and appropriately established depending on the child's mental and physical abilities (Funderburk and Eyberg 2011). On the other hand, do not lock the child in a closet. Often, just having the child sit in a special chair or go to a separate room is enough. There are certain guidelines for time-out, such as specifying a time limit. An egg timer is great to help with time out. One to five minutes is usually adequate for time out (Morawska and Sanders 2011). Do not let the child come back into the situation if he or she is still crying or misbehaving. For example, if he or she is cursing, send the child back out of the room for 3 to 5 min. This is usually adequate. The effective time range for a time out will vary depending on the child and also should accurately reflect the reason why the child is being punished (Morawska and Sanders 2011). If the child continues to curse, explain the time will begin when the cursing stops. Start the timer when the child is quiet. Be firm. Be consistent. Approach the implementation in a nonemotional manner and maintain this behavior throughout the whole process (Morawska and Sanders 2011). It will be tough at first, but will pay off later.

If you cannot execute the time out process in this manner, do not even attempt it. If you really feel frustrated and feel like you want to physically assault the child, take a time out. There are certain limitations to your time out, too. Do not leave the children in a shopping center. Instead, drop them off somewhere, such as a relative's house or a friend's house. Call a neighbor. Call a crisis nursery. Nevertheless, you take a timeout, and you get out of the environment. Take a walk or jog, have a glass of tea. When you cool off, come back and settle the situation. This can be done through talking, ignoring, or punishment-but only when you are in control of the situation.

Have all participants make a list of neighbors, friends, and relatives who could be used as time-out helpers. Have each prewarn the friend to facilitate the process. Encourage parents within the group to serve as back up friends for time-out. They can certainly relate to the situation. Also, have all participants make a list of different time-out activities that they can engage in (walking, singing, jogging, and so forth). Role-play a situation in which time-out would be appropriate. If needed, you, the trainer, take part in the role-play. Then discuss it.

Next, try this exercise. Below are certain examples of misbehaviors. Circle the ones that are appropriate situations for time-out.

1. When Billy spits on his sister, lock him in the closet for 5 to 10 min.
2. When Suzanne smacks her brother, ask her to sit in her special chair for 5 min while the rest of the family plays games, eats, talks, and so forth.
3. When Lucy begins to cry and throw a tantrum at a neighbor's house, remove her from the situation, but let her come back after 5 min even though she is still crying.
4. After Joanie uses a stream of curse words, send her to her room where her TV, stereo, and phone are.
5. When Al cries and pounds his fists, sit him in a corner. Start timing when he stops crying and pounding. Have him sit quietly for 5 min in the corner. Explain the rationale to him.
6. After a long day, the kids are screaming, one child is sick and you have had it. Throw up your hands and announce, "I'm leaving".
7. Your two boys have been fighting all day and you are ready to gag them and tie them up. Call a neighbor over for 20 min while you take a walk in the woods or down the street.
8. After a long day at work you come home and your wife starts nagging. You leave to go get drunk.

Review time-out and answer questions that participants might have. Talk about the examples and exercise.

Session X

One very important part of behavior modification is listening. Everyone talks, but how many people can really listen to their children, spouses, or their relatives? In addition, do these people listen to you? Many people sit and talk at each other. They never really listen to what the other person is saying. To really hear what your child is saying, you must actively listen.

This exercise will help you learn to actively listen. Divide the group into pairs of people. Person 1 will state a problem. Person 2 must not interrupt or speak until person 1 is finished. Then, the listener should repeat what person 1 has just stated, almost word for word. It is good to start with a statement like, "what I hear you saying is…." or "I hear you saying that you need…". Explain that participants should do whatever is comfortable for them. Each person should send two or three messages for the other person to repeat. Then switch the listener to the teller.

After this exercise, ask the participants how they felt about it. Then stress the following: repeating message does several things; it makes the listener listen, because he or she will have to perform by repeating, the listener is more likely to listen to what is being said. It also clarifies the message. Often people do not hear the message clearly, the listener may have heard the problem wrong, or the teller may not be saying what he or she thinks. In any event, this direct feedback of problems will clear up the message being sent between participants.

Now, role-play this exercise in front of the group. The trainer is to whisper or state a problem to each trainee. The trainee must restate the problem to the trainer and the rest of the group. Just go quickly around the room with this one. See if anyone is hearing what you are saying. Also, see if everyone is listening to what is being said.

Next, try this exercise: State a problem to the whole class. Ask everyone to restate the problem, verbally or in writing. Check to see if the messages are being sent clearly, and heard clearly. Discuss any misconceptions in the exercise. Review the listening techniques. Talk about any problems that have come up in the last few sessions.

Session XI

The next logical question that your participants may have is "how do all of these wonderful principles affect me?" How do participants apply the techniques in order to work for them? How do they apply them in specific situations? Create the expectation that the participants can use these techniques at home, and with good results.

The next step is to actually implement the reinforcement guides at home that the trainer has been elaborating in the classroom. Indicate that they must follow them faithfully. If they, as parents, use them sometimes but forget sometimes, the procedures will be ineffective. Children will just think that they are crazy and unpredictable. Be consistent. Listen to your children and to yourself and follow the procedures as we have practiced them.

Select a problem. Ask parents to write down three real problems at home. Each parent should have a list. The first step is for each person to admit the difficulty. Is it the child's problem or is it a problem of yours? What are things that you will have to change to help change the overall situation? Discuss the lists. Check to see if the spouse's list agrees. If not, be sure to discuss them.

Here is an example to get parents started:

Your husband does not come home right after work. Maybe it is because you:

1. Look like a truck hit you when he walks in the door.
2. Have numerous children lined up for him to punish.
3. Have not started dinner yet.
4. Are always away from home.
5. Or maybe it is not your fault at all.

In the majority of instances, it takes at least two people to have a problem. Mutual concessions have to be made for a problem to be solved. After discussing who owns the problems on everyone's list, tell each participant to pick one problem to work on. It can be one of his or her own problems, or their child's. Ask the parents to write the problem down. Now, everyone must define what the problem is. Defining a problem may be just a bit more complicated than it may seem. The problem must be broken down into observable, countable behaviors for the program to work. This can be very tricky and hard for rural individuals and will take patience and time. Some good examples of behaviors to work on include cursing, spitting, not fixing dinner, and not picking up clothes from the floor.

Write this example on the board, "I want my husband to be nicer to me." What is nicer? What does nicer really mean? It is much too broad of a word. Get everyone to list what they think "nicer" means. Read everyone's list aloud. Pick five definitions. Write them on the board. A list of things nicer means might include:

Coming home after work.
A kiss at the door.
Spending 15 min with you before dinner.
Talking together during those 15 min.
Helping to wash the dishes.
Spending time with the children.
Appropriate compliments for task accomplished.

Break the problem of the statement into small, countable behaviors. This will help you to measure success and to be successful. After you break the problem into behaviors, decide how each person will reinforce the behavior, and what other techniques to use. Decide exactly how you define the behavior to be worked on, what amount and type of reinforcement you will use, and when you will reinforce.

Remember that consistency and immediacy is very important in this problem. Moreover, remember that punishment is used as a last resort. An easy way to keep track of successes and failures is to keep a chart. In this session, everyone should practice setting up a chart for the specific behavior. Mark off each day, each behavior, and how many times the participant reinforced the behavior. The chart will help to get into the reinforcement routine, and it will show you just how successful you are. You, the trainer, can make out a sample chart on the board to help your group understand, as illustrated in Table 12.2. Ask the class to fill in the missing information.

Talk about the problem with your spouse or child. Discuss the types of rewards-tell your child or husband the rules for the system. For parents with older children, behavior contracts may be in order. Discuss the contract with the child and write it up like a formal contract. Write in specific things to which you both agree. Make the expectations as specific as possible. Be sure that you both understand the terms of the contract and live up to them. For example:

I, ______________________________(the parent) agree to the following:

- I will pay $5.00 weekly for these chores to be done by my child______________________
  - Take the trash out daily
  - Feed the dog after supper
  - Pick up clothes daily
  - Make the bed daily.

In return, I ___________________________________(the child) agree to do these chores for the sum of $5.00 weekly to be paid in cash to me on Fridays at 5:00 p.m.

For an excellent discussion of the formulation of contracts see the text by W. DeRisi and G. Butz (1976) entitled *Writing Behavioral Contracts*. Use of behavioral contracts is also discussed in Tighe et al. (2012).

Getting everyone to sign a contract impresses upon him or her just how important this contract is. Review the idea of charts. Help everyone get a notion of a chart for his or her specific behavior problem. If possible, help them set up the chart during class. The starting date for the charts will be the day after this session. Tell participants that you will check the charts next week.

Session XII to XV

Discuss the charts and check them. Make charts for new behaviors to work on. Talk about the problems that are occurring at home. Praise good things that are going on at home. Review any points about the techniques that are unclear. Have the children come to one session during this time frame. Make videotape schedules for the group. On Child Nights have parents and children watch the videotape of the family. Videotaping of parent-child sessions is one factor that may contribute to the success of a parent modification program (Phaneuf and McIntyre 2011). A group discussion on how to handle a certain type of problem at home is very beneficial. Weekly home visits should be continued for 1 to 2 months after behavior change. Once a behavior is altered it is no longer necessary to reinforce it every time it occurs (Brotman et al. 2011). Such a procedure ensures that the behaviors will continue as reinforcement becomes intermittent. After these tasks are completed, the group can terminate, or it can continue as a parent support group.

Parent Training via CD-ROM and Technology

In his 2000 article published in *The Journal of Primary Prevention,* Donald Gordon hailed the success of CD-ROM technology in the dissemination of effective parent-training programs. In fact, Gordon suggests that interactive videodisk programs are more effective in increasing knowledge and performance than any previous method of instruction.

CD-ROM interactive programs can carry high treatment integrity (Gordon 2000). Gordon's interactive program *Parenting Wisely* has been chosen as an exemplary model program by the Substance Abuse and Mental Health Services Association (SAMHSA), and there is evidence that it has been effective in treating teenage parents, poor families in Appalachia, and parents of children with conduct disorders (Family Works, Inc. 2006; Barth et al. 2005).

As mentioned earlier, one of the major hindrances to the effectiveness of parent-training programs is the difficulty of child welfare settings. The use of CD-ROM training programs can help to ameliorate the problems posed by these difficult situations. The technology requires minimal agency resources, comes at a low cost, and requires very little computer skill. The program can be implemented in private, eliminating the stigma associated with attending training programs and providing the client with a level of convenience that accommodates real world time constraints. The use of CD-ROM technology can also make the learning process less confrontational, since the user receives feedback from a computer and not a person. Also, given the versatility and capacity of modern computer technology, CD-ROM programs can be equipped with enough options to satisfy the cultural demands of most ethnicities.

There are some barriers that stand in the way of CD-ROM technology. Many social service and mental health professionals remain apprehensive of computer technology and resist implementation of such programs. Many clients are also intimidated by the prospect of using computer-based programs, as well as have limited access to computers (Gordon 2000). Despite these behaviors, however, the use of CD-ROM technology is a low-cost, effective, and overall viable option when implementing an effective parent training program.

Another way to use technology is through televised programs. In the United Kingdom, researchers tested how effective it was to use the media as a source of intervention. Their attention was gained when a television series, *Driving Mum and Dad Mad,* discussed parenting techniques in a documentary style and caught the attention of 4.2 million viewers. Their question became, "can this parenting intervention work?" The findings of the study revealed there were significant improvements in child behavior problems, dysfunctional parenting, parental anger, parental self-efficacy, and parental mood. These are all key areas in preventing child maltreatment. They were also able to reach parents who traditionally were more likely to drop out or not attend classes. This retention rate could possibly be due to a less threatening environment. They do state that this approach is not beneficial for all families and more research would be useful, but they present a unique alternative to how we address parenting training (Calam et al. 2008). These instances show that technology is providing trainers with new ways to involve parents.

Additional Resources

Preventing Child Abuse and Neglect with Parent Training: Evidence and Opportunities. http://futureofchildren.org/publications/journals/article/index.xml?journalid=71&articleid=513.

Training on Child Abuse and Neglect Prevention. http://www.childwelfare.gov/preventing/developing/training.cfm.

Circle of Parents. http://www.preventchildabusenc.org/?fuseaction=cms.page&id=1005.

Active Parenting. http://www.nrepp.samhsa.gov/ViewIntervention.aspx?id=110.

Cultural Competence and Child Maltreatment. http://www.childwelfare.gov/systemwide/cultural/can.cfm.

Cultural Competence: Preventing Child Abuse and Neglect. http://www.childwelfare.gov/systemwide/cultural/preventing.cfm.

References

Aarons, G. A., Hurlburt, M., & Horwitz, S. M. (2011). Advancing a conceptual model of evidence-based practice implementation in public service sectors. *Administration and Policy in Mental Health, 38*(1), 4–23.

Barth, R. P. (2009). Preventing child abuse and neglect with parent training: Evidnce and opportunities. *The Future of Children, 19*(2), 95–118.

Barth, R. P., Landsverk, J., Chamberlain, P., Reid, J. B., Rolls, J. A., Hurlburt, M. S., Farmer, E., James, S., McCabe, K. M., & Kohl, P. L. (2005). Parent-training programs in child welfare services: Planning for a more evidence-based approach to serving biological parents. *Research on Social Work Practice, 15*(5), 353–371.

Brotman, L. M., Calzada, E., Huang, K. Y., Kingston, S., Dawson-McClure, S., Kamboukos, D., Rosenfelt A., Schwab A., & Petkova, E. (2011). Promoting effective parenting practices and preventing child behavior problems in school among ethnically diverse families from underserved, urban communities. *Child Development, 82*(1), 258–276.

Calam, R., Sanders, M. R., Miller, C., Sadhnani, V., & Carmont, S. (2008). Can technology and the media help reduce dysfunctional parenting and increase engagement with preventive parenting interventions? *Child Maltreatment, 13*(4), 347–361.

Coard, S. I., Wallace, S. A., Stevenson, H. C. Jr, & Brotman, L. M. (2004). Towards culturally relative preventive interventions: The consideration of racial socialization in parent training with African American families. *Journal of Child and Family Studies, 13*(3), 277–293.

Cohen, D. (2010). *An examination of group parent training with contextualized coaching on positive parenting practices*. Unpublished master's thesis, University of Oregon, Dept. of Special Education and Clinical Sciences. Retrieved from https://scholarsbank.uoregon.edu/xmlui/handle/1794/10622. May 18, 2013.

DeRisi, W. & Butz, G. (1976). Writing behavioral contracts. Champaign: IL. *Research Press*.

Doughty, A. H., & Shields, M. C. (2009). The power of reinforcement: A review. The Psychological Record. Vol. 59, 2(11).

Dumas, J. E., Moreland, A. D., Gitter, A. H., Pearl, A. M., & Nordstrom, A. H., (2008). Engaging parents in preventive parenting groups: Do ethnic, socioeconomic, and belief match between parents and group leaders matter? *Health Education and Behavior, 35*(5), 619–633.

Eyberg, S. M., & Robinson, E. A. (1982). Parent-child interaction therapy: Effects on family functioning. *Journal of Clinical Child Psychology, 11,* 130–137.

Eyberg, S. M., Funderburk, B. W., Hembree-Kigin, T. L., McNeil, C. B., Querido, J. G., & Hood, K. K. (2001). Parent-child interaction therapy with behavior problem children: One and two year maintenance of treatment effects in the family. *Child and Family Behavior Therapy, 23*(4), 1–20.

Family Works, Inc. (2006). Parenting wisely. http://www.parentingwisely.com/about/index.html. Accessed 15 April 2006.

Forehand, R., & Kotchick, B. A. (2002). Behavioral parent training: Current challenges and potential solutions. *Journal of Child and Family Studies, 11*(4), 377–384.

Funderburk, B. W., & Eyberg, S. (2011). Parent–child interaction therapy.

Gershoff, E. T. (2002). Corporal punishment by parents and associated child behaviors and experiences: A meta-analytic and theoretical review. *Psychological Bulletin, 128*(4), 539–579.

Gordon, D. A. (2000). Parent training via CD-ROM: Using technology to disseminate effective prevention practices. *Journal of Primary Prevention, 21*(2), 227–251.

Gordon, T. (2008). *Parent effectiveness training: The proven program for raising responsible children*. New York: Random House Digital.

Henggeler, S. W., Rowland, M. D., Halliday-Boykinds, C., Shadow, A. J., Ward, D. M., Randall, J., et al. (2003). One-year follow up of multisystemic therapy as an alternative to the hospitalization of youths in psychiatric crisis. *Journal of the Academy of Child and Adolescent Psychiatry, 42,* 543–551.

Kaminski, J. W., Valle, L. A., Filene, J. H., & Boyle, C. L. (2008). A meta-analytic review of components associated with parent training program effectiveness. *Journal of Abnormal Child Psychology, 36,* 567–589.

Le, H., Ceballo, R., Chao, R., Hill, N. E., Murry, V. M., & Pinderhughes, E. E. (2008). Excavating culture: Disentangling ethnic differences for contextual influences of parenting. *Applied Developmental Science, 12*(4), 163–175.

Lemmens, M. (2011). Parent effectiveness training. *Issues in Mental Health Nursing, 32*(2), 137–139.

Mabe, P. A., Turner, M. K., & Josephson, A. M. (2001). Parent management training. *Child and Adolescent Psychiatric Clinics of North America, 10*(3):451–464.

Mersky, J. P., Berger, L. M., Reynolds, A. J., & Gromoske, A. N. (2009). Risk factors for child and adolescent maltreatment: A longitudinal investigation of a cohort of inner-city youth. *Child Maltreatment, 14*(1), 73–88.

Morawska, A., & Sanders, M. (2011). Parental use of time out revisited: A useful or harmful parenting strategy. *Journal of Child and Family Studies, 20,* 1–8.

Pfiffner, L., & Kaiser, N. (2010). Behavioral parent training. In M. K. Dulcan (Ed), *Dulcan's textbook of child and adolescent psychiatry*. Arlington: American Psychiatric Publishing

Phaneuf, L., & McIntyre, L. L. (2011). The application of a three-tier model of intervention to parent training. *Journal of Positive Behavior Interventions, 13*(4), 198–207.

Pinsker, M., & Geoffroy, K. (1981). A comparison of parent effectiveness training and behavior modification parent training. *Family Relations, 30*(1), 61–68.

Sanders, M. R. (2008). Triple P-Positive Parenting Program as a public health approach to strengthening parenting. *Journal of Family Psychology, 22*(4), 506.

Sandler, I., Schoenfelder, E., Wolchik, S., & MacKinnon, D. (2011). Long-term impact of prevention programs to promote effective parenting: Lasting effects but uncertain processes. *Annual Review of Psychology, 62,* 299.

Serketich, W. J., & Dumas, J. E. (1996) The effectiveness of behavioral parent training to modify antisocial behavior in children: A meta-analysis. *Behavior Therapy, 27,* 171–186.

Shaffer, A., Lindhiem, O., Kolko, D. J., & Trentacosta, C. J. (2013). Bidirectional relations between parenting practices and child externalizing behavior: A cross-lagged panel analysis in the context of a psychosocial treatment and 3-year follow-up. *Journal of Abnormal Child Psychology, 41*(2), 199–210.

Smagner, J. P., & Sullivan, M. H. (2005). Investigating the effectiveness of behavioral parent training with involuntary clients in child welfare settings. *Research on Social Work Practice, 15*(6), 431–439.

Sorkhabi, N. (2005). Applicability of Baumrind's parent typology to collective cultures: Analysis of cultural explanations of parent socialization effects. *International Journal of Behavioral Development, 29*(6), 552–563.

Tighe, A., Pistrang, N., Casdagli, L., Baruch, G., & Butler, S. (2012). Multisystemic therapy for young offenders: Families' experiences of therapeutic processes and outcomes. *Journal of Family Psychology, 26*(2), 187.

Ward, J. V. (2000). *The skin we're in: Teaching our teens to be emotionally strong, socially smart, and spiritually connected.* New York: Simon and Schuster.

Webster-Stratton, C. (1994). Advancing videotape parent training: a comparison study. *Journal of Consulting and Clinical Psychology, 62*(3), 583–593.

Webster-Stratton, C. (1998). Parent training with low-income families: Promoting parental engagement through a collaborative approach. In J. R. Lutzger (Ed.), *Handbook of child abuse research and treatment* (pp. 183–210). New York: Plenum.

Webster-Stratton, C., & Reid, M. J. (2010). The Incredible Years parents, teachers, and children training series: A multifaceted treatment approach for young children with conduct disorders. In J. R. Weisz & A. E. Kazdin (Eds.), *Evidence-based psychotherapies for children and adolescents* (2nd ed., pp. 194–210). New York: Guilford.

Chapter 13
Adolescent Employment Intervention

Shauna Cook, Cindy McCleary-North, Shannon Waldrup and Carrie Fair

Introduction

The passage of a young person from adolescence to adulthood is marked by a number of events. Of these, none is more important than the young person's finding work and becoming economically independent. Today in the USA, this transition is often painful and frustrating, and a large number of youth are failing to achieve it (Zarrett and Eccles 2006). Americans place enormous emphasis on employment and financial security (Wodarski and Wodarski 1993). This is still a fundamental premise used in the literature.

In 2008, the Gallup Organization reported that the job market continues to weaken. It reports, "jobless claims will exceed 565,000 up from the 542,500 report last week (January 17–24, 2008) and reflecting the continued disappearance of jobs in the United States."

Research indicates that for the majority of people, employment constitutes the single most defining aspect of living in American society. Indeed, work has special meaning to the psychosocial development of adolescents (Wodarski and Dziegielewski 2002), representing an opportunity to gain independence and establish an independent identity, contribute to family finances, acquire prestige, and try out adult roles. Accepting responsibility for self, making independent decisions, and being financially independent have been identified as the top criteria for the

---

This chapter discusses the skills and education needed prior to entering the job market including social skills training, communication skills training, problem solving techniques, and vocational enrichment training.

S. Cook (✉)
Children's Mental Health Services Research Center,
University of TN, Knoxville, TN, USA
e-mail: cooks@utk.edu

C. McCleary-North · S. Waldrup · C. Fair
The University of Tennessee, Knoxville, TN, USA

J. S. Wodarski et al. (eds.), *Evidence-Informed Assessment and Practice in Child Welfare*, DOI 10.1007/978-3-319-12045-4_13

transition to adulthood (Arnett 2000). This process varies in length depending on a variety of circumstances in the adolescent's life. Things such as culture, family history, and childhood affect the manner in which adolescents respond to employment. Being unemployed has a negative effect on the psychological development and expression of many people (Cole et al. 2009). This problem is currently compounded by the volume and length of unemployment that exists today.

Educational Elements

In this chapter, the effect of education was not specifically identified. However, we found that low performing high schools—particularly those serving low-income communities and students of color—are often characterized by high absentee and course failure rates, and substantial dropout rates. Even high school graduates are faced with inadequate preparation for postsecondary education and the labor market. While the stage is often set for these problems in elementary and middle schools, the devastating effects become more visible in ninth grade. As many as one-half to three-quarters of ninth-graders in low-performing high schools embark on their freshmen year with significant reading difficulties, lacking the skills needed to comprehend complex texts assigned in their content courses. Students who face marked literacy deficits are unlikely to do well in high school. Poor reading ability is a key predictor of academic disengagement and, ultimately, dropping out (Manpower Demonstration Research Corporation 2006). Conversely, unemployment at this age (18–26 years) lowers feelings of self-esteem; long spells of unemployment may precipitate psychological problems and chemical dependency. This guide and comprehensive study meticulously reinforces the effects of these issues on adolescents and the disabled (Timmons et al. 2004).

Similar to their adult counterparts, adolescents experience feelings of desperation, hostility, frustration, and even fatigue and malaise as a result of being unemployed. In addition to being bored, frightened, insecure, depressed, and confused—certain adolescents claimed that unemployment caused them to have problems with alcohol, eating, and sleeping (Mean Patterson 1997). Increases in family conflicts were also reported. Drug addiction, teenage pregnancy, and family violence have also been associated with adolescent unemployment (1997). Existing literature indicates that work enhances one's mental health and emphasizes that many adolescents are motivated to work, but lack knowledge about how to accurately assess their own interests and abilities, how to plan for employment, and how to find and secure jobs. Many adolescents, especially those with negative school experiences, may experience alienation from society and a lack of self esteem. Employment during adolescence is associated with both negative and positive consequences. As mentioned earlier, employment can positively affect one's self esteem and it also provides adolescents with the opportunity to develop valuable time management skills and workforce experience. High school jobs may be beneficial for youth who are less engaged in academics and less interested in college, as well as those lacking familial or personal resources (high aspirations and engagement in schools) to successfully pursue a 4-year college degree (Mortimer 2010). In this situation, obtaining a steady job with career potential can be a positive accomplishment for a young adult. Potential negative consequences are that employment decreases time available for homework and family, increases the number of school absentees, and can lead to conflict surrounding how earnings are being spent (Hansen and Jarvis 2000). The Tennessee Department of Education (2006) provided information on new "wellness" programming in the state of Tennessee, discussing the effects of "limited" work time to improve adolescent grades and identity formation through work programs.

Employment Prerequisites

Adolescents successfully gain employment by preparing both psychologically and socially for the job market (Wodarski et al. 1989; Wolf-Branigin et al. 2007). An examination of developmentally disabled adolescents (Wodarski et. al. 1989; Wolf-Branigin et. al. 2007) was also broadly applicable to able-bodied adolescents regarding employment conditions and stipulations. A job preparation program mainly focuses on preparing adolescents for employment through training of skills and behaviors that constitute employability as well as by arranging for appropriate job placement. *Employability* refers to the skills, attitudes, and work behaviors necessary to obtain a job and to perform satisfactorily in order to maintain a job. *Placeability* refers to the perceived attractiveness of an applicant to an employer. Labor market conditions and an employer's willingness to fire a person with a disability affect a client's placeability. The Tennessee Department of Labor and Workforce Development confirms that attitudes, appearance, and behaviors have not changed regarding the employment of adolescents and disabled individuals (Crudden et al. 2005).

The most comprehensive operational definition for employability and placeability are provided by the Vocational Behavior Checklist (Walls and Werner 1977). Assessment includes examination of 39 behaviors, covering seven areas of employment-related competencies: prevocational skills, job-related skills, work performance skills, on-the-job social skills, financial security skills, job-seeking skills, and interview skills. Although it has been revised, the Vocational Behavior Checklist has not required any extreme modifications since its inception. Following is a comprehensive list of the operational definition of each of the employment competencies as measured on the Vocational Behavior Checklist:

Prevocational Skills Include knowledge about the need for work, what a job is, and the trainee's vocational interest (e.g., folding, sorting, etc.).

Job-Related Skills Refer to the skills that each worker must have to "get around," or to locate particular characteristics of the work setting.

Work Performance Skills Include setting up and keeping a clean work station, starting on time, following instructions and models, sorting and using materials, using and caring for tools, working safely, and seeking help when needed.

On-the-Job Social Skills Include being friendly to others, following accepted policy and protocol, being able to deal constructively with criticism, refraining from socially destructive or annoying behaviors, and appropriate employee relations and boundaries.

Financial Security Skills Refer to behaviors involved in locating and applying for employment, such as matching skills with jobs, completing applications, and preparing a résumé.

Interview Skills The behaviors involved in preparing to be interviewed and in presenting a favorable and accurate impression of oneself during the job interview.

According to the National Association of Colleges and Employers (NACE) (2009), the following are the results from a 5-point Likert scale survey conducted in 2008 of the most desired characteristics of an employee; communication skills (4.7 average), honesty/integrity (4.7), teamwork skills (4.6), interpersonal skills (4.5), motivation/initiative (4.5), and strong work ethic (4.5).

A Conceptual Model for Employment

To secure and maintain employment, adolescents must exhibit behaviors that are valued and considered appropriate in an employment setting. Production skills and effective social skills represent two paramount behavioral categories for ensuring employment success.

Social Skills Training

The comprehensive employment preparation approach is based on an amalgamation of the following structured learning models: "Skill streaming the Adolescent" (Goldstein et al. 1980), Gazda's (1982), life-span development skills training approach, and Schinke and Gichrist's (1984) program of life skills counseling with adolescents. These studies have been revised, but we have found that the premise of the studies has not changed. The terminology has been modified, but the structural aspects and application have remained the same. Social skills training programs are still based on the fundamentals recognized by Goldstein et al. (1980). Examples of sampling of these programs, including the 4 step modules adopted by the state of Tennessee, can be found in current "wellness" educational curriculums all around the country. Today, many social skills training modules are based on Social Learning Theory (Moote et al. 1999; Wodarski and Feit 1995). The Social Learning

Theory broadly states that people learn by observing others (Bandura 1977). Adolescents learn by watching others, so positive role modeling is extremely important in developing social skills and preparing them for the work force.

These theories and programs emphasize the value of transferable work-skills attitudes rather than the training for either specific vocational skills or basic skills, such as reading and mathematics. Vocational training teaches skills specific to one job whereas, frequently in today's market of technological advancements, these skills quickly become outdated. During the past decade, the vocational training in America has dominated its traditional postsecondary academics (Silberman 2004). Many reasons exist for this transition; however, the economy has certainly played a major role. Postsecondary schools are being more selective regarding enrollment and students are becoming increasingly interested in gaining direct, hands-on experience in a structured manner rather than learning distant concepts, such as those typical of higher education. Schools have thus begun to counteract this shift by increasing internships and work opportunities within the academic curriculum (Fallows and Stephen 2000).

Adolescents need life management skills that are transferable from one job to the next and from work to home (Fallows and Stephen 2000). However, social skills training is not enough to enable high-risk adolescents to cope with present stresses and to facilitate their development, thus individual and group counseling is essential to success (Bolton et al. 2010).

Social skills may be categorized as overt (verbal and nonverbal components of explicit social behaviors) or covert (internal skills affecting self-control and problem-solving abilities across all social settings and circumstances) learned behaviors that maximize the chances for obtaining positive reinforcement from social interactions while minimizing perceived cost to self and others (Mazur 2002). Social skills trainings often emphasize the following topics: communication, problem-solving skills, anger management, and conflict resolution (Moote et al. 1999). One effective method of teaching these skills is to use the Teams-Game-Tournament method of group education (Wodarski and Feit 1995). This method uses a cooperative learning strategy designed to increase basic skills, increase student achievement, facilitate positive interactions between students, and enable acceptance of mainstreamed classmates and self-esteem (Ke and Grabowski 2006). These are necessary skills for success in many life domains and once learned, they can be applied to any number of settings.

Training in social skills typically consists of rationale as to why a particular social behavior is desirable; an opportunity to observe examples of the behavior, usually through role-play situations followed by corrective feedback regarding performance (Adams et al. 2002).

Teaching adolescents work skills and good ethical attitudes enables them to not only successfully compete in the job market, but to effectively manage current problems and stressors, including anticipation and prevention of future problems, and advancing their mental health, social functioning, and economic viability (Valentine 2004).

During the first session of social skills training, a professional counselor should assess an adolescent's vocational aptitude and work-skills attitudes. Subsequently, the adolescent should participate in a series of psycho-educational courses, to include vocational enrichment (Azrin 1980), enhancing interpersonal relationships (Martin and Dowson 2009), managing stress and building social responsibility (Compas et al. 2001), determining alternatives to aggression and dealing with feelings (Goldstein et al. 1997), and general problem solving (Timmons et al. 2004). Various psychoeducational methods are employed in these courses for increased effectiveness, including individual and group counseling, self-assessments, live and videotaped demonstrations, behavioral rehearsal with a therapist, peer and videotaped feedback, written materials, positive reinforcement, individual and group contracts, buddy systems, and progress logs. Most of these therapeutic strategies are delivered through a group work approach (Chong 2005).

The Group Context for Training

Even though recent years have witnessed a growing emphasis on group treatment, relatively few adolescents were treated using this approach. This has changed substantially with group treatment ranging from job training skills programs, behavioral/conduct issues, and substance abuse or sexual assault issues being used to assist the youth. The provisions for services in group therapy offer certain positives aspects. The group interaction typifies many types of daily interactions. Activities that facilitate the development of behaviors that enable people to interact in groups are likely to prepare them for participation in real world activities (Malekoff 2004). According to social learning theory, if an employment preparation behavior is learned in a group context, it is likely to come under the control of a greater number of discriminative stimuli; therefore, greater generalization of the behavior can occur for a broader variety of interactional context, including the work environment.

The group context of the Comprehensive Employment Preparation (CEP) program is designed to capitalize on the adolescent's dependence on peers. Group identity and cohesion should be fostered within groups of adolescents. Group support can be mobilized to aid individuals at moments of particular difficulty (Wodarski and Feit 1995; Wodarksi et al. 2004). As stated, the group interaction situation typifies many kinds of daily living situations, and the group provides a context whereby new behaviors can be tested in a realistic atmosphere (1995; 2004).

There are additional substantiated rationales for working with adolescents in groups. Adolescents can obtain immediate peer feedback and support regarding their problem-solving behaviors. Groups provide a more valid locus for accurate diagnosis and a more potent means for changing client behavior (Malekoff 2004). Groups can be utilized in many diverse and cost effective ways that individual therapy cannot. This factor is becoming increasingly more important in a struggling economy, where Managed Care necessitates the most cost effective manner to treat clients (Oxman and Chambliss 2003).

Lack of interpersonal relationship skills plays a significant role in an adolescent's ability to secure and maintain employment and in his or her general dissatisfaction with life. Services structured in a group manner should help these teenagers practice necessary social skills to facilitate their acquisition, thus enhancing their interpersonal relationships and increasing employment opportunities. In addition, many adolescents experience feelings of emptiness, social isolation, and a sense of failure, and may benefit from the support derived from the group. Finally, the provision of services through groups greatly increases the number of clients who can be served by an effective treatment program (Dwived 1993)

Specific Elements of the Employment Paradigm

To secure and maintain employment, it is necessary to help adolescents and young adults acquire socially sanctioned skills and train them to interact appropriately with their peers and employers on the job. The CEP program offers an exciting and functional method of preparing adolescents and young adults to become productive members of society by building a repertoire of positive behaviors that have a higher probability of reducing dependence. Much of the new research focuses on adolescents with developmental disabilities who use this program.

The CEP program begins 3 months prior to employment and continues for 3 months after the adolescent is in the workplace. This plan bridges the transition between pre-employment and the workplace community. Programs to accomplish the acquisition of requisite skills in each of the general target areas are selected from the technology of Applied Behavioral Analysis and Social Psychology. Reviews of problem-solving training programs (D'Zurilla and Nezu 1982) and cognitive anger control and interpersonal skills training (Spence 2003) have shown that their effectiveness is substantial when compared with other treatment programs for the acquisition of such behaviors. Data supporting vocational enrichment programs from this applied perspective are impressive.

Problem Solving

Adolescents and young adults who have difficulty maintaining employment are often deficient in their ability to cope with daily problems of living in terms of personal care, domestic skills, or budgeting skills (Osgood et al. 2010). These adolescents would, indeed, benefit from the basic instruction of the core components of the CEP program. The general components emphasized are how to generate information; how to generate possible solutions; how to evaluate possible courses of action; how to choose and implement strategies; and how to verify the outcome of the chosen course of action. Adolescents who have the drive and honesty to identify their faults and reform their behavior will enter the job force as successful problem solvers and diligent workers.

Rationale: data indicate that from an early age, high-risk adolescents and young adults do not solve problems as efficiently as their peers (Lewis et al. 2004).

Cognitive Anger Control

A significant number of adolescents lack the means to control anger (Feindler 1990). Professionals must be prepared to help at-risk adolescents in the following ways; identify stressors that provoke anger and subsequent violent behavior, develop cognitive relaxation skills to reduce the effects of stress, learn how to receive contentions and deal with the anger of others, develop appropriate communication and assertion skills, and to practice alternative behavior in frustrating situations, such as stimulus removal.

Rationale: Recent data suggest that within 6 weeks of employment, high-risk adolescents have altercations that lead to termination of employment (Lochman et al. 2003).

The Social Skills Program

The social skills program, based on the work of De Lange et al. (1982), involves interpersonal skills training and the development of assertive behavior for appropriate situations. Specific elements include self introductions, how to initiate and continue conversations, giving and receiving compliments, enhancing appearance, appropriately making and refusing requests, spontaneous expression of feelings, appropriate use of nonverbal cues such as body language, facial expression, hand and foot movements, or smiling, and appropriate expressions of sexuality.

Rationale: Data indicate that from an early age, high-risk adolescents are disliked by their peers and do not develop the interpersonal skills necessary to interact productively with others (Kuperminc and Allen 2001).

Vocational Enrichment Program

The vocational enrichment program is based on the work of Azrin (1980). General components worth emphasis include group discussions, employment-securing aids, and specific aspects of the program.

Group discussions should involve strong motivation for vocational achievement and include mutual assistance among job seekers, development of a supportive buddy system, family support, sharing job leads, and widening the variety of positions considered.

Employment-securing aids include searching "help-wanted" ads, role-playing interview situations, instructions in telephoning for appointments, procedures for motivating the job seeker, developing appropriate conversational competencies, emphasizing strong personal attributes in terms of dress and grooming, and securing transportation for job interviews. With advances in technology, utilizing the Internet to search for employment is also an important skill. Many websites exist where you can post your resume (monster.com), or where local employers advertise online for available positions (betterknoxvillejob.com).

Specific aspects of the program include how to benefit from therapy, the role of therapy, how to operate the job club, initial contact with prospective employers, finding employment leads, arranging interviews and analogous activities, applying for the job, completing an application, simulating a job interview, learning how to answer questions by presenting strong points, learning how to ask appropriate questions, securing and maintaining the job in terms of interpersonal skills, and dealing with rejection.

Rationale: Data indicate that adolescents who have work or string leads for employment can become more independent (Timmons et al. 2004; Manpower Demonstration Research Corporation, MDRC 2006).

Career Development Skills Intervention with Inner City Adolescents

Researchers have suggested that adolescents who live in an inner city environment face multiple career development barriers related to their entering the workforce (Turner and Conkel 2010). Many of these adolescents face greater challenges and have fewer resources than adolescents from other levels of society. Issues such as high unemployment rates, low levels of educational attainment, family poverty, lack of work experience, and underdeveloped social skills are some of the barriers encountered by inner city youth. Therefore, it is imperative that these youth receive adequate preparation to enter the workforce.

The Integrative Contextual Model of Career Development (ICM) helps young people develop a more adaptive, resilient, and proactive approach to both current situations and future career opportunities (Turner et al. 2006). The model focuses on adolescents learning and employing skills necessary for career development. Certain skill sets addressed by ICM include: self and career exploration, personal interests, values and abilities related to occupational opportunities, goal-setting, social skills, work readiness, and self-regulated learning skills. A study of career development skills by Turner and Conkel (2010), showed that adolescents living in an inner city, who participated and completed activities of ICM reported greater emotional support than did adolescents who only completed more traditional career counseling activities.

The Job Club

The *Job Club Counselor's Manual: A Behavioral Approach to Vocational Counseling* (Azrin and Besalel 1980) is a good model that many companies still use today.

In order to effectively implement it, counselors should allocate 3 h sessions to allow enough time to complete each activity.

Specific Procedures and Activities

The job club allows people to join other job seekers and work with each other toward mutual goals. Job seekers are under the guidance of a counselor and receive encouragement, support, information, supplies, and facilities within a noncompetitive atmosphere. Following are the procedures and strategies provided to the participants.

Job Seeking as a Full-Time Job About half of the day is spent getting job leads and arranging interviews and the remainder of the day is spent on interviews. This is followed every day until a job is obtained.

Friends, Relatives, and Acquaintances as Sources of Job Leads The job seeker makes an effort to contact relatives, friends, and other acquaintances as a main source of job leads.

Standard Scripts and Forms The job seeker is given forms and scripts to follow when contacting friends or employers. They will write letters, make telephone calls, and keep records of each contact.

Facilities and Supplies The program provides all the services and supplies necessary for a job search; a telephone, postage, newspapers, access to making copies, and a work area.

Group Support from Other Job Seekers This program is offered in a structured group setting where job seekers can help each other. Members are encouraged to look for leads for and from other members, and leads from previous members are made available to current members.

Buddy System Members are paired with a "buddy" who provides advice and help in monitoring telephone calls, writing letters, looking at help wanted ads, and practicing for interviews.

Obtaining Unpublicized Jobs The club teaches members how to obtain interviews for jobs that have not been advertised or that do not yet exist. This allows for the discovery and creation of job openings.

Use of Technology as the Primary Contact for Leads Technology is used as the main method of obtaining job leads and arranging interviews.

Classified Directory (Yellow Pages) of the Telephone Book The Yellow Pages is used daily to obtain new lists of employers.

Emphasis on Personal and Social Skills This teaches job seekers how to emphasize their personal and social skills, not just work skills. Personal skills are stressed in the resume, in making contacts, and in the interview.

One Job Lead Uncovers Others This teaches seekers to turn unsuccessful inquiries into new leads to regenerate the supply of leads and contacts.

The Call Back The seeker is taught to arrange a second contact with an employer after an interview. This helps to facilitate the employers' decision.

Transportation This teaches job seekers how to find transportation to otherwise inaccessible job locations. Other members of the group can assist each other with transportation.

Former Employers Job seekers are trained to go to previous employers for job leads as well as job openings.

Open Letter of Recommendation The job seekers obtain letters of recommendations to give potential employers the information needed for making an immediate decision upon an interview.

Resume This helps the seekers build a resume that stresses their personal and work skills rather than simply listing their previous job titles.

Employment Application This teaches the job seeker how to stress positive attributes on the application.

Interview Training This teaches seekers how to act in an interview and how to respond to questions.

Interview Checklist A list of actions to be covered during the interview is given to the job seeker. This list is reviewed after the interview to address any problems that might require correction.

Job Wanted Ads This program places a job wanted ad in the paper for job seekers who have a hard time finding a job. The ad emphasizes the seeker's positive personal attributes.

Non Employment-Derived Work Skills This helps the seeker identify work-related skills that may not have been acquired from previous employment.

Structured Job-Seeking Schedule Job seekers use a form to plan the schedule for each day.

Leads List The seeker maintains a record of leads to organize contacts and call potential employers.

Progress Chart The seeker keeps a record of activities to allow for quick evaluation of progress and to address possible reasons for difficulties in finding a job.

Job Supervisor Job seekers learn how to contact supervisors who might play a role in hiring decisions and who can sometimes create a job geared toward the attributes of an applicant.

Relocation This teaches the seeker how to find a job in another location if no suitable jobs are available locally.

Handicaps This shows the seeker how to discuss any handicaps they may have and how to frame the handicaps in terms of their positive attributes.

Letter Writing for Job Leads This provides sample letters to be used by the job seeker in writing to people for job leads.

Family Support The job seeker gets support from family members and lets them know the ways in which they can help.

Photograph (Optional) Sometimes the job seeker can personalize their resumes by attaching a photograph.

Capability for Many Positions The job seeker learns to look at many different positions, so they are not restricting themselves to one particular type of job.

Continued Assistance This program can give assistance to job seekers until they have found a job. The seeker can also return to the club if they leave a job.

Scheduling

A new group of job seekers enrolls in a club every 2 weeks. This could change depending on the agency. If there are too many job seekers still attending, the next group should be postponed for another week because it is harder to provide attention to each individual when the number of job seekers becomes too large.

There should be fewer than 20 job seekers in the group at one time. This would include members from previous groups added to the number in the current group. Only 10–12 new job seekers are included in each new group, and after the first week, up to 20 can be accommodated.

Therapists should impress upon job seekers to consider the club itself a new full-time job when they begin attending. By doing this, job seekers develop habits of consistency and promptness.

In scheduling the beginning sessions of a job club group, the therapist should remember that the participants who have been out of work for a while might be accustomed to getting up late in the morning, and may get discouraged by early morning sessions. To help accustom the job seekers to attend regularly, the first five sessions should be held in the afternoons.

A new group meets every afternoon during the first week and then switches to morning sessions. The morning sessions include the job seekers from previous groups. After the first five days, the newest members will be asked to arrive for the morning sessions. Job seekers from the previous groups are joined by the job seekers from the new group during the second week. No afternoon sessions are conducted during the second week.

If a new group is organized every 3 weeks, the new group still starts with afternoon sessions for the first week and then changes to morning sessions. The extra week of sessions should see more people finding employment. It is recommended that session hours be posted in a visible place for all to see. The therapist should not meet with job seekers at times other than what is posted. Job seekers arriving early should wait until the designated time for the session. If a job seeker asks a question after the session is over, the therapist should defer the question to the next session. These questions are usually relevant to everyone and others would benefit from listening to the therapist's reply.

Each session should last from 2 to 3 h. In making up a daily schedule, enough time should be allowed for counseling and "free time" for other tasks. The therapist should give undivided attention to job seekers during each session. The therapist must ensure that all other duties are scheduled during free time periods. No telephone interruptions should be allowed. If other duties are important, allow more free time. Other companies use this model with some modifications.

The Social Center for Psychiatric Rehabilitation: Adapting to Change

Job location assistance is provided through the combination of two vehicles, the job developer and the job club. The job club uses a modification of Azrin and Besalel's (1980) work and focuses on getting a job in the community through active participation in structured activities. These activities include locating job leads, interview practice, evaluating, grooming, writing resumes, and making daily contacts with prospective employers with the assistance and support of vocational staff and fellow job seekers. To help facilitate a successful job search, a wide variety of resources are readily provided. This may include the use of a telephone, computer, newspapers, or stationary supplies. After initial openings are identified, job developers engage in extensive outreach to the business community to secure jobs for members. If requested, job developers will go to interviews with members and then provide feedback and additional training and practice as indicated (Cobb and Mellen 1995).

The National Institute of Drug Abuse

Satisfying, gainful employment or career activities can play an important role in achieving and maintaining abstinence from cocaine and other drugs of abuse. Work quality is found to be positively related to teen self-concepts and attitudes. Work experiences give opportunity for advancement and promote a stronger sense of self-efficacy over time, whereas, stressors at work can diminish self-esteem and self-efficacy and appear to foster a depressed mood (Mortimer 2010). Therefore, vocational counseling is an important component of CRA + Vouchers. The procedures are based on those outlined in Azrin and Besalel's "Job Club Counselor's Manual" (1980). We have adapted it for use in individual rather than group settings. Counselors providing this vocational component will benefit from familiarizing themselves with the Job Club manual (Azrin 1976; Chambless et al. 1998).

A job counselor is available to work with clients throughout the week, and therapists use Job Club procedures in individual counseling sessions when appropriate. This counseling focuses on helping unemployed clients locate work and on improving the employment situation of clients who consider their jobs unsatisfactory or have jobs that place them at high risk for continued drug use (Azrin 1976; Chambless et. al. 1998).

For the Unemployed Client

- Make eight job contacts per week.
- Develop a resume.
- Send out two resumes with a cover letter each day.
- Go to the job service twice a week.
- Enroll in a job training twice a week.
- Enroll in a job training program.
- Enroll in a vocational exploration program.
- Take a job-skills-related class.
- Collect and consider information on education possibilities.

The Narrative Model for Career Counseling

This is an individual counseling approach that has been successful with adolescents affected by parental divorce. Approximately 1.5 million children and adolescents in the USA experience parental divorce each year, and 40 % of children are estimated to live with a divorced parent before they reach the age of 16 (Haine et al. 2003).

Adolescents of divorced families often display lower levels of academic and vocational attainment (Thomas and Gibbons 2009). Parental divorce has been associated with maladaptive academic and behavioral outcomes for children, such as depression, anxiety, dropping out of school, drug and alcohol use, and poor academic performance (Wolchik et al. 2000). These effects can continue on into adulthood. Children of divorce tend to earn less income and achieve lower educational status over the course of their life (Amato and Cheadle 2005).

Use of the narrative model allows career counselors a way to empower adolescents to proactively write the next chapters of their lives. It requires the adolescent to be the primary author and actor, which can provide a feeling of control over their lives, a component that is often missing in children of divorce. Narrative counseling allows adolescents to explore family reflections and recognize emotions (Thomas and Gibbons 2009).

Summary

Adolescents that have a higher ability to succeed in the job market demonstrate the ability to be honest about their own abilities and limitations. They also have the ability to adjust to the needs of an employer. The need for a college education is increasing as the job market continues to become more competitive. Workers 18 years and older with a bachelor's degree earned an average of $ 56,788 in 2006, while those with a high school diploma earned $ 31,071 (US Census Beaurea 2008).

Adolescents in 2006, just as in previous times, were motivated to work but lacked adequate knowledge to succeed in a progressive media and computerized environment. Students today face a selective job market that places immeasurable value on experience. Hands-on experience cannot be gained through lectures. Internships play a crucial role in students gaining this experience as well as advancing their professional development (Bailey et al. 2000). In 2008, many university programs include an internship program to aid students in the development of these skills.

Unemployment and the lack of constructive activities correlate with youth experience of low self-esteem, problems with alcohol, depression, unhealthy eating habits, and sleep disorders. Still a fundamental premise—drug addiction, teenage pregnancy, and family violence maintain a strong association with adolescent unemployment. These concerns are reiterated with the rising unemployment rates. Unemployment among teens in December 2008 rose to 20.7 % (Department of Labor 2009).

Work is excellent for the psychosocial development of adolescents. It encourages independence; family contribution to finances, prestige among family and peers, and practice in adult roles. To be sure, the data on an appropriate amount of invested time for youth to work is currently disputed (Pickering and Vazsonyi 2004).

Literacy is a prime resource to transition youth into the growing cyber community and enhances potential to be competitive in the emerging job markets.

New evidence is now surfacing that work may be a distraction from the importance of academic pursuits of youth.

Overall however, limited employment still represents a constructive outlet to adolescent development.

Future Research Implications

Vast research has been done to identify skills employers value most in their employees. Many of these skills fall under the social skills umbrella. As mentioned earlier, communication skills, teamwork skills, and interpersonal skills are among the most desired characteristics sought in employees. These are all skills that can be developed through social skills trainings. Ensuring skills are transferred from the learning environment to the work place is important. This can be done through group processing after each session, as well as using work related situations during group activities. Also, relating tasks to specific jobs skills that can be generalized across jobs would be most effective. Research must isolate the relevant corresponding social behaviors for employment situations (Heckman et al. 2006).

Because the family exerts a powerful influence on the career attitudes and options of adolescents, parent–professional partnerships may be one of the most critical elements in a vocational training program. One study found that disabled individuals aged 16–24 experienced lower workforce participation, higher rates of unemployment, and lower mean earnings than their able-bodied peers (Schultz and Liptak 1998). Families have been only slightly involved in gaining employment for their children, despite the desperate need for collaboration between the individual, the family, and professional assistance.

Additional Resources

Developing Socially Acceptable Skills
http://www.education.com/reference/article/social-strategies-parents-teachers/
The Center for Cognitive Behavioral Therapy
http://www.centreforcbtcounselling.co.uk/anger.php
Program for the Education and Enrichment of Relational Skills (PEERS) program
http://www.semel.ucla.edu/peers/teens
Social Skills Ideas for Children and Teenagers: Ideas Inspired by Research
http://www.parentingscience.com/social-skills-activities.html

References

Adams, A., Franklin, S., & Taylor, R. (2002). *Case management: A resource manual.* (Employment and Training Administration (DOL)), Washington, DC: Office of Youth Opportunities.

Amato, P. R., & Cheadle, J. (2005). The long reach of divorce: Divorce and child well being across three generations. *Journal of Marriage and Family, 67,* 191–206.

Arnett, J. (2000). Emerging adulthood: A theory of development from the late teens through the twenties. *American Psychologist, 55*(5), 469–480.

Azrin, N. H. (1976). Improvements in the community-reinforcement approach to alcoholism. *Behaviour Research and Therapy, 14*(5), 339–348.

Azrin, N. H. (1980). *Job counselors manual: A behavioral approach to vocational counseling.* Austin: Pro-Ed.

Azrin, N. & Besalel, V. (1980). *Job club counselor's manual: A behavioral approach to vocational counseling.* Baltimore, Maryland: Univ. Park Press

Bailey, T., Hughes, K., & Barr, T. (2000). Achieving scale and quality in school-to-work internships: Findings from two employer surveys. *Educational Evaluation and Policy Analysis, 22*(1), 41–46.

Bandura, A. (1977). *Social learning theory*. Englewood Cliffs: Prentice Hall.
Bolton, L. R., Becker, L. K., & Barber, L. K. (2010). Big five trait predictors of differential counterproductive work behavior dimensions. *Personality and Individual Differences, 49*(5), 537–541.
Chambless, D. L., Baker, M. J., Baucom, D. H., Beutler, L. E., Calhoun, K. S., Crits-Christoph, P., & Woody, S. R. (1998). Update on empirically validated therapies, II. *Clinical Psychologist, 51*(1), 3–16.
Chong, W. (2005). The Role of Self-Regulation and Personal Agency Beliefs: A Pychoeducational Approach with Asian High School Students in Singapore. *Journal of Specialist in Group Work, 30*(4), 343–361.
Cobb, S., & Mellen, V. (1995). The Social Center for Psychiatric Rehabilitation: adapting to change. http://www.findarticles.com/p/articles/mi_m0842/is_n1_v21/ai_17299650/pg_4. Accessed 3 April 2006
Cole, K., Daly, A., & Mak, A. (2009). Good for the soul: The relationship between work, wellbeing, and psychological capital. *The Journal of Socio-Economics, 38*(3), 464–474.
Compas, B. E., Connor-Smith, J. K., Saltzman, H., Thomsen, A. H., & Wadsworth, M. E. (2001). Coping with stress during childhood and adolescence: Problems, progress, and potential in theory and research. *Psychological Bulletin, 127*(1), 87–127.
Crudden, A., Sansing, W., & Butler, S. (2005). Overcoming Barriers to Employment: Strategies of Rehabilitation Providers. *Journal of Visual Impairment and Blindness, 99*(6), 325–335.
De Lange, J. M., Barton, J. A., & Lanham, S. L. (1982). The WISER way: A cognitive-behavioral model for group social skills training with juvenile delinquents. *Social Work with Groups, 4*(3–4), 37–48.
Department of Labor. (2009). Economic news release. http://www.bls.gov/news.release/empsit.nr0.htm. Accessed 27 Jan 2009.
Dwived, K. N. (1993). *Group work with children and adolescents: A handbook*. Philedelphia: Jessica Kingsley.
D'Zurilla, T. J., & Nezu, A. (1982). Social problem-solving. In P. C. Kendall (Éd), *Advances in cognitive-behavioral research and therapy* (pp. 201–274). London: Academic Press.
Fallows, S., & Stephen, C. (2000). *Integrating key skills in higher education: Employability, transferable skills, and learning for life*. Sterling: Stylus Publishing.
Feindler, E. L. (1990). Adolescent anger control: Review and critique. *Progress in Behavior Modification, 26,* 11–59.
Gallup Organization. (2008). Gallup's Measure Suggests More Jobless Claims. http://www.gallup.com/tag/Jobs.aspx. Accessed 2 Feb 2009.
Gazda, G. (1982). Basic Approaches to Group Psychotherapy and Group Counseling. Charles C Thomas Pub Ltd; 3rd Ed.
Goldstein, A. P., Sprafkin, R., Gershaw, N., & Klein, P. (1980). *Skill streaming the adolescent.* Champaign, IL: Research Press.
Goldstein, A. P., McGinnis, E., Sprafkin, R. P., Gershaw, N. P., & Klein, P. (1997). *Skillstreaming the adolescent: New strategies and perspectives for teaching prosocial skills*. Champaign: Research Press.
Haine, R. A., Sandler, I. N., Wolchik, S. A., Tein, J., & Dawson-McClure, S. R. (2003). Changing the legacy of divorce: Evidence from prevention programs and future directions. *Family Relations, 52,* 397–405.
Hansen, D. M., & Jarvis, P. A. (2000). Adolescent employment and psychosocial outcomes: A comparison of two employment contexts. *Youth & Society, 31,* 417–436.
Heckman, J. J., Stixrud, J., & Urzua, S. (2006). *The effects of cognitive and noncognitive* abilities on labor market outcomes and social behavior (No. w12006). National Bureau of Economic Research.
Ke, F., & Grabowski, B. (2006). Game playing for math learning: Cooperative or not? *British Journal of Educational Technology, 38*(2), 249–259.

Kuperminc, G., & Allen, J. (2001). Social orientation: Problem behavior and motivation toward interpersonal problem solving among high risk adolescents. *Journal of Youth and Adolescence, 30*(5), 597–622.
Lewis, T., Hudson, S., Richter, M., & Johnson, N. (2004). Scientifically supported practices in emotional and behavioral disorders: a proposed approach and brief review of current practices. *Behavioral Disorders, 29*(3), 247–259.
Lochman, J. E., Boxmeyer, C. L., Powell, N. P., Barry, T. D., & Pardini, D. A. (2003). Anger control training for aggressive youths. *Evidence-Based Psychotherapies for Children and Adolescent* 263–281. 2nd Ed.
Malekoff, A. (2004).*Group work with adolescents: Principles and practice*. New York: The Guildford Press.
Manpower Demonstration research Corporation, MDRC (2006). *Evaluation of Adolescent Literacy Intervention Strategies*. http://www.mdrc.org/project_29_70.html. Accessed 12 March 2013.
Martin, A. J., & Dowson, M. (2009). Interpersonal relationships, motivation, engagement, and achievement: Yields for theory, current issues, and educational practice. *Review of Educational Research, 79*(1), 327–365.
Mazur, J. (2002).*Learning and behavior: Fifth edition*. Upper Saddle River: Prentice Hall/Pearson Education.
Mean Patterson, L. J. (1997). Long-term unemployment amongst adolescents: A longitudinal study. *Journal of Adolescence, 20*(3), 261–280.
Moote, G., Smyth, N., & Wodarski, J. (1999). Social skills training with youth in school settings: A review. *Research in Social Work Practice, 9*(4), 427–465.
Mortimer, J. T. (2010). The benefits and risks of adolescent employment. *Prevention Researcher, 17*(2), 8–11.
National Association of Colleges and Employers (NACE). (2009). http://www.naceweb.org/press/display.asp?year=2003&prid=169. Accessed 27 Jan 2009.
Osgood, D. W., Foster, E. M., & Courtney, M. E. (2010). Vulnerable populations and the transition to adulthood. *The Future of Children, 20*(1), 209–229.
Oxaman, E., & Chambliss, C. (2003). Tailoring treatments for diverse inpatient population. Retrieved from ERIC database (ED475588).
Pickering, L., & Vazsonyi, A. (2004). The impact of adolescent employment on family relationships. *Journal of Adolescent Research, 17*(2), 196–218.
Schinke, S. P., & Gilchrist, L. D. (1984). *Lifeskills counseling with adolescents*. Baltimore: University Park Press.
Schultz, A. W., & Liptak, G. S. (1998). Helping adolescents who have disabilities negotiate transitions to adulthood. *Issues in Comprehensive Pediatric Nursing, 21*(4), 187–201.
Silberman, H. (2004). Academic versus vocational education in the United States. *International Review of Education, 24*(2), 167–176.
Spence, S. (2003). Social skills training with children and young people: Theory, evidence, and practice. *Child and Adolescent Mental Health, 8*(2), 84–96.
Tennessee Department of Education. (2006). Lifetime Wellness Programming Grades 9-12 course description. http://www.tennessee.gov/education/ci/cipewellhiv/cilifetimewellness.html. Accessed 1 April 2006.
Thomas, D. A., & Gibbons, M. M. (2009). Narrative theory: A career counseling approach for adolescents of divorce. *Professional School Counseling, 12*(3), 223–229.
Timmons, J., Podmostko, M., Bremer. C., Lavin, D., & Wills, J. (2004). Career planning begins with assessment: A guide for professionals serving youth with education and career development challenges. Nation Collaborative on Workforce and Disability for Youth, funded under a grant by the U.S. Department of Labor, Office of Disability Employment Policy (grant Number E-9-4-1-0070).
Turner, S. L., & Conkel, J. L. (2010). Evaluation of a career development skills intervention with adolescents living in an inner city. *Journal of Counseling & Development Fall 2010, 88,* 457–465.

Turner, S. L., Trotter, M. J., Lapan, R. T., Czajka, K. A., Yang, P., & Brissett, A. E. (2006). Vocational skills and outcomes among native American adolescents: A test of the integrative contextual model of career development. *The Career Development Quarterly, 54,* 216–226.
Census Bureau, U. S. (2008). Newsroom. http://www.census.gov/Press-Release/www/releases/archives/education/011196.html. Accessed 27 Jan 2009.
Valentine, S. (2004). Employment Counseling and Organizational Ethic Value. *Journal of Employment Counseling, 41*(4), 146.
Walls, R. & Werner, T. (1977). Vocational behavior checklist. *Mental Retardation, 15*(4), 30–35.
Wodarski, J., Wodarski, L., & Kim, T. (1989). Comprehensive employment preparation for adolescents with developmental disabilities: An empirical paradigm. *Adolescence, 24*(96), 821–836.
Wodarski, J., & Wodarski, L. (1993). *Curriculums and practical aspects of implementation: Preventive health services for adolescents.* Lanham: University Press of America, Inc.
Wodarski, J., & Feit, M. (1995). *Adolescent substance abuse: An empirical-based group preventative health paradigm.* Binghamton: Haworth Press, Inc.
Wodarski, J., & Dziegielewski, S. (2002). *Human behavior in the social environment: An empirical approach.* New York: Springer.
Wodarski, J., Wodarski, L., & Parris, H. (2004). Adolescent preventive health and teams-games-tournaments: A research and development paradigm entering its fourth decade of research. *Journal of Evidence-based Social Work, 1*(1), 101–124.
Wolchik, S. A., Wilcox, K. L., Tein, J., & Sandler, I. N. (2000). Maternal acceptance and consistency of discipline and buffers of divorce stressors on children's psychological adjustment problems. *Journal of Abnormal Child Psychology, 28,* 87–102.
Wolf-Branigin, M., Schuyler, V., & White, P. (2007). Improving quality of life and career attitudes of youth with disabilities experiences from the adolescent employment readiness center. *Research on Social Work Practice, 17*(3), 324–333.
Zarrett, N., & Eccles, J. (2006). The passage to adulthood: Challenges of late adolescence. *New Directions for Youth Development, 2006*(111), 13–28. doi:10.1002/yd.179.

Chapter 14
The Empirical Base for the Implementation of Social Skills Training with Maltreated Children

Michael J. Holosko

Children's peer relationships are increasingly recognized as critical to healthy adjustment both in childhood and later in life. Without effective social interaction skills, children experience rejection by peers, social isolation, and limited opportunities to benefit from play and work with others. Moreover, research suggests that children do not outgrow social skills deficits. Disturbances in peer relationships can predict difficulties in later life such as delinquency, dropping out of school, and mental health referrals (Cowen et al. 1973). Children and adolescents with poor social skills have been shown to be at heightened risk for engaging in delinquent behaviors (Fixsen et al. 2010; Patterson et al. 1992; Parker and Asher 1987), depression or social withdrawal (Christoff et al. 1985), poor academic performance (Hinshaw 1992), and other serious emotional and behavioral difficulties (Newman et al. 1996) than youth who are socially competent. Social skills deficits that result from social-behavioral difficulties, often lead to short- and long-term adjustment difficulties in educational, psychosocial, and vocational domains (Kupersmidt et al. 1990; Newcomb et al. 1993; Parker and Asher 1987).

Social skills are the specific behaviors that an individual exhibits to perform competently on a social task (e.g., active listening skills, reciprocal communication, ignoring, etc.) (Gresham 2002). Deficits in social skills may result from developmental delays in language acquisition or motor performance or from faulty learning. Studies have repeatedly shown that children with social competence deficits are at greater risk for poor school adjustment and adult psychopathology than students who are socially competent (Newman et al. 1996; Patterson et al. 1992). Social Competence is an evaluative term based on judgments that a person has performed a social task completely (Cook et al. 2008). Children who fail to respond appropriately in social situations may have been exposed to inappropriate models in their environments; parents of withdrawn children tend to display low rates of pro-social behavior with their children (Finch and Rogers 1984), and parents of aggressive children tend to be aggressive themselves (Pfeffer et al. 1983; Reid et al. 1981).

M. J. Holosko (✉)
University of Georgia, Athens, GA, USA
e-mail: mholosko@uga.edu

J. S. Wodarski et al. (eds.), *Evidence-Informed Assessment and Practice in Child Welfare,* DOI 10.1007/978-3-319-12045-4_14

Further, children with social skills deficits are often reared in dysfunctional families in which members feel isolated and respond to each other in a passive, ineffective fashion (Webster-Stratton and Reid 2010).

Social Skills Deficits in Maltreated Children

The Berkeley Planning Associates' large-scale evaluation study of demonstration treatment projects found that 70% of maltreated children who entered treatment did not relate well with their peers (Cohn 1979). Another study investigated the specific types of social deficits in maltreated children, and found that when compared to their nonmaltreated peers, maltreated children were significantly less able to maintain self-control during play and significantly less likely to initiate social interactions with peers during play. These children also exhibited a significantly greater number of problem behaviors, such as physical and verbal aggression and temper tantrums (Darwish et al. 2001). Furthermore, neglected and abused children have been found to exhibit developmentally delayed social skills, decreased spontaneous playfulness, and behavioral issues during play (Cooper 2000). A large body of maltreatment research has identified marked social skills deficits in abused and neglected children, including both aggressive and withdrawal behaviors. As social learning theory had predicted, abused and neglected children have been found to display different patterns of dysfunctional social behavior; abused children are more likely to display high rates of aggression with peers, and neglected children are more likely to display low rates of interaction with peers (Hoffman-Plotkin and Twentyman 1984). Other studies, however, have found that abused children also exhibit low rates of social interaction and neglected children exhibit elevated levels of aggression (Aber and Allen 1987; Bousha and Twentyman 1984; Straker and Jacobson 1981).

These mixed findings could be a result of the lack of conceptual clarity of the terms *abuse* and *neglect* (Burgess and Conger 1978; Giovannoni and Becera 1979). Indeed, evidence exists that abusive and neglectful families are more similar than they are different (Erickson et al. 1987). For example, observational research has found that both types of families have low rates of interaction and emphasize negative interactions (Burgess and Conger 1978). A number of researchers recently have suggested that the psychological maltreatment that underlies both abuse and neglect accounts for the effects of child maltreatment (Garbarino and Vondra 1987; Hart and Brassard 1987). The work of Egeland, Sroufe, and their associates (Egeland and Sroufe 1981; Erickson and Egeland 1987) supports this view. Their prospective, longitudinal study comparing nonmaltreated children with children whose mothers were abusive, neglectful, or "psychologically unavailable" found not only severe cognitive and social deficits in all groups of maltreated children, but also remarkable similarities among children in all maltreatment groups.

Children who fail to respond appropriately in social situations may have been exposed to inappropriate models within their environments. Parents of socially withdrawn or aggressive children have been found to display lower rates of prosocial behaviors themselves (Weisz and Kazdin 2010). Without positive and consistent parental examples of social interactions, children become more likely to develop deficits in attachment and less likely to explore within their environment. Issues regarding poor attachment development can affect how the maltreated child perceives caregivers, authority figures, and peers (Elliott et al. 2005). In addition to appropriate modeling of social interactions by parental figures, the attachment style is dependent on parental response to stressful situations. If an infant learns that she can rely on her parents to soothe her when she is stressed, she will develop a secure attachment style and eventually be able to learn self-soothing and emotional regulation. Conversely, if the home environment is chaotic and parental response to stress is unpredictable or inconsistent, the infant will develop a disorganized attachment style and be less able to cope later in life. Disorganized attachment prevents children from forming healthy relationships with others, which negatively affects peer interactions and social development (Putnam 2005).

In addition, considerable evidence exists that both abusive (Garbarino and Crouter 1978; Parke and Collmer 1975) and neglectful (Giovannoni and Billingsley 1970; Polansky et al. 1981) parents have social skills deficits that leave them isolated from formal and informal social supports. It seems unlikely that the much discussed intergenerational cycle of child maltreatment can be broken without focusing on the social deficits that maltreated children and their parents have in common (Barahal et al. 1981). For instance, a study comparing mother-infant play in maltreating and nonmaltreating families found significant differences in the behaviors of mothers and children from these groups. When compared to their nonmaltreated counterparts, maltreated infants were more likely to engage in imitative play and were less likely to engage in independent play, both of which indicate delayed social development. Researchers also found that mothers of maltreated children were significantly more likely to be less attentive during play than were mothers of nonmaltreated children (Valentino et al. 2006). Empirical research on the psychosocial sequelae of child maltreatment has identified specific social deficits in abused and neglected children that may be amenable to treatment. Maltreated children have been characterized as shy and inhibited in interpersonal contacts (Oates et al. 1984) and lacking in self-confidence (Martin and Beezley 1977) and in receptive and expressive language skills (Allen and Oliver 1982). Evidence exists that maltreated children socially isolate themselves even as toddlers (George and Main 1979), and that by school age, these children may have great difficulty comprehending complex social roles and evaluating the feelings and motives of others (Barahal et al. 1981; Straker and Jacobson 1981). The elementary-age abused children in Kinard's (1980) study described themselves as being sad, unpopular, and unhappy. Further, when compared with control groups, maltreated children are more likely to believe that negative outcomes are primarily due to external factors rather than self action (Slade et al. 1984). Curiously, another study found that maltreated children did not perceive themselves as having poor social skills or peer interactions, but their mothers perceived their maltreated children as being socially incompetent when compared to their nonmaltreated peers (Milling 1999).

Aggression, poor impulse control, and low frustration tolerance have been noted consistently in maltreated children, particularly abused children (Aber and Allen 1987; Bousha and Twentyman 1984; Burgess and Conger 1978; George and Main 1979; Straker and Jacobson 1981). McCord and Sanchez's (1983) longitudinal study found higher rates of delinquency among children who had been abused or neglected than among those raised in loving homes. Further, much evidence exists that abused and neglected children are exposed to frequent and severe stress as a result of their families' poverty, restricted educational and occupational opportunities, unemployment, social isolation, marital conflict, and unstable family situations (Conger et al. 1979; Plansky et al. 1981; Straus 1979). The effects of such environmental stressors may be exacerbated by the inability of the maltreated child to cope adequately with frustrating situations (Egeland et al. 1983; Herrenkohl and Herrenkohl 1981).

Social Skills Training (SST)

Most SST programs have the following four objectives: (1) promoting skill acquisition, (2) enhancing skill performance, (3) reducing or eliminating competing problem behaviors, and (4) facilitating generalization and maintenance of social skills. Thus, the common features shared by most SST programs are that they emphasize the acquisition, performance, generalization, and/or maintenance of pro-social behaviors and the reduction or elimination of competing problem behaviors (Cook et al. 2008). Theoretically, social skills deficits that result from faulty learning can be remedied through instruction in specific components of social interaction; the effectiveness of this approach has been demonstrated for adults, socially withdrawn children (Asher et al. 1981; Ladd 1981), and aggressive children (Elder et al. 1979). As Bandura (1977) postulated, specific skills are enhanced by providing encouragement and opportunities to perform new skills for which standards of performance are increased gradually. Furthermore, evidence exists that improvements in a child's social behavior lead to more positive attitudes toward the child by peers (Oden and ERIC Clearinghouse on Elementary and Early Childhood Education, U. I. 1986). A number of maltreatment researchers have suggested that social skills training may be especially appropriate for abused and neglected children (Barahal et al. 1981; Keller and Erne 1983). Thus far, however, the effectiveness of this approach has not been evaluated systematically with children from this population.

Maltreatment interventions generally focus on improving the child's circumstances through changing parental behaviors. Typically, child welfare agencies are mandated to work with abusive or neglectful parents but not with the maltreated child. Until recently, very few maltreated children received direct services (Cohn and Daro 1987). Interventions focused on the parents may be insufficient to overcome established social deficits in the maltreated child (Howes and Espinosa 1985). Treatment services provided for child victims of maltreatment, however, have led to notable gains (Daro 1988). The recent National Clinical Evaluation Study of demonstration treatment projects found that 70 % of the children and adolescents treated achieved gains on all the study's outcome measures. Among the most effective services provided were therapeutic day care, personal skills development classes, and group counseling, all of which offer implicit opportunities to learn socialization skills. One group of researchers found that in addition to having parents involved in social skills training, it was critical to have the support and modeling of more resilient and socially well-adjusted peers as well. Researchers randomly assigned maltreated children to either the resilient peer treatment (RPT) group or the control group, and found that those who had been exposed to positive peer role models exhibited significant increases in positive social interactions and significant decreases in socially isolated behaviors (Fantuzzo et al. 1996). What are needed now are programs offering explicit social skills training for maltreated children.

Designing Social Skills Training Programs for Maltreated Children Management

Skill Selection: The Theoretical Base

Social skillfulness often is viewed as a trait-like feature (that is, a person is said to be "high" or "low" in social skillfulness across a broad range of situations and over time). Empirical research has not supported such a view, which is of little use in specifying points of intervention (Bornstein et al. 1977). A more useful approach begins with the identification of specific tasks that are relevant and critical for a person or group, followed by an analysis of the cognitive, affective, motor, and physiological components necessary for competent performance of that task (McFall 1982).

As the first part of this formulation suggests, developmental, cultural, and situational considerations are of critical importance in designing intervention programs (that is, the skills selected must reflect the age-appropriate issues and "real life" needs of the target population (Hops et al. 1985). Thus, the common practice of selecting skills to teach children by extrapolating downward from successful adult models has been justly criticized (Hops et al. 1994).

To be effective, social skills training programs should identify specific deficits in the target population and design interventions to address them (Beelmann et al. 1994; Wodarski et al. 1990; La Greca 1993; Lochman et al. 1993). Skill selection for children must begin with an empirical identification of skills that are functional for a given age and peer group. When the target population consists of maltreated children, a critical examination of the literature on skill deficits that have been identified in abused or neglected children of the same developmental state is in order. Maltreatment research that categorizes children of varying ages as one group is less helpful because it may obscure critical developmental differences (Aber and Cicchetti 1984).

The second part of the formulation—the analysis of the components necessary for successful completion of the task—also has implications for skill selection; tasks must be divisible into identifiable sequences of behavior. Thus, a general task, such as "becoming more sociable," should be broken into more manageable subtasks, such as "introducing yourself" or "initiating a conversation." These subtasks should be stated in terms of sequential, observable behaviors for which appropriate instructional strategies can be identified (Cartledge and Milburn 1986).

Recently, McConnell (1987) discussed a third factor that must be considered in selecting skills to teach children. To ensure that skills are generalized and maintained beyond the training setting, the skills selected should be ones that will be reinforced naturally by persons in the child's environment. Thus, taught behaviors should be of intrinsic value and benefit not only to the child, but also to his or her peers, parents, teachers, or significant others, who will then reinforce their occurrence. The reciprocal nature of social interaction suggests that program planning should begin with specification of the type of persons from whom reinforcement is desired. If peer skills are the focus of the training and program, program planners should recognize that behaviors considered desirable by adults (such as orderliness and following rules) may not be as highly valued or reinforced by peers. On the other hand, skills training for maltreated children may target parents as the intended reinforcers to develop skills in the child that could reduce the likelihood that maltreatment will recur (Azar et al. 1984). In this case, however, parent involvement in the treatment process is vital. As Azar and Twentyman (1986) warn, "changing the child without intervening with the family as a whole may prove not only fruitless, but harmful to the child… if verbal initiations on his/her part are punished" by parents (p. 260).

There is some evidence that interventions involving peer-initiated interactions produced more positive responses among maltreated children than did those involving adult-initiated actions or no intervention (Fantuzzo et al. 1988). Even when skills training focuses on improving peer relationships, it may be important, especially for older children, to supplement training with environmental manipulations aimed at changing peer responses to the target child (McConnell 1987). Such manipulations go back to the importance of positive reinforcement to encourage pro-social behaviors (Gresham et al. 2004). In terms of using peers in the reinforcement aspect of social skill training, the developmental age of the child must be taken into account as the influence of peer groups holds different significance over time (Wodarski et al. 2004; Wodarski and Feit 2012). During the period of preadolescence, when peer acceptance patterns have begun to crystallize, changes in a target child's behavior may have less effect on peer attitudes (Bierman and Furman 1984). Considering the difficulties maltreated children have in dealing with failure (Slade et al. 1984), providing examples of strategies for coping with negative peer responses is crucial (Ladd and Mize 1983). Further, maltreated children may have particular problems, such as language deficits or distractibility that require different approaches to implementing social skills training programs (Wodarski et al. 1990).

Skills Training: The Practice Base

A number of group- oriented intervention packages with multiple skills training components have been developed to improve children's social skills (LaGasse 2014; Rodriguez and Anderson 2014; Rosselet and Stauffer 2013; Schinke and Gilchrist 1984), but few have been empirically validated, with the exception of Hops et al. (1978). The development and validation of programs designed around developmental and situational factors specific to abused and neglected children should be a priority for researchers in the field of child maltreatment interventions. Components that may be particularly appropriate for this population involve interpersonal communication, problem-solving, self-control, appropriate assertiveness, and stress management. The authors' recommendations identify appropriate starting points for developing new programs, but application of the skill components with other groups of maltreated children should not be ruled out.

Interpersonal Communication

Nonverbal and verbal behaviors are integral to the successful social adjustment of children. Effective communication depends on postures, facial mannerisms, gestures, and voice inflections, as well as verbal content. A number of researchers have developed programs for teaching interpersonal communication skills (Ladd 1981; LaGreca and Santogrossi 1980; Lange and Jakubowski 1976), which include the following seven elements: (1) introducing oneself; (2) initiating and maintaining conversations; (3) giving and receiving compliments; (4) enhancing appearance; (5) making and refusing requests; (6) spontaneously expressing feelings; and (7) appropriately using distance, body language, face, hand and foot movement, and smiles.

Kinard (1999) suggests maltreated children have difficulties in relationships with others and thus may lack the interpersonal skills necessary to establish successful relationships. Training in interpersonal communication skills may be particularly beneficial for withdrawn maltreated children of preschool or early elementary age, before self-concept has begun to crystallize (Collins 1984). Neglected children, who tend to interact minimally with peers and adults, are good candidates for this type of training. The language deficits common to abused and neglected children suggests that nonverbal techniques may need to be emphasized initially in training programs for these children. An emphasis on nonverbal skills is further justified by findings that, in contrast with their middle-class counterparts, popularity among lower-class school children is associated more with positive nonverbal than with positive verbal interactions (Hartup 1984). The vast majority of children who are identified as physically abused or neglected, come from low-income families.

Problem Solving

It is common for maltreated children to struggle with executive functioning, such as abstract thinking, decision-making, and problem solving. This is due to the fact that abuse and neglect in early childhood can have detrimental effects on brain development, which is rapid and critical during this time of life. In particular, the prefrontal cortex develops and makes important connections in early childhood, and abuse and neglect can cause deficits in this part of the brain, where problem-solving happens (Bolen and Gergely in press). Children who exhibit interpersonal problem solving skills are less likely to experience peer relationship disturbances (Asarnow and Callan 1985; Asher et al. 1981; Kazdin 2010). A number of researchers have developed procedures for teaching children the problem-solving steps of problem identification, issue clarification, brainstorming, decision making, and verification to provide the child with general strategies to apply in a variety of situations (Spivak and Shure 1974; Weissberg et al. 1980). A growing body of research has established the usefulness of problem-solving training with adolescents, including adjudicated delinquents (Hazel et al. 1985; Sarason and Sarason 1984). Skills that are enhanced include the following five: (1) generating alternative solutions to interpersonal problems, (2) identifying the steps necessary to reach a goal, (3) considering the means and ends of social acts, (4) examining the consequences of various courses of action, and (5) recognizing differences in motives and view points (similar to empathy).

Problem-solving skills training may be best suited for impulsive maltreated children age 12 and over. The heightened capacity for abstract thinking that appears in most children by age 12 may facilitate the structured learning of problem-solving skills. Further, the increased challenges of adolescence often become overwhelming for young people who lack parental and peer support. Physically abused adolescents may display emotional instability, poor coping skills and impulse control, helplessness, depression, acting out, or serious adjustment problems (Hjorth and Ostrov 1982). The authors' own current research shows that adolescents, (age 12–16) abused girls, in particular, tend to display impulsive, under-controlled behavior (Wodarski et al. in press; Wodarski and Feit 2012). Other research has found that, without intervention, boys' problems are likely to improve during adolescence, while girls' problems are likely to become worse (Werner and Smith 1982). Thus, physically abused adolescent girls might benefit from problem-solving skills training.

Self-Control

Aggressive children are likely to be rejected by peers (Coie et al. 1982; Dodge 1983) and are at risk for a variety of maladjustment problems, including delinquency (Loeber and Dishion 1983; Roff et al. 1972) and psychiatric problems (Cowen et al. 1973; Roff and Wirt 1984). Although aggressive children are notoriously difficult to treat, researchers have developed and used social learning approaches and training models for this population (Camp and Bash 1981; Goldstein et al. 1978; Kendall and Brawswell 1985). Self-control training includes five elements: (1) identifying stressors that can provoke anger and subsequent violent behavior; (2) developing relaxation skills to reduce the effects of stress; (3) learning to handle assertions from others and deal with others' anger; (4) developing appropriate communication and assertion skills, and (5) practicing alternative behavior, such as stimulus removal, in anger-provoking situations.

Despite a marked degree of stability in aggressive behavior, particularly among boys, aggressive reactions are thought to be a result more of environmental interaction than of genetic influence and thus may be modified if intervention takes place at an early age (Olweus 1984). Interventions to control aggression in later childhood or adolescence have frequently been unsuccessful (Patterson 1979). Unfortunately, aggressive patterns that continue past middle childhood may be a prelude to delinquency and adult criminality (Rutter and Garmezy 1983). Thus, the development of models to facilitate the early identification and treatment of aggressive maltreated children should be a priority for researchers and program planners. Physically abused preschool and early elementary age abused boys may be particularly appropriate targets for social skills remediation programs that emphasize self-control training.

Appropriate Assertiveness

Studies have shown that socially maladjusted children resort to both withdrawal and aggression because they are unable to be appropriately and effectively assertive (Bornstein et al. 1977). Although the literature on assertiveness training with adults is extensive, and although skills training programs for children often include an assertiveness component, the empirical base for such training with children is limited. Several studies by Bornstein et al. (1977), however, did report improvement in the assertiveness skills of elementary-age children after individual training, which focused on maintaining eye contact while speaking, speaking with appropriate loudness, increasing speech duration, and requesting new behavior from the interpersonal partner.

Withdrawal and aggression have been identified as major components in the social maladjustment of abused and neglected children at every age level. Assertiveness training, perhaps combined with interpersonal skills training or self-control training, could prove an effective means of teaching maltreated children to increase their interactions and to express strong feelings of aggression in appropriately prosocial ways.

Stress Management

Research on the effects of childhood stress had consistently found a significant relationship between stressful life events and psychological and behavioral problems in children and adolescents (Compas 1987). Self-relaxation training is an effective treatment for stress-induced anxiety in children and youth (Koeppen 1974; Ollendick and Cerny 1981). Training in cognitive coping techniques is also considered useful (Meichenbaum 1993; Schinke and Gilchrist 1984). These procedures focus on skills such as learning muscle relaxation and deep-breathing exercises to reduce tension, using self-talk to get through stressful episodes, recognizing and modifying self-limiting internal dialogue, and rewarding effective coping performance through self reinforcement.

Stress management training may be especially appropriate for adolescent and preadolescent abused or neglected children. It appears that children between the ages of 6 and 12 are more able than older children to cope well with a variety of problems (Berger 1986). For older maltreated children, the normative stressors of adolescence are compounded by the stressors endemic to maltreating families. Further, there is evidence that the separate effects of major childhood stressors (such as low social status, severe marital discord, and overcrowding) are markedly potentiated by each other (Rutter 1979). Children who face more than one such stressor are much more likely to have psychiatric problems than children who face only one. Adolescent girls seem to be particularly vulnerable to the effects of stress (Compas 1987). Thus, abused or neglected girls over age 12 may be particularly good candidates for stress management training, perhaps in combination with problem-solving skills training. Disorganized attachment, which commonly results from abusive or neglectful environments, prevents children from learning self-soothing and emotional regulation. For this reason, it is especially important for maltreated children to learn developmentally appropriate coping skills (Putnam 2005).

Group Format

The group format is a natural context for teaching interpersonal skills to children. It provides an arena in which children can observe a variety of models and receive ongoing peer reinforcement as they acquire new skills (Feldman and Wodarski 1975). Unlike individual treatment, the group context offers interactional situations that reflect the structure and constantly changing demands of the child's world. According to social learning theory, behaviors learned in a group are more likely to come under the control of a greater number of discriminative stimuli, increasing the probability that learned skills will be used in situations outside the group. Furthermore, the provisions of services through groups greatly increases the number of children that can be served and, consequently, the cost-effectiveness of treatment services.

Groups are seen as appropriate for children of all ages, even preschool children (Steward et al. 1986). Small groups of 10 or fewer children are thought to be more effective than larger groups (McGinnis and Goldstein 1984), and regular skill instruction at least twice a week is recommended (Michelson et al. 1983); daily programs that are in effect for at least 2 months have the greatest impact (Hops 1983; Thyer and Wodarski 2007). McGinnis and Goldstein (1984) suggested that the use of more than one trainer (preferably a male and a female) facilitates generalization of new skills, Barth and Ash (1986) reported that the use of peer leaders has been encouraging.

Several other factors should be considered in structuring groups for maltreated children. LeCroy (1983) reported that leaders of children's groups ranked boredom and inattentiveness as primary barriers to the groups' smooth functioning. Because abused and neglected children tend to be more distractible than control groups (Egeland et al. 1983), special efforts may be required to involve these children in the group process. Cartledge and Milburn (1986) suggested that almost any social content can be put into game format through very simple means, for example, picking a skill out of a hat to role play, or having teams take turns playing a form of charades in which a specific emotion or coping strategy is pantomimed (p. 144). Such an approach may be especially appropriate for maltreated children. Additionally, the language deficits common to these children require special attention. Memory enhancement procedures, such as reducing children's rehearsed examples of new skills into shorter phrases or memory codes (Oden and Asher 1977), may prove effective with this population.

Given their similar social skills deficits, abused and neglected children could arguably be included in the same group. In addition, the inclusion of higher-functioning peers (if they are not functioning at levels the target children consider unattainable) may provide motivation for lower-functioning members (Schellenbach and Guerney 1987). On the other hand, Furman et al. (1979) suggested that as a result of developmental lags, certain maltreated children may respond more effectively in a group of slightly younger children.

Evaluation

Process evaluation measures, such as videotapes of children practicing their new skills, provide an ongoing record of progress that can be shared with children to reinforce learning (Ladd and Mize 1983). Outcome evaluation procedures can be used to demonstrate that a social skills training program was effective in changing the behaviors of target children. The impact of a program is increased immeasurably if these procedures are empirically sound and if the findings are disseminated. The rapid increase in the reported incidence of child maltreatment (up to 66 % from 1980 to 1986 according to the National Center on Child Abuse and Neglect 1988) underscores the critical importance of such evaluation research to society. Child welfare practitioners need to know which components of social skills training, delivered in what manner and by whom, are successful in changing the social behaviors of maltreated children. Thus, statistical procedures and planned variations that can document the separate contributions of these factors to the obtained outcomes are needed (Ladd and Mize 1983).

It is beyond the scope of this chapter to discuss research designs and data collection strategies in detail, but this information is available elsewhere (for example, Barlow et al. 1982). Generally, the most useful approaches compare children on measures of social competence before and after training or compare the target children's pretest and posttest scores with those children from the same population who did not receive training. In either case, follow-up testing is essential to show whether the effects of training are maintained after termination of the training.

Training effectiveness may be measured in a variety of way (Hops et al. 1985). Direct observation of children in social situations can provide fine-grained data and behavior role-play tests can be used to assess child behaviors in situations that correspond to real life. These tests can be videotaped to reinforce learning and to provide data on the processes by which social skills are acquired. Reports from the child, parents, teachers, peers, or others in the form of interviews, behavior checklists, or self-reports can elicit information on a child's functioning in diverse settings. Whichever procedures are used, the criteria of assessment should relate directly to the behaviors targeted for change and should take into account the stage-specific developmental tasks of the target children (Aber and Cicchetti 1984). Evaluation measures should focus on both the quality of children's skill performance and their effectiveness at achieving peer acceptance (Foster and Ritchey 1979). Finally, multisource and multicriterion evaluation is far superior to the use of a single measure; thus, a combination of assessment procedures is recommended.

Conclusion

Every treatment program should be established on the best theoretical and empirical rationale in existence. On the basis of both theory and research findings, social skills training appears to offer a promising approach for intervention with maltreated children. Not all children who have been abused or neglected are deficient in the social skills that have been discussed, but an extensive body of research has found that a great many are. This consistent finding suggests that remedial programs should be implemented. Social skills training programs that depend on social learning principles have proven effective with a variety of clinical populations. Present evidence clearly warrants extending such training to maltreated children.

Additional Resources

Developmental problems of Maltreated Children
http://aspe.hhs.gov/hsp/07/children-cps/litrev/part1.htm
Child Maltreatment
http://www.uiowa.edu/~c07p224/abstracts/child_maltreatment.htm
Understanding the effects of Maltreatment on Brain Development
https://www.childwelfare.gov/pubs/issue_briefs/brain_development/effects.cfm
Social Skills Training Project
http://www.socialskillstrainingproject.com/

The Role of Educators in Preventing and Responding to Child Abuse and Neglect
https://www.childwelfare.gov/pubs/usermanuals/educator/educatorf.cfm
Preventing Child Maltreatment: Evidence and Opportunities
http://futureofchildren.org/publications/journals/article/index.xml?journalid=71&articleid=513&sectionid=3500
Adults and Children Together (ACT) Raising Safe Kids Program
https://www.crimesolutions.gov/ProgramDetails.aspx?ID=311

References

Aber, J. L, & Allen, J. P. (1987). Effects of maltreatment on young children's socioemotional development: An attachment theory perspective. *Developmental Psychology, 23*(3), 406–414.

Aber, J. L., & Cicchetti, D. (1984). The socio-emotional development of maltreated children: An empirical and theoretical analysis. In H. Fitzgerald, B. Lester, & M. Yogman (Eds.), *Theory and research in behavioral pediatrics* (Vol. 2, pp. 147–205). New York: Plenum Press.

Allen, R. E., & Oliver, J. M. (1982). The effects of child maltreatment on language development *Child Abuse & Neglect,* 6(3), 299–305.

Asarnow, J. R., & Calan, J. R. (1985). Boys with peer adjustment problems: Social cognitive processes. *Journal of Consulting and Clinical Psychology, 53,* 80–87.

Asher, S. R., Hymel, S., & Renshaw, P. D. (1981). Loneliness in children. *Child Development, 55*(4), 1456–1464.

Bandura, A. (1997). *Self-efficacy: The exercise of control.* New York: W. H. Freeman.

Barahal, R. M., Waterman, J., & Martin, H. P. (1981). The social cognitive development of abused children. *Journal of Consulting and Clinical Psychology, 49,* 508–516.

Barth P., & Ash, R. (1986). Identifying, screening and engaging high-risk clients in private nonprofit child abuse prevention programs. *Child Abuse & Neglect, 10,* 99–109.

Beelmann, A., Pfingsten, U., & Lösel, F. (1994). Effects of training social competence in children: A meta-analysis of recent evaluation studies. *Journal of Clinical Child Psychology, 23,* 260–271.

Berger, B. G. (1986). Use of jogging and swimming as stress reduction techniques. In J. H. Humphrey (Ed.), *Human stress: Current selected research in human stress* (Vol. 1). New York: AMS.

Bierman, K. L., & Furman, W. (1984). The effects of social skills training and peer involvement on the social adjustment of preadolescents. *Child Development, 55*(1), 151–162.

Bolen, R. M., & Gergely, K. B. (in press). Child sexual abuse. In J. Conte (Ed.), *Child abuse and neglect worldwide.* ABC-CLIO.

Bornstein, M. R., Bellack, A. S., & Hersen, M. (1977). Social-skills training for unassertive children: A multiple-baseline analysis. *Journal of Applied Behavioral Analysis, 10*(2), 183–195. doi:10.1901/jaba.l977.10–183.

Bornstein, M., Bellack, A. S., & Hersen, M. (1980). Social skills training for highly aggressive children: Treatment in an inpatient psychiatric setting. *Behavior Modifications, 4*(2), 173–186.

Bousha, D. M., & Twentyman, C. T. (1984). Mother-child interaction style in abuse, neglect, and control groups. *Journal of Abnormal Psychology, 93*(1), 106–114.

Burgess, R. L., & Conger, R. D. (1978). Family interaction in abusive, neglectful and normal families. *Child Development, 49,* 1152–1175.

Camp, B. W., & Bash, M. A. (1981). *Think aloud.* Champagne: Research Press.

Cartledge, G., & Milburn, J. F. (1986). *Teaching social skills to children: Innovative approaches* (2nd ed.). New York: Pergamon Press.

Christoff, K. A., Scott, W. O., Kelley, M. L., Schlundt, D., Baer, G., & Kelly, J. A. (1985). Social skills and social problem-solving training for shy young adolescents. *Behavior Therapy, 16,* 468–477.
Cohn, A. H. (1979). Essential elements of successful child abuse and neglect treatment. *Child Abuse & Neglect, 3*(2), 491–496.
Cohn, A. H., & Daro, D. (1987). Is treatment too late: What ten years of evaluative research tell us. *Child Abuse & Neglect, 11*(3), 433–442.
Coie, J., Dodge, K., & Coppotelli, H. (1982). Dimensions and types of social status: A cross-age perspective. *Developmental Psychology, 18,* 557–570.
Collins, N. L, & Read, S. J. (1984). Adult attachment, working models and relationship quality in dating couples. *Journal of Personality and Social Psychology, 58,* 644–663.
Compas, B. E. (1987). Coping with stress during childhood and adolescence. *Psychological Bulletin, 101,* 393–403.
Conger, R. D., Burgess, R. L., & Barrett, C. (1979). Child abuse related to life change and perceptions of illness: Some preliminary findings. *The Family Coordinator, 28*(1), 73–78.
Cook, C., Gresham, F., Kern, L., Barreras, R., Thornton, S., & Crews, S. (2008). Social skills training for secondary students with emotional and/or behavioral disorders: A review and analysis of the meta-analytic literature. *Journal of Emotional and Behavioral Disorders, 16*(3), 131–144. (Retrieved February 16, 2009, from Academic Search Premier database).
Cooper, R. J. (2000). The impact of child abuse on children's play: A conceptual model. *Occupational Therapy International, 7*(4), 259–276.
Cowen, E. L., Pederson, A., Babigren, H., Izzo, L. D., & Trost, M. A. (1973). Long-term follow-up of early detected vulnerable children. *Journal of Consulting and Clinical Psychology, 4,* 438–446.
Daro, D. (1988). Confronting child abuse: Research for effective program design. New York: Free Press.
Darwish, D., Esquivel, G. B., Houtz, J. C., & Alfonso, V. C. (2001). Play and social skills in maltreated and non-maltreated preschoolers during peer interactions. *Child Abuse & Neglect, 25*(1), 13–31.
Dodge, K. (1983). Behavioral antecedents of social status. *Child Development, 54,* 1386–1399.
Egeland, B., & Sroufe, L. A. (1981). Attachment and early maltreatment. *Child Development, 52,* 44–52.
Egeland, B., Sroufe, L. A., & Erickson, M. (1983). The developmental consequence of different patterns of maltreatment. *Journal of Child Abuse & Neglect, 7,* 459–469.
Elder, G. H., Jr., & Rockwell, R. C. (1979). Economic depression and postwar opportunity in men's lives: A study of life patterns and health. In R. G. Simmions (Ed.), *Research in community and mental health.* Greenwich: JAI Press.
Elliott, G., Cunningham, S., Linder, M., Colangelo, M., & Gross, M. (2005). Child physical abuse and self-perceived social isolation among adolescents. *Journal of Interpersonal Violence, 20*(12), 1663–1684.
Erickson, M. F., Sroufe, L. A., & Egeland, B. (1985). The relationship between quality of attachment and behavior problems in preschool in a high-risk sample. In I. Bretherton & E. Waters (Eds.), *Growing points in attachment theory and research: Monographs of the Society for Research in Child Development* (pp. 147–166). Chicago: University of Chicago Press.
Erickson, M. R., Egeland, B., & Pianta, R. C. (1987). The effects of maltreatment on the development of young children. In D. Cicchetti & V. Carlson (Eds.), *Child maltreatment: Theory and research on the causes and consequences of child abuse and neglect.* New York: Cambridge University Press.
Fantuzzo, J. W., Jurecic, L., & Stovall, A. (1988). Effects of adult and peer social initiations on the social behavior of withdrawn, maltreated preschool children. *Journal of Consulting and Clinical Psychology, 56,* 34–39.
Fantuzzo, J. W., Sutton-Smith, B., Atkins, M., Meyers, R., Stevenson, H., Coolahan, K., Weiss, A., & Manz, P. (1996). Community-based resilient peer treatment of withdrawn maltreated preschool children. *Journal of Consulting and Clinical Psychology, 64*(6), 1377–1386.

Feldman, R. A., & Wodarski, J. S. (1975). *Contemporary approaches to group treatment*. San Francisco: Jossey-Bass.
Finch, A. J., Jr., & Rogers, T. R. (1984). Self-report instruments. In T. H. Ollendick & M. Hersen (Eds.), *Child behavioral assessment: Principles and procedures* (pp. 106–123). New York: Penguin.
Fixsen, D. L., Blase, K. A., Duda, M. A., Naoom, S. F., & Van Dyke, M. K. (2010). Implementation of evidence-based treatments for children and adolescents: Research findings and their implications for the future. In J. R. Weisz & A. E. Kazdin (Eds.), *Evidence-based psychotherapies for children and adolescents* (2nd ed.). New York: Guilford.
Foster, S. L., & Ritchey, W. L. (1979). Issues in the assessment of social competence in children. *Journal of Applied Behavior Analysis, 12,* 625–638.
Furman, W., Rahe, D., & Hartup, W. (1979). Rehabilitation of socially withdrawn preschool children through mixed age and same age socialization. *Child Development, 50,* 915–922.
Garbarino, J., & Crouter, A. (1978). Defining the community context for parent-child relations: The correlates of child maltreatment. *Child Development, 49,* 604–616.
Garbarino, J., & Vondra, J. (1987). Psychological maltreatment: Issues and perspectives. In M. R. Brassard, R. Germain, & S. N. Hart (Eds.), *Psychological maltreatment of children and youth* (pp. 22–24). New York: Pergamon Press.
George, C., & Main, M. (1979). Social interactions of young abused children: Approach, avoidance, and aggression. *Child Development, 50,* 306–318.
Giovannoni, J. M., & Becera R. M. (1979). *Defining child abuse*. New York: The Free Press.
Giovannoni, J. M., & Billingsley, A. (1970). Child neglect among the poor: A study of parental adequacy in families of three ethnic groups. *Child Welfare,* XLIZ, *4,* 196–204.
Goldstein, A. P., Sherman, M. N., Gershaw, N. J., Sprafkin, R. P., & Glick, B. (1978) Training aggressive adolescents in prosocial behavior. *Journal of Youth and Adolescence, 7,* 73–92.
Gresham, F. M. (2002). Teaching social skills to high-risk children and youth: Preventive and remedial strategies. In M. R. Shinn, H. M. Walker, & G. Stoner (Eds.), *Interventions for academic and behavior problems II: Preventive and remedial approaches* (pp. 403–432). Bethesda: National Association of School Psychologists.
Gresham, F. M., Cook, C. R., Crews, S. D., & Kern, L. (2004). Social skills training for children and youth with emotional and behavioral disorders: Validity consideration and future directions. *Behavioral Disorders, 30,* 19–23.
Hart, S. N., & Brassard, M. R. (1987). A major threat to children's mental health. Psychological maltreatment. *American Psychologist, 42,* 160–165.
Hartup, W. W. (1983). Peer relationships. In P. H. Mussen (Ed.), *Handbook of child psychology* (Vol. 4, 4th ed. pp. 103–196). New York: Wiley.
Hazel, J. S., Sherman, J. A., Shumaker, J. B., & Sheldon, J. (1985). Group social skills training with adolescents: A critical review. In D. Upper & S. Ross (Eds.), *Handbook of behavioral group therapy* (pp. 203–246). New York: Plenum Press.
Herrenkohl, R. C., Herrenkohl, E. C., Egolf, B., & Seech, M. (1979). The repetition of child abuse: How frequently does it occur? *Child Abuse & Neglect, 3,* 67–72.
Herrenkohl, R. C., Herrenkohl, E. C., Egolf, B. P. (1983). Circumstances surrounding the occurrence of child maltreatment. *Journal of Consulting and Clinical Psychology, 51*(3), 424–431.
Hinshaw, S. P. (1992). Academic achievement, attention deficits, and aggression: Comorbidity and implications for intervention. *Journal of Consulting and Clinical Psychology,* 60, 893–903.
Hjorth, C. W., & Harway, M. (1981). The body-image of physically abused and normal adolescents. *Journal of Youth and Adolescence, 11,* 71–76.
Hoffman-Plotkin, D., & Twentyman, C. (1984). A multimodal assessment of behavioral and cognitive deficits in abused and neglected preschoolers. *Child Development, 52,* 13–30.
Hops, H. (1983). Children's social competence and skill: Current research practices and future directions. *Behavior Therapy, 14*(1), 3–18. doi:10.1016/50005-7894(83)80084-7.
Hops, H., & Finch, M. (1985). Social competence and skill: A reassessment. In B. H. Schneider, K. H. Rubin, & J. E. Ledingham (Eds.), *Children's peer relations: Issues in assessment and intervention* (pp. 23–39). New York: Springer.

Hops, H., Wills, T, Patterson, G. R., & Weiss, R. L. (1972). *Marital interaction coding system (MICS)*. Unpublished manuscript, University of Oregon and Oregon Research Institute, Eugene.
Hops, H., Biglan, A., Sherman, L., Arthur, J., Friedman, L., & Osteen, V. (1987). Home observations of family interactions of depressed women. *Journal of Consulting and Clinical Psychology, 55*(3), 341–346.
Hops, H., Greenwood, C. R., Rudolph, K. D., Hammen, C., & Burge, D. (1994). Social behavior scale. *Journal of Abnormal Child Psychology, 22,* 355–371.
Howes, C., & Espinosa, M. P. (1985). The consequences of child abuse for the formation of relationships with peers. *Child Abuse & Neglect, 9,* 397–404.
Howing, P. T., Wodarski, J. S., Kurtz, P. D., & Gaudin, J. M., Jr. (1990). The empirical base for the implementation of social skills training with maltreated children. *Social Work, 35,* 460–467.
Kazdin, A. E. (2001). Problem-solving skills training and parent management training for oppositional defiant disorder and conduct disorder. In J. R. Weisz & A. E. Kazdin (Eds.), *Evidence-based psychotherapies for children and adolescents* (2nd ed.). New York: Guilford.
Keller, H., & Erne, D. (1983) Child abuse—Toward a comprehensive model [from prevention and control of aggression, P 1-36, 1983]. In A. P. Goldstein & L. Krasner (Eds.), [See NCJ-104683 CJ-104683] [serial online]. Available from: National Criminal Justice Reference Service Abstracts, Ipswich, MA. Accessed November 20, 2014.
Kendall, P. C., & Brawswell, L. (1985). *Cognitive-behavioral therapy with impulsive children.* New York: Guildford Press.
Kinard, E. M. (1980). Emotional development in physically abused children. *American Journal of Ortho-psychiatry, 50,* 686–696.
Kinard, E. (1999). Perceived social skills and social competence in maltreated children. *American Journal of Orthopsychiatry, 69*(4), 465. (Retrieved February 16, 2009, from Academic Search Premier database).
Koeppen, A. S. (1974). Relaxation training for children. *Elementary School Guidance and Counseling, 9,* 14–21.
Kupersmidt, J. B., Coie, J. D., & Dodge, K. A. (1990). The role of poor relationships in the development of disorder. In S. R. Asher & J. D. Coie (Eds.), *Peer rejection in childhood* (pp. 17–59). New York: Cambridge University Press.
Ladd, G. (1981). Effectiveness of a social learning method for enhancing children's social interaction and peer acceptance. *Child Development, 52,* 171–178.
Ladd, G. W., & Mize, J. (1983). A cognitive-social learning model of social skill training. *Psychological Review, 90,* 127–157.
LaGasse, A. B. (2014). Effects of a music therapy group intervention on enhancing social skills in children with autism. *Journal of Music Therapy, 51*(3), 250–275. doi:10.1093/jmt/thu012.
La Greca, A. M. (1993). Social skills training with children: Where do we go from here? *Journal of Clinical Child Psychology, 22,* 288–298.
Lange, A. J., & Jakubowski, P. (1976). *Responsible assertive behavior.* Champaign: Research Press.
LeCroy, C. W. (1983). *Social skills training for children and youth.* New York: Haworth.
Lochman, J. E., Coie, J. D., Underwood, M. K., & Terry, R. (1993). Effectiveness of a social relations intervention program for aggressive and nonaggressive, rejected children. *Journal of Consulting and Clinical Psychology, 61,* 1053–1058.
Loeber, R., & Dishion, T. J. (1983). Early predictors of male delinquency: A review. *Psychological Bulletin, 94,* 68–99.
Martin, H. P., & Beezley, P. (1977). Behavioral observations of abused children. *Developmental Medicine and Child Neurology, 19,* 373–387.
McConnell, S. R. (1987). Entrapment effects and the generalization and maintenance of social skills training for elementary school students with behavior disorders. *Behavioral Disorders, 12,* 252–263.
McCord, W., & Sanchez, J. (1983). The treatment of deviant children: A twenty-five year follow-up study. *Crime and Delinquency, 29,* 238–253.

McFall R. M. (1982). A review and reformulation of the concept of social skills. *Behavioral Assessment, 4,* 1–33.
Meichenbaum, D. (1993). Stress inoculation training: A twenty year update. In R. L. Woolfolk & P. M. Lehrer (Eds.), *Principles and practices of stress management.* New York: Guilford Press.
Milling, K. E. (1999). Perceived social skills and social competence in maltreated children. *American Journal of Orthopsychiatry, 69*(4), 465–481.
Newcomb, A. F., Bukowski, W. M., & Pattee, L. (1993). Children's peer relations: A meta-analytic review of popular, rejected, neglected, controversial, and average sociometric status. *Psychological Bulletin, 113,* 99–128.
Newman, D. L., Moffitt, T. E., Caspi, A., Magdol, L., Silva, P. A., & Stanton, W. R. (1996). Psychiatric disorder in a birth cohort of young adults: Prevalence, comorbidity, clinical significance, and new case incidence from ages. *Journal of Consulting and Clinical Psychology, 64,* 552–562.
Oates, R. K., Peacock, A., & Forrest, D. (1984). Development in children following abuse and nonorganic failure to thrive. *American Journal of Diseases of Children, 138,* 764–767.
Oden, S., & Asher, S. R. (1977). Coaching children in social skills for friendship making. *Child Development, 48,* 495–506.
Oden, S., & ERIC Clearinghouse on Elementary and Early Childhood Education, U. I. (1987). *The Development of Social Competence in Children.*
Ollendick, T. H., & Cerny, J. A. (1981). *Clinical behavior therapy with children.* New York: Plenum Press.
Olweus, D. (1984). Stability in aggressive and withdrawn, inhibited behavior patterns. In R. Kaplan, V. Konecni, & R. Novaco (Eds.), *Aggression in children and youth* (pp. 104–137). The Hague: Nijhoff.
Parke, R., & Collmer, C. (1975). Child abuse: An interdisciplinary analysis. In E. M. Hetheringlon (Ed.), *Review of child development research* (Vol. 5). Chicago: University of Chicago.
Parker, J. G., & Asher, S. R. (1987). Peer relations and later personal adjustment: Are low-accepted children at risk? *Psychological Bulletin, 102*(3), 357–389.
Patterson, G. R. (1979). Treatment for children with conduct problems: A review of outcome studies. In S. Feshbach & A. Fraczek (Eds.), *Aggression and behavior change: Biological and social processes.* New York: Preager.
Patterson, G. R., Reid, J. B., & Dishion, T. J. (1992). *Antisocial boys.* Eugene: Castalia.
Pfeffer, C., Plutchik R., & Mizruchi M. (1983). Predictors of assaultiveness in latency age children. *American Journal of Psychiatry, 140,* 31–34.
Plansky, N. A. (1981). *Integrated ego psychology.* Hawthorne: Aldine de Gruyter.
Polansky, N. A., Chalmers, M. A., Williams, D. P., & Buttenwieser, E. W. (1981). *Damaged parents: An anatomy of child neglect.* Chicago: University of Chicago Press.
Putnam, F. W. (2005). The developmental neurobiology of disrupted attachment. Lessons from animal models and child abuse research. In L. J. Berlin, Y. Ziv, L. Amaya-Jackson., & M. T. Greenberg (Eds.), *Enhancing early attachments: Theory, research, intervention, and policy* (pp. 79–99). New York: Guilford.
Reid, J. B., Taplin, P. S., & Lorber, R. (1981). A social interaction approach to the treatment of abusive families. In R. B. Stuart (Ed.), *Violent behavior: Social learning approaches to prediction, management and treatment.* New York: Brunner/Mazel.
Rodriguez, B. J., & Anderson, C. M. (2014). Integrating a social behavior intervention during small group academic instruction using a total group criterion intervention. *Journal of Positive Behavior Interventions, 16*(4), 234–245. doi:10.1177/1098300713492858.
Roff, J. D., & Wirt, R. D. (1984). Childhood aggression and social adjustment as antecedents of delinquency. *Journal of Abnormal Child Psychology, 12*(1), 111–126. doi:10.1007/BF00913464.
Roff, M., Sells, S. B., & Golden, M. M. (1972). *Social adjustment and personality development in children.* Minneapolis: The University of Minnesota.
Rosselet, J. G., & Stauffer, S. D. (2013). Using group role-playing games with gifted children and adolescents: A psychosocial intervention model. *International Journal of Play Therapy, 22*(4), 173–192. doi:10.1037/a0034S57.

Rutter, M. (1979). Protective factors in children's responses to stress and disadvantage. In M. W. Kent & J. Rolf (Eds.), *Primary prevention of psychopathology, Vol. III: Social competence in children* (pp. 49–74). Hanover: University Press of New England.
Rutter, M., & Garmezy, N. (1983). Developmental psychopathology. In E. M. Hetherington (Ed.), *Mussen's handbook of child psychology:* (Vol. 4). *Socialization, personality, and social development* (4th ed., pp. 775–911). New York: Wiley.
Sarason, I. G., & Sarason, B. R. (1981). Teaching cognitive and social skills to high school students. *Journal of Consulting and Clinical Psychology, 49,* 908–918.
Schinke, S. P., & Gilchrist, L. D. (1984). Preventing cigarette smoking with youth. *Journal of Primary Prevention, 5,* 48–56.
Shure, M. B., & Spivack, G. (1972). Means-end thinking, judgment, and social class among elementary school-aged children. *Journal of Consulting and Clinical Psychology, 38*(1972), 348–353.
Shure, M. B., & Spivack, G. (1974). *The Hahnemann preschool behavior (HPSB) rating scale.* Philadelphia: Department of Mental Health Sciences, Hahnemann University.
Slade, B. B., Steward, M. S., Morrison, T. L., & Abramowitz, S. I. (1984). Locus of control, persistence, and use of contingency information in physically abused children. *Child Abuse & Neglect, 8*(4), 447–457.
Straker, G., & Jacobson, R. (1981). Aggression, emotional maladjustment and empathy in the abused child. *Developmental Psychology, 17,* 762–765.
Straus, M. A. (1979a). Measuring intrafamily conflict and violence: The conflict tactics scales. *Journal of Marriage and Family, 41,* 75–88.
Straus, M. A. (1979b). Family patterns and child abuse in a nationally representative American sample. *Child Abuse & Neglect, 3,* 213–222.
Steward, M., Farquhar, L., Dicharry, D., Glick, D., & Martin, P. (1986). Group therapy: A treatment of choice for young victims of child abuse. *International Journal of Group Psychotherapy, 36,* 261–277.
Thyer, B. A., & Wodarski, J. S. (Eds.). (2007). *Social work in mental health: An evidence based approach.* Hoboken: Wiley.
Valentino, K., Cicchetti, D., Toth, S. L., & Rogosch, F. A. (2006). Mother-child play and emerging social behaviors among infants from maltreating families. *Developmental Psychology, 42*(3), 474–485.
Walker, H. M., Greenwood, C. R., Hops, H., & Todd, N. (1979). Differential effects of reinforcing topographic components of free play social interaction: Analysis and systematic replication. *Behavior Modification, 3,* 291-321.
Webster-Stratton, C., & Reid, M. J. (2010). Adapting the incredible years, an evidence-based parenting program, for families involved in the child welfare system. *Journal of Children's Services, 5*(1), 25–42.
Weisz, J. R., & Kazdin, A. E. (2010). *Evidence-based psychotherapies for children and adolescents.* New York: The Guilford Press.
Weissberg, R. P., Gesten. E. L., Liebenstein, N, L., Schmid, K. D., & Hutton, H. (1980). *The Rochester social problem solving (SPS) program.* Rochester: Primary Mental Health Project, Center for Community Study.
Werner, E. E., & Smith, R. S. (1989). *Vulnerable but invincible: A longitudinal study of resident children and youth.* New York: Adams-Bannister-Cox. (Original work published 1982).
Wodarski, J. S., & Feit, M. D. (2012). Social group work practice: An evidence-based approach. *Journal of Evidence-Based Social Work, 9,* 414–420.
Wodarski, J. S., Wodarski, L. A., & Parris, H. N. (2004). Adolescent preventive health and Teamgames-tournaments: A research and development paradigm entering its fourth decade research. *Journal of Evidence-based Social work, 1*(1), 101–124.
Wodarski, J. S., Kurtz, P., Gaudin, J., & Howing, P. (1990) Maltreatment and the school-age child: Major academic, socioemotional, and adaptive outcomes. *Social Work, 35*(6), 506–513.

Chapter 15
Preventative Services for Children and Adolescents

Marvin D. Feit, Jennifer Holmes, Jason Minor, Renee Strong and Kat Murphy

Introduction

The years surrounding the turn of the century have been years in which our country has focused greatly on the well-being of young children and mental health of the youth. Policy makers, practitioners, and scientists have been working together to find interventions to promote the health of our country's young people. The contemporary concept of prevention gained ground in the nineteenth and twentieth century to combat mental illnesses, but in the past two decades, new scientifically based approaches have moved to the forefront (Weisz et al. 2005).

The prevention approach to intervention has implications for the traditional role of the social worker and for the timing of the interventions. Social workers attempt to help clients learn how to exert control over their own behaviors and over the environments in which they live. Practitioners do not take a passive role in the intervention process. Instead they use their professional knowledge, expertise, and understanding of human behavior theory and personality development in the conceptualization and implementation of intervention strategies. Since their training equips them to evaluate scientifically any treatment procedure they have instituted, there is continual assessment of the treatment process (Steinberg 2010).

Prevention is especially appropriate for dealing with the problems of the adolescent. It provides early developmental focus for intervention, which may forestall development of future problems. These problems usually intensify later and become harder to alter. Prevention provides a view of the person that is optimistic. The approach is mass-oriented rather than individual-oriented, and it seeks to build health from the start rather than to repair.

M. D. Feit (✉)
Norfolk State University, Norfolk, VA, USA
e-mail: mdfeit@nsu.edu

J. Holmes · J. Minor · R. Strong · K. Murphy
The University of Tennessee, Knoxville, TN, USA

J. S. Wodarski et al. (eds.), *Evidence-Informed Assessment and Practice in Child Welfare,* DOI 10.1007/978-3-319-12045-4_15

Problem behaviors of the young and their undesirable consequences are extensive and well documented. Teenagers' experimentation with drugs and alcohol can lead to overindulgence and abuse. Serious short- and long-term effects include risk-taking and daredevil behavior that increases risks to mental and physical health, including accidents, a leading cause of death among adolescents. Likewise, they may increase the incidence of irresponsible sexual activity, which eventuates in venereal disease, unwanted pregnancy, and premature parenthood (Ozer et al. 2011). In 2006, research was conducted to determine the connection between delinquency, drug use, sexual activity, and pregnancy of urban adolescents. The results of this study showed that in adolescents the above are co-occurring problem behaviors (Smith and Thornberry 2006). Prevention during childhood and the adolescent developmental period would reduce these serious physical and social problems.

There is confusion in the field as to what prevention approaches are effective in prevention with children and adolescents. Research in the area of prevention of adolescent substance abuse shows that the programs which focus on factual information, self-esteem, or decision making are less effective than prevention programs that follow a social (or peer) influence model (Skiba et al. 2004). Resilience should also be taken into account when seeking proper interventions. Resilience protects adolescents against psychological risks that are associated with negative environmental factors. Resilience has some advantages for adolescents. Good intellectual functioning, close supportive families, and positive role models outside the family are all factors that help increase resilience which aids the child in overcoming negative environmental factors (Santrock 2003). Research conducted on resilience finds that most young children from resource-deprived communities who have high amounts of resilience do become successful and develop their own strengths regardless of their harsh childhoods (Benard 2006).

This chapter will define prevention and review the three approaches to prevention: primary, secondary, and tertiary. From a life span developmental approach, skills an adolescent must master such as social, cognitive, and academic, should provide the focus for the intervention. The life skills approach is proposed as the treatment of choice. This approach has rational elements in common with other prevention programs that are based on public health orientation. These consist of three essential components: health education, skills training, and practice applying skills. The teams-games-tournaments (TGT) model consists of the same components except that in addition it uses peers as parallel teachers (Wodarski and Feit 2011).

Prevention Defined

Prevention is defined as the act of discouraging a problematic behavior or illness before it actually happens or before it becomes a problem. As there is a gradual shift away from the band-aid, after-the-fact approach to mental health, programs designed to prevent more serious consequences of present and/or future mental health problems or to prevent the recurrence of mental dysfunction are beginning to emerge in rural as well as in urban areas. Since it is more cost-effective to prevent or reduce social problems, these programs proposed during a period of tight funds are sure to continue gaining appeal.

Social problems are the by-product of undesirable or ineffective behaviors. For adolescents, these behaviors, such as the abuse of drugs and alcohol, may be the result of poor coping mechanisms, peer pressure, and lack of self-esteem (Wodarski and Feit 2011). Furthermore, research shows that there are several factors that place youth at risk for drug use including school climate, peer influence, and lack of parental monitoring. Protective factors against drug use in youth have also been identified, such as intellectual and social skills (Hanlon et al. 2002). Frequent communication between parents and teenagers about the dangers of alcohol use can also serve as a protective factor against adolescent alcohol use (Abar et al. 2011). Similarly, the frequency of eating meals together as a family is related to decreased alcohol and tobacco use in teenagers, particularly in girls (White and Halliwell 2011).

Approaches to Prevention

Preventative programs should focus on those adolescents who will require services in the future if no ameliorating activities occur. Preventative programs must teach alternate ways of dealing with environmental conditions. Prevention programs should not only focus on information or attitude change, but should have multiple components to address many aspects of the individual and community (Skiba et al. 2004). This type of substance abuse prevention strategy is part of a new generation of primary prevention programs that have proven effective in reducing the initiation of one or more forms of substance use.

Primary prevention is concerned with methods of reducing the overall incidence of social problems. These preventions can also be referred to as universal interventions which are targeted at the general public, not selected because of individual risk factors (Wodarski and Feit 2011). Primary prevention has a group focus, targets at-risk adolescents, has a solid knowledge base, and can be used to prevent school, learning, and behavioral problems (Baker 2001). An example of primary prevention of physical need deficits could be testing newborns for phenylketonuria (PKU) to prevent mental retardation and providing adolescent parents with information regarding child rearing. Primary prevention of psychosocial need deficits could focus on acquisition of studying skills (Fisak et al. 2011).

Secondary prevention takes on a different approach to the issue of social problems. This approach uses organizational and community supports to select candidates for intervention. These interventions are generally targeted at groups and individuals who are at risk (Durlak et al. 2011). Examples of secondary prevention programs include school-based programs, family therapy, and interventions (Elliot et al. 2005). Secondary prevention strategies should focus on communities and youth who are exposed to greater risk factors. Community-level secondary prevention intervention has shown a decrease in the gang problem among adolescents who reside in impoverished communities (Esbensen 2000). Adolescents who are children of alcoholics might be an appropriate group for a secondary prevention program, as they have been identified as being at a high risk for developing alcoholic tendencies (Belles et al. 2011). Another at-risk group that might benefit from secondary prevention programs are adolescents in the child welfare system, who have been found to be more likely to experiment with and become addicted to drugs (Casanueva et al. 2011).

Tertiary Prevention deals with adolescents who have had previous social problems. The goal is to maintain the individual in the community and to prevent problems from recurring. The effort here is to reduce the recidivism rate for adolescents who have been institutionalized. Such efforts might include helping a student reintegrate back into a school setting following a treatment program as well as giving relapse prevention support (Lewis et al. 2010).

Adolescent Developmental Tasks

The adolescent is preoccupied with rapid physical and intellectual maturation, heightened emotional sensitivity, and acceptance by social groups. Abstract thinking is possible and the adolescent is capable of conceptualizing changes that may occur in the future. The adolescent can anticipate the consequences of behavior and is especially sensitive to consistent and inconsistent parental behavior. Membership in peer groups that are more structured and organized than they were in earlier stages are extremely important. Group membership is most frequently based on physical attractiveness. The adolescent also begins engaging in heterosexual relationships. Forming relationships with boys at this age has specifically been found to increase the likelihood of cigarette smoking in adolescent girls (Mrug et al. 2011). Parents and significant adults influence the child's identity and self-esteem less than the all-important peers.

The psychological crisis at this stage is "group identity versus alienation." The adolescent receives pressure from parents, peers, and school to identify with a group. A positive resolution of the crisis results in the individual allying with a group that is perceived as meeting social needs and providing a sense of belonging. A negative resolution results in the adolescent experiencing a sense of isolation and continually feeling uneasy in the presence of peers. The central process in adolescence is peer pressure (Harrell et al. 2009).

Peer Influence

The peer group serves as a transitional world for the adolescent. Data suggests that participation in extracurricular activities is the most important determination of the adolescent's status with peers (Wodarski and Feit 2011). The self-concept of the adolescent is very susceptible to status fluctuations that occur with family transience and high school transitions. The worker should encourage the adolescent undergoing such transitions to become involved in extracurricular activities because they can provide support (Crean 2012).

For teenagers, detrimental behaviors frequently occur in situations involving peers. The influence of peer groups on adolescent behavior is well known and for many adolescents, strong social pressure provokes participation in peer-sanctioned behaviors such as smoking, drinking, and sexual intercourse. Although teenagers may understand the health risks involved in these activities, this understanding is insufficient to counter the social significance of indulging (Ozer et al. 2011).

A recent study found that popularity at school is related to a teenager's willingness to conform to the drinking behaviors of peers. For boys, popularity is further increased when they drink alcohol excessively to the point of intoxication (Balsa et al. 2011). However, peer influence can also have positive consequences. Research has shown that contraceptive use among adolescents increases when they are aware that peers are also using contraceptives (Ali et al. 2011). In other words, peer pressure tends to cause adolescents to conform to whatever behavior is the norm for their peer group, whether that behavior is positive or negative.

When taking parental and peer influence into account in substance abuse cases, research shows that the adolescent reacted more negatively when parents monitored drug use than when their peers did so. The more active their peers were in using substances, the more the adolescent was to participate in substance abuse. However, the study shows that the less an adolescent's drug use was monitored by parents or peers, the more likely they were to increase their substance use. It is very important for peers and parents to work together to steer the adolescent on the right path (Brown and Bakken 2011)

Specific cognitive and behavioral skills are needed to resist external pressures and to successfully negotiate interpersonal encounters where pressure occurs. Adolescents often lack these skills not because of individual pathology but for developmental reasons. Age brings increased opportunity to engage in previously unknown or prohibited activities. Lack of experience and prior learning opportunities hampers youths' ability to deal with a new situation and behavioral requirements (Romer 2010)

There is confusion among the helping professionals about whether or not prevention programs have been effective. It is clear that prevention intervention should not focus on one aspect of an individual, but should focus on the person in the environment (Skiba et al. 2004; Weisz et al. 2005). A recent program that utilized this prevention approach successfully was the Health Wise program in South Africa. This program used education and enhancement of social skills to prevent substance abuse and the spread of HIV in adolescents (Tibbits et al. 2011). In addition, because prevention educational intervention is frequently poorly designed, with vague goals compounding difficulties, prevention program effects are hard to evaluate, further diminishing the likelihood of public and legislative support. A new conceptualization is required if prevention and health promotion services are to become effective components of service systems (Cameron and Keenan 2010)

There is an accurate database to provide rational and empirical support for development prevention and health education programs for children and adolescents. This is based on the Skills Training Intervention Model and the use of TGT, a teaching method with successful empirical history (Wodarski and Feit 2011)

The social development prevention model focuses on "effects of empirical predictors ("risk factors" and "protective factors") for antisocial behavior and attempts to synthesize the most strongly supported propositions of control theory, social learning theory, and differential association theory" (Gavazzi 2011). This model has also been used to predict drug use in adolescents. The social development model is much like the TGT prevention plan. The social development model states that positive socialization is achieved when youth interact and are rewarded by peers for positive behaviors. This theoretical model creates bounds that can prevent delinquent behavior (Hawkins and Weis 2005).

Skills Training Intervention Model

The skills model described here has rationale and elements in common with other preventative approaches. The interventive goal is skill building to strengthen adolescents' resistance to harmful influence in advance of their impact. Three components comprise this preventative model: health education, skill training, and practice applying information and skills in troublesome situations (Aarons et al. 2011).

Health Education That adolescents need accurate information to make informed choices is clear. Equally clear is the inadequacy of simply exposing teenagers to facts about unhealthy consequences of certain behavior. One fault with past health education programs is their assumption that exposure to training materials guarantees learning. Information-only programs have few lasting effects (Skiba et al. 2004). Particularly among younger adolescents, perceptual errors such as selectively ignoring, misreading, or mishearing certain facts or selectively forgetting information can create discrepancies between facts presented and facts received and remembered. The model proposed here addressed this potential problem by asking teenagers to periodically summarize presented content in written and verbal quizzes. Correct responses are then reinforced and errors are detected and clarified. Also, peers are used as teachers, which enhances their commitment to healthy behaviors.

Skills Training Even personalized information is of little value if adolescents lack the skills to use it. Translating health information into everyday decision-making and behavior involves cognitive and behavioral skills. Therefore, this model emphasizes skills for making effective short- and long-term decisions and assertive and communications skills needed to implement decisions (Kazdin 2011).

Training also focuses on behavior skills necessary to transform decisions into action. Based on established assertive and communication skills-training procedures, training presents verbal and nonverbal aspects of good communication to help adolescents learn to initiate difficult interactions, to practice self-disclosure and positive and negative feelings, to refuse unreasonable demands, to request changes in another's behavior, to ask others for relevant information and feedback, and to negotiate mutually acceptable solutions (Rakovshik and McManus 2010).

Practice Applying Skills In the final and most important phase of the model, adolescents practice applying skills in a variety of potentially risky interpersonal situations. Extended role-played interactions provide adolescents with opportunities to recall and make use of health information, decision-making techniques, and communication skills. The following is an example of a vignette that might be used in this phase: You are at a party with someone you've been dating for about 6 months. The party is at someone's house; their parents are gone for the weekend. There is a lot of beer and dope and couples are going into upstairs bedrooms to make out. Your date says, "Hey, Lisa and Rom have gone upstairs. It's real nice up there—let's go, come on."

Role playing is an important tool that can be used to help adolescents develop confidence needed to foster refusal skills and to provide assistance in developing communication skills (Hamby et al. 2011).

In role-playing, teenagers practice responding to increasingly insistent demands and receive feedback, instructions, and praise to enhance performance. Practice applying skills also takes the form of "homework" assignments involving written contracts to perform certain tasks outside the training environment such as meeting with a family planning counselor and initiating discussion of birth control with a dating partner.

Teams-Games-Tournament (TGT) Model

The most important socialization agent in an adolescent's life is his/her peer, and schools provide a natural environment for peer influence. Virtually all attempts to educate teenagers about health topics have taken an education lecture model approach aimed at general education of all teenagers. Nearly all instruction in educational techniques is aimed at the individual pupil, ignoring the potential usefulness of the peer group in motivating students to learn and to acquire new skills or behaviors. Research has shown that students participating in learning teams in the classroom have uniformly positive effects (Wodarski and Feit 2011).

TGT is an innovative, small group teaching technique. The method is grounded in current theory, applies to diverse problems and settings, and provides clear criteria for evaluating program effects. The technique alters the traditional classroom structure and gives each student an equal opportunity to achieve and to receive positive reinforcement from peers by capitalizing on team cooperation, the popularity of games, and the spirit of the competitive tournaments. Group reward structures set up a learning situation wherein the performance of each group member furthers the overall group goals. This has been shown to increase individual members' support for group performance, to increase performance itself under a variety of similar circumstances, and to further increase the group's goals. This program has been found to be successful in helping students acquire and retain knowledge in such areas as nutrition, alcohol, and drug abuse (Wodarski and Feit 2011).

Peer relationships play a significant role in the adolescent's socialization and health behavior. Therefore, the information is provided in a group context to help students practice necessary social skills to develop adequate health behavior. Moreover, it capitalizes on the power of peers to influence the acquisition and subsequent maintenance of behavior, which data indicate, is the most potent influencing faction in an adolescent's life. It capitalizes on peers as teachers and this changes the normative peer structure to support healthy behavior (Wodarski and Feit 2011).

Components of Teams-Games-Tournament (TGT) Model The components of the program are as follow:

1. Drug education. This aspect includes biological, psychological, and sociocultural determinates of drug abuse. Basic knowledge about drug consumption and usage is in the next section. The final area is the ten-session curriculum. These are thought group discussion and participatory activities.
2. Self-Management and Maintenance. The comprehensive educational program provides instruction in self-management.

This component is based on social learning theory concepts. Adolescents also need training in terms of coping with daily problems of living. They are taught a problem-solving approach based on the work of Robin and Foster (Siu and Shek 2010). The general components emphasized are:

1. Problem definition
2. How to generate possible solutions
3. Decision making
4. How to choose and implement strategies through the following procedures:
    a. General introduction as to how the provision of certain consequences and stimuli can control problem-solving behavior.
    b. Isolation and definition of a behavior to be changed
    c. Use of stimulus control techniques to influence rates of problem solving behavior
    d. Use of appropriate consequence to either increase or decrease a behavior
5. Verification of the outcome and renegotiation

Cognitive Foci

Cognitive theories propose, in their stage development, that a child is at a concrete operations stage early in school and moves into more abstract, formal operational thought during adolescence. By utilizing cognitive-behavioral methods the worker is able to adjust the service mode according to the child's cognitive developmental stage. The ultimate goal of most cognitive intervention methods is to control his/her own outcomes, through techniques such as desensitization, self-observation, and in-vivo exposure, all of which are geared toward showing that the individual has a large amount of control over the situation (Chen et al. 2010). For adolescents, the achievement of adequate self-concept and self-esteem can foster relationship building and strengthen resiliency (Myers et al. 2011).

Various cognitive theories originated from Bandura's 1950s social learning theory. Bandura demonstrated that modeling, imitation, or observational learning is an important basis for children's behavior (Berk 2003; Pratt et al. 2009). Cognitive theorists have proposed several major approaches, many of which overlap. These approaches focus both on particular sets of cognitive deficits or ways in which thinking may deviate from the logical, and on the methods by which these errors or deficits may be corrected. The ultimate aim in cognitive intervention is to produce change in the negative attitudes an adolescent has, thus reducing cognitive blocks to appropriate behavior (Gibbons et al. 2012).

Cognitive theorists' investigation of the client's thinking is based on two premises. First, clients think in an idiosyncratic way (that is, they have a systematic negative bias in the way they regard themselves, their world, and their future). Second, the way clients interpret events maintains their cognitive distortions (Tolin 2010).

Cognitive therapists continue to view cognition in the treatment process as the behavior that needs to be modified or as an area that is indirectly changed when the overt behavior is treated, which is what many studies continue to show (Dobson and Dozios 2001). The cognitive therapist attempts to alter what the adolescent thinks in order to effect a change in behavior. The belief is that the therapy should aim at reducing the maladaptive behavior through the carefully guided lead of the therapist using cognitive-behavioral techniques. The focus is on the cognitive beliefs that the client has created, and these faulty beliefs are viewed as a pattern of thinking that needs to be changed in order to alter the maladaptive behavior (McGowan et al. 2005).

Formerly there were believed to be only four types of cognitive distortions (arbitrary interference, overgeneralization, magnification, and cognitive deficiency). However, recent studies by Leahy (2003), and Najavits and colleagues, modified Beck's (1976) scale to make 20 total cognitive distortions. These distortions include: (1) instant satisfaction, (2) mind reading, (3) shoulds, (4) fooling yourself, (5) overreacting, (6) arbitrary interferences, (7) fortune-telling, (8) confusing needs and wants, (9) focusing on the negatives, (10) all or none thinking, (11) catastrophizing, (12) discounting positives, (13) over generalizing, (14) personalizing, (15) regret orientation, (16) short-term thinking, (17) emotional reasoning, (18) negative filtering, (19) labeling, and (20) blaming (Najavits et al. 2004).

To address these distortions, the worker may have the client utilize problem-solving skills that are used throughout his/her life (Gitterman and Heller 2011). In addition, a number of behavioral therapy procedures can be adapted to modify cognitive statements (Tolin 2010). For example, cognitive theorists have emphasized the following cognitive aspects of depression. Beck assigned a primary position to a cognitive triad consisting of a very negative view of the self, of the outside world, and of the future (Gitterman and Heller 2011). This triad is seen as the key to the consequences of depression, such as the lack of motivation, the affective state, and other ideational and behavioral manifestations. The depressed person's cognitions lead to misinterpretations of experience; hence many of the secondary responses are logical sequences of such misinterpretations. The depressed person is locked in an unsolvable situation, the result of which is further despair which has been shown to be treated significantly well by cognitive-behavioral therapy, especially when followed up by a continuation phase to prevent relapse (Jarret et al. 2001). Research has shown that cognitive behavioral therapy is particularly effective with adolescents suffering from comorbid major depressive disorder and alcoholism (Cornelius et al. 2011). Thus, cognitive responses that can be altered by the therapist are: (1) sense of hopelessness, (2) self-condemnation and self-defeating thoughts, (3) low self-esteem, (4) tension, (5) death wishes, and (6) sense of helplessness.

Successful interventions have been found to have to address the client, the family, school, work, community, the media, as well as other system factors that affect the client's ability to overcome the situation (Skiba et al. 2004). The individual's expectations and assumptions will play a significant role in the success he/she will experience in therapy (Goldfried 2012). In relation to success in therapy, Pratt and colleagues (2009) noted that regardless of the methods used, treatments implemented through the individual's actual performance achieve consistently superior results to those based on symbolic forms of the same approach.

Social Networks

Data suggests that adolescents are at less social risk to develop mental distress if they are socially connected to other peers and family, i.e., these supports can buffer stress, help with stressful events, generally help promote good physical health, provide emotional support, material support, informational support, and several other beneficial effects (Cohen 2004). Alarmingly, however, recent research has also found that best friend dyads tend to report similar levels of depression, so it is critical for adolescents to be socially connected to a variety of people and networks (Giletta et al. 2011).

One of the most perplexing yet critical problems confronting social work professionals interested in prevention is the use of networking for adolescents at risk (Gibbons et al. 2012). Questions that need to be resolved include the following: How can adolescents be tied to the networks available in the community? What peer characteristics may be matched with adolescent attributes to facilitate networking and enhancement of an individual's functioning? What support systems such as the church, extended family, and friends are available to enhance the adolescent networks?

This aspect of prevention would involve developmental programs to utilize efficacious and cost effective assessment procedures to isolate physical, psychological, and social factors that lead to networking. Possible procedures include

(1) assessment of adolescent's attributes; (2) enlistment of social networks and support groups such as family, peers, ministers, and significant adult models to provide necessary support; (3) preparation of the adolescent in terms of emphasizing appropriate social behaviors that will be rewarded and will facilitate integration into the social structure of their peer community; (4) educating the adolescent about support services available and whom to contact and gradually introducing the individual to appropriate and available support systems; and (5) developing appropriate preventative intervention (Goldfried 2012).

Family Prevention

One empirically supported theoretical perspective is anchored within a broad base of a social learning framework (Crittendan 2005). From this viewpoint, the adolescent learns appropriate and inappropriate behavior from the context (that is, parents and peers) in which he/she functions by modeling and reinforcement (Grusec 2011). That is, by observing the behaviors demonstrated by parents who receive or do not receive reinforcement/punishment for engaging in such behaviors, adolescents acquire certain behavior patterns. Furthermore, and of particular importance, if an adolescent functions within a context in which good communications and/or adequate cognitive skills are lacking (e.g. he/she has inadequate knowledge and unrealistic beliefs, expectations or attributions) he/she is more likely to engage in maladaptive behavior patterns through modeling and reinforcement (Grusec 2011).

One of the critical variables that influence an adolescent's development is the family. The particular types of parenting behavior (lack of positive reinforcement, communication skills, and problem-solving skills) can serve as predictors of adolescent problems, and can discriminate between adolescents at high risk who are or developing subsequent interpersonal difficulties (Oliver et al. 2009).

Basically, problem solving involves four steps: problem identification, generation of alternative solutions, decision making, and planning solution implementation (Siu and Shek 2010). Communication involves skills which can be used during problem solving discussions and at other times. Siu and Shek (2010) have identified 20 behaviors that may interfere with effective communication. These include accusing, putting down, interrupting, getting off topic, dwelling on the past, and threatening. Siu and Shek have conducted three well-controlled studies which support the effectiveness of a problem solving communication skills training program for parents. Relative to waiting list control groups and a family therapy approach, problem solving communication skills increase communication and decrease conflicts (Siu and Shek 2010). Furthermore, at follow-ups, improvements achieved with problem solving skills were maintained. Therefore, it would appear that teaching parents to provide appropriate models and improving parents' problem solving and communication skills would be critical ingredients of an adolescent prevention program.

Research Foci

Few would deny the controversy surrounding the efficacy of current social work preventive services aimed at changing adolescent behavior. Issues pertain to where services should be provided and by whom, what is the proper duration of services, and what are appropriate criteria for evaluation. The legal emphasis on providing effective services to clients and the expressed desire to provide social services on an empirical and rational basis are motivating factors in the development of a sound theoretical base (Wodarski and Feit 2011).

Critical questions center on the following issues: What are the relevant human behavior variables that can provide a solid base for structuring prevention services to adolescents? What guidelines can be furnished for structuring services for an organizational perspective? What criteria can be utilized in the evaluation services? How can one delineate the level of intervention of the micro-macro level continuum? Results and products culminating from a number of research projects over the last decade indicate rationale for a more elaborate comprehensive theory of prevention.

It is evident that more elaborate theories of human behavior are needed to provide the rationale for complex therapeutic intervention systems that are based on principles derived from empirical knowledge, with the goal being to prevent adolescent dysfunction. These theories must consider biological, sociological, economic, political, and psychological factors as they interact in the human matrix to cause behavior (Wodarski and Feit 2011). It is a definite challenge for any theory of human behavior to isolate those components that lead to prevention, such as the specific aspects of an intervention package in terms of expectations for change, role of cognitive processes, particular client and social work characteristics, interventions, context of intervention, and so forth. Once this knowledge is developed, the choice of prevention techniques can be made on such criteria as client and worker characteristics, context of intervention, and type of intervention.

Recent evidence suggests that in order for prevention to be successful, macro-level intervention variables have to be considered. An adequate theory of prevention will isolate the social system variables (i.e., legal, political, health, financial, social services, educational, housing, unemployment, etc.) and their effects on human behavior. Moreover, these variables have to be addressed in a manner that focuses on the attainment of prevention and maintenance of behavior. Current theories fall far short of this goal.

Summary

A major challenge to the community mental health approach is the question of timing of the intervention. Prevention places great emphasis on the teaching of components of the interceptive process with social workers attempting to help clients learn how to exert control over their own behaviors and the environment in which they live. In recognition of the critical role of prevention in improving the mental health of all citizens, it has been suggested that a special staff be set up in each mental health center for prevention programs (Haggerty and Shapiro 2013). The setup of such a branch of programs in mental health centers has been implemented, and while costly, it will surely have been shown, relative to the cost of remedial programs, to have been a bargain to the mental health field.

Additional Resources

Raising Teens
http://hrweb.mit.edu/worklife/raising-teens/ten-tasks.html
Developmental Tasks facing adolescents
http://www.education.com/reference/article/Ref_Adolescence/
Preventative Services for Children
http://www.hhs.gov/healthcare/prevention/children/
Guidelines for Adolescent Children Services
http://www.uptodate.com/contents/guidelines-for-adolescent-preventive-services
Framework for Prevention of Child Maltreatment
https://www.childwelfare.gov/preventing/overview/framework.cfm
Preventive Services
http://www2.monroecounty.gov/hs-preventative.php

References

Aarons, G. A., Hurlburt, M., & Horwitz, S. M. (2011). Advancing a conceptual model of evidence-based practice implementation in public service sectors. *Administration and Policy in Mental Health and Mental Health Services Research, 38*(1), 4–23.
Abar, C. C., Fernandez, A. C., & Wood, M. D. (2011). Parent-teen communication and pre college alcohol involvement: A latent class analysis. *Addictive Behaviors, 36,* 1357–1360.
Ali, M. M., Amialchuk, A., & Dwyer, D. S. (2011). Social network effects incontraceptive behavior among adolescents. *Journal of Developmental and Behavioral Pediatrics, 32*(8), 563–571.
Baker, S. B. (2001). Coping-skills training for adolescents: Applying cognitive behavioral principles to psychoeducational groups. *The Journal for Specialists in Group Work, 26*(3), 219–227.
Balsa, A. I., Homer, J. F., French, M. T., & Norton, E. C. (2011). Alcohol use and popularity: Social payoffs from conforming to peers' behavior. *Journal of Research on Adolescence, 21*(3), 559–568.
Belles, S., Budde, A., Moesgen, D., & Klein, M. (2011). Parental problem drinking predicts implicit alcohol expectancy in adolescents and young adults. *Addictive Behaviors, 36,* 1091–1094.
Benard, B. (2006). Using the strengths based practice to tap the resilience of families. Boston
Berk, L. E. (2003). Child Development. Boston: Illinois State University.
Brown, B. B., & Bakken, J. P. (2011). Parenting and peer relationships: Reinvigorating research on family-peer linkages in adolescence. *Journal of Research on Adolescence, 21*(1), 153–165.

Cameron, M., & Keenan, E. K. (2010). The common factors model: Implications for transtheoretical clinical social work practice. *Social Work, 55*(1), 63–73.
Casanueva, C., Stambaugh, L., Urato, M., Fraser, J. G., & Williams, J. (2011). Lost in transition: Illicit substance use and services receipt among at-risk youth in the child welfare system. *Children and Youth Services Review, 33,* 1939–1949.
Chen, A. C., Thompson, E. A., & Morrison-Beedy, D. (2010). Multi-system influences on adolescent risky sexual behavior. *Research in Nursing and Health, 33*(6), 512–527.
Cohen, S. (2004). Social relationships and health. *American Psychologist, 11,* 676–684.
Cornelius, J. R., Douaihy, A., Bukstein, O. G., Daley, D. C., Wood, S. D., Kelly, T. M., & Salloum, I. M. (2011). Evaluation of cognitive behavioral therapy/motivational enhancement therapy (CBT/MET) in a treatment trial of comorbid MDD/AUD adolescents. *Addictive Behaviors, 36,* 843–848.
Crean, H. F. (2012). Youth activity involvement, neighborhood adult support, individual decision making skills, and early adolescent delinquent behaviors: Testing a conceptual model. *Psychology, 33*(4), 175–188.
Crittenden, W. F. (2005). A social learning theory of cross-functional case education. *Journal of Business Research, 58*(7), 960–-966
Dobson, K. S., & Dozois, D. J. (2001). Historical and philosophical bases of the cognitive-based behavioral therapies. In K. S. Dobson (Ed.), *Handbook of cognitive behavioral therapies* (2nd ed.). New York: Guilford.
Durlak, J. A., Weissberg, R. P., Dymicki, A. B., Taylor, R. D., & Schellinger, K. B. (2011). The impact of enhancing students' social and emotional learning: A meta-analysis of school- based universal interventions. *Child Development, 82*(1), 405–432.
Elliot, L., Orr, L., & Watson, L. (2005). Secondary prevention interventions for young drug users: A systematic review of the evidence. *Adolescence, 40,* 1–22.
Esbensen, F. (2000). Preventing adolescents gang involvement. Office of juvenile justice and delinquency prevention.
Fisak, B. R., Richard, D., & Mann, A. (2011). The prevention of child and adolescent anxiety: A meta-analytic review. *Prevention Science, 12*(3), 255–268.
Gavazzi, S. M. (2011). *Families with adolescents: Bridging the gaps between theory. Research and practice*. New York: Springer.
Gibbons, F. X., Kingsbury, J. H., & Gerrard, M. (2012). Social-psychological theories and adolescent health risk behavior. *Social and Personality Psychology Compass, 6*(2), 170–183.
Giletta, M., Scholte, R. H. J., Burk, W. J., Engels, R. C. M. E., Larsen, J. K., Prinstein, M. J., & Ciairano, S. (2011). Similarity in depressive symptoms inadolescents' friendship dyads: Selection or socialization? *Developmental Psychology, 47*(6), 1804–1814.
Gitterman, A., & Heller, N. R. (2011). Integrating social work perspectives and models with concepts, methods and skills with other professions' specialized approaches. *Clinical Social Work Journal, 39*(2), 204–211.
Goldfried, M. R. (2012). On entering and remaining in psychotherapy. *Clinical Psychology and Practice, 19*(2), 125–128.
Grusec, J. E. (2011). Socialization processes in the family: Social and emotional development. *Annual Review of Psychology, 62,* 243–269.
Haggerty, K. P., & Shapiro, V. B. (2013). Science-based prevention through communities that care: A model of social work practice for public health. *Social Work in Public Health, 28*(3–4), 349–365.
Hamby, A., Pierce, M., Daniloski, K., & Brinberg, D. (2011). The use of participatory action research to create a positive youth development program. *Social Marketing Quarterly, 17*(3), 2–17.
Hanlon, T. E., Bateman, R. W., Simon, B. D., O'Grady, K. E., & Carswell, S. R. (2002). An early community based intervention for the prevention of substance abuse and other delinquent behavior. *Journal of Youth and Adolescence, 31*(6), 459–472.
Harrell, A. W., Mercer, S. H., & DeRosier, M. E. (2009). Improving the social-behavioral adjustment of adolescents: The effectiveness of a social skills group intervention. *Journal of Child and Family Studies, 18*(4), 378–387.

Hawkins, J. D., & Weis, J. G. (2005). The social development model: An integrated approach to delinquency prevention. *The Journal of Primary Prevention, 6*(2), 73–97.
Jarret, R. B., Kraft, D., Doyle, J., Foster, B. M., Eaves, G. G., & Silver, P. C. (2001). Preventing recurrent depression using cognitive therapy with and without a continuation phase. *Arch Gen Psychiatry, 58,* 381–388 (Journal of Business Research, 58, 960–966).
Kazdin, A. E. (2011). Evidence-based treatment research: advances, limitations, and next steps. *American Psychologist, 66*(8), 685–698.
Leahy, R. L. (2003). Cognitive therapy techniques: A practioner's guide. New York: Guilford.
Lewis, T. J., Jones, S. E. L., Horner, R. H., & Sugai, G. (2010). School-wide positive behavior support and students with emotional/behavioral disorders: Implication for prevention, identification and intervention. *Exceptionality: A Special Education Journal, 18*(2), 82–93.
McGowan, J. F., Lavender, T., & Garety, P. A. (2005). Factors in outcome of cognitive-behavioural therapy for psychosis: Users' and clinician's views. *The British psychological society journal, 78,* 513–529.
Mrug, S., Borch, C., & Cillessen, A. H. N. (2011). Other-sex friendships in late adolescence: Risky associations for substance use and sexual debut? *Journal of Youth and Adolescence, 40,* 875–888.
Myers, J. E., Willse, J. T., & Villalba, J. A. (2011). Promoting self-esteem in adolescents: The influence of wellness factors. *Journal of Counseling and Development, 89*(1), 28–36.
Najavits, L. M., Gotthardt, S., Weiss, R. D., & Epstein, M. (2004). Cognitive distortions in the dual diagnosis of PTSD and substance use disorder. *Cognitive Therapy and Research, 28,* 159–172.
Oliver, P. H., Guerin, D. W., & Coffman, J. K. (2009). Big five parental personality traits, parenting behaviors, and adolescent behavior problems: A mediation model. *Personality and Individual Differences, 47*(6), 631–636.
Ozer, E. M., Adams, S. H., Orrell-Valente, J. K., Wibbelsman, C., Lustig, J. L., Millstein, S. G., Garber, A. K., & Irwin, C. E. (2011). Does delivering preventive services in primary care reduce adolescent risky behavior? *Journal of Adolescent Health, 49*(5), 476–482.
Pratt, T. C., Cullen, F. T., Sellers, C. S., Winfree, L. T., Madensen, T. D., Daigle, L. E., Fearn, N. E., & Gau, J. M. (2009). The empirical status of social learning theory: A meta-analysis. *Justice Quarterly, 27*(6), 765–802.
Rakovshik, S. G., & McManus, F. (2010). Establishing evidence-based training in cognitive behavioral therapy: A review of current empirical findings and theoretical guidance. *Clinical Psychology Review, 30*(5), 496–516.
Santrock, J. W. (2003). Psychology 7ed. New York: McGraw Hill
Siu, A. M. J., & Shek, D. T. L. (2010). Social problem solving as a predictor of well-being in adolescents and young adults. *Social Indicators Research, 95*(3), 393–406.
Skiba, D., Monroe, J., & Wodarski, J. (2004). Adolescent substance use: Reviewing the effectiveness of prevention strategies. *Social Work, 49*(3), 343–353.
Smith, C. & Thornberry, T. P. (2006). The relationship between childhood maltreatment and adolescent involvement in delinquency. *Criminology, 33*(4), 451–481.
Steinberg, D. M. (2010). Mutual aid: A contribution to best-practice social work. *Social Work with Groups, 33*(1), 53–68. (Strengths Perspective in Social Work Practice. Boston: Pearson Press).
Tibbits, M. K., Smith, E. A., Caldwell, L. L., & Flisher, A. J. (2011). Impact of Health Wise South Africa on polydrug use and high-risk sexual behavior. *Health Education Research, 26*(4), 653–663.
Tolin, D. F. (2010). Is cognitive-behavioral therapy more effective than other therapies? A meta-analytic review. *Clinical Psychology Review, 30*(6), 710–720.
Weisz, J. R., Sandler, I. N., Durlak, B. S., & Anton, B. S. (2005). Promoting and protecting youth mental health through evidence-based prevention and treatment. *American Psychologist, 60*(6), 628–648.
White, J., & Halliwell, E. (2011). Family meal frequency and alcohol and tobacco use in adolescence: Testing reciprocal effects. *The Journal of Early Adolescence, 31,* 735–749.
Wodarski, J. S., & Feit, M. D. (2011). Adolescent preventive health and Team-Game- Tournament: Five decades of evidence for empirically based paradigm. *Social Work in Public Health, 26*(5), 482–512.

Chapter 16
Summary: Field-Tested Evidence-Informed Assessment and Treatment for Practice in Child Welfare

Michael J. Holosko

Mahatma Gandhi, among others like Aristotle, is often credited with the famous quote: “a society’s greatness is measured by how it treats its weakest members.” More recently, Hurbert H. Humphrey’s last speech in his office (December 30, 1964) echoed this sentiment … “the moral test of a government is how that government treats those who are in the dawn of life, the children; those who are in shadows of life; the sick, the needy, and the handicapped.” These vulnerable and in turn, more dependent populations in our society have been the lifeblood of North American social work practice since its inception. Going back further, they were also mentioned in the social policies of the *Elizabethan Poor Laws* of 1601 in the UK.

The centerpiece of the development of professional social work practice in the USA, around the turn of the century up until today has been the social welfare of children and their families. Thus, this book is about our profession’s core raison d’etre (or reason for being) that is, social welfare practice. It is written for BSW and MSW students whose likely first job, and for some their last, will be in federal or state run departments of social welfare services. Although these governmental and their complementary nongovernmental initiatives are designed to prevent and treat these vulnerable clients, due to continued annual budget cuts and reforms, paired with increased and disproportionate numbers of clients who need these services to just barely survive, let alone thrive—it appears that for many prevention is an ideal, but not an attainable goal.

In this text, we present field-tested assessments and interventions framed in evidence-informed (EI) practice approaches defined by the Institute of Medicine as the consideration of empirical research evidence, clinician expertise, and client values in addition to contextual variables used in clinical decision-making (Jordan and Franklin 2008). We consciously selected this broader EI term to anchor the chapters in this text, as the “other term” evidence-based practice (EBP): (a) is differentially defined in the social work profession, (b) is temporal and still iterative in its consensual use in the profession, and (c) when used, often opens the debate door wide

M. J. Holosko (✉)
University of Georgia, Athens, GA, USA
e-mail: mholosko@uga.edu

J. S. Wodarski et al. (eds.), *Evidence-Informed Assessment and Practice in Child Welfare,* DOI 10.1007/978-3-319-12045-4_16

for polemic discussions about hierarchies of evidence, and value judgments about what constitutes "good," "better," or "bad" evidence. Our contention about this was that *any empirical evidence* that directs and informs practice, to assist our front-line workers in their noble and altruistic work is acceptable, as long as it achieves just that—it did direct and inform their practice.

Another content feature of the text, where we tried hard to "stay the course" (as reflected in the title) was the incorporation of selected field-tested EI assessments and interventions. All of these were indeed implemented by social workers in a variety of social welfare settings. These then, reflect pragmatic approaches to rendering comprehensive EI assessments and interventions tied to specifically targeted client problems. We tried to offset the pervasive "research conundrum" articulated by Wordarski (2011) which refers to the indiscriminate slapping of homogenous or "off-the-shelf" interventions to heterogeneous client groups. The importance of linking these field-tested integrative assessments to interventions that have a greater likelihood of achieving success as measured by specific short and long-term outcomes was another "story behind the thinking and writing" of this text.

The 15 chapters are partitioned into three subsections: (i) the context for providing EI assessments and interventions, (ii) field-tested EI assessments, and (iii) field-tested EI interventions. Subsection one has five chapters, subsection two has three, and subsection three has seven. For each, we will try to provide a brief rationale for their conceptualization and inclusion.

Earlier, we noted that national and state political reforms and their ensuing economic social welfare annual financial cutbacks are driven by not only the increasing numbers of children and the families who need more and more services daily, but also the need for more social workers to serve them adequately. This paradoxical social welfare reality occurs not just in the USA, but in many other democratic and "not-so-democratic" countries all over the world (Holosko and Barner, In Press). How these trends actually trickle down to our "factories" or institutions of social welfare, the largest single employer of Bachelor of Social Work (BSW) and Master of Social Work (MSW) certified social workers, presents a rather interesting picture of the day-to-day of our practicing professionals.

Our institutions of child welfare in the USA have come under much scrutiny of late, in trying to provide effective child welfare and protective services in every state in America. The prevailing trends in such institutions include increased caseloads, more multiproblem and complex families, more violent cases, budget cutbacks, community capacity building, retooling and modernizing service delivery systems, outsourcing services, more computerization and paperwork, partnering more actively with community stakeholders to assist in the delivery of their mandates, performance contracting for all partner agencies with clearly defined outcomes, evaluating programs with cost-effectiveness data, devolving levels of decision-making organizationally to the local community level, and developing plans for the recruitment and retention of better trained front-line child welfare professionals. Taken together, these trends have resulted in numerous lawsuits that have cost many state departments dearly, public outcry about the credibility of such departments and their ability to deliver their service mandates, and greater levels of public scrutiny and accountability which in turn, have resulted in stressful working conditions for many social work employees who work within their walls (Holosko 2006). In a nutshell, this was the rationale for us presenting the contextual chapters in subsection 1 as frankly, it is this very context that shapes the policies and practices in our social welfare settings.

Earlier on, we referred to the essential (and not taken for granted) linkage between more precise/accurate and comprehensive EI assessments impacting more selective and measureable outcome-based interventions. EI assessments utilize simultaneously: (a) the best empirical evidence with (b) critical thinking skills, and with (c) client input (Gibbs and Gambrill 2002). In plying our social work craft, effective social workers skillfully braid these three elements together to help move clients to an eventual end point with sufficient data and information—to affect a planned intervention.

Currently, our social welfare assessments are normally characterized by: brief, rapid assessment scales and instruments; using both quantitative and qualitative approaches; using multiple techniques such as interviewing, testing, and benchmarking clinical diagnosis; using observations, collateral and confirmatory interviewing of individuals in the client's environment; being conducted in compressed time frameworks, using computer technology with interfacing diagnostic codes specific to the agency and client populations; more integrative and holistic approaches; reframing and focusing on assets/strengths and options; and last but not least, involving our clients and their families as full partners in the process for not only their assessment and diagnosis, but also their eventual planned treatment. Generally, such assessments are conducted as part of a clearly defined, and/or regulatory agency protocol, or they are done to gather additional information about the client, and/or their families for a more comprehensive understanding of their various situations/problems/needs/issues/concerns. These assessment issues provide the backdrop for the three chapters presented in subsection two.

Finally, we move to the end of the first foremost reason why a client and his/her family arrives on the doorstep of a social welfare agency. That is, to receive "treatment," normally for a defined particular problem or need. This is not to say that after clients receive various EI interventions like the six presented in the third subsection of the text, that "they are finally helped," and can "move out of the system." For many it is the opposite, as this is just the beginning of a long and arduous process in which the child welfare agency is but one institution in their treatment journey, in tandem with a variety of other local health and human agencies. For some, this is a short journey but for others more typically, it is a long one. For many, the journey does not only include these children and families, but their extended families as well. The 2013 U.S. Department of Commerce reported that of the 26.9% of 46,700,000 persons on Aid to Families with Dependent Children (AFDC), 27% stay on this form of welfare on average for 2–5 years, and 20% stay on for over 5 years.

Due to increasingly more complex problems seen daily in our social welfare agencies, the search for help, treatment, hope, and "moving forward" for the majority of clients becomes one that taxes the individuals and families who are "in the system," is challenging for those practitioners who work with them daily, perplexes policymakers who allegedly craft policies to shape reform efforts toward more efficient services, and frustrates those in upper level decision-making who annually allocate expenditures for social welfare clients and their programs. Despite such overt frustration, perplexing confusion, uncertainty, and all that goes with it, if asked the rhetorical question—are we in the business of people processing, people sustaining, or people changing?—social welfare workers would be one of the only cohorts identified in this frustration group that would say "people changing." That is because our profession's strengths, perspective, and adherence to core values look beyond the labels of the two former answers. That is, we see strength in simply processing individuals, as we are not dealing with manufactured goods, but actual people. Second, to sustain people in vulnerable situations on our child welfare caseloads who frankly don't or can't change, is more positive than negative for many.

In conclusion then, we offer this text and its timely evidence to BSW and MSW students and social work professionals alike, to have information at hand, so they may better understand their clients and data to direct and inform them in their day-to-day valued and important work.

References

Gibbs, L. E., & Gambrill, E. (2002). Evidence-based practice: Counterarguments to objections. *Research on Social Work Practice, 12,* 452–476.

Holosko, M. J. (2006). Why don't social workers make better child welfare workers than non-social workers? *Research on Social Work Practice, 16(4),* 426–430.

Holosko, M. J., & Barner, J. (2013). Neoliberal globalization: Social welfare policy and institutions. In M. Vidal de Haymes, S. Haymes, & R. Miller (Eds.), *The routledge handbook on poverty in the United States*. London: Taylor & Francis.

Jordan, C. & Franklin, C. (2008). Assessment. Encyclopedia of social work. file:///C:/Documents%20and%20Settings/sswxp/Desktop/HK/Negotiation%20Mediation/PPT%20for%202%20courses/2014 %20HK%20Assess & %20Inter/Assessment%20-%20Encyclopedia%20of%20Social%20Work.htm. doi:10.1093/acrefore/9780199975839.013.24. Accessed June 16, 2014.

Wodarski, J. S. (2011). The social work practice research conundrum. *Journal of Human Behavior in the Social Environment, 21,* 577–600.

Index

J. S. Wodarski et al. (eds.), *Evidence-Informed Assessment and Practice in Child Welfare,* DOI 10.1007/978-3-319-12045-4

D

E